business solutions

Managing **Data**

with

Microsoft® Excel

Conrad Carlberg

800 East 96th Street
Indianapolis, Indiana 46240

Managing Data with Excel

International Standard Book Number: 0-7897-3100-2

Library of Congress Catalog Card Number: 2004100887

Printed in the United States of America

First Printing: May 2004

07   06   05   04   4   3   2   1

Trademarks

Warning and Disclaimer

Bulk Sales

Que Publishing offers excellent discounts on this book when ordered in quantity for bulk purchases or special sales. For more information, please contact

U.S. Corporate and Government Sales
1-800-382-3419
corpsales@pearsontechgroup.com

For sales outside the U.S., please contact

International Sales
1-317-428-3341
international@pearsontechgroup.com

Publisher
Paul Boger

Associate Publisher
Greg Wiegand

Acquisitions Editor
Stephanie J. McComb

Development Editor
Laura Norman

Managing Editor
Charlotte Clapp

Project Editor
Tonya Simpson

Copy Editor
Mike Henry

Indexer
Erika Millen

Proofreader
Kathy Bidwell

Technical Editors
Debra Dalgleish
Jon Price

Publishing Coordinator
Sharry Lee Gregory

Interior Designer
Anne Jones

Cover Designer
Anne Jones

Page Layout
Eric S. Miller

Contents

About the Author

Conrad Carlberg is president of Network Control Systems, a firm that develops event and statistical analysis software for the health care industry. He holds a doctorate from the University of Colorado and has authored nine books on Excel, including Que's *Business Analysis with Excel*. Carlberg lives near San Diego, and would go sailing more frequently if his loved one would just take the man overboard drill again.

Dedication

Once again, this is for Toni Messer and for Tabben—who are still with me, thank heaven. And it's for Tigger and for Button—who left us far too early but will live in our hearts forever.

Acknowledgments

My thanks go to this book's technical editors, Debra Dalgleish and Jon Price, who curbed some of my wilder flights of fancy. To its development editor, Laura Norman, who tactfully handled my optimistic page counts and my other editorial ineptitudes. And to Stephanie McComb for pulling it all together.

It's long past time that I acknowledge people who have taught and encouraged me. Gene Glass, who thought better than he might have of my early attempts to get Excel to extract principal components. Dave Derby and Bev Monigal, who taught me relational database theory in the context of a very different version of Excel—not Microsoft's but SBC's. My fellow Microsoft MVPs from the CompuServe forum days, Rob Bovey, David Hager, Tom Ogilvy, Jim Rech, Bob Umlas, and others who showed me the elegance that Microsoft built into Excel, as well as the errors, both egregious and subtle, that seem to never go away. Finally, of course, John LaTour, who ran the forum with such grace when we let him and such persuasiveness when we didn't.

We Want to Hear from You!

As the reader of this book, *you* are our most important critic and commentator. We value your opinion and want to know what we're doing right, what we could do better, what areas you'd like to see us publish in, and any other words of wisdom you're willing to pass our way.

As an associate publisher for Que, I welcome your comments. You can email or write me directly to let me know what you did or didn't like about this book—as well as what we can do to make our books better.

Please note that I cannot help you with technical problems related to the topic of this book. We do have a User Services group, however, where I will forward specific technical questions related to the book.

When you write, please be sure to include this book's title and author as well as your name, email address, and phone number. I will carefully review your comments and share them with the author and editors who worked on the book.

Email: feedback@quepublishing.com

Mail: Greg Wiegand
           Associate Publisher
           Que Publishing
           800 East 96th Street
           Indianapolis, IN 46240 USA

For more information about this book or another Que Publishing title, visit our Web site at www.quepublishing.com. Type the ISBN (0789731002) or the title of a book in the Search field to find the page you're looking for.

Introduction

About Excel

In the late 1990s, I read a *whitepaper*—a market research report—that found that most Excel worksheets use no formulas. That is, most Excel users employ Excel more as a storehouse of data than as a tool for analysis.

That finding troubled me. Excel isn't designed as a means of storing or retrieving data. Yes, you can use Excel in that way and, according to the market research, many people do so.

That's not how Excel's developers intended it to be used. They meant us to use Excel to *analyze* data, not to manage it. If you used Excel, you were expected to use functions like AVERAGE(), RATE(), and PI(), not to just stuff letters and numbers into worksheet cells.

But it's the marketplace that decides how a product is used, not the design team. And the marketplace has decided to use Excel to store data, regardless of its designers' intentions.

Okay, I can understand that. The marketplace finds that Excel is a good device for storing and arranging data, and the marketplace is usually right. I agree with the marketplace and I suspect you do too. Excel worksheets are a wonderful place to put data.

So, this question arises: Given that we want to use Excel to store and manage data, what are the best ways to go about doing that?

There's no good answer to that question, at least none that's simultaneously short and clear and informative. The answer depends in part on how much data you have to deal with, and in part on how you need to structure the data, and in part on whether you can use worksheet formulas to summarize and analyze the data.

Excel can offer you a terrific way to store data, as most of its users have found. It's flexible enough to let you define how you want to store your data. You need not comply with structures that are forced on you by other applications, such as Access and SQL Server.

Excel, for example, does not require that you put different records in different rows. It does not, as do other applications, require that you put different variables in different columns. This flexibility can be very handy, especially when the way that the data appears is important.

But that flexibility comes at a cost. Suppose that you want to put mailing addresses into an Excel worksheet, as shown in Figure I.1.

Figure I.1
This arrangement makes the most sense if you want to see how mailing labels might look.

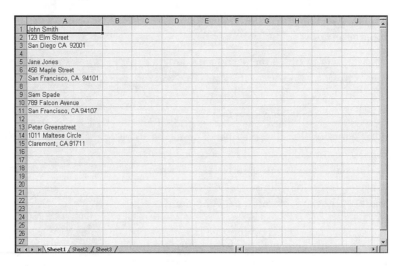

The data layout shown in Figure I.1 is a handy one. In particular, it mimics the way that you would want the information to appear on envelope labels.

But, as usual, you pay for your convenience. For example, what if you wanted to know how many addresses were in California? Or in San Francisco? Or on Falcon Street in San Francisco? The layout used in Figure I.1 isn't a good basis for that sort of analysis—or, for that matter, any sort of analysis.

Although it's not a good basis, you can deal with it. The right formula can, for example, count the number of addresses, laid out as in Figure I.1, in any given state, in any given city, on any given street. This book shows you how to create those formulas.

More importantly, this book shows you how to manage your data in ways that make it easier to analyze and summarize the information. For example, another possible layout of the data in an Excel worksheet appears in Figure I.2.

The difference between Figure I.1 and Figure I.2 underscores the flexibility that Excel offers you. It's great that you can decide to put a recipient's name in rows 1, 5, 9, and so on, as in Figure I.1, or to put them all in the same column, as in Figure I.2. Excel lets you decide. Other applications, database management systems in particular, don't let you make that sort of design decision.

Figure I.2
This layout is best if you want to summarize or otherwise manage your data.

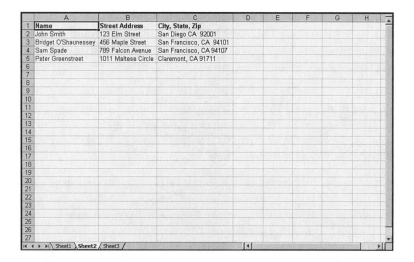

There are good reasons that database management systems are so persnickety, and those reasons also apply to Excel. When it comes to analyzing the data, it's much more efficient to lay it out as in Figure I.2 than I.1.

But when it comes to viewing the data as individual records, layouts such as the one shown in Figure I.1 can be much more effective. So, how do you choose between the two?

You might not have to choose. The right approach can give you the best of both layouts. If you manage your data correctly, you can have the convenience of layouts such as the one shown in Figure I.1 *and* the efficiency of layouts such as the one shown in Figure I.2.

So, you can have your cake and eat it too, but first you need to make the right arrangements. You'll need to know how to use Excel's array formulas. You'll need to get acquainted with Excel's data management functions. Visual Basic for Applications is required in many cases, as are its near neighbors, Data Access Objects and ActiveX Data Objects.

The intent of this book is to give you the tools you need to decide how to store your data—using Excel, using a database management system such as Access—and how best to implement the choice you make. That puts you in the best position to manage the data.

How to Use This Book

A good place to start is with bad choices. Chapter 1, "Misusing Excel as a Database Management Tool," gives you the details of several horrid examples.

Chapter 2, "Excel's Data Management Features," discusses ways to use Excel's worksheet functions to locate and rearrange data on the worksheet.

There are some ways to set up a worksheet—that is, to lay out its entries—that make it much easier for you to manage the data. Chapter 3, "Excel's Lists, Names, and Filters," shows you how to arrange your data effectively.

Excel has a variety of ways for you to get data from other sources into your worksheets. Chapter 4, "Importing Data: An Overview," walks you through one of the most powerful of these: external data ranges. This chapter also introduces Microsoft Query and establishing pivot tables based on imported data.

Chapter 5, "Using Microsoft Query," goes much further into using Microsoft Query to acquire external data. You'll see how to connect external data tables together and use selection criteria to design exactly the data import you're after. You'll also see how to manage the external data range so that it refreshes itself automatically, fills down adjacent formulas, maintains password protection, and so on.

As good as Excel's data import capabilities are, there are a few tricks and traps to be aware of. Chapter 6, "Importing Data: Further Considerations," discusses how to avoid null values, grouping fields in pivot tables, changing your criteria each time you run a query, and how to set up and refresh Web queries.

The remainder of *Managing Data with Excel* is concerned with automating the exchange of data between Excel and true relational databases. Especially when you're moving data out of Excel into another container, the most powerful methods involve Visual Basic for Applications, or VBA. Chapter 7, "VBA Essentials Reviewed," uses lots of sample code to show you how to use loops, understand the object model, declare variables, establish With structures, and work with the macro recorder. All these techniques are discussed in terms of their use in managing data.

Chapter 8, "Opening Databases," introduces two important libraries that you use in VBA so that your code will have direct access to structures in databases—tables, fields, records, queries, and so on. By using these libraries with VBA, you can manage databases entirely from the context of Excel.

If you're going to manage data in a database from inside Excel, it helps to know how to do it from a database management system. Chapter 9, "Managing Database Objects," shows you how to create tables, fields, and queries directly, using the database management system's user interface.

With Chapter 9's review of managing data structures from inside a database as a basis, the next chapter shows you how to do the same thing from inside Excel. Chapter 10, "Defining Fields and Records with ActiveX Data Objects and Data Access Objects," has plenty of examples of manipulating them using a combination of VBA and DAO, and of VBA and ADO.

Chapter 11, "Getting Data from Access and into Excel with ADO and DAO," examines the most efficient ways to use VBA, ADO, and DAO to move data from a database and into an Excel worksheet. These techniques are especially important when the data can't just be brought back all at once, as with an external data range, but when your code needs to do additional work with the data. You're walked through the development of a lengthy block of VBA code that places the data retrieved from the database in precise locations on the worksheet.

Chapter 11 focuses on getting data into Excel from a database. Chapter 12, "Controlling a Database from Excel Using ADO and DAO," looks at the other direction of data flow—from Excel to the database. You'll see how to add new records to database tables, edit existing records, and delete those you no longer need—all by using a combination of VBA and DAO or VBA and ADO.

Special Elements

There are several different types of information that we've included in this book to help you along.

Case Studies

A case study is a problem or situation that you might encounter in the course of your work with Excel—almost always, one that requires some extra ingenuity to deal with. All the case studies in this book come directly from situations I've encountered at my company's client sites. But because I really want to do more work for them, I'm not mentioning any names.

Notes, Tips, and Cautions

> **NOTE**
>
> A note is just an extra little tidbit about the topic being discussed. You can easily skip over these, but you might miss a gold nugget!

> **TIP**
>
> A tip is the spot where I can relay my own experiences with Excel in the real world and offer suggestions and tricks to help you use Excel more effectively.

> **CAUTION**
>
> These are the ones you don't want to skip. The caution will help keep you out of common pitfalls or alert you to potential problems.

Cross References

You'll find helpful references to other parts of the book when a topic is covered in more than one way in different chapters or when there is related information to the discussion at hand.

→ A cross reference is formatted like this and points you to other useful areas in the book.

Conventions

You'll find that we've employed some specific conventions to help you easily find what you are looking for and to distinguish certain elements from the rest of the text. The following list outlines those conventions:

- `Mono Font`: Mono font is used on most of the code you'll find in this book. Whether it's a function name, VBA code, SQL statements, or any other type of code listing, you'll see it in the mono font.
- *Italic*: When you see a word in *italics* that is to let you know that the word is a new term that is being defined in that location.
- **Bold**: In numbered lists, we've bolded items such as menus, buttons, and check boxes so that you can easily pick out the items as you work through the steps.

Pitfalls in Data Management

Misusing Excel as a Database Management Tool

1

Putting Data Management into Context

Excel is a superb application. Its user interface is comfortable and effective—at least, you can make it match your own sense of comfort and effectiveness. The worksheet layout is flexible. You can make the rows and columns stand for whatever you want: records and variables, weeks and days, accounts and debits or credits, and so on.

Excel offers a huge selection of *functions*: prefabricated formulas that have already done the heavy lifting for you. Its charts help you visualize what's going on with your data. Its pivot tables make it a snap to synthesize and analyze large collections of records. You can even control its appearance so that other users can't tell that what they're looking at is an Excel worksheet.

And Excel offers you plenty of ways to manage and manipulate data. You can filter data to focus in on details, sort data into subsets, and make use of various lookup and reference functions that make Excel act something like a true database management system.

Over the years, Excel has been so successful that many people never want to use anything else. In many cases, they don't have to. For small-to-medium data sets, Excel gives you most everything you need to manage and analyze data. It's when the data sets get large that things start to get out of hand.

Beginning with Chapter 2, "Excel's Data Management Features," *Managing Data with Excel* shows you how to use different Excel features—in particular, its worksheet functions—to make Excel act like a database management system. Parts III, "Managing External Data from Inside Excel," and IV, "Managing Databases from Inside Excel," show you how to deal with situations that involve more data than Excel can handle effectively by itself.

This chapter is meant to convince you that there comes a point when more data becomes too much of a good thing. When you recognize that one of your own projects has reached that point, you'll be well placed to apply one or more of the data management solutions you'll read about in this book.

CASE STUDY

Overworking Functions

You've taken on The Sisyphus Corporation as a client to help it solve a data tracking problem. Sisyphus wants to track information about purchase orders (POs) that it has prepared for its vendors. As the vendors send invoices for payment, the Sisyphus staff enters information into an Excel workbook. The information includes data such as PO number, PO date, invoice number, invoice amount, invoice date, and so on.

Over time, Sisyphus acquires a considerable amount of information, some of which appears in Figure 1.1.

Figure 1.1
Not all records with the same PO number are grouped together; the sort is by column F, Date Invoice Received.

	A	B	C	D	E	F	G	H
1	PO #	DATE	MGR ID	Amount	Vendor	INV REC	INV DATE	INV AMT
1	PO #	DATE	MGR ID	Amount	Vendor	INV REC	INV DATE	INV AMT
2	020022	1/10/2002	6	$ 18,952.00	A1 WINDOW CLEANERS	7/5/2000	6/29/2002	$ 3,502.00
3	020155	1/2/2002	7	$ 1,095.61	TELECO	1/2/2001	12/25/2001	$ 1,095.61
4	020010	1/15/2002	7		SPECIALTY UNIFORM	1/15/2001	12/27/2001	$ 212.42
5	021189	5/2/2002	3	$ 1,050.00	CONSUMERS OPTIONS	5/2/2001	5/2/2002	$ 1,050.00
6	021225	5/7/2002	1	$ 200.00	TIRCO INDUSTRIES	6/2/2001	5/14/2002	$ 172.62
7	020278	1/17/2002	3	$ 1,560.00	MOTTEL VOICE & DATA	12/17/2001	12/3/2001	$ 1,560.00
8	020277	1/17/2002	3	$ 1,560.00	MOTTEL VOICE & DATA	12/19/2001	12/10/2001	$ 1,560.00
9	020204	1/8/2002	7		WEBERN PRINTING COMPANY	12/21/2001	12/12/2001	$ 1,063.80
10	020203	1/8/2002	3	$ 231.50	UNAVATEC	12/24/2001	12/14/2001	$ 231.50
11	020226	1/11/2002	7	$ 75.00	INT'L ASSOC. FOR FACILITIES	12/27/2001	12/19/2001	$ 75.00
12	020377	1/29/2002	3	$ 920.00	TRI-CO SERVICES	12/27/2001	1/23/2002	$ 920.00
13	020001	1/15/2002	8		PROPERTY INNOVATIONS, INC.	12/28/2001	12/30/2001	$ 539.63
14	020002	1/15/2002	8		PROPERTY INNOVATIONS, INC.	12/28/2001	12/30/2001	$ 630.76
15	020003	1/15/2002	8		PROPERTY INNOVATIONS, INC.	12/28/2001	12/30/2001	$ 1,700.00
16	020003	1/15/2002	8		PROPERTY INNOVATIONS, INC.	12/28/2001	12/30/2001	$ 245.78
17	020004	1/15/2002	8		PROPERTY INNOVATIONS, INC.	12/28/2001	12/30/2001	$ 157.42
18	020263	1/15/2002	8	$ 250.00	WESTERN GROUNDS MAINTENANCE	12/28/2001	12/27/2001	$ 250.00
19	020264	1/15/2002	8	$ 224.00	WESTERN GROUNDS MAINTENANCE	12/28/2001	12/27/2001	$ 224.00
20	020007	12/25/2001	6	$ 11,440.00	SHORE'S OF BELLFLOWER	12/31/2001	12/25/2001	$ 210.78
21	020151	1/2/2002	3		TOM KEPLER	1/2/2002	12/31/2001	$ 840.00
22	020280	1/17/2002	3	$ 1,560.00	MOTTEL VOICE & DATA	1/2/2002	12/18/2001	$ 1,560.00
23	020001	1/15/2002	8		PROPERTY INNOVATIONS, INC.	1/3/2002	1/1/2002	$ 2,250.00
24	020001	1/15/2002	8		PROPERTY INNOVATIONS, INC.	1/3/2002	1/1/2002	$ 415.00

Ready · · · NUM

NOTE
Although the vendors' names have been altered, the information shown in Figure 1.1 is genuine, taken from a workbook maintained by a mid-sized company (which is *not* named Sisyphus). All the case studies, and most of the figures, in this book are taken from real-world examples.

The data shown in Figure 1.1 actually extends from Row 1 to Row 6045. As part of your client's management and control process, Sisyphus wants to compare periodically the total amount paid on each PO with the amount for which the PO was originally drawn. To make that comparison, Sisyphus needs the total amount of all the invoices submitted for each PO.

The staff who created the worksheet inserted new rows in the midst of the worksheet to hold PO totals. This approach was reasonable, if rudimentary, when the worksheet contained only a few PO and invoice records. When a new invoice arrived, they took the following steps, using a worksheet with the same data as Figure 1.1, but with extra rows to show invoice totals:

1. Sort the entire data range by PO number.

2. Choose **Find** from the **Edit** menu to locate the first record with a PO number matching the current invoice.

3. Scroll down to find the totaling row for that PO.

4. Insert a blank row just above the totaling row.

5. Enter information about the current invoice in the new row.

6. Correct the range address in the totaling formula so that it captures the new invoice amount (see Figure 1.2).

Figure 1.2
This intuitively obvious approach creates huge problems when it comes time to analyze the data more fully.

	A	B	C	D	E	F	G	H	
1	PO #	DATE	MGR ID	Amount	Vendor	INV REC	INV DATE	INV AMT	
2	020001	1/15/2002	8		PROPERTY INNOVATIONS, INC.	12/28/2001	12/30/2001	$ 539.63	
3	020001	1/15/2002	8		PROPERTY INNOVATIONS, INC.	1/3/2002	1/1/2002	$ 2,250.00	
4	020001	1/15/2002	8		PROPERTY INNOVATIONS, INC.	1/3/2002	1/1/2002	$ 415.00	
5	SUM							$ 3,204.63	
6	020002	1/15/2002	8		PROPERTY INNOVATIONS, INC.	12/28/2001	12/30/2001	$ 630.76	
7	020002	1/15/2002	8		PROPERTY INNOVATIONS, INC.	1/3/2002	1/1/2002	$ 3,242.53	
8	020002	1/15/2002	8		PROPERTY INNOVATIONS, INC.	1/3/2002	1/1/2002	$ 648.32	
9	SUM							$ 4,521.61	
10	020003	1/15/2002	8		PROPERTY INNOVATIONS, INC.	12/28/2001	12/30/2001	$ 1,700.00	
11	020003	1/15/2002	8		PROPERTY INNOVATIONS, INC.	12/28/2001	12/30/2001	$ 245.78	
12	SUM							$ 1,945.78	
13	020004	1/15/2002	8		PROPERTY INNOVATIONS, INC.	12/28/2001	12/30/2001	$ 157.42	
14	020004	1/15/2002	8		PROPERTY INNOVATIONS, INC.	1/3/2002	1/1/2002	$ 1,250.00	
15	SUM							$ 1,407.42	
16	020007	12/25/2001	6	$ 11,440.00	SHORE'S OF BELLFLOWER	12/31/2001	12/25/2001	$ 210.78	
17	SUM							$ 210.78	
18	020010	1/15/2002	7		SPECIALTY UNIFORM	1/15/2001	12/27/2001	$ 212.42	3
19	SUM							$ 212.42	
20	020012	12/4/2001	7	$370,000.00	PACIFIC EXTRUSION SYS	1/7/2002	1/4/2002	$ 9,469.75	
21	020012	12/4/2001	7	$370,000.00	PACIFIC EXTRUSION SYS	1/7/2002	1/4/2002	$ 10,233.04	
22	020012	12/4/2001	7	$370,000.00	PACIFIC EXTRUSION SYS	1/7/2002	1/4/2002	$ 1,090.04	
23	020012	12/4/2001	7	$370,000.00	PACIFIC EXTRUSION SYS	1/7/2002	1/4/2002	$ 514.42	
24	SUM							$ 21,307.25	
25	020013	12/4/2001	8		PACIFIC EXTRUSION SYS	1/7/2002	12/20/2001	$ 235.00	

The arrangement shown in Figure 1.2 causes several problems:

- Sorting the data—for example, to get subtotals by month instead of by PO—becomes clumsy. Those extra totaling rows get in the way.

- Putting in new data, and pointing the SUM function at the proper cells, is subject to keying errors.

- Each time a new row is inserted, and new data is entered, and a SUM formula is edited, all the SUM formulas recalculate. Sisyphus now has so much data that the process is unacceptably slow.

- The user can't get a total of *all* invoices via something like `=SUM(H1:H7000)` because the PO subtotals get included.

When the worksheet contained roughly 50 POs, and 100 to 200 invoices, this approach wasn't a bad idea. It was quick and dirty, true, but it was quick.

By the time the worksheet grew to contain more than 3,000 POs and more than 6,000 invoices, things had gotten out of hand and Sisyphus called you in. These situations are insidious: They worm their way into how a department does business, people get trained to use them and give them up only reluctantly, and a "that's the way we've always done it" mindset takes over.

A slightly more sophisticated approach might have been more straightforward in the long run. Here's one possibility:

1. Use a pivot table, or the Advanced Filter, to create a list of unique PO numbers. Figure 1.3 shows a pivot table with the unique PO numbers; see Chapter 3, "Excel's Lists, Names, and Filters," for information on how to use Excel's Advanced Filter.

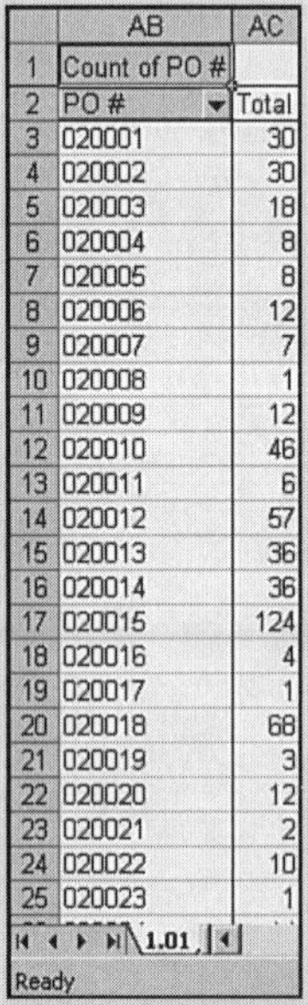

Figure 1.3
This pivot table counts the number of invoice records associated with each PO.

	AB	AC
1	Count of PO #	
2	PO # ▼	Total
3	020001	30
4	020002	30
5	020003	18
6	020004	8
7	020005	8
8	020006	12
9	020007	7
10	020008	1
11	020009	12
12	020010	46
13	020011	6
14	020012	57
15	020013	36
16	020014	36
17	020015	124
18	020016	4
19	020017	1
20	020018	68
21	020019	3
22	020020	12
23	020021	2
24	020022	10
25	020023	1

`|◄ ◄ ► ►|\ 1.01 ,|◄`
`Ready`

2. Suppose that the list created in step 1 is in AB3:AB3540. In (for instance) cell AE1, you might array-enter this formula:

```
=SUM(IF($A$3:$A$6045=AB3,$H$3:$H$6045,0))
```

and then copy and paste that formula into AE3:AE3540. Figure 1.4 shows the result.

This array formula begins with a conditional:

```
IF($A$3:$A$6045=AB3,
```

The conditional evaluates as TRUE when a value in A2:A6045 equals the value in cell AB3. The formula continues:

```
$H$3:$H$6045,0))
```

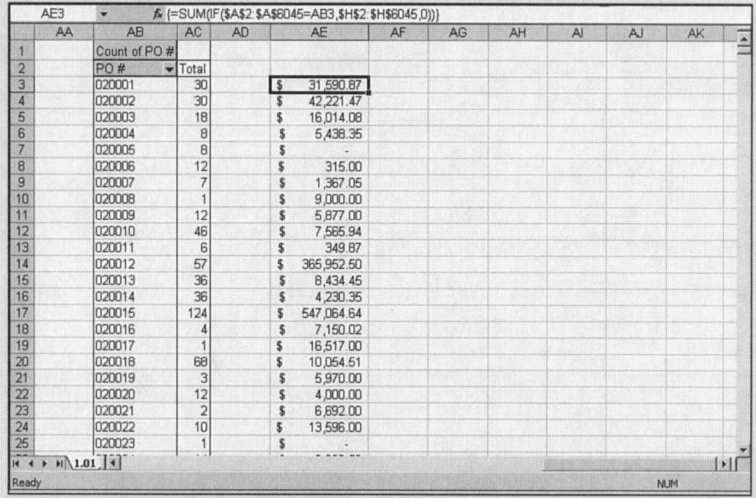

Figure 1.4
The curly brackets
around the formula in
the Formula Bar show
that it's an array formula.

	AA	AB	AC	AD	AE	AF	AG	AH	AI	AJ	AK
					AE3 {=SUM(IF($A$2:$A$6045=AB3,$H$2:$H$6045,0))}						
1		Count of PO #									
2		PO #	Total								
3		020001	30		$ 31,590.87						
4		020002	30		$ 42,221.47						
5		020003	18		$ 16,014.08						
6		020004	8		$ 5,438.35						
7		020005	8		$ -						
8		020006	12		$ 315.00						
9		020007	7		$ 1,367.05						
10		020008	1		$ 9,000.00						
11		020009	12		$ 5,877.00						
12		020010	46		$ 7,565.94						
13		020011	6		$ 349.87						
14		020012	57		$ 365,952.50						
15		020013	36		$ 8,434.45						
16		020014	36		$ 4,230.35						
17		020015	124		$ 547,064.64						
18		020016	4		$ 7,150.02						
19		020017	1		$ 16,517.00						
20		020018	68		$ 10,054.51						
21		020019	3		$ 5,970.00						
22		020020	12		$ 4,000.00						
23		020021	2		$ 6,692.00						
24		020022	10		$ 13,596.00						
25		020023	1		$ -						

In words, for a row in column A where the conditional is true, the formula returns the corresponding value from column H, and otherwise it returns a zero. Finally, that logic is submitted to the SUM function:

=SUM(IF($A$3:$A$6045=AB3,$H$3:$H$6045,0))

which adds the value in column H when the PO number in cell AB3 is found in column A, and adds zero otherwise.

> **NOTE**
> You array-enter a formula with the key combination Ctrl+Shift+Enter, instead of merely pressing the Enter key. You'll see several more examples of array formulas in Chapter 2.

This sequence of steps results in 3,538 array formulas, each providing the sum of the invoice amounts for each PO number. You can compare the results with the amount for which each PO was drawn—this comparison tells you which PO amounts have been overrun and which have not yet been used up.

After brief consideration, you realize that this approach won't work. The problem is that it's going to take what seems like forever for all those formulas to calculate. And the moment that Sisyphus makes any change to the content of the worksheet, the formulas all have to recalculate (unless you've had the foresight to set Calculation to Manual, and later remembered to turn it back to Automatic). On a 1.80GHz Pentium 4, that recalculation takes more than a minute with the data shown in Figure 1.1.

Even a minute is too long to wait. Your client has already acquired far too much data for Excel to handle comfortably and effectively. A much better approach is to use a pivot table with PO Number as the row field and Invoice Amount as the data field (see Figure 1.5).

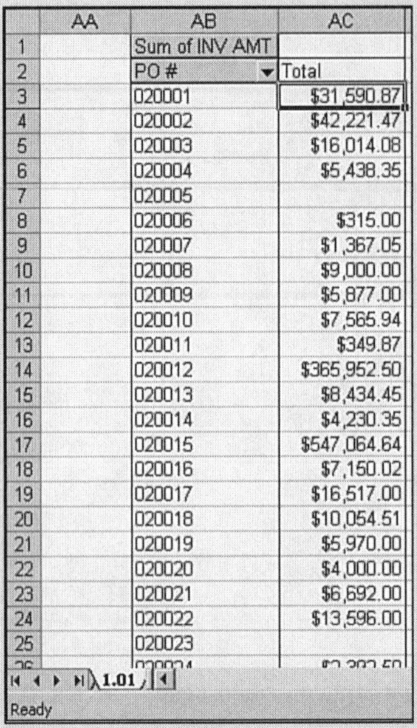

Figure 1.5
The figures shown in pivot tables are values, not formulas that must be recalculated.

	AA	AB	AC
1		Sum of INV AMT	
2		PO # ▾	Total
3		020001	$31,590.87
4		020002	$42,221.47
5		020003	$16,014.08
6		020004	$5,438.35
7		020005	
8		020006	$315.00
9		020007	$1,367.05
10		020008	$9,000.00
11		020009	$5,877.00
12		020010	$7,565.94
13		020011	$349.87
14		020012	$365,952.50
15		020013	$8,434.45
16		020014	$4,230.35
17		020015	$547,064.64
18		020016	$7,150.02
19		020017	$16,517.00
20		020018	$10,054.51
21		020019	$5,970.00
22		020020	$4,000.00
23		020021	$6,692.00
24		020022	$13,596.00
25		020023	
26		020024	$2,393.50

Better yet would be to store the PO and invoice data in a true relational database, because doing so keeps all the individual detail records out of the workbook. With that arrangement, you could

- Return the data to the workbook in a pivot table, specifying External Data Source as your data location.
- Return the data to the workbook in an external data range, using a Select query as the data source and grouping on PO number. (See Chapters 4, "Importing Data: An Overview," and 5, "Using Microsoft Query," for information about Select queries.)

In either case, you wind up with values, not formulas, showing the total invoice amount for each PO. This means that Sisyphus doesn't need to wait for 3,538 recalculations to complete whenever there's a change in the underlying data, or when someone edits the worksheet, kicking off a recalculation. Even without recalculating formulas, it's quick and easy to update the totals as new invoices arrive or new POs are created; all your client needs to do is refresh the pivot table or the external data range.

Transposing Rows and Columns

Excel is not a database management system. It is not, for example, designed to manage the relationship between parent and child records. To extend the example in the previous section, a PO is a parent record and invoices are child records because each invoice—the child record—belongs to a PO—the parent record.

Still, Excel has some rudimentary database features, among them the AutoFilter and the Advanced Filter. These two filters in particular depend on a particular orientation of your data, called *lists*. In Excel, a list has these characteristics:

- Each record (each person, each product, each invoice) occupies a different row.
- Each variable (for example, name and address, or model and price, or invoice date and amount) occupies a different column.
- Each column begins with the name of the variable that's located in that column.

Figure 1.1 is an example of a list. It has different records—invoices—in different rows, different variables—dates, amounts, and so on—in different columns, and each column is headed by the name of that column's variable.

Changing the Orientation with Paste Special

Many of Excel's tools work best, and some work *only*, when the data you point them at are arranged in lists. Tools such as pivot tables and data filters will not work properly with any other arrangement.

From time to time, a user might decide to enter data using a different layout. When this happens, it's often a 90-degree rotation from the normal list arrangement; that is, he puts different records in different columns and different variables in different rows. Figure 1.6 shows an example.

Figure 1.6
A user might lay out his data this way for any reason from aesthetics to lack of experience with list structures.

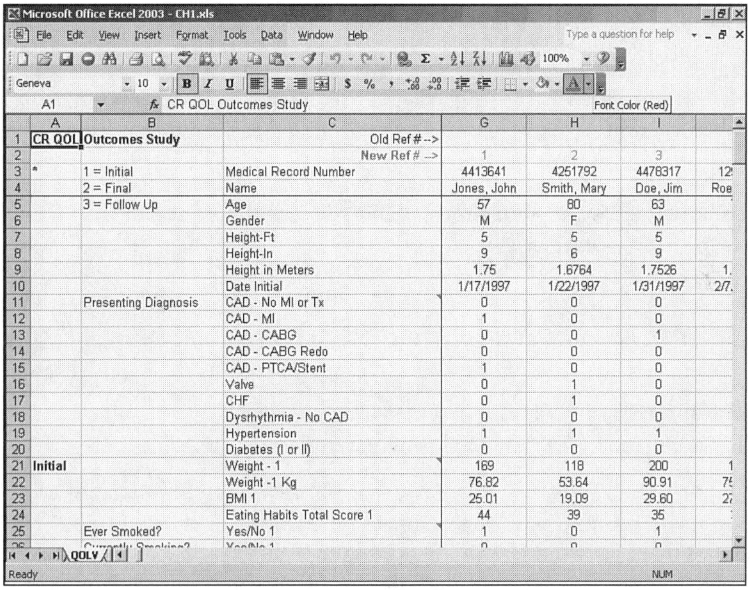

This arrangement is unwise for several reasons, but the strongest is that the user will run out of columns long before he runs out of rows. An Excel worksheet has 256 columns only, and there's no way to add more. But it has 65,536 rows. (No, you can't add more rows either, but 65,536 is pretty roomy. 65,536 is 2 to the 16th power, by the way.)

There are many situations in which you would have more than 256 records. For example, a company of any appreciable size has more than 256 invoices to deal with. But it is rare to have as many as 256 variables that describe the records. So, the dimensions of the worksheet itself argue for using the list structure.

Nevertheless, you frequently encounter worksheets laid out as in Figure 1.6. If only a few formulas are based on the data as it's shown in the figure, there are a couple of easy fixes:

1. Select the entire data range.
2. Choose **Copy** from the **Edit** menu.
3. Select a cell that has empty columns to its right.
4. Choose **Paste Special** from the **Edit** menu, fill the **Transpose** check box, and click OK.
5. Repair the range addresses used in the formulas.

> **CAUTION**
>
> Be careful when transposing data using Paste Special. In some cases, you can transpose formulas so that they depend on cells that don't exist. Chapter 2 discusses this problem in detail.

Changing the Orientation with the TRANSPOSE Function

Sometimes the user has structured the worksheet as shown in Figure 1.6 because it's easier to enter the data that way—perhaps the data comes in a hardcopy format with records in columns and variables in rows. Then it's much easier on the person entering the data to follow the arrangement of the hard copy.

To preserve the data entry format and yet reconfigure the data so that it forms a list, you could take these steps:

1. Count the number of rows and columns in the existing data range.
2. Select an entire range of blank cells. This new range should have as many columns as the original range has rows, and as many rows as the original range has columns.
3. In the Formula Bar, type **=TRANSPOSE(** followed by the address of the original range (for example, A1:Z5), and a closing parenthesis.
4. Array-enter the formula using the key combination Ctrl+Shift+Enter.

Now you have two ranges: One is laid out as in Figure 1.6, where more data can be entered as it becomes available, and the other appears as in Figure 1.7.

To accommodate more records as they're entered into the original range, just select more rows in the new range before you enter the TRANSPOSE formula. That way, as more records are entered in columns in the original range, they'll appear in new rows in the transposed range.

Figure 1.7
The data seen in Figure 1.6 has been transposed and is now ready for analysis.

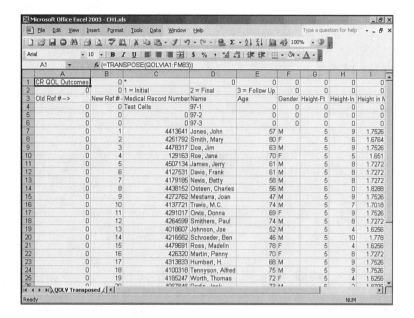

Using Labels Instead of Codes

Traditionally, true databases have used numeric codes instead of text labels for fields that can take on only a fairly restricted set of values. For example, the label "Ford" might be represented by the number 1, "Chrysler" by the number 2, and "Toyota" by the number 3.

This approach had a special advantage when the availability of storage media was at a premium. If you have 1,000 records, you can store 1,000 byte values (1, 2, or 3, for example) in 1000 bytes. But if you store the car make in a text field, the value "Chrysler" forces that field to be at least seven characters—8 bytes, or 8000 bytes for 1,000 records. Years ago, that was a significant amount of space.

The idea—just as in chess—was to trade time for space. It takes the processor a little more time to look up what label is associated with a number, and return that label: give it a 1, for example, and wait for it to figure out that the associated label is "Ford" and to return the label. If you could afford to wait that long, you'd save a significant amount of space.

Today, though, storage space is relatively cheap and readily available, so perhaps there's less reason to associate labels with codes. On the other hand, processors are very much faster now. They're so fast that our eyes and brains can't tell, when viewing a record, whether they're seeing a label that's part of the record or one that has been returned by looking up a code.

That seems to make it tough to decide, when you're designing either a workbook or a true database, whether to use lookups or to store labels directly with their associated records. The benefits and drawbacks are covered more fully in Part II, "Managing Data Inside Excel." For now, the next section shows what can happen when you make the wrong choice—or, when you make what might be the right choice at the outset but it turns wrong as more and more data comes in.

Setting Up a Lookup

Here's an example of advice you might have received—or given—in 1996. Suppose that you want to enter, by hand, sales results in an Excel worksheet. You might want the result to appear as shown in Figure 1.8.

Figure 1.8
Using the lookup functions can save time and prevent typing errors.

	A	B	C	D	E	F	G	H	I	J
1	Branch	Sales								
2	Tulsa District Office	$59,957.23								
3	St. Louis District Office	$13,955.49								
4	Southern Plains Regional Office	$52,430.18								
5	Southwest Regional Office	$93,489.15								
6	Southern Plains Regional Office	$90,178.65								
7	Los Angeles District Office	$13,898.81								
8	North Plains Regional Office	$33,722.62								
9	North Plaines Regional Office	$36,262.37								
10	Tulsa District Office	$53,977.90								

The main drawback to the setup shown in Figure 1.8 is that someone has to type some fairly long labels in column A, and that can bring about a couple of problems. One is that it might take a long time to do all that typing. Another problem is that the typist is likely to make keystroke errors. If and when you want an analysis of the data, such as calculating total sales by branch, the North *Plans* regional office will be treated separately from the North *Plains* regional office. Excel's Cell AutoComplete feature helps out with some of these problems, but not all of them.

> **NOTE** The AutoComplete feature can finish cell entries for you. For example, if you've already entered **`Lenny`** in a worksheet, under some circumstances Excel will finish it for you if you begin to enter it again. You must have the option selected—choose Tools, Options, click the Edit tab, and fill the AutoComplete check box. The entry must be text (not numbers or dates), must be in the same column, and usually cannot be separated from other data in the column by a blank cell. So, if **`Lenny`** is in A6, typing **`L`** or **`l`** in A7 causes Excel to supply the remaining four characters.

Way back then, long before the Y2K kerfuffle focused everyone's attention on storage space, you might have arranged things as in Figure 1.9.

Notice the use of the VLOOKUP function in Figure 1.9 (see the Formula Bar, found right above the worksheet's column headers). The VLOOKUP function largely solves the problems of typographical errors and wasted time entering data.

Figure 1.9
In Excel, a lookup range functions much as a lookup table in a database.

B2 fx =IF(A2="","",VLOOKUP(A2,$E$2:$F$9,2,0))

	A	B	C	D	E	F	G
1	Code	Branch	Sales		Code	Branch	
2	8	Tulsa District Office	$59,957.23		1	Los Angeles District Office	
3	7	St. Louis District Office	$13,955.49		2	Minneapolis District Office	
4	5	Southern Plains Regional Office	$52,430.18		3	North Plains Regional Office	
5	6	Southwest Regional Office	$93,489.15		4	Seattle District Office	
6	5	Southern Plains Regional Office	$90,178.65		5	Southern Plains Regional Office	
7	1	Los Angeles District Office	$13,898.81		6	Southwest Regional Office	
8	3	North Plains Regional Office	$33,722.62		7	St. Louis District Office	
9	3	North Plains Regional Office	$36,262.37		8	Tulsa District Office	
10	8	Tulsa District Office	$53,977.90				

Chapter 2 has much more on the VLOOKUP function, but this is its effect as it's used in Figure 1.9:

- The typist looks at the table of region names and finds the appropriate code.

- That code is entered in column A; for example, 8 to represent the Tulsa district office.

- The VLOOKUP function finds the label associated with the code in column A and displays that label in column B.

Mission accomplished? Well, yes and no. You've saved time and you've largely prevented errors (and there's a spinoff benefit from this approach, which is discussed in the next section).

But nothing's free. You've avoided lots of typing, and in so doing you've created the need for a lengthy set of VLOOKUP formulas. Furthermore, what if there's nothing in column A for some of the formulas to look up? Those formulas are going to return #N/A error values in any row that has no value in column A. And what of a nonexistent code? That is, what if the typist enters a 9 as the code in Figure 1.9? That causes an #N/A error as well.

Yes, you can get around one of those problems by modifying the VLOOKUP formulas to follow this pattern:

```
=IF(A1="","",VLOOKUP(A1,$J$1:$K$10,2,0))
```

This minor modification causes Excel to display nothing if A1 itself is blank, and to display the result of the lookup otherwise.

That disposes of one cause of the annoying problem of rampant #N/A error values on the worksheet, but it doesn't help you decide how many rows should contain the formula. Suppose that you put it in B1:B200. Periodically, someone has to check to see whether the person entering the data has gotten past the 200th row, and if so to extend the range as far as necessary.

You could, of course, extend the formula all the way to row 65,536. But that significantly increases the space required to store the file: from perhaps 500KB to well over 7MB—a 14-fold increase. That's a fairly large file, even on a standalone computer. If yours is a workstation on a network, it's not a good idea to force the network to transmit all those bytes every time you want to open the file.

Using Data Validation

If you've used versions of Excel released since 1996, you might have used data validation to speed up data entry and to better ensure its accuracy (see Figure 1.10).

As Figure 1.10 shows, you can arrange things so that a cell, or range of cells, has a dropdown whose contents depend on a list. (You'll see how to set up this arrangement in Chapter 2.) You don't need to get formulas involved, and by setting up the data validation for an entire column, you don't need to worry about the extent of the range of cells as you do using the VLOOKUP approach. It takes only trivially more file space to apply data validation to 65,536 cells than to 65 cells.

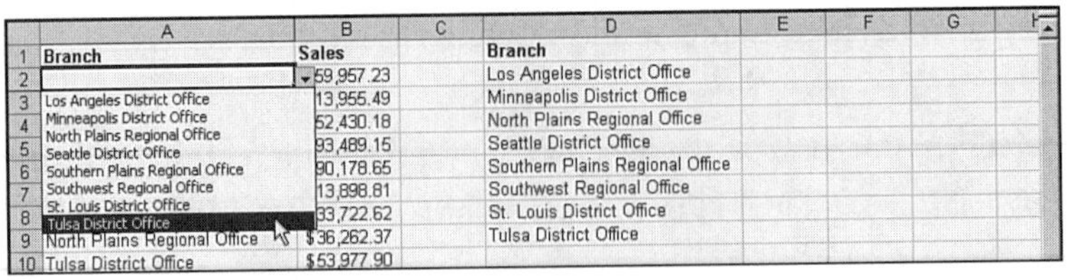

Figure 1.10
A data validation list limits your choices to the elements in the list.

But suppose that at some point you want or need to move the data to a true database manager: Access, say, or SQL Server, or Oracle, or some similar application. In that environment, you almost surely want to use a numeric code—or at least a very brief alphanumeric one—to identify each branch office. Database management systems like those are designed to make efficient use of codes and labels.

But using data validation, you no longer have a one-to-one correspondence on your worksheet between a concise code and a descriptive label. The VLOOKUP approach forces you to let some code value represent Northwest Seattle, another value represent Northwest Boise, and so on. But the data validation approach doesn't require codes, and so if you want to move the data to a relational database and take advantage of its power, you'll need to develop codes for your labels.

In turn, this means you'll need to associate codes with your validation list, create VLOOKUP formulas to put a code with each record, and finally move the records with their codes to the database. Figure 1.11 gives an example of how you might set this up.

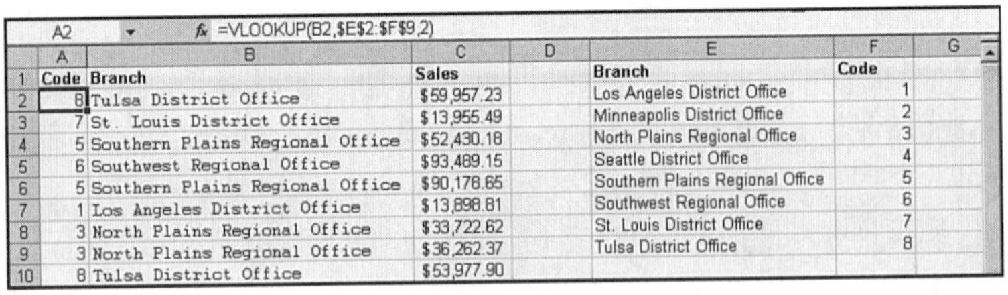

Figure 1.11
This reverses the situation shown in Figure 1.9; now, VLOOKUP returns codes instead of labels.

After you've put codes representing branch locations together with data such as sales figures, you can move the sales data into a table in the database. You'll also want to move the lookup table, which pairs the codes with the labels, into the database—then the database can associate branch location sales values with the appropriate branch name.

All this implies that you should give real thought before deciding to rely on Excel's data validation feature. If you have perhaps 100 records or so, and something like 10 possible labels, data validation might well be the right approach. This is especially true if you *don't* expect your data set to grow to several hundred or even thousands of records.

But if you have, or know that you will eventually have, a much larger data set, it probably makes sense to start out with the code-and-label VLOOKUP approach. Eventually you're likely to decide to move the data to a true database and keep the analysis in the Excel workbook. When you make that decision, you'll already have the codes associated with the proper labels, and it will be easy to move them into the database.

Handling Variable Numbers of Records per Category

Excel presents a real headache when you have some number of records in different categories, and not all categories have the same number of records. Figure 1.12 continues the example first shown in Figure 1.1.

Figure 1.12
This is what a relational structure can look like when it gets shoehorned into a worksheet.

	A	B	C	D	E	F	G	H
1	PO #	DATE	MGR ID	Amount	Vendor	INV REC	V DATE	INV AMT
833	020062	3/25/2002	3	$ 11,340.00	DADE BEARINGS	6/5/2002	4/13/2002	$ 2,835.00
834	020063	3/26/2002	1	$ 7,344.00	WEST COAST FILTER	4/3/2002	3/29/2002	$ 404.82
835	020063	3/26/2002	1	$ 7,344.00	WEST COAST FILTER	4/29/2002	4/25/2002	$ 306.00
836	020063	3/26/2002	1	$ 7,344.00	WEST COAST FILTER	5/3/2002	4/26/2002	$ 674.70
837	020063	3/26/2002	1	$ 7,344.00	WEST COAST FILTER	8/19/2002	8/16/2002	$ 269.88
838	020068	4/9/2002	1	$ 28,840.80	BARRY'S GREEN THUMB	5/29/2002	5/22/2002	$ 1,953.15
839	020068	4/9/2002	1	$ 28,840.80	BARRY'S GREEN THUMB	5/30/2002	5/22/2002	$ 265.00
840	020068	4/9/2002	1	$ 28,840.80	BARRY'S GREEN THUMB	6/7/2002	4/22/2002	$ 278.25
841	020068	4/9/2002	1	$ 28,840.80	BARRY'S GREEN THUMB	6/24/2002	6/21/2002	$ 2,051.76
842	020068	4/9/2002	1	$ 28,840.80	BARRY'S GREEN THUMB	7/18/2002	7/17/2002	$ 278.25
843	020068	4/9/2002	1	$ 28,840.80	BARRY'S GREEN THUMB	7/18/2002	7/17/2002	$ 2,051.76
844	020068	4/9/2002	1	$ 28,840.80	BARRY'S GREEN THUMB	7/18/2002	1/17/2002	$ 115.06
845	020068	4/9/2002	1	$ 28,840.80	BARRY'S GREEN THUMB	7/18/2002	4/22/2002	$ 2,051.76
846	020068	4/9/2002	1	$ 28,840.80	BARRY'S GREEN THUMB	5/29/2002	5/22/2002	$ 92.00
847	020068	4/9/2002	1	$ 28,840.80	BARRY'S GREEN THUMB	7/18/2002	5/22/2002	$ 96.60
848	020068	4/9/2002	1	$ 28,840.80	BARRY'S GREEN THUMB	7/18/2002	6/21/2002	$ 96.60
849	020068	4/9/2002	1	$ 28,840.80	BARRY'S GREEN THUMB	7/8/2002	7/1/2002	$ 498.78
850	020068	4/9/2002	1	$ 28,840.80	BARRY'S GREEN THUMB	7/18/2002	7/17/2002	$ 96.60
851	020068	4/9/2002	1	$ 28,840.80	BARRY'S GREEN THUMB	7/18/2002	4/22/2002	$ 96.60
852	020069	4/9/2002	8	$ 819.00	BARRY'S GREEN THUMB	7/18/2002	7/17/2002	$ 68.25
853	020069	4/9/2002	8	$ 819.00	BARRY'S GREEN THUMB	7/18/2002	2/22/2002	$ 65.00
854	020069	4/9/2002	8	$ 819.00	BARRY'S GREEN THUMB	7/18/2002	4/22/2002	$ 68.25
855	020070	4/9/2002	8	$ 1,020.00	BARRY'S GREEN THUMB	6/20/2002	5/22/2002	$ 65.00
856	020070	4/9/2002	8	$ 1,020.00	BARRY'S GREEN THUMB	6/24/2002	6/21/2002	$ 68.25

POs / 1.1

Ready NUM

Notice in Figure 1.12 that some rows repeat information: rows 834 through 837, for example, and rows 838 through 851. Rows that have the same value for the PO Number have the same PO Date, Vendor, Manager ID, and PO Amount in columns A through E. From Column F and on to the right, rows with the same PO Number might have different values, depending on the invoice's date, amount, and so on.

This arrangement isn't as effective as another one might be. Look at all that repetition! All that's really needed to uniquely identify a purchase order is the PO number (assuming that the issuer takes the elementary precaution of avoiding duplicate PO numbers). Knowing the PO number tells you its issue date, the vendor's name, the manager's ID, and its amount.

And yet, as vendors' invoices enter the system, this layout requires repetition so that the user can see all the pertinent information. For example, how would you know that a $5,000 invoice exceeded the original PO amount of $4,000 unless you could see both figures?

The approach shown in Figure 1.12 assigns one row to each invoice, multiple rows to each PO, and one column to each field—whether or not that field contains information concerning a PO or an invoice. Another way to approach the problem is to assign exactly one row to a PO and to string out information about the associated invoices in columns. Figure 1.13 shows one way of doing this.

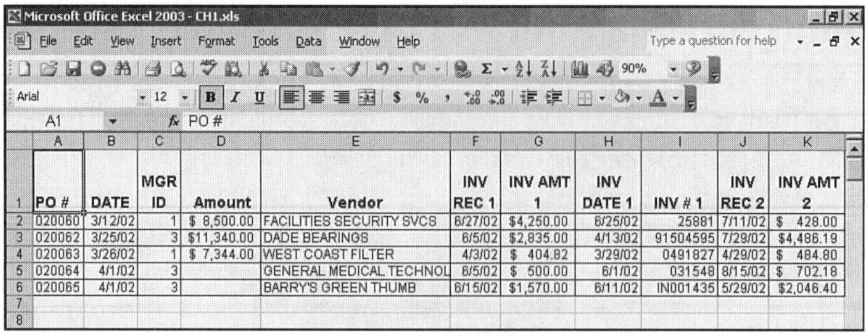

PO #	DATE	MGR ID	Amount	Vendor	INV REC 1	INV AMT 1	INV DATE 1	INV # 1	INV REC 2	INV AMT 2
020060	3/12/02	1	$ 8,500.00	FACILITIES SECURITY SVCS	6/27/02	$4,250.00	6/25/02	25881	7/11/02	$ 428.00
020062	3/25/02	3	$11,340.00	DADE BEARINGS	6/5/02	$2,835.00	4/13/02	91504595	7/29/02	$4,486.19
020063	3/26/02	1	$ 7,344.00	WEST COAST FILTER	4/3/02	$ 404.82	3/29/02	0491827	4/29/02	$ 484.80
020064	4/1/02	3		GENERAL MEDICAL TECHNOL	6/5/02	$ 500.00	6/1/02	031548	8/15/02	$ 702.18
020065	4/1/02	3		BARRY'S GREEN THUMB	6/15/02	$1,570.00	6/11/02	IN001435	5/29/02	$2,046.40

Figure 1.13
Instead of an indeterminate number of rows per PO, here you get an indeterminate number of columns.

In one way at least, the layout shown in Figure 1.13 is better than that in Figure 1.12: It doesn't repeat the PO information for every invoice that references the same PO. But it introduces new drawbacks. One is that you can't sensibly get invoice amounts into a range of contiguous cells, such as G980:G995, where it's easy to total them. Instead, you have to create a formula that adds each cell separately—for example

```
=G970 + L970 + Q970 + V970 + AA970 . . .
```

and so forth until you reach the final possible invoice amount (yes, after you've created this formula it's easy to copy into new rows). More important, suppose that 14 columns are needed to completely describe an invoice. What happens when you get to the eighteenth invoice? With 17 invoices entered, you've used 243 columns: 238 for the invoice data plus 5 for the PO. That leaves 13 columns of the 256 on a worksheet, and you can enter only 17 invoices.

Seventeen invoices might seem like plenty, but the worksheet from which Figure 1.12 was taken had 15 different purchase orders with more than 17 invoices each. And visually, a repeating sequence of columns is a nightmare.

This gets us back to the problem discussed in the earlier section, "Transposing Rows and Columns." And if you switch rows and columns in this layout, distributing invoice records across columns instead of across rows, you deny yourself the list structure (records in rows, fields in columns) that is so useful in Excel. How, for example, would you go about charting invoice amount against invoice date given the layout in Figure 1.13? You'd have to create a chart using one pair of columns, and then add data to that chart from another pair of columns, and so on—instead of creating the chart in a single step as a list layout would let you.

Another approach might be to use different workbooks for different vendors, and a different worksheet within each workbook for each purchase order. That's a recipe for chaos.

The root cause of the problem is that Excel is asked to account for three dimensions when only two are available. One dimension is purchase orders. Another is invoices, which are nested within each purchase order. The third dimension is the set of fields that describes a purchase order or an invoice; this set of fields crosses purchase orders and invoices.

But a worksheet has two dimensions: rows and columns, and you can't represent purchase orders, invoices, and fields on a worksheet without distributing information across rows, as in Figure 1.12, or alternating fields across invoices so that it's impractical to do any charting or analysis, as in Figure 1.13.

This is one of the reasons that relational databases are so useful: You use them to *relate* a set of *child records* (here, the invoices) to the *parent records* they belong to (here, the purchase orders). One major goal of this book is to show you how to harness the management power of a relational database to the analytic power of Excel, so that you can bring to bear the best of both applications.

Changing Horses

This chapter has taken a brief look at overworking functions, ineffective data orientation, codes versus labels, and flat file workarounds that try to manage relational structures. There are more problems that you've probably run into already—for example, managing multiple simultaneous users and working with data outlines instead of pivot tables. Subsequent chapters in this book deal with these issues in greater detail.

If this chapter leaves you with the sense that Excel is the wrong application for data management, it has misled you. Worksheet functions, transposed lists, code lookups, and other features are sensible, valuable tools for data management. Nevertheless, they can go wrong and often do. That happens usually, if not always, when you find yourself working with more data than your original setup anticipated.

You'll eventually save yourself a lot of time and grief if you're willing to recognize when your current data set has outgrown the data management setup that you started with. If you'll change horses when that time comes, you'll wind up with a system that works rapidly and smoothly, with a minimum of fits and starts.

Of course, the problem is in recognizing the need for a redesign. You get that only with experience, but subsequent chapters in this book will give you some pointers. A good place to start is with Excel's family of lookup and reference functions, coming up in Chapter 2.

Managing Data Inside Excel

II

Excel's Data Management Features

Using the Worksheet Functions: An Overview

Using worksheet functions to help manage data might seem, at the outset, a little odd. It's natural to think of functions that you enter on the worksheet to do calculations and return values, such as the average of a set of numbers, a monthly payment amount, or pi.

But there is a class of worksheet functions, valuable ones indeed, that help you find data and display it in different configurations. Some of the lookup and reference functions are presented in the following list, along with a description of how they're used. This is intended not as a comprehensive discussion of the functions, but as a brief summary of the sort of thing that's available to you right on the worksheet.

- ADDRESS returns a cell reference when given a row number and a column number. `ADDRESS(3,4)` returns $D$3, which is the third row and fourth column. Optional arguments enable you to specify a fixed, mixed, or relative reference; an A1 or R1C1 style; and a worksheet name.

- AREAS returns the number of areas in (usually) multiple references. An area is a range of contiguous cells. `AREAS((A1:C3,E4:G6))` returns 2. The extra pair of parentheses is required with multiple references. If you leave out the extra parentheses--for example, `AREAS(A1:C3,E4:G6)`--Excel thinks you are providing more than one argument when it expects one argument only.

- COLUMN returns the column number of a reference. `COLUMN(E6)` returns 5. `COLUMN(F8:G9)` returns {6,7}, but you see only the 6 unless you array-enter the formula in two horizontally adjacent cells. For example, you might select A1:B1, type this formula

  `=COLUMN(F8:G9)`

  and enter it with Ctrl+Shift+Enter, instead of just pressing the Enter key.

- COLUMNS returns the number of columns in a reference. `COLUMNS(F8:G10)` returns 2.

- GETPIVOTDATA returns a data field value from a pivot table, given the data field's name, a cell reference that identifies the pivot table, a field name, and an item name. In Excel 2002 and 2003, this formula

  `=GETPIVOTDATA("Voters",$A$1,"Affiliation","Independent")`

  returns information about Voters (the count, perhaps; it depends on what summary statistic you've called for in the pivot table itself) whose Affiliation is Independent, in the pivot table that includes cell $A$1.

- VLOOKUP finds a value in the first column of a lookup range, and returns the corresponding value in a different column of that range. If A3 contains Smith and C3 contains $5,000, `VLOOKUP("Smith",A1:D10,3)` returns $5,000.

- HLOOKUP returns results in much the same way that VLOOKUP does. The difference is that the lookup table is rotated 90 degrees: Instead of occupying, say, A1:B10 as it might if used by VLOOKUP, the table might occupy A1:J2 if used by HLOOKUP. Because Excel's list structure calls for records in rows and fields in columns, you're much more likely to have use for VLOOKUP than for HLOOKUP.

- INDEX returns a value from a worksheet range (more generally, from an array, which is often a worksheet range). If cell C23 contains the value 3, `INDEX(B20:C26,4,2)` returns 3. This is the value in the fourth row (row 23) and second column (column C) of the range B20:C26.

- INDIRECT returns a cell address, given a string. Often, the string is in another cell. If A20 contains the string E28, and cell E28 contains 5, `INDIRECT(A20)` returns 5. In tandem with ROW or COLUMN, INDIRECT is also a handy way to get an array of integers: `ROW(INDIRECT("1:5"))` returns {1;2;3;4;5}. This has broad applicability. Suppose that A1 contains a string of indeterminate length. Then `ROW(INDIRECT("1:" & LEN(A1)))` returns an array of as many integers as there are characters in A1. If A1 contains "Fred", `ROW(INDIRECT("1:" & LEN(A1)))` returns {1;2;3;4}.

- MATCH returns the position of a value in an array. If A1:A5 contains A, B, C, D, and E, `MATCH("C",A1:A5)` returns 3--the position that C occupies in the range A1:A5. Contrast this with INDEX: Given a value, MATCH returns a position; given a position, INDEX returns a value.

- OFFSET returns the contents of a cell or range that is shifted--*offset*--from another cell, sometimes termed the *basis cell*. Suppose that cell C4 contains 42. Then `OFFSET(A1,3,2)` returns 42: the contents of the cell that is offset three rows and two columns from A1, the basis cell.

- ROW returns the row number of a reference. `ROW(E6)` returns 6. If you array-enter this formula

    `=ROW(F8:G9)`

    it will return the array {8;9}. You would begin by selecting two vertically adjacent cells, such as A1:A2, and type the ROW formula as shown, finishing up with Ctrl+Shift+Enter.

> **TIP**
>
> Notice how, in contrast to COLUMN, the ROW function returns an array of numbers separated by a semicolon. In general, Excel uses commas to separate cell references that occupy different columns; it uses semicolons to separate cell references that occupy different rows. You can see this directly by selecting a cell that the array formula occupies, and choosing Insert, Function.

- ROWS returns the number of rows in a reference. `ROWS(F8:G10)` returns 3.
- TRANSPOSE switches the orientation of rows and columns in a range. Except when the original range contains one cell only (and then there's no point to using TRANSPOSE), the function *must* be array-entered with Ctrl+Shift+Enter. It's much easier to see what TRANSPOSE does than to read it (see Figure 2.1).

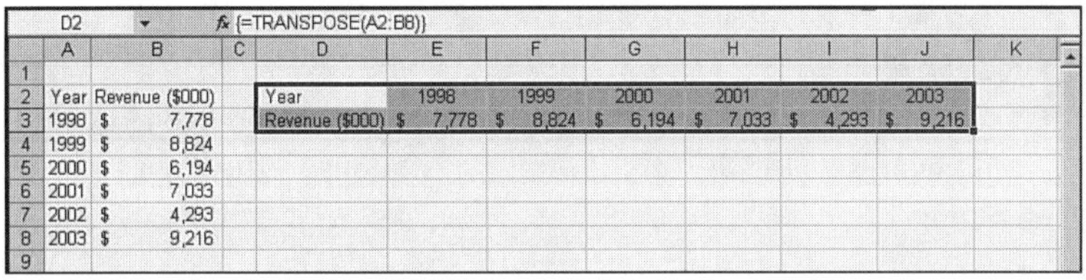

Figure 2.1
Before you enter the TRANSPOSE function, select a range with as many rows as the original range has columns, and as many columns as the original range has rows.

With the preceding overview as a backdrop, the next few sections go into considerably more detail about how to use the worksheet functions to help manage data.

Locating Data with OFFSET

The OFFSET function returns a reference to a cell, or to a range of cells, and it displays their contents. Figure 2.2 has a basic example of OFFSET.

Understanding the Basis Cell

OFFSET needs a cell reference to use as a basis. You will also tell OFFSET how many rows and how many columns to shift, or *offset*, but first it needs to know which cell to shift from.

The whole idea behind the OFFSET function is that you want the address of a range of cells that are near to some other cell. For example, you might want to use the address of the range of cells in a table so that you can get their sum, but you *don't* want to include the row of labels at the top of the table. You could use the cell in the table's upper-left corner as the basis cell to tell OFFSET where to start.

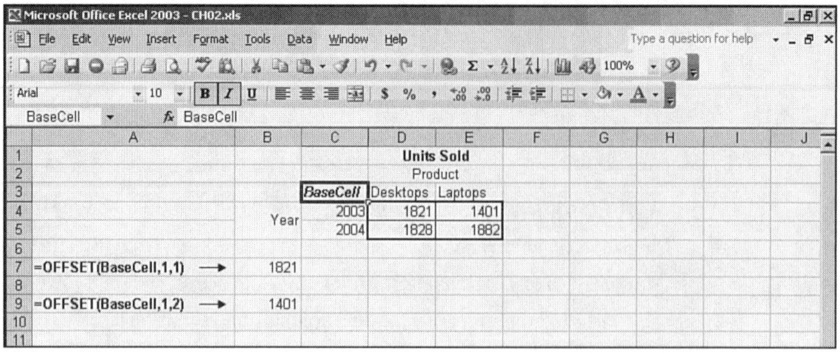

Figure 2.2
OFFSET is one good way to rearrange data from a table.

In Figure 2.2, OFFSET uses a cell named *BaseCell* as its basis. For example, the formula with the OFFSET function, as used in cell B9, is

```
=OFFSET(BaseCell,1,2)
```

So, cell B9 uses the OFFSET function to

- Start with the cell named BaseCell, which is cell $C$3.

- OFFSET's second argument tells it how many rows to shift. In this case, the second argument is 1, so OFFSET shifts down one row below BaseCell, into row 4.

- OFFSET'S third argument tells it how many columns to shift. In this case, the third argument is 2, so OFFSET shifts two columns to the right from BaseCell, into column E.

In other words, cell B9 displays the contents of the cell that is one row below and two columns right of BaseCell. That is cell E4, and its value, 1401, is the one you see in B9.

Array-Entering OFFSET to Return Several Cells

OFFSET has two other arguments: Height and Width. These refer to the height of the range in rows, and the width of the range in columns, that you want OFFSET to return. (They need to be positive numbers: Excel doesn't know how to interpret a range that's –2 rows high.) So, this formula

```
=OFFSET(BaseCell,1,1,2,2)
```

would return a range that's offset from BaseCell by one row and one column, and that is two rows high and two columns wide, as shown in Figure 2.3.

Typically, OFFSET is used to return just some of the rows or some of the columns in a source range. It can also be used to return, say, a 3–by–3 section of a 7-by–7 source range.

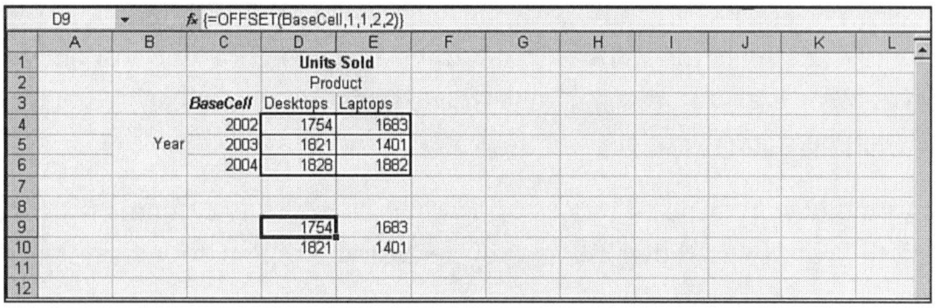

Figure 2.3
The curly brackets around the formula tell you that it's an array formula.

OFFSET's Height and Width arguments are particularly powerful when used to return successively larger square sections of an array of values, as is often required in quantitative analysis. For example

```
=OFFSET(A1,0,0,2,2)
=OFFSET(A1,0,0,3,3)
=OFFSET(A1,0,0,4,4)
```

But notice in Figure 2.3 that there are curly brackets, sometimes termed *French braces*, around the formula. This means that it is not a regular Excel formula, but an *array formula*. Array formulas often, but not always, occupy a range of multiple cells. They usually take arrays as one or more arguments.

Array formulas were mentioned (without much explanation) in the first section of this chapter. You enter an array formula with a special key combination: Ctrl+Shift+Enter. In words, you hold down the Ctrl and Shift keys simultaneously, and press Enter. Your formula appears in the formula bar surrounded by curly braces, just as shown in Figure 2.3.

CAUTION

Don't type the curly braces yourself. If you do, Excel will interpret the formula as text.

You find array formulas in many Excel worksheets that have intermediate to advanced uses. In fact, several Excel functions *require* that you array-enter them or they won't work as intended; among them are MMULT, MDETERM, LINEST, LOGEST, and FRE-QUENCY. Also keep in mind that you need to select the range that the formula will occupy before you begin to enter it. Of course, this requires that you know the dimensions of the array that the function will return. To array-enter the OFFSET function shown in Figure 2.3, follow these three steps in this specific order:

1. Using Insert, Name, Define, name cell $C$3 **BaseCell**.
2. Select the range D9:E10.
3. Click in the Formula Bar, and type this: **=OFFSET(BaseCell,1,1,2,2)**.
4. Hold down **Ctrl** and **Shift**, and press **Enter**.

This array-entered formula, with the help of the OFFSET function, returns a reference to D4:E5--the range that is offset from the basis cell C3 by one row and one column, and that is two rows high and two columns wide. If instead you had array-entered this formula

```
=OFFSET(BaseCell,1,1,2,3)
```

it would have returned a range two rows high and *three* columns wide. But you would have had to begin by selecting a 2–row by 3–column range before array-entering the formula.

Finding Data with INDEX

Both the INDEX function and the OFFSET function return data from a subset of an array. They differ in several ways, including what it is you want to accomplish:

- It's typical to use OFFSET when you can specify several rows and columns that you want to get at. For example, you might use this

  ```
  =OFFSET(BaseCell, 0, 0, 2, 2)
  ```

  to get the cells in the first two rows and the first two columns of a range of cells.
- It's typical to use INDEX when you can specify a particular row or column and you want the value where they intersect. For example, this

  ```
  =INDEX(D4:E6, 3, 2)
  ```

  returns the contents of cell E6; that is, the third row of the second column of the range D4:E6. See Figure 2.4.

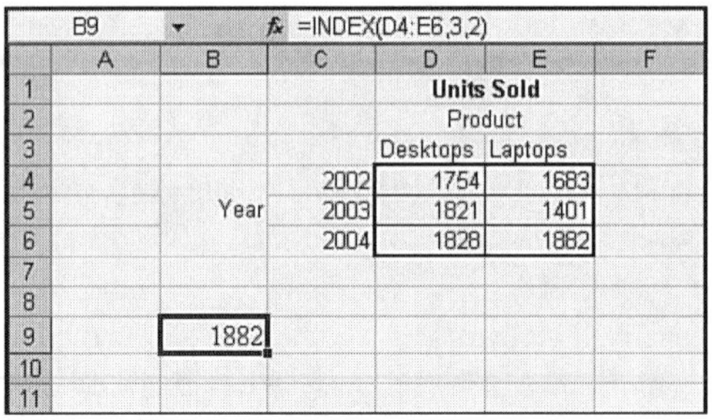
B9 =INDEX(D4:E6,3,2)

	A	B	C	D	E	F
1				Units Sold		
2				Product		
3				Desktops	Laptops	
4			2002	1754	1683	
5		Year	2003	1821	1401	
6			2004	1828	1882	
7						
8						
9		1882				
10						
11						

Figure 2.4
Using INDEX in this way is similar to using a formula with constants, such as =6 + 2--its usefulness is limited.

That last example, finding the value in the third row and second column of a range of cells, is almost trivial. How many times do you think you'll need to find that your company sold 1882 laptops in 2004? The INDEX function begins to get really useful when you combine it with other functions, which tell INDEX where to look. One such is MATCH.

Finding Data with MATCH

OFFSET and INDEX both return values from a range--more generally, from an array--given information about where to look. In contrast, MATCH tells you where in a range to look, given information about values.

> **NOTE**
>
> What's the difference between an array and a range? An *array* refers to any arrangement of one or more rows crossed by one or more columns. It needn't exist on a worksheet. It could be and often is a memory array used by code written in VBA (or C or FORTRAN or Java); your VBA code can use the worksheet functions described here on memory arrays. A *range* is an array that's located on a worksheet. You can, and often do, use VBA to move data back and forth between worksheet ranges and memory arrays.

For example, this formula

```
=MATCH(20,$B$2:$B$6,0)
```

says to find the value 20 in the range $B$2:$B$6 and return 20's position in that range. The third argument, 0, means that you want an exact match (see Figure 2.5).

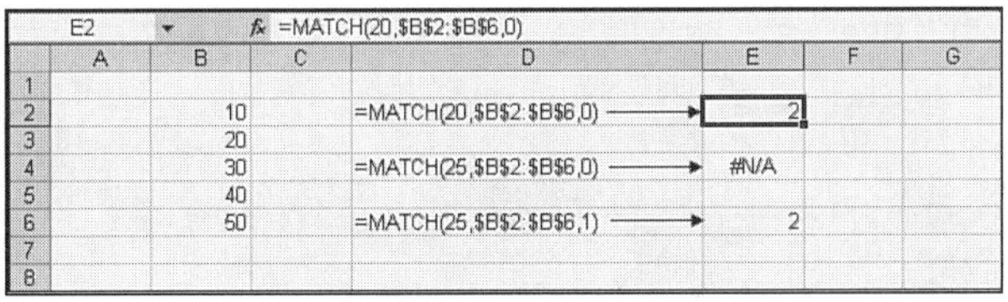

Figure 2.5
If you ask MATCH for an exact match, and it can't find one, it returns the error value #N/A.

As Figure 2.5 shows, you can use MATCH to find an exact match or an approximate match. In the figure, cells E2 and E4 use MATCH to find an exact match. Cell E6 uses 1 as its third argument, to find an approximate match. Notice that

- In cell E2 and E4, MATCH's third argument is 0 (zero). This requests an exact match.
- In cell E2, MATCH successfully finds an exact match; 20 is in the second position in the range, so MATCH returns 2 (to indicate the second position).
- In cell E4, MATCH cannot find an exact match; 25 is not found in any position in the range. MATCH therefore returns the error value #N/A.
- In cell E6, MATCH's third argument is a 1. This value does two things: It asks for an approximate match, and it promises that the range's values are sorted in ascending order.

The phrase *approximate match* is only approximately accurate. When you supply a 1 as MATCH's third argument, you tell MATCH to find the largest value that is less than or equal to the value you're looking for.

Suppose that you're looking for the value 5 in the array {2, 4, 6, 8}. Supplying a 1 as MATCH's third argument causes MATCH to return 2. The value 4 is the array's largest value that is equal to or less than 5, and 4 is in the second position.

It's important to remember that the sort order of the array can make a difference to an approximate match. Again, suppose that you're looking for 5, but that the array is {2, 4, 6, 8, 5}. MATCH still returns 2 (the position that 4 occupies), even though the value 5 itself is in the array. By giving 1 as the third argument, you've promised that the array is in ascending order, so when it finds the 6, MATCH assumes that it doesn't need to look any further. If, as promised, the array is in ascending order, MATCH won't find a value that is less than or equal to 5 by looking past 6. You have to keep your promises.

Using MATCH with Other Functions

You probably won't have much use for the MATCH function all by itself. Think back: How often have you wondered where to find the number 5 in the range C10:C100 by means of a worksheet function? But when you use MATCH as an argument to another function, such as INDEX or OFFSET, you begin to appreciate how valuable it is.

Combining MATCH and INDEX

That aspect of MATCH--being able to find the largest value less than or equal to the value you're looking for--is useful when you have to deal with grouped values as seen in Figure 2.6.

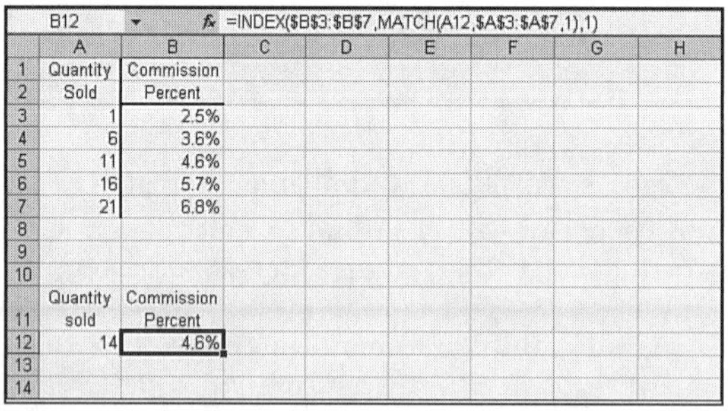

Figure 2.6
Consider using MATCH whenever several values (such as 11 through 15) are associated with one value (such as 4.6%).

In Figure 2.6, the user is looking for the proper commission rate to pay for a sale of 14 items. The proper rate is 4.6%: the rate that applies when 11, 12, 13, 14, or 15 units are sold. You get that rate by looking for the right group of units by means of MATCH, and then using MATCH's result to find the value you're after.

The formula shown in Figure 2.6 is

```
=INDEX($B$3:$B$7,MATCH(A12,$A$3:$A$7,1),1)
```

Look first at the MATCH part of the formula:

```
MATCH(A12,$A$3:$A$7,1)
```

This tells Excel to look for the value in A12 (which is 14) in the range $A$3:$A$7, and return the position of the largest value that's less than or equal to 14 (the third argument to MATCH, 1, calls for the less-than or equal-to approximate match).

The value 11 is the largest value that's less than or equal to 14 in $A$3:$A$7, and it's in position number 3 in that range. So, MATCH returns the value 3. In the original formula

```
=INDEX($B$3:$B$7,MATCH(A12,$A$3:$A$7,1),1)
```

you could replace the MATCH function and its arguments with 3, the value it returns, as follows:

```
=INDEX($B$3:$B$7,3,1)
```

So, by using MATCH to approximately locate the value 14, you tell INDEX to return the value in the third row, first column of $B$3:$B$7, or 4.6%.

> **TIP**
>
> If you're using Excel 97 or 2000, you can select a cell containing a formula such as the one discussed here, and in the Formula Bar, use your mouse pointer to drag across some portion of it, such as MATCH(A12,$A$3:$A$7,1). Then press the F9 key to see how Excel evaluates the highlighted portion. Press Esc to leave the formula as is. (If you press Enter, you might unintentionally convert the highlighted portion to a constant.)
>
> If you're using Excel 2002 or 2003, you can do the same thing, but instead you can choose Tools, Formula Auditing, Evaluate Formula to see, step by step, how Excel evaluates each portion of the formula.

The following list outlines the main points you need to remember:

- Make sure that the array (in Figure 2.6, that's B3:B7) is in ascending order. This is because you will call for an approximate match.
- To call for the approximate match, use 1 as MATCH's third argument.
- Make sure to convert the position (what MATCH actually returns) to a value (what you're really after). In many cases, including this one, that means passing the result of the MATCH function as an argument to the INDEX function.

> **TIP**
>
> This way of using functions--that is, using the result of one function as an argument to another-- has broad applicability in Excel, particularly in the text functions. For example, you could get an email address stripped of its domain with something such as
> ```
> =LEFT(D1,FIND("@",D1)-1)
> ```

Fooling the Approximate Match

It's not unusual to use functions and their arguments in ways that they weren't originally intended. One good example involves MATCH, OFFSET, and the MAX function. The MAX function returns the largest numeric value in a range. For example, this formula

```
=MAX(A1:C200)
```

returns the largest value in A1:C200.

Suppose that you want to know the location of the final value in, say, Column A. One way to do that is to activate cell A65536, the final cell in Column A. Hold down the Ctrl key and press the up arrow key. Assuming that A65536 is an empty cell, this will take you to the bottommost nonempty cell in Column A.

> **NOTE**
> This chapter makes frequent use of the terms *bottommost* and *rightmost*, so it's good to define them, if only by example. Suppose that column A has the value 8 in row 25 and nothing at all in rows 26 through 65536. In that case, A25 is column A's bottommost cell. If row 4 has the value "EBCDIC" in column AD and nothing at all in columns AE through IV, AD4 is row 4's rightmost cell.

Fine, but that's not very convenient, especially if there are several columns of interest. And if you want to use the last value in a column in another formula, you want to be able to redetermine that value as more cells are filled in. Further, you might want to test whether some extraneous value has found its way into a column, well below the area where your work normally occurs. A fairly ingenious use of the approximate match solves the problem (see Figure 2.7).

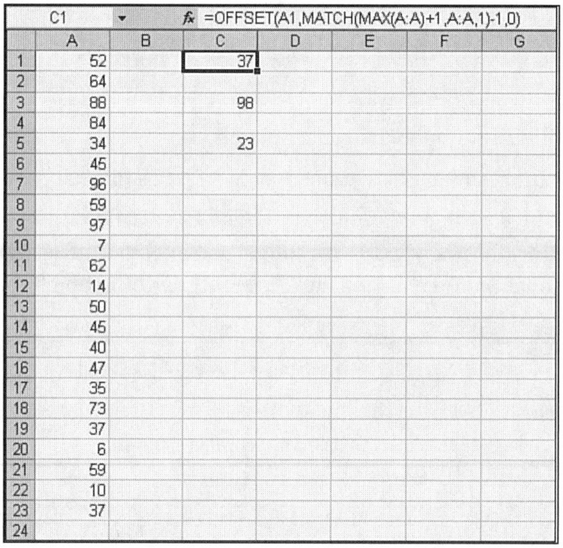

	A	B	C	D	E	F	G
1	52		37				
2	64						
3	88		98				
4	84						
5	34		23				
6	45						
7	96						
8	59						
9	97						
10	7						
11	62						
12	14						
13	50						
14	45						
15	40						
16	47						
17	35						
18	73						
19	37						
20	6						
21	59						
22	10						
23	37						
24							

Figure 2.7
This technique does not work with text values.

The formula in cell C1 of Figure 2.7 is

```
=OFFSET(A1,MATCH(MAX(A:A)+1,A:A,1)-1,0)
```

and it returns 37, the last (bottommost) value in column A. This would normally be a trivial usage because you can see it. But suppose that the last value were in cell A4500, where it wouldn't be quite so obvious. Or suppose that the formula returned 2432, against your expectations. That would cue you to look further to see how that 2432 value got in there.

To see what's going on, take the formula apart. Cell C3 contains this fragment from the complete formula

```
=MAX(A:A)+1
```

which returns 98. The value 97 is the largest value in column A, and adding 1 to it results in 98. Substituting that value for the MAX function in the complete formula leaves this:

```
=OFFSET(A1,MATCH(98,A:A,1)-1,0)
```

Now, what does the MATCH function return? This fragment is in cell C5

```
=MATCH(98,A:A,1)
```

and it returns the value 23.

As you've seen, the value 1 as MATCH's third argument requests the largest value in the lookup range that is less than or equal to the lookup value. Here, though, the MATCH function is confronted with a lookup value that is larger than any value in the lookup range. It has to be, because it's the result of adding 1 to the maximum value in the range.

Because the lookup type of 1 promises that the range is in ascending order, MATCH locates the range's final value: According to the promise of an ascending sort, that's its largest value. By using one more than MAX as the lookup value, the final value must be less than or equal to the lookup value. So, the MATCH function returns the position of that final value; here, that's 23.

Notice that if you wanted to, you could stop at this point. You might do that if you were interested less in the actual value than in where it's located. You already know that the final value is in the 23rd position of the lookup range (which is Column A).

But if you want to know the value itself, take one more step. Here are two versions of the original formula, simplified by using the results of the MAX and the MATCH functions:

```
=OFFSET(A1,23-1,0)
```

or

```
=OFFSET(A1,22,0)
```

That is, the value that is 22 rows below and zero columns to the right of A1, and that's 37.

TIP

A good way to test your understanding of the material in this section is to change the original formula so that it searches for the rightmost value in a row, rather than the bottommost value in a column. If you do, remember to switch the position of the row and column arguments in the OFFSET function. Also, bear in mind that while you refer to the first column as A:A, you refer to the first row as 1:1.

Extending the Last Cell Search

The technique described in the prior section is fine for single columns and single rows, but what about a full range such as A1:G200? And what about text values, which the MAX function isn't able to locate?

Figure 2.8 demonstrates one approach, attributed to Bob Umlas. To show the idea in book format, the range that contains values is kept small, A1:G20, although the range actually searched is much larger, A1:G500. Of course, if you use this in your own work, the range that contains values is likely to be much larger.

Figure 2.8

If these formulas were entered normally, they would return the #VALUE! error value.

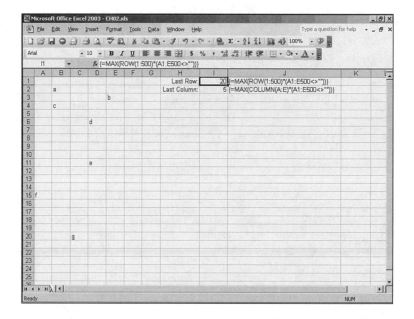

The formula in J1 of Figure 2.8 is

```
{=MAX(ROW(1:500)*(A1:E500<>""))}
```

Note the curly braces indicating an array formula. Excel adds them automatically when you array-enter a formula with Ctrl+Shift+Enter instead of pressing just the Enter key.

The formula in J1 returns 20, the row in which the bottommost value in the range A1:E500 is found. It's helpful to parse the formula to better understand how it works. This portion

```
ROW(1:500)
```

returns an array of row numbers, separated by semicolons (recall that Excel separates row references by semicolons and column references by commas). It looks like this:

```
{1;2;3;4; ... ;499;500}
```

Or it would if you could see it all.

> **NOTE** Using the Excel 97 and 2000 technique, dragging across `ROW(1:500)` to highlight it in the Formula Bar and then pressing F9 results in the message that the formula is too long. The Excel 2002 and 2003 technique, using the Formula Evaluator, does not result in an error, but returns a single value only when applied to the `ROW(1:500)` expression.

So far, the formula has created an array of 500 row numbers. The next portion is

`(A1:E500<>"")`

It returns this array

`{FALSE,FALSE,FALSE,FALSE,FALSE;FALSE,TRUE,FALSE,FALSE,FALSE; . . .;}`

which shows FALSE if a cell equals "" (that is, the cell contains a blank), and TRUE if a cell does *not* equal "" (so, the cell contains anything other than a blank, including numbers and text, but not error values such as #REF!).

Notice that the first five values in the array are separated by commas. They represent cells A1:E1, which are in different columns but in the same row, so they are separated by commas. The first through fifth values and the sixth through tenth values are separated by a semicolon. Collectively, they represent A1:E1 and A2:E2, which are in different rows, so the first five are separated by a semicolon from the second five.

Also notice that the seventh value in the array is TRUE. This corresponds to cell B2, which Figure 2.8 shows to contain the value *a*. It's not a blank cell, so the formula returns a TRUE.

By now two portions of the formula have been evaluated, and we have an array of numbers from 1 through 500, and an array of TRUE or FALSE values. The original formula calls for those two portions to be multiplied together.

When you multiply the value TRUE times a number, the result is that number. So, 7*TRUE equals 7. When you multiply the value FALSE times a number, the result is 0. Multiplying the two arrays together, then, returns 0s where the cell contains a blank (and so the second array contains a FALSE). It returns the row number from the first array when the cell contains a nonblank, nonerror value (the row number times TRUE gives the row number). Here's what the first part of the array looks like:

`{0,0,0,0,0;0,2,0,0,0;`

Notice that the array contains 0s where the cell is blank, and the cell's row number where the cell is neither blank nor an error. In the fragment shown above, the row number is 2.

By now ,the formula has returned an array consisting of 0s and the numbers of rows that contain values. By applying MAX to the result, it's possible to learn the largest value in that array: the largest row number in the range that contains a legitimate value. Substituting the prior array for the formula fragments that create it

`=MAX({0,0,0,0,0;0,2,0,0,0; . . . ,0;})`

returns what the formula's after: the bottommost row in a multi-column range that contains a legitimate value.

Of course, the formula in cell J2 works in much the same way, except that it deals with the maximum column number instead of the maximum row number.

Distinguishing the Bottommost Cell from the Last Cell

There's a subtle difference between what the prior two sections have meant by the term *bottommost cell* (and *rightmost cell*) and what Excel means by *last cell*. As used in this chapter, the bottommost cell is the one that contains a value and that is farthest down the worksheet-- that is, the value that occupies the row with the largest row header.

By *last cell*, Excel means the bottommost, rightmost cell that has been used since the workbook was last saved. The phrase *has been used* needs some clarification. The following actions are all considered *using* a cell:

- Entering a value in a cell

- Formatting a cell, even an empty one

- Changing a row's height or a column's width

- Changing a cell's protection--for example, from locked to unlocked

One implication of this is that an empty cell could be considered the last cell. To demonstrate this to yourself, take the following steps:

1. Open a new workbook.
2. Select some cell other than A1, such as **E5**.
3. Choose **Format**, **Cells** and click the **Number** tab. Give the cell any format other than General--in other words, change the cell's default format.
4. Select cell **A1**.
5. Choose **Edit**, **Go To** and click the **Special** button. Fill the **Last Cell** option and click **OK**. Excel selects the cell you formatted.

This definition of *last cell* is not the same as that used in the prior two sections, where a bottommost or a rightmost cell was defined by the presence of a value in the cell. And it's more persistent as well. Clear a value from the bottommost cell in Column A, for example, and the formula

```
=OFFSET(A1,MATCH(MAX(A:A)+1,A:A,1)-1,0)
```

no longer displays that value. Rather, it displays the new bottommost value.

In contrast, click the Select All button on the worksheet you used to test for the location of its last cell, and choose Edit, Clear, All. Even though you've reset the format of all the worksheet's cells to General, you still activate the same last cell by means of Edit, Go To, Special, Last Cell.

You force Excel to redefine the last cell by closing the workbook (saving changes) and then reopening it. No matter whether you enter and then clear a value from a cell, or format and then clear the format from a cell, or reset the row height or column width, Excel continues to activate that cell as the last cell until you close and then reopen the workbook.

Using MATCH and INDEX in Two-Way Arrays

Figure 2.9 extends the example, begun in Figure 2.6 and implying one product line only, to several product lines.

Figure 2.9
Here you use MATCH to find both the proper row and the proper column.

C12 =INDEX($C$3:$H$7,MATCH(B12,$B$3:$B$7,1),MATCH(A12,$C$2:$H$2,0))

	A	B	C	D	E	F	G	H	I
1		Quantity			Product Line				
2		Sold	Laptops	Desktops	Scanners	Routers	Monitors	Printers	
3		1	2.5%	8.6%	3.8%	3.3%	7.2%	5.7%	
4		6	3.6%	10.8%	6.2%	5.4%	9.4%	8.3%	
5		11	4.6%	13.0%	8.6%	7.6%	11.6%	10.9%	
6		16	5.7%	15.2%	11.0%	9.7%	13.9%	13.5%	
7		21	6.8%	17.4%	13.4%	11.8%	16.1%	16.1%	
8									
9									
10									
11	Product	Quantity sold	Commission Percent						
12	Desktops	8	10.8%						
13	Routers	2	3.3%						
14	Printers	4	5.7%						
15	Monitors	12	11.6%						
16	Laptops	14	4.6%						
17									
18									

Figure 2.9 shows that MATCH works with both numeric and text values. As shown, the formula in cell C12 is

```
=INDEX($C$3:$H$7,MATCH(B12,$B$3:$B$7,1),MATCH(A12,$C$2:$H$2,0))
```

Again, break the formula down into its components. The first instance of MATCH is

```
MATCH(B12,$B$3:$B$7,1)
```

That is, return the position occupied in $B$3:$B$7 by the largest value that's less than or equal to the value in B12. B12 contains 8, and the largest value in $B$3:$B$7 less than or equal to 8 is 6. The value 6 occupies the second position in $B$3:$B$7, so this instance of MATCH returns 2.

The second instance of MATCH is

```
MATCH(A12,$C$2:$H$2,0)
```

That is, return the position occupied in $C$2:$H$2 by the value in A12, and return an exact match. (The third argument, 0, calls for an exact match.) The value in A12 is Desktops, and Desktops occupies the second position in $C$2:$H$2. So, this instance of MATCH also returns 2.

> **NOTE**
>
> The reason that the second instance of MATCH calls for an exact match is that approximate matches are seldom sensible with text values. In Figure 2.9, for example, you would not want MATCH to return *Scanners* if you had it look for *Software*.

To see more clearly what's happening in the full formula, replace the two MATCH functions with the values they return. Again, you can do this by dragging across MATCH(B12,$B$3:$B$7,1) in the Formula Bar and pressing F9. Follow that up, if you wish, by doing the same with MATCH(A12,$C$2:$H$2,0). Or in Excel 2002 or 2003, use Tools, Formula Auditing, Evaluate Formula.

When you do so, the INDEX function simplifies to this:

```
=INDEX($C$3:$H$7,2,2)
```

In words, return the value in the second row and second column of the range $C$3:$H$7. That value is 10.8%, which is the commission rate indicated for selling eight desktops.

When you use MATCH in this way, it's not necessary that the range you're looking in to find the proper row occupy the same rows as the values you want to return. For example, the range $B$3:$B$7, with the quantity sold, could just as easily be in $GW$200:$GW$204 and the actual commission percentages could stay in $C$3:$H$7. But it's a lot easier to arrange your data as Figure 2.9 shows.

> **NOTE**
>
> This chapter hasn't mentioned it yet because it's so seldom used, but the *lookup type* argument to the MATCH function has another possible value. This chapter has examined the effect of 0 (return an exact match) and of 1 (return an approximate match, the largest one that's less than or equal to the lookup value in an array that's sorted in ascending order). A third possibility is −1, and it also requests an approximate match: find the smallest one that's *greater than or equal to* the lookup value in an array that's sorted in *descending* order. It takes an idiosyncratic data layout to require this approach, but bear in mind that it's available if you ever encounter one.

Using VLOOKUP

The last section discussed one way to manage arrays of data using INDEX along with MATCH. Another closely related technique uses VLOOKUP. Unlike MATCH, VLOOKUP returns a value, not a position in a range, so it's seldom necessary to pair VLOOKUP with a function such as INDEX.

As a practical matter, VLOOKUP requires a range of at least two columns, but you often use it to return a value from a range with three or more columns. The distinction is similar to one you've just seen. Compare Figure 2.6 (two columns: one for quantity and one for percentages) with Figure 2.9 (seven columns: one for quantity and six for percentages).

Using VLOOKUP with a Two-Column Range

To use VLOOKUP with a two-column range, you need lookup values in the first column, just as with MATCH combined with INDEX. Similarly, the second column should contain the values you want it to return. Figure 2.10 gives an example.

Figure 2.10
VLOOKUP is usually more convenient than MATCH when just two columns are involved.

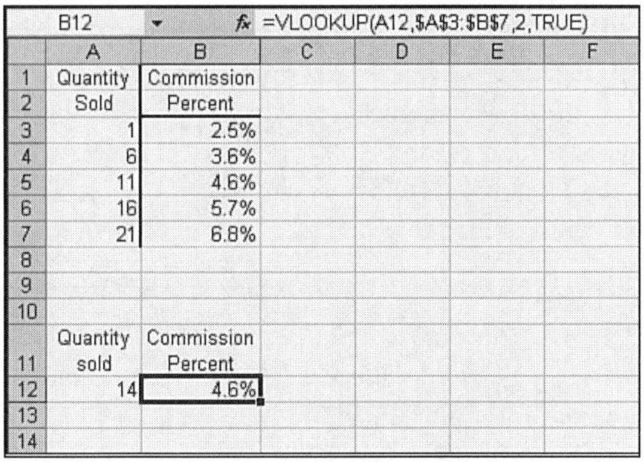

	A	B	C	D	E	F
B12		*fx* =VLOOKUP(A12,$A$3:$B$7,2,TRUE)				
1	Quantity	Commission				
2	Sold	Percent				
3	1	2.5%				
4	6	3.6%				
5	11	4.6%				
6	16	5.7%				
7	21	6.8%				
8						
9						
10						
11	Quantity sold	Commission Percent				
12	14	4.6%				
13						
14						

It's useful to assign terms to VLOOKUP's arguments:

- VLOOKUP's first argument is the *lookup value*. It is the value that VLOOKUP will look for. It can be an actual value, a cell address, or even a defined name.

- VLOOKUP'S second argument is the *lookup array*. It is a range of at least one column and one row; normally, the lookup array contains two or more columns and at least several rows.

- VLOOKUP's third argument is the *column number*. It is the column that VLOOKUP uses to find the value it returns.

- VLOOKUP's fourth argument is the *lookup type*. As in MATCH, it tells Excel whether to make an exact or an approximate match.

In Figure 2.10, the VLOOKUP function is used instead of INDEX and MATCH, which were used in Figure 2.6. In Figure 2.10, the formula in cell B12 is

```
=VLOOKUP(A12,$A$3:$B$7,2,TRUE)
```

The process works as described in the following list:

- VLOOKUP is asked to find the value in A12, the lookup value.

- VLOOKUP *always* looks in the first column of the lookup array to find a matching value. The lookup array is in $A$3:$B$7; the first column in the array is column A, so that's where VLOOKUP searches for a matching value--more specifically, in A3:A7.

- After the value in A12 has been found in A3:A7, VLOOKUP needs to know which column to return. The column number argument (here, the value 2) provides that. In the example, VLOOKUP is asked to return the value in the second column of the lookup array.

■ The fourth argument tells VLOOKUP whether to find an exact or an approximate match in the lookup array. Here the value TRUE specifies an approximate match, looking for the largest value that's less than or equal to the lookup value. This is the same as in the MATCH function, except that VLOOKUP uses TRUE where MATCH uses 1. The TRUE in VLOOKUP and the 1 in MATCH are the defaults.

VLOOKUP looks for the value 14 in the first column of the range A3:B7. Because the lookup type specifies an approximate match, VLOOKUP uses 11: the third value in the first column and the largest value that is less than or equal to 14.

VLOOKUP then looks in the second column of the lookup array, as specified by the column number argument. In the lookup array's third row, second column is the value 4.6%, which is the value that VLOOKUP returns.

You'll probably find VLOOKUP more convenient than the combination of MATCH and INDEX for lookup arrays with only two columns. It's not quite as clear what's going on because it's not intuitively obvious that VLOOKUP always looks to the first column of the lookup array to find a matching value. But it is nice to take advantage of VLOOKUP's brevity: You need only one function instead of two.

CASE STUDY

Calculating Commissions with VLOOKUP

As the sales manager for a local distributor of computing equipment, Debra Brown wants to guide her sales force toward sales that involve more units. Selling one desktop here and a couple of routers there is well and good, but the fulfillment costs eat into the profit margins. Brown would prefer one sale of five monitors, for example, to seven sales of one monitor each.

Accordingly, she draws up a commission schedule that gradually increases the commission percentage according to the number of units sold. The percentages vary both by product line and by quantity sold. Her table of commission percentages is shown in cells C2:H7 of Figure 2.11.

After setting up the table, Brown starts to enter VLOOKUP formulas to determine actual commission dollars. She encounters a typical problem: VLOOKUP is less convenient when you're working with more than two columns than it is when you're working with exactly two. The problem with multiple columns is to get the correct column number into the VLOOKUP arguments.

> NOTE
>
> It will become clear that the sales manager could use a combination of MATCH and INDEX in this case study, just as was shown in Figure 2.9, instead of VLOOKUP. The choice is largely a matter of style and personal preference. Your formulas are somewhat more explicit when you go to the trouble of passing the results of MATCH functions to INDEX. But they are also inevitably lengthier, and many expert users prefer the terser VLOOKUP syntax to the more verbose MATCH-INDEX combination.

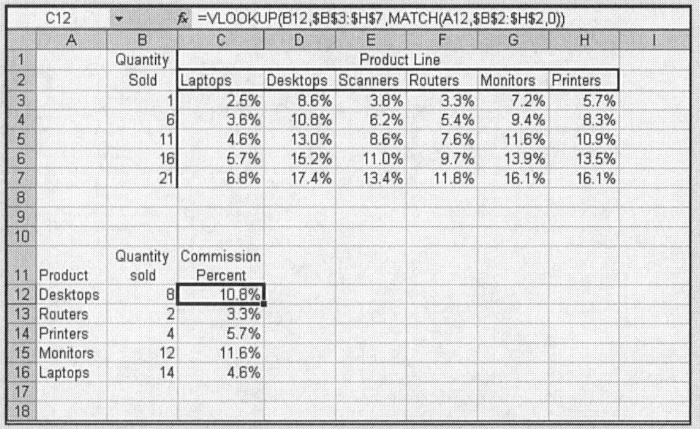

Figure 2.11
If you have more than two columns in the lookup array, you're probably back to requiring MATCH.

In Figure 2.11, cell C12 is intended to show the commission percentage for selling some number of Desktops. VLOOKUP is able to figure out which row in the lookup table to use: It finds that 6 is the largest value that's less than or equal to the lookup value. But VLOOKUP doesn't automatically know which column to use--it's up to the user to give it that information.

Unless the situation is simple enough that you can get by with constants such as 2, 3, and 4 for the column number, you need a way to identify the column to use. In Figure 2.11, Ms. Brown has used the MATCH function to find the column, just as was done in the earlier section on MATCH and INDEX in two-way arrays. The formula is

`=VLOOKUP(B12,$B$3:$H$7,MATCH(A12,$B$2:$H$2,0))`

The MATCH function looks for the value in A12, Desktops, in the range $B$2:$H$2. It finds Desktops in the third position of that array, so the VLOOKUP function simplifies to this:

`=VLOOKUP(B12,$B$3:$H$7,3)`

Compare the VLOOKUP approach with the INDEX and MATCH approach; to review, you use INDEX and MATCH in this way:

`=INDEX($C$3:$H$7,MATCH(B12,$B$3:$B$7,1),MATCH(A12,$C$2:$H$2,0))`

There's no question that the VLOOKUP approach is a little more concise, and many users prefer it. Others prefer the INDEX and MATCH approach because it makes what's going on a little clearer--you match one value to get a row, another to get a column, and return their intersection. As you become familiar with using Excel functions to locate data, you're likely to develop your own preference.

Brown completes the formulas needed to determine the applicable percentage for a given quantity in a product line and enters them in cells C12:C16. She still has to determine the actual dollar amounts, and that's simple compared to determining the commission percentage.

Brown enters a new table, shown in cells J2:K6 of Figure 2.12, to associate a sales price with each product. She picks up the product price using a combination of MATCH and INDEX, and then multiplies the quantity in column B times the percentage in column C times the price. That formula appears in cell D12 of Figure 2.12.

Figure 2.12
This is a good opportunity to use range names, discussed in Chapter 3, in place of absolute addressing.

	D12	▼		fx =B12*C12*INDEX($J$2:$K$6,MATCH(A12,$J$2:$J$6,0),2)								
	A	B	C	D	E	F	G	H	I	J	K	
1		Quantity			Product Line					Product Line	Unit Price	
2		Sold	Laptops	Desktops	Scanners	Routers	Monitors	Printers		Desktops	$ 863.00	
3		1	2.5%	8.6%	3.8%	3.3%	7.2%	5.7%		Routers	$ 245.00	
4		6	3.6%	10.8%	6.2%	5.4%	9.4%	8.3%		Printers	$ 110.00	
5		11	4.6%	13.0%	8.6%	7.6%	11.6%	10.9%		Monitors	$ 236.00	
6		16	5.7%	15.2%	11.0%	13.9%	13.9%	13.5%		Laptops	$1,154.00	
7		21	6.8%	17.4%	13.4%	11.8%	16.1%	16.1%				
8												
9												
10	Weekly Commission, 10/11/2004 - 10/17/2004, R. Smith											
11	Product	Quantity sold	Commission Percent	Commission								
12	Desktops	8	10.8%	$ 748.11								
13	Routers	2	3.3%	$ 16.16								
14	Printers	4	5.7%	$ 25.14								
15	Monitors	12	11.6%	$ 329.78								
16	Laptops	14	4.6%	$ 748.97								
17			Total	$ 1,868.16								
18												
19	Weekly Commission, 10/11/2004 - 10/17/2004, A. Jones											
20	Product	Quantity sold	Commission Percent	Commission								
21	Desktops	6	10.8%	$ 561.08								
22	Routers	4	3.3%	$ 32.31								
23	Printers	3	5.7%	$ 18.86								

Ready | NUM

Rearranging Data with TRANSPOSE

On the Web and on Usenet, there are various forums and newsgroups devoted to the asking and answering of questions about the use of Excel. And there are plenty of FAQ lists that summarize the answers to the most popular of those questions. One common question goes something like this: "I have a range of data that I imported from a database into Excel. I want to print it, but even in Landscape mode the range is too wide for the paper. I'd be okay if I could print the rows as columns and the columns as rows--that is, if I could reverse the orientation. Is there a way to do that?"

That question has lots of variations. Sometimes it's convenient to key in the data with one orientation, but it turns out that it's the wrong setup for charting the data, or analyzing the data with a pivot table, or some other activity that won't cooperate with the data's layout. There are a couple of good ways of dealing with this situation, both involving the term *transpose* (see Figure 2.13).

Figure 2.13
Transposing values has various uses in numeric analysis, but it's also helpful for managing data.

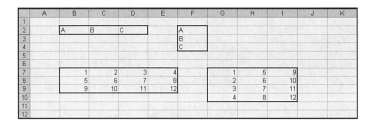

In Figure 2.13, the values in cells B2:D2 have been *transposed* into the range F2:F4. But transposing data isn't limited to ranges that have only one row, or only one column: The range B7:E9 has been transposed into G7:I10. In both cases, the rows of the original range become the columns of the transposed range.

Transposing with Paste Special

Here's one way to transpose a range:

1. Select the source range. In Figure 2.13, that might be B7:E9.
2. Choose **Edit**, **Copy**.
3. Select the cell that will be the upper-left cell of the transposed range. In Figure 2.13, that might be G7.
4. Choose **Edit**, **Paste Special** (see Figure 2.14). Fill the **Transpose** check box, and click **OK**.

Figure 2.14
The Paste Special window has several special uses; for example, convert text values to numeric by adding zeros to cells.

If your source range (B7:E9 in Figure 2.13) contains formulas that depend on the contents of other cells, you should also make sure that the Values option button is filled in the Paste Special dialog box. This option converts formulas to values in the range that you're pasting into. If you don't select the Values option, the result depends on where the source range formulas point, and is generally unpredictable, but it probably isn't what you want.

One predictable result is shown in Figure 2.15. Cells B1:D4 are the original range. In cells B7:D10 are formulas that point at B1:D4, as shown in cells F7:H10. Cells A12:D14 show the result of using copying B7:D10, selecting A12, and choosing Edit, Paste Special, Transpose. The effect is to force the formulas to point at columns that are to the left of Column A. Those columns are undefined, and Excel returns the #REF! error value. In contrast, cells A16:D18 show the result of choosing the Value option: Edit, Paste Special, Transpose *and* Values.

Figure 2.15
This is similar to copying the formula =A1 from B2 and pasting it into A2.

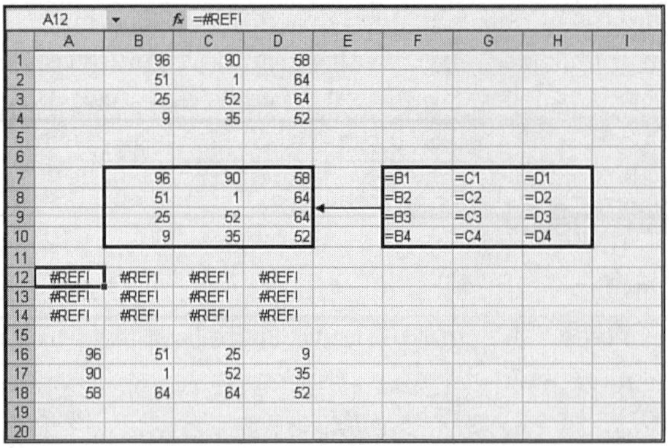
A12 =#REF!

	A	B	C	D	E	F	G	H	I
1		96	90	58					
2		51	1	64					
3		25	52	64					
4		9	35	52					
5									
6									
7		96	90	58		=B1	=C1	=D1	
8		51	1	64		=B2	=C2	=D2	
9		25	52	64		=B3	=C3	=D3	
10		9	35	52		=B4	=C4	=D4	
11									
12	#REF!	#REF!	#REF!	#REF!					
13	#REF!	#REF!	#REF!	#REF!					
14	#REF!	#REF!	#REF!	#REF!					
15									
16	96	51	25	9					
17	90	1	52	35					
18	58	64	64	52					
19									
20									

To replicate the problem (and the solution) shown in Figure 2.15, take these steps:

1. Enter a range of values in B1:D4.
2. In B7, enter this formula: `=B1`.
3. Copy cell **B7** and paste it into **C7:D7**.
4. Now select **B7:D7**, copy it, and paste into cells **B8:D10**. You now have a replica of B1:D4, but made entirely of formulas.
5. Select **B7:D10**, and copy it.
6. Select cell **A12**, choose **Edit**, **Paste Special**, fill the **Transpose** checkbox, and click **OK**.

Your transposed range consists of nothing but #REF! errors. You can avoid this effect by filling the Values option button as well as the Transpose check box to convert the formulas to values before transposing the range. The result is shown in A16:D18 of Figure 2.15.

Transposing with the Worksheet Function

Another way to avoid the problem of pivoting off the worksheet is to use the TRANSPOSE worksheet function, which you can use whether your source range consists of formulas or values. Here's the sequence, based on Figure 2.13:

1. Select the range **G7:I10**. This is the range that you want to contain the transposed cells.
2. Type this formula: `=TRANSPOSE(B7:E9)`.
3. Then instead of simply entering the formula, array-enter it. (Array-entry was described earlier in the section titled "Array-Entering OFFSET to Return Several Cells"; use **Ctrl+Shift+Enter** instead of just **Enter**.)

You wind up with a transposed range that looks as though you had used Edit, Copy, and Edit, Paste Special, but there are two important differences:

- You get the transposition of the source range, no matter whether it contains values or formulas that point to other cells.
- You have a volatile formula, not static values. So, if a value in the source range changes, it will also change in the transposed range. If you have tried out the preceding three-step example, try changing any cell in the source range; you'll see that the change is reflected in the transposed range.

> **TIP**
>
> If you use the TRANSPOSE worksheet function as described to change the orientation of a source range, remember that you need to start by selecting a *range* of cells. The range should have as many rows as the source range has columns, and as many columns as the source range has rows. (This will sound all too familiar to you if you ever took matrix algebra.)

Getting Data from a Pivot Table: GETPIVOTDATA

A pivot table is the most powerful means of analyzing data available in Excel.

That might sound over the top, but it's true. Consider that a pivot table enables you to

- View a data field (such as age, weight, revenues, costs, and so on) as a sum, an average, a standard deviation, a count of cases, and seven other types of summary
- Categorize the records according to many different fields (such as sex, product line, political affiliation, region, and so on)
- Combine and recombine categories (such as male Republicans, or routers sold from northwest offices) just by dragging a cell
- Base the pivot table on a list in an Excel workbook, or an external data source such as a database or a data cube
- Display the data in a chart in addition to a table--a chart that pivots its dimensions just as a pivot table does

It starts to become apparent that you've put your hands on a powerful tool indeed.

But if you've used pivot tables much, you know that they can give you more information than you need. Suppose that your pivot table analyzes revenues and costs by region and product. An example appears in Figure 2.16.

If you wanted to insert comments among the results of the pivot table, you'd be out of luck. Instead, you have to copy the results you want into other cells and insert your comments where you want them. In Figure 2.16, in cells A27:D34, the user wants to focus on costs and revenues for Desktops in both regions and intersperse comments about the gross margin.

The GETPIVOTDATA function is ideal for this. The function returns a value from a pivot table to the cell where you enter it. Its syntax depends on the Excel version you're using.

Figure 2.16

Pivot tables don't always offer the perfect format for reports.

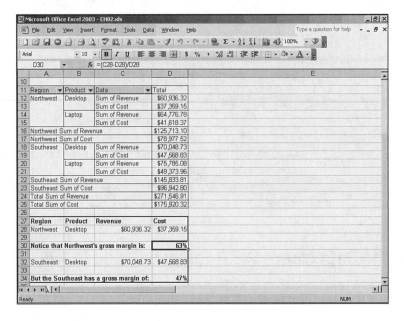

Using GETPIVOTDATA in Excel 97 and Excel 2000

The syntax is

```
GETPIVOTDATA(pivot table, name)
```

Here, the `pivot table` argument is a reference to a pivot table. It can be any of these:

- A cell that the pivot table occupies, such as $B$14
- A range name that identifies the full pivot table, such as PivotRange, where the name itself might refer to $A$11:$D$25, as in Figure 2.16
- The name of a pivot table such as PivotTable3, as specified in the pivot table's options

The *name* argument is one or more items in the pivot table, entered as a single string. Using the data as shown in Figure 2.16, you could enter

```
=GETPIVOTDATA($A$11,"Northwest Desktop Sum of Cost")
```

to get the value shown in cell D13. Notice that the `name` argument includes items from two different fields (the Northwest item from the Region field, and the Desktop item from the Product field), as well as the name of the data field (Sum of Cost). When a pivot table has more than one data field, you have to specify the one you want--otherwise, you'll get a #REF! error.

Using GETPIVOTDATA in Excel 2002 and Excel 2003

The syntax is

```
GETPIVOTDATA(data field, pivot table, field1, item1, field2, item2 . . .)
```

You can specify as many as 14 fields and associated items in the argument list.

Just as in the Excel 97 and 2000 version, you specify the pivot table you're after with the `pivot table` argument: a cell in the pivot table, or the name of the range the pivot table occupies, or the name of the pivot table.

In contrast to the Excel 97 and 2000 versions, the arguments in Excel 2002 and 2003 call out the fields separately, instead of all together in a single `name` argument. One possible 2002/2003 version of the formula to return the value in cell D13 of Figure 2.16 is

```
=GETPIVOTDATA("Sum of Cost", $A$11, "Region","Northwest","Product","Desktop")
```

Entering GETPIVOTDATA Automatically

Excel 2002 and 2003 give you a way to avoid the tedium of entering the arguments for GETPIVOTDATA. Just enter an equal sign in a cell and then click in a data field cell in a pivot table. Again using the layout in Figure 2.16, you might select cell D37, type an equal sign, and then click any cell in the range D12:D25. Excel generates the GETPIVOTDATA arguments automatically. For example, if you typed an equal sign in some blank cell and then clicked in cell D18, Excel would generate this formula for you:

```
=GETPIVOTDATA("Sum of Revenue",$A$11,"Region","Southeast","Product","Desktop")
```

This automatic formula generation is optional (although it is the default option). If you want a simple cell link instead--such as =D18--you can just type the cell reference instead of using point and click. Or toggle the option by taking these steps:

1. If necessary, choose **View**, **Toolbars** and show the PivotTable toolbar. (This step is needed only if you want to use the PivotTable toolbar and it's not currently visible.)
2. Choose **Options**, **Customize** and click the **Commands** tab.
3. Click **Data** in the Categories list box.
4. In the Commands list box, scroll down until you see **Generate GetPivotData**.
5. Click on **Generate GetPivotData**, hold down the mouse button, and drag it to a toolbar. Release the mouse button.

Now you can click the Generate GetPivotData button to toggle the option on and off.

Pivoting the Table: Why Use GETPIVOTDATA?

It might seem pointless to use GETPIVOTDATA, with all its arguments, instead of a simple cell link. Figure 2.17 shows a pivot table along with two formulas. Both formulas return the same value from the pivot table.

Figure 2.17
Using GETPIVOTDATA looks a lot more tedious than a simple cell link.

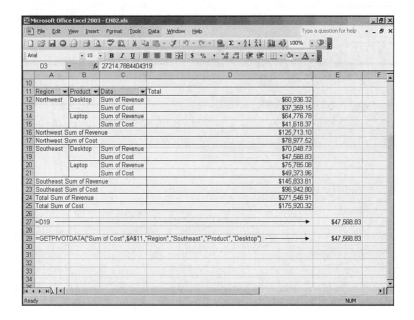

The formula in E27 is =D19. It is a simple cell link, and displays whatever value is in D19. In Figure 2.17, that value is $47,568.83.

The formula in E29 is

```
=GETPIVOTDATA("Sum of Cost",$A$11,"Region","Southeast","Product","Desktop")
```

This lengthy formula also returns the value in D19, $47,568.83, but it does so by way of naming the fields and items.

Figure 2.18 shows what happens when you decide to pivot the table, making Product a column field instead of an inner row field as in Figure 2.17.

After pivoting the table, as Figure 2.18 shows, the simple cell link in E27 still points to cell D19, but because it's empty, the link returns $0.00. However, the GETPIVOTDATA function still looks up its value using field and item names, so it continues to return the value it did before pivoting.

GETPIVOTDATA is no cure-all. If you rename a field (for example, rename *Product* to *Product Line*) or an item (for example, rename *Desktop* to *Desktops*), GETPIVOTDATA won't know where to look to find the data field value you're after.

Figure 2.18
The pivot table no longer occupies cell D19, and the simple cell link now returns zero.

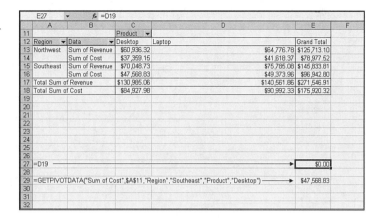

Looking Ahead

This chapter focused heavily on using worksheet functions to help you locate data, reorient ranges, and identify the extent of the area that your data occupies. In particular, the chapter explored the technique of using Excel functions in combination with one another to bring about the results you're after.

This by no means exhausts the role that worksheet functions have in managing data. As shown in the next chapter, "Excel's Lists, Names, and Filters," you use worksheet functions such as OFFSET and COUNT to build worksheet structures that respond automatically when you add or remove data.

Excel's Lists, Names, and Filters

3

Creating Lists

In Excel, a *list* is a set of data, arranged in a certain way. Many of Excel's features—the Data Form, pivot tables, filters, and others—will not work properly if data is not arranged as a list. And while other features such as charts will work with data that's not in list format, they become more difficult to use.

Furthermore, it's typical for data that has been imported into Excel from an external data source to enter the workbook in the form of a list. So, it's useful to know what a list is and how to set one up.

A list is a rectangular range of cells on a worksheet. It has one or more adjacent columns and two or more rows. The list is usually separated from other data on the worksheet by blank rows and columns.

In versions of Excel prior to Excel 2003, a list is an informal structure. It's more a way of arranging data and following a few conventions than something readily identifiable, such as a print area or a pivot table. There's no command to select or button to click to create a list.

Still, as informal as they are, list structures make it much easier to manage your data. For just one example of several in this chapter, see the section titled "Using Data Forms."

In Excel 2003, list structures remain informal, but a set of commands has been added to Excel's worksheet menu structure. These commands make it easier to set up lists, edit their data, and extend their reach. This section describes lists in general, and Excel 2003's new commands in particular.

Understanding List Structures

Lists have three fundamental characteristics, shown in Figure 3.1.

Figure 3.1
The data in cells A1:C21 make up a *list*.

	A	B	C	D	E	F
1	Party	Sex	Age			
2	Democrat	Female	40			
3	Democrat	Female	52			
4	Republican	Male	75			
5	Democrat	Male	47			
6	Republican	Male	56			
7	Republican	Female	27			
8	Republican	Male	46			
9	Republican	Male	66			
10	Democrat	Female	72			
11	Republican	Male	34			
12	Democrat	Male	54			
13	Republican	Female	56			
14	Democrat	Female	78			
15	Democrat	Female	42			
16	Democrat	Male	36			
17	Democrat	Male	41			
18	Republican	Female	29			
19	Democrat	Male	88			
20	Republican	Female	24			
21	Republican	Female	39			
22						
23						

NOTE
If you've worked with a database management system such as Access, SQL Server, or even dBASE, you probably recognize the layout shown in Figure 3.1. In datasheet view, most database management systems display data in the same fashion: records occupying separate rows and fields occupying separate columns.

Notice the following in Figure 3.1:

- The variable (also called a *field*) named Party is in column A, the variable Sex is in column B, and the variable Age is in column C. The variables' names aren't important, nor are the particular columns. It *is* important that each variable is in a different column, and that the columns are adjacent.

- Each record is in a different row. Just by looking at the data, you can infer that row 3 represents a 52-year-old female who is a Democrat, row 11 represents a 34-year-old Republican male, and so on. No matter whether the data describe people, products, or plant life, in a list, each person, product, or plant is in a different row.

- Variable names occupy the list's first row. In Figure 3.1, the variable names are Party, Sex, and Age, and they are in the first row of the list. They do not have to be in row 1 of the worksheet, but they must be in row 1 of the list.

> **NOTE**
>
> Excel's Help, and other Microsoft documentation, variously use the terms *column labels* and *header row* (among others) to represent the first row of a list. To avoid confusion with the letters at the top of each worksheet column (which Excel terms *column headings*), this book uses the term *variable names* to mean the values, normally text, in a list's first row.

Figure 3.2 shows two data ranges that are not lists. In the range A1:C22, the first row does not contain variable names in each column. In the range F1:I21, there is an empty column so that not all the columns are adjacent.

Figure 3.2
Neither A1:C22 nor F1:I21 is a list.

	A	B	C	D	E	F	G	H	I	J
1	Party	Sex				Party	Sex		Age	
2	Democrat	Female	Age			Democrat	Female		40	
3	Democrat	Female	40			Democrat	Female		52	
4	Republican	Male	52			Republican	Male		75	
5	Democrat	Male	75			Democrat	Male		47	
6	Republican	Male	47			Republican	Male		56	
7	Republican	Female	56			Republican	Female		27	
8	Republican	Male	27			Republican	Male		66	
9	Republican	Male	66			Republican	Male		46	
10	Democrat	Female	46			Democrat	Female		72	
11	Republican	Male	72			Republican	Male		34	
12	Democrat	Male	34			Democrat	Male		54	
13	Republican	Female	54			Republican	Female		56	
14	Democrat	Female	56			Democrat	Female		78	
15	Democrat	Female	78			Democrat	Female		42	
16	Democrat	Male	42			Democrat	Male		36	
17	Democrat	Male	36			Democrat	Male		41	
18	Republican	Female	41			Republican	Female		29	
19	Democrat	Male	29			Democrat	Male		88	
20	Republican	Female	88			Republican	Female		24	
21	Republican	Female	24			Republican	Female		39	
22			39							
23										
24										

3

However, just because these ranges violate a couple of rules for list making doesn't necessarily mean that you'll get an error message, or that Excel will quit unexpectedly. It just means that the tools you want to use with lists won't work as readily.

For example, suppose that you click in cell A2 of Figure 3.1; then you choose Filter from the Data menu and click AutoFilter. A dropdown will appear next to each variable name: Party, Sex, and Age.

But if you do the same with the data as shown in columns A:C of Figure 3.2, Excel ignores the first row and puts dropdowns in the second row, next to Democrat, Female, and Age. Excel puts the dropdowns in the first row in the range that has nonblank values, making the assumption that they are variable names. (You'll find much more information about Excel's data filters in this chapter's sections titled "Filtering Data with the AutoFilter" and "Using the Advanced Filter.")

But that behavior is not consistent. Suppose that you click in cell A2 as shown in Figure 3.2, and choose Sort from the Data menu. If you tell Excel that your sort range has a header row, it will sort the range A3:C22. If you specify *no* header row, it will sort starting one row higher: A2:C22. In neither case will it pick up the first row. This isn't the behavior you want. When you structure your worksheet, be sure to put the names of the variables in the same row.

You can force the sort to pick up the first row by selecting the entire range before choosing Sort from the Data menu, but you've still inconvenienced yourself. Excel will then let you sort on Party, Sex, and column C—and if you sort on column C, Excel sorts what it regards as the value "Age" to the bottom of the range.

> **TIP**
> Excel's ascending sort order puts numbers first, and then text values, and then logical values (TRUE comes before FALSE), and then error values such as #REF!, and finally blanks. Except blanks, the order is reversed for a descending sort. Regardless of the sort order, blanks always come last.

To further illustrate the point, in Figure 3.2, click in cell G5 and choose Data, Filter, AutoFilter. Excel puts the dropdowns in F1 and G1, but ignores I1. Column I is not regarded as part of the list because it's separated from the rest of the data by a blank column. You can select the entire range F1:I21 before you start the AutoFilter, and then you'll get dropdowns in cells F1:I1. But what's the point of doing that? Where possible, make the columns in your list adjacent.

Again, the poorly designed lists cause no error messages in these examples, but Excel does not behave as you'd want when it encounters list structures that it doesn't expect.

On the other hand, try selecting A1:C22 as shown in Figure 3.2, and choose PivotTable and PivotChart Report from the Data menu. In step 2 of the wizard, make sure that A1:C22 is in the Range box: Excel will try to avoid using a range that contains a blank variable name, and the way it resolves its difficulty depends on the version you're using.

At some point (again, the point at which this occurs depends on the version that you have installed), Excel complains that The PivotTable field name is not valid and you won't be able to complete the pivot table. All the columns in a list that you use for a pivot table have to have variable names. Another way to violate list structure appears in Figure 3.3.

Figure 3.3
This arrangement transposes the list from records in rows to records in columns.

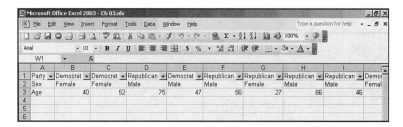

Suppose that you began by selecting the entire range seen in Figure 3.3. Now, if you try to use AutoFilter on the range as shown, Excel will put dropdowns in each cell in the first row. The assumption will be that you have a variable named Party, one named Democrat, another named Democrat, another named Republican, and so on.

In other words, although you won't cause an error message using AutoFilter with this layout, you won't get what you're after, either.

Your life with lists will be much easier if you put variable names in the first row, different records in different rows, and different variables in different, adjacent columns.

Setting Up Lists in Excel 2003

The title of this section is a little misleading. You set up lists in Excel 2003 exactly as you do in earlier versions. The difference is that after you've arranged your list, you can click any cell in the list, and then choose List from the Data menu and Create List from the cascading menu. The window shown in Figure 3.4 appears.

Figure 3.4
Excel automatically proposes all adjacent, non-blank columns and rows for your list.

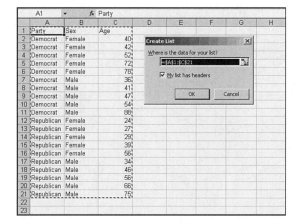

If Excel finds values in the first row that it can interpret as headers, it fills the My List Has Headers check box for you. Use the window to edit the list's range address if necessary, and use the check box to describe the list accurately. Then click OK. When you do so, several things happen:

- A border is drawn around the list, including its header row.
- The AutoFilter is turned on; you can tell this from the drop-down arrows in the header cells. (See this chapter's section titled "Filtering Data with the AutoFilter" for more information.)
- A row for entering additional records is established at the bottom of the list. Excel terms this the *insert row*. You can identify it from the asterisk in the list's first column. (If you're familiar with Microsoft Access, you'll recognize the asterisk as the indicator for adding records.)
- If you did not provide variable names, Excel supplies them for you, using the labels Column1, Column2, and so on.
- With a list active, right-click in it, choose List from the shortcut menu, and click Total Row in the cascading menu. Excel adds a row to the list that can show eight different types of total, including Sum, Average, and Count. Click a cell in the Total row to choose the total you want from a drop-down list.

See Figure 3.5 for an example of how a list appears after you've used the Create List command.

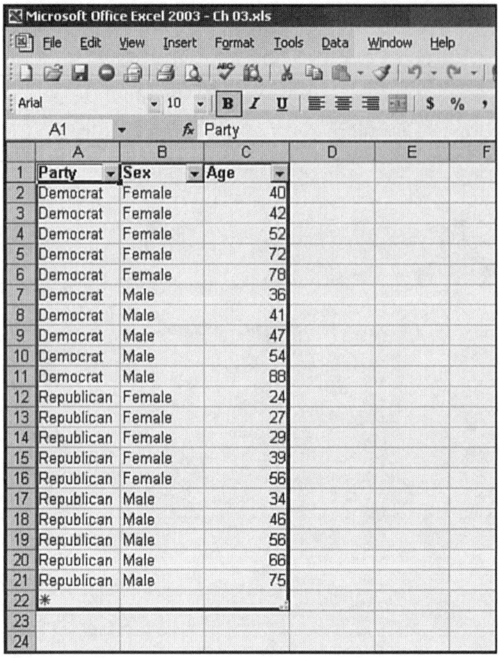

	A	B	C	D	E	F
1	Party	Sex	Age			
2	Democrat	Female	40			
3	Democrat	Female	42			
4	Democrat	Female	52			
5	Democrat	Female	72			
6	Democrat	Female	78			
7	Democrat	Male	36			
8	Democrat	Male	41			
9	Democrat	Male	47			
10	Democrat	Male	54			
11	Democrat	Male	88			
12	Republican	Female	24			
13	Republican	Female	27			
14	Republican	Female	29			
15	Republican	Female	39			
16	Republican	Female	56			
17	Republican	Male	34			
18	Republican	Male	46			
19	Republican	Male	56			
20	Republican	Male	66			
21	Republican	Male	75			
22	*					
23						
24						

Figure 3.5
When you add a new value in any column in row 22, Excel expands the border and moves the insert row.

You can expand the list directly by clicking and dragging the resize handle in the bottom-right corner of the list.

Excel 2003 also provides automatic subtotals for your list. To get them, select any cell in the list, choose Data, List, and then click Total Row in the cascading menu. It's a toggle, so to remove the total row, just click Total Row again. (You can also get to the List menu by right-clicking any cell in the list.)

Using Data Forms

After you have a list set up, you can immediately start browsing through records, adding records, deleting records, and editing fields. You can use a form that Excel constructs for you automatically (see Figure 3.6).

All you need to get the Data Form to appear is to have a list, select any cell in the list, and choose Data, Form. A form that looks like the one shown in Figure 3.6 appears, and using it you can take any of the following actions:

- Click New to establish a new record in the list.
- See which record you're currently viewing by glancing at the record counter just above the New button.

Figure 3.6
The Data Form is automatically tailored to your list's variable names and number of records.

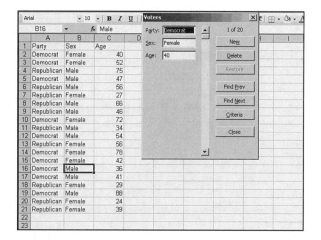

- Click Delete to delete the selected record. You're prompted to confirm that you want to delete it, and you can cancel the deletion if you want.

- Change a value in one or more of the edit boxes. After you've done so, click Restore to return all variables in the current record to their prior values. After you move to another record, you can no longer use Restore on the edited record.

- Move from edit box to edit box by using hot keys. Notice in Figure 3.6 that the edit box labels have hot keys on the form, indicated by the underscores. To move from, say, P<u>a</u>rty to A<u>g</u>e, hold down Alt and simultaneously press Age's hot key, g.

- Click Criteria to set a selection criterion on any of the variables in your list (see Figure 3.7).

Figure 3.7
Clicking the Clear button clears all the boxes.

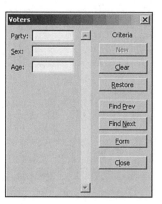

- Enter a value in one or more boxes to establish selection criteria.

- With criteria established, Find Prev takes you to an earlier record that matches the criteria and Find Next takes you to a subsequent matching record. If no match is found, the currently selected record remains selected.

- Return to Form view by clicking Form.
- Scroll through records by using the scrollbar.
- Click Close to remove the Data Form.

The Data Form is a handy way to manage records and variables that are set out in list format. Using it requires only a list structure and knowing to choose Data, Form (and it's an easy way to impress someone who doesn't know it's there).

Sorting Lists

This chapter wouldn't have insisted that you be so fastidious about structuring lists if there weren't plenty of good reasons. Many of those reasons have to do with data management, but they don't stop there.

The list first shown in Figure 3.1 is repeated in Figure 3.8. Suppose that you wanted to sort the list, first by Sex, and then by Party within Sex, and finally by Age within Party within Sex. You would click any cell inside the list—as shown in Figure 3.8, that might be C8 or B18—and choose Sort from the Data menu.

Figure 3.8
You can choose No Header Row if you're not sorting a true list: one without variable names, perhaps.

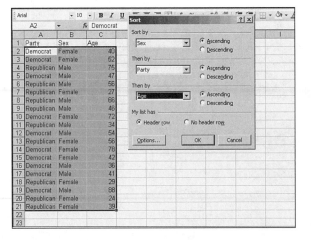

In the first row of the range of contiguous cells, if Excel can find values that could be variable names, it treats those names as a header row. As Figure 3.8 shows, Excel excludes the variable names from the range of cells to be sorted. It lets you know by *not* highlighting the first row and by choosing (on your behalf) the Header row option button on the Sort dialog box.

This makes sorting very convenient. You use the dropdowns in the Sort dialog box to select the variables you want to use as the first, second, and third sort keys. If, as in Figure 3.8, you choose to sort by Age within Party within Sex, your choices appear in the dropdowns.

Suppose that you choose to sort in ascending order for all three variables: first by Sex, and then by Party, and then by Age. This pattern would sort all Females into one group of adjacent rows. Within the group of Females, it would sort the Female Democrats together and, in a different group of rows, the Female Republicans. Finally, within the Female Democrats, the pattern would sort the records in ascending order by Age.

When you have a range of cells that's so wide that its columns disappear off your screen, using a header row becomes especially convenient. Suppose that your range runs from column A to column J, and that you can see only columns A through E on your screen. You want to sort on, say, Product (column B), Sales Office (column G), and Revenue (column I). Without a header row that has variable names, you need to remember which columns are occupied by Sales Office and by Revenue—because you can't see them, you need to remember that your sort involves columns G and I. But if you're using a header row, you can see the variable names in the Sort dropdowns, and you don't need to remember where anything is.

Here's yet another reason to set your data up as a list. Assume that the data layout is as shown in Figure 3.9.

Figure 3.9
The layout is a simple transposition of the data in Figure 3.8.

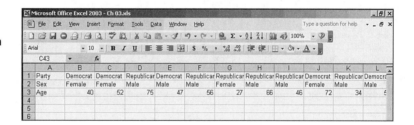

As you might know, you can choose to sort left-to-right as well as top-to-bottom. Use the following to do so:

1. Choose **Data**, **Sort**.
2. Click the **Options** button.
3. Fill the **Sort Left to Right** option button.
4. Click **OK** to return to the Sort menu and continue as before.

The problem is that left-to-right sorts don't support header rows. Notice in Figure 3.9 that the variable names are in the first column of each row instead of in the first row of each column. If you don't exclude that column from the range to be sorted, the headers will be sorted as though they were values.

> **NOTE**
> Notice that if you specify a left-to-right sort, Excel disables the Header Row and the No Header Row option buttons.

To preserve the headers in this layout, you would have to begin by selecting the entire range of values, excluding the headers in A1:A3. If you start by selecting a single cell only, Excel insists on treating the first column's variable names as values to be sorted.

Working with Names

Names are enormously useful in Excel. They make it easier to work with everything from worksheet ranges to arrays to constants to formulas and more.

There's no brief, crisp definition of the term *name* as it's used in Excel. It's best to look at examples of names to see how they're used and how they function. This book is concerned mainly with names as they apply to worksheet ranges, but keep in mind that names have a variety of uses.

Naming Formulas

Suppose that you frequently work with data that consists of a person's first name and last name: For example, you might have *George Washington* in cell A1 and *John Adams* in cell A2. You might want to strip off the person's first name, perhaps for use in a salutation. One way would be to use this combination of functions:

```
=LEFT(A1,FIND(" ",A1)-1)
```

If *George Washington* is in cell A1, this formula would return *George*. In words, it finds a blank space in the value in cell A1, and notes the position of that character in the string (here, that's 7). It subtracts 1 from that position, and returns that many characters. To simplify the formula:

```
=LEFT(A1,6)
```

or *George*.

That's useful, of course, but it's not very intuitive. Here's a way, involving a name, that's more cumbersome at first but lots easier in the long run:

1. Select cell **B1**.
2. Choose **Insert**, **Name**, **Define**. You'll see the window shown in Figure 3.10—this is a window you'll become very familiar with if you make effective use of names in Excel.
3. In the Names in Workbook box, type a handy mnemonic such as `FirstName`.
4. In the Refers To box, type
   ```
   =LEFT(A1,FIND(" ",A1)-1)
   ```
   If, instead of typing the cell address **A1**, you click in the cell, Excel will fill in the address for you. But Excel will add the dollar signs that make the reference absolute ($A$1). For the present purpose, you don't want that. Either type the address yourself or remove the dollar signs supplied by Excel.
5. Click **OK**.

Figure 3.10
You can put a combination of worksheet ranges, functions, and even other names in the Reference box.

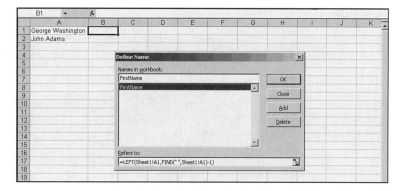

Now, in cell B1, type =FirstName. If *George Washington* is in A1, you'll see *George* in B1. Select cell B2 and type =FirstName. If *John Adams* is in A2, you'll see *John* in B2.

The name *FirstName* is standing in for the formula that combines the LEFT and FIND functions. You have defined a name that refers to a formula.

Furthermore, it's a formula whose results depend on—are relative to—where you enter it. This is the reason that you took in step 1, and step 4 where you avoided using dollar signs. You selected cell B1, and the formula you entered refers to A1. By selecting a cell immediately to the right of the one you want the formula to refer to, you arrange for any instance of the formula to refer to the cell immediately to its left. If you enter =FirstName in cell AC27, it will refer to the value in cell AB27.

Especially if it's been some time since you used this worksheet, it's a lot easier to recognize, remember, and understand this

```
=FirstName
```

than this

```
=LEFT(A1,FIND(" ",A1)-1)
```

and that's typical of names in Excel. That is, you can usually choose a name for something that's much easier to remember and use than is the thing itself.

Naming Constants

Another use for names is to refer to constants. You might establish the name DollarsPerMile by typing that name in the Names in Workbook box and =.365 in the Refers To box. This would let you use the name DollarsPerMile in any calculation where you wanted to know how much to expense (in this example, 36.5 cents) per mile driven. P 65For example

```
=100*DollarsPerMile
```

to return $36.50. (If you're really nuts and have a scientific disposition, you might enter Planck in the Names in Workbook box, and =6.62606891 * 10^(-34) in the Refers To box.)

Naming Ranges

As useful as named formulas and named constants are, it's likely that the most frequent use of names in Excel is to refer to ranges of cells, including single cells. Figure 3.11 repeats the lookup situation originally shown in Figure 2.9.

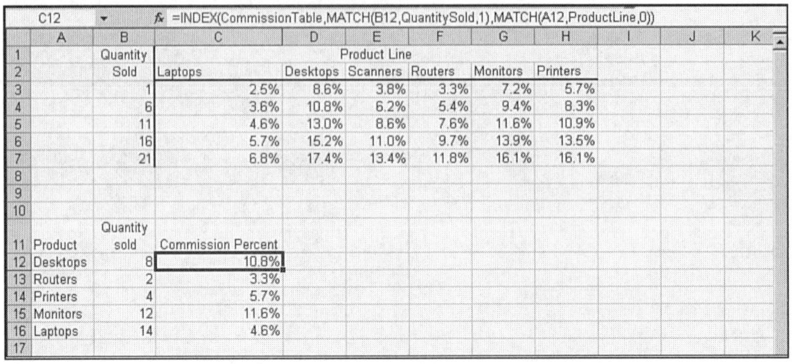

Figure 3.11

A little care in naming ranges goes a long way toward clarifying what your formulas are intended to do.

	C12	▾		ƒx	=INDEX(CommissionTable,MATCH(B12,QuantitySold,1),MATCH(A12,ProductLine,0))						
	A	B	C	D	E	F	G	H	I	J	K
1		Quantity			Product Line						
2		Sold	Laptops	Desktops	Scanners	Routers	Monitors	Printers			
3		1	2.5%	8.6%	3.8%	3.3%	7.2%	5.7%			
4		6	3.6%	10.8%	6.2%	5.4%	9.4%	8.3%			
5		11	4.6%	13.0%	8.6%	7.6%	11.6%	10.9%			
6		16	5.7%	15.2%	11.0%	9.7%	13.9%	13.5%			
7		21	6.8%	17.4%	13.4%	11.8%	16.1%	16.1%			
8											
9											
10											
11	Product	Quantity sold	Commission Percent								
12	Desktops	8	10.8%								
13	Routers	2	3.3%								
14	Printers	4	5.7%								
15	Monitors	12	11.6%								
16	Laptops	14	4.6%								
17											

In Figure 3.11, as in Figure 2.9, the value in cell C12 is 10.8%. In Figure 2.9, the formula in C12 is based on the INDEX function, and it uses columns and rows as its arguments:

```
=INDEX($C$3:$H$7,MATCH(B12,$B$3:$B$7,1), _
MATCH(A12,$C$2:$H$2,0))
```

That's not a formula that's rich in intuitive meaning. If you entered it on Monday and had another look at it on Friday, you'd spend a few seconds figuring out what it's intended to do.

Now suppose that you define some names, so that

- The name CommissionTable refers to $C$3:$H$7.
- The name ProductLine refers to $C$2:$H$2.
- The name QuantitySold refers to $B$3:$B$7.

Notice that the ranges that the names refer to are the ranges used in the INDEX formula, repeated from Figure 2.9. But now those ranges have names, and you can use this formula as shown in Figure 3.11:

```
=INDEX(CommissionTable,MATCH(B12,QuantitySold,1), _
MATCH(A12,ProductLine,0))
```

That's a lot easier to interpret. You can look at it and see almost at once that it returns from the commission table the value that is found at the intersection of a particular quantity and a particular product.

There are several good methods you can use to define these names. The method shown next gives you the most control. Using the layout shown in Figure 3.11, follow these steps:

1. Choose **Insert**, **Name**, **Define**.
2. In the Names in Workbook box, type CommissionTable.

3. Click in the Refers To box and then, using the mouse pointer, drag through the worksheet range **C3:H7**. (Notice that when you use the worksheet in this way to establish a reference, Excel makes the reference absolute.)

4. Click **OK**, or click **Add** if you're not through defining names.

Another convenient method to establish a named range involves the Name box. Begin by selecting the worksheet range C3:H7. Now click in the Name box—that's the box with the drop-down arrow, at the left edge of the Excel window and on the same row as the Formula Bar. Type the name CommissionTable and then press Enter.

Similarly, you could begin by selecting B3:B7, clicking in the Name box, typing QuantitySold, and pressing Enter.

> **TIP** The Name box is a convenient way to tell whether the active range or cell has a name and, if so, what the name is. After naming the QuantitySold range, for example, the Name box shows that name if you select the range B3:B7. Turning it around, you can choose a name from the Name box's dropdown in order to select that range on the worksheet.

The Name box displays only names that refer to worksheet cells and ranges, and you can use it to define only range and cell names.

Using Implicit Intersections

Suppose that you define the name Quantity as referring to the range B12:B16 in Figure 3.11. Now, select a cell in some column other than B, and in a row anywhere from 12 through 16, you enter this formula:

=Quantity

That formula will return the corresponding value in the range named Quantity. For example, suppose that you entered that formula in cell F14. It would return the value 4: the value in the cell where the range named Quantity (that is, B12:B16) intersects the row where you enter the formula (here, row 14). That value is 4, so that's what the formula returns.

This is an example of an implicit intersection. It's implicit because the row is *implied* by the location of the formula. If you entered the same formula in row 16, it would return the value 14, where row 16 intersects the range named Quantity.

Suppose that the range that you name Quantity occupies several columns in one row, rather than several rows in one column. You enter the same =Quantity formula in one of its columns but in a row that's outside the named range. In that case, you would get the same effect: an implicit intersection, but with one of the range's columns instead of one of its rows.

The implicit intersection is useful in the current example on sales commissions. If you give the name Quantity to the range B12:B16 in Figure 3.11, you can enter this formula in C12:

```
=INDEX(CommissionTable,MATCH(Quantity,QuantitySold,1),MATCH(A12,ProductLine,0))
```

Note the difference from the earlier example. In the first MATCH, the argument B12 has been replaced with a reference to Quantity. Because you have entered it in cell C12, the implicit intersection picks up the value 8 from cell B12 and returns the original result, 10.8%. When you copy and paste that formula into C13:C16, the implicit intersection again gets the necessary values from B13:B16, and again returns the proper results.

In the same way, you could give the name Product to the range in A12:A16. Then you could completely dispense with cell and range references:

```
=INDEX(CommissionTable,MATCH(Quantity,QuantitySold,1), _
MATCH(Product,ProductLine,0))
```

Now the formula has become self-documenting. You need not go back and forth between cell references in the formula and their contents in the worksheet to figure out what's going on.

> **NOTE**
>
> If a formula that relies on an implicit intersection is entered *outside* the rows or columns that the named range occupies, the formula returns the #VAL! error.

Defining Static Range Names

A name is *static* if it refers directly to a cell or range of cells. It's useful to distinguish a static name from a *dynamic* name, which refers to a range that can change size automatically as new data arrives (see the next section for more information).

You've already seen a couple of ways to define static range names: using the Name box, and using Insert, Name, Define. You can also use the Create item in the Name menu.

If you have an Excel list, you can easily create static range names based on the list's variable names. Select the entire list, choose Name from the Insert menu, and click Create. The window shown in Figure 3.12 appears.

By filling the Top Row check box and clicking OK, you create three names: the name Party refers to $A$2:$A$21, Sex refers to $B$2:$B$21, and Age refers to $C$2:$C$21.

If your variable names are in the range's left column, instead of its top row, fill the Left Column check box. To create names that occupy rows as well as names that occupy columns, fill both the Left Column and the Top Row check boxes before clicking OK.

The Create Names window even allows for eccentrically placed variable names: If you've put them in the rightmost column or bottommost row, just fill the appropriate check boxes.

Figure 3.12
Filling the Left Column check box misleads Excel into treating the values *Democrat* and *Republican* as Names.

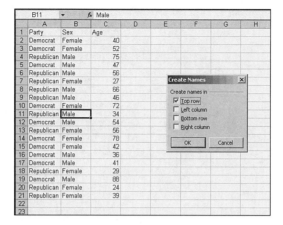

Defining Dynamic Range Names

Dynamic names are those that change the dimensions of the ranges they refer to, depending on how much data the ranges contain. Figure 3.13 gives an example.

Figure 3.13
Dynamic range names are effective in formulas and charts based on data that you update frequently.

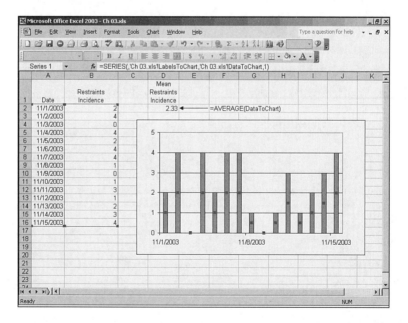

There are two named ranges in Figure 3.13: one named LabelsToChart and one named DataToChart. The name LabelsToChart refers to the date values in column A. These are dates on which observations were made. The name DataToChart refers to the counts in column B. These count the incidents of the use of restraints in a hospital on a given date. The user wants to know the average daily incidence of the use of restraints, and to chart the actual daily incidence over time.

Both range names were defined by choosing Insert, Name, Define. This is the only way to define a dynamic range name; the Name box won't help you here.

Here's the definition of the range LabelsToChart, as found in the Refers To box of the Define Names window:

```
=OFFSET(Restraints!$A$1,1,0,COUNT(Restraints!$A:$A),1)
```

> **TIP**
>
> The easiest way to enter this reference is to click in the Refers To box. Type =**OFFSET(** and then click in cell A1. Excel will put `Restraints!$A$1` in the formula for you. When you get to the argument to the COUNT function, click the column label A. Excel automatically puts the reference `Restraints!$A:$A` into the formula.

This is another useful instance of the OFFSET function, already discussed in Chapter 2, "Excel's Data Management Features." In words, here's what it does:

- The COUNT function, as used in the name definition, returns the number of numeric values found in column A of the worksheet named Restraints. In the case shown in Figure 3.11, that result is 15. The 15 dates found in A2:A16 are all numbers, and the one label in cell A1 is a text value.

- The definition can now be simplified to

```
=OFFSET(Restraints!$A$1,1,0,15,1)
```

- Using the syntax of the OFFSET function, the definition refers to the range that's offset from $A$1 by one row and zero columns, that's 15 rows high and one column wide—in other words, A2:A16.

Suppose now that you have reached November 16 on the calendar and it's time to enter another day's worth of data. You type 11/16/2003 in cell A17. Notice what happens to the definition of the dynamic range name LabelsToChart: The COUNT function in the definition now finds 16, not 15, numeric values in column A. So the definition now refers to the range that's offset from $A$1 by one row and zero columns, *that's 16 rows high* and one column wide—that is, A2:A17.

This is why the name is termed a *dynamic* range name. The COUNT function makes it sensitive to the number of numeric values in column A. The more values in that column, the more rows in the named range.

The other named range in Figure 3.13, DataToChart, is defined as

```
=OFFSET(LabelsToChart,0,1)
```

in the Define Names window's Refers To box. This makes the name dependent on the name LabelsToChart: It is offset from that range by zero rows and one column. Because the (optional) height and width arguments are not provided, the DataToChart range automatically assumes the same number of rows and columns as LabelsToChart. So, as the number of rows in LabelsToChart increases (or decreases), so does the number of rows in DataToChart.

After all this hand-waving, you're in a position to take advantage of the dynamic range names. In cell D2 of Figure 3.13, you find the formula =AVERAGE(DataToChart), which—with the data as shown in column B—returns the value 2.33.

Suppose that you now enter 11/16/2003 in cell A17 and 4 in B17. This increases the average restraints incidence from 2.33 to 2.44. It also causes both ranges to increase by one row, and the formula =AVERAGE(DataToChart) recalculates accordingly.

Another effect appears in the chart. An additional column appears on the chart to reflect the new values entered in A17:B17. This is because the charted series is defined in the chart as

=SERIES(,'Ch 03.xls'!LabelsToChart,'Ch 03.xls'!DataToChart,1)

> **TIP**
>
> To view or edit what a chart's data series refers to, click on the series to select it. You can then see what it refers to, and edit that information, in the Formula Bar.

So, as each range gets more data, the names are dynamically redefined to capture the new information, and the chart updates to show more labels on its x-axis and more values in its columns.

There are a couple of aspects to dynamic range names that it pays to keep in mind, and we'll discuss them in the following sections.

Looking Out for Extraneous Values

Notice in Figure 3.13 that the formula =AVERAGE(DataToChart) is outside column A. If it were in column A, it would count as a numeric value, and would contribute to the number of numeric values returned by the COUNT function in the definition of LabelsToChart.

Suppose, for example, that =AVERAGE(DataToChart) were in column A. Then =AVERAGE(DataToChart) would involve a circular reference: The formula would contribute to the definition of the range it refers to. (There are situations in which this can be a good thing, but this isn't one of them.)

Or suppose that you somehow let an extraneous numeric value get into column A—as far away, perhaps, as cell A60000. Then column A would have 15 dates and one extra, unwanted number, each counting as a numeric value. The COUNT function would return 16, not 15, and LabelsToChart would extend from A2:A17.

To use dynamic range names effectively, you need to make sure to keep extraneous values out of the range that COUNT looks at.

Selecting Dynamically Defined Ranges

Static range names are available in the Name box: You can click the Name box's dropdown and choose a range name to select that range. They're also available via the Go To item in the Edit menu. The list box shows all accessible range names; just select one of them and then click OK to select its range.

Dynamic range names don't behave that way. You'll never see one in the Name box—not, at least, through the 2003 version of Excel. And if you choose Go To from the Edit menu, you won't see dynamic range names in the list box. You can, however, choose Go To from the Edit menu, and type an already existing dynamic range name in the Reference box. When you click OK, Excel selects the range that's currently defined by that dynamic name.

Understanding the Scope of Names

Names can be either *workbook-level* or *worksheet-level* names. Workbook-level names are the default, and are the type that this chapter has discussed so far.

Workbook-level names (often referred to more briefly as *book-level names*) are accessible from any worksheet or chart sheet in a workbook. So, if the book-level name DataToChart refers to a range on Sheet1, you can use that name in any sheet in the workbook. For example, the formula =AVERAGE(DataToChart) could be used on Sheet2 or Sheet3, and would return the same result each time.

You define a book-level name using any of the methods discussed so far in this chapter: by means of the Name box, using the Define Names dialog box, or with the Create Names dialog box.

One possible drawback to a book-level name is that only one instance of that name can exist in a workbook. For example, you can't use the book-level name DataToChart to refer to A1:A20 on Sheet1 and also to some other range, such as C1:C20 on Sheet1, or A1:A20 on Sheet2, or to a constant or a formula. A book-level name can exist only once in a workbook and can have one reference only.

In contrast, a worksheet-level name (also termed a *sheet-level name*) can exist once in a workbook for each sheet in that workbook. One sheet-level name DataToChart can exist for Sheet1, and another sheet-level name DataToChart can exist for Sheet2, and so on.

Here's how to define the sheet-level name DataToChart for Sheet1 and Sheet2 (you can extend it to as many worksheets as you like):

1. Activate Sheet1.
2. Choose **Insert**, **Name**, **Define**.
3. In the Names in Workbook box, type Sheet1!DataToChart.

   That is, qualify the range name by the name of the worksheet it is to belong to. Separate the name of the worksheet from the range name itself with an exclamation point.

4. In the Refers To box, assign whatever reference you want: a constant, formula, or worksheet range. (If you cause the name to refer to a worksheet range, bear in mind that you can choose a range on any worksheet—not just Sheet1. That is, the name Sheet1!DataToChart can refer to B1:B10 on Sheet2.)

5. Click **OK**, or click **Add** to continue defining names.

You could also use the Name box: Select the range you want to refer to, then type, for example, Sheet1!DataToChart in the Name box.

When you're through entering sheet-level names, it's a good idea to double-check them in the Define Names window (see Figure 3.14).

Figure 3.14
Which sheet-level names are visible depends on which sheet is active when you choose Insert, Name, Define.

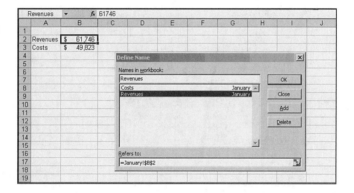

Notice that the name of the sheet to which the name belongs (in Figure 3.14, that's January) appears to the right of the sheet-level name in the Names in Workbook list box.

Sheet-level names are very handy when you assign similar kinds of data to different sheets in a workbook. For example, you might place a different income statement for each month in a year on a different worksheet. Each worksheet might be named according to its month. Then, you could have January!Revenues, February!Revenues, March!Revenues, and so on.

Keep these points in mind as you work with sheet-level names:

- You don't need to qualify a sheet-level name when you use it on the sheet that it's defined for. That is, if the worksheet named January is active, the formula =SUM(Revenues) is equivalent to =SUM(January!Revenues).

- If you want to refer to a sheet-level name, and the sheet that it's defined for is not active, you must qualify the name. If the February worksheet is active, and you want it to show the sum of January's revenues, you would need to enter =SUM(January!Revenues). This is true even if there is no sheet-level name February!Revenues.

Filtering Data with the AutoFilter

When you're working with a large amount of data, you sometimes want to hide certain records so that you can focus on others. This is called *filtering*: You filter out the records that you want to ignore.

Excel's worksheets offer two approaches to filtering data: the AutoFilter and the Advanced Filter. (There's nothing really complicated about the Advanced Filter; it just takes an extra step to set up.) Both filters require that you arrange data in list form: different records in different rows, different variables in different columns, and variable names in the first row of each column.

> **NOTE**
> If you don't put variable names in the list's first row, Excel's filters ask you whether you want to treat the first row as names. Excel calls these *column names*. To avoid confusion with the A, B, C, D, ... at the top of worksheet columns, we call them *variable names*.

Fast Filtering: Using the AutoFilter's Dropdowns

The idea behind AutoFilter is to make it easy to focus on a subset of records in your list. AutoFilter does this by temporarily hiding the records that don't belong to the subset you're interested in (see Figure 3.15).

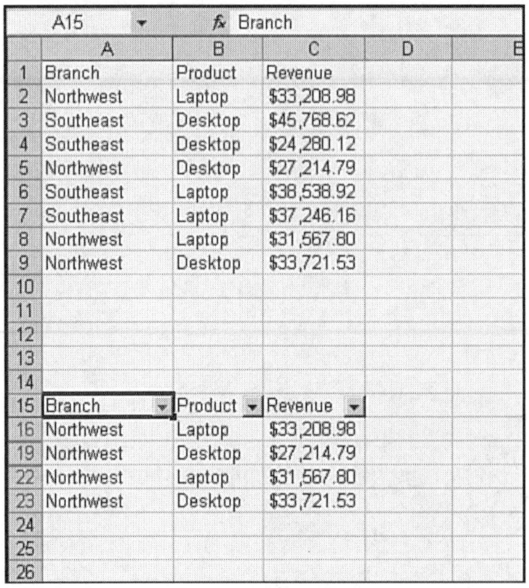

Figure 3.15
Notice that the records in the unfiltered list are not sorted, nor need they be.

	A	B	C	D	E
	A15		fx Branch		
	A	B	C	D	E
1	Branch	Product	Revenue		
2	Northwest	Laptop	$33,208.98		
3	Southeast	Desktop	$45,768.62		
4	Southeast	Desktop	$24,280.12		
5	Northwest	Desktop	$27,214.79		
6	Southeast	Laptop	$38,538.92		
7	Southeast	Laptop	$37,246.16		
8	Northwest	Laptop	$31,567.80		
9	Northwest	Desktop	$33,721.53		
10					
11					
12					
13					
14					
15	Branch	Product	Revenue		
16	Northwest	Laptop	$33,208.98		
19	Northwest	Desktop	$27,214.79		
22	Northwest	Laptop	$31,567.80		
23	Northwest	Desktop	$33,721.53		
24					
25					
26					

In Figure 3.15, the list in the range A1:C9 is unfiltered. That data is repeated in A15:C23, where the user has applied AutoFilter on the Branch variable so as to display only the Northwest branch's records. Notice that rows 17, 18, 20, and 21 are hidden: AutoFilter does this by setting their height to zero. And, although you can't tell in a black-and-white figure, the drop-down triangle in a field that has been used as a filter turns from black to blue.

> **TIP**
>
> You can easily activate a cell even if it's in a hidden row. Click in the Name box, type the cell's address, and press Enter. You'll see the cell's contents, if any, in the Formula Bar.

Suppose that you have a worksheet with the data shown in the range A1:C9 of Figure 3.15. To prepare to use AutoFilter, just do this:

1. Select any cell in the list.

2. Choose **Data**, **Filter**, **AutoFilter**.

This puts a series of dropdowns into the first row of your list. Each dropdown, when clicked, displays the *unique* values found in its column (see Figure 3.16).

Figure 3.16

Each unique value in a dropdown appears once only.

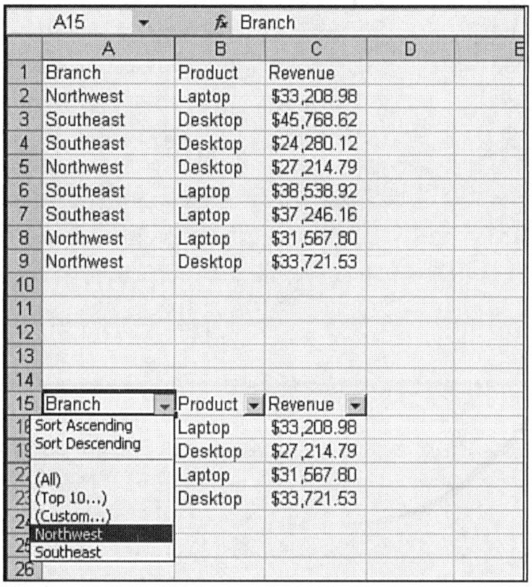

By clicking the Northwest value in column A's dropdown, you can filter the records in the entire list so that only the Northwest branch's records appear.

If your list has more than one column, you can use AutoFilter to select two or more values simultaneously, one from each column's dropdown (see Figure 3.17).

In Figure 3.17, the user has focused on both the Northwest branch and the Desktop product line. The two dropdowns act as though they were connected by an *and*: "If Branch is Northwest *and* Product is Desktop …".

Bear in mind that the effect of AutoFilter is to hide the rows that don't meet the filtering criteria that you set by means of the dropdowns. In Figure 3.17, for example, you can no longer see rows 16 through 18 and 20 through 22. But the values in the hidden records are still there. Formulas that depend on values in the hidden records are unchanged by AutoFilter.

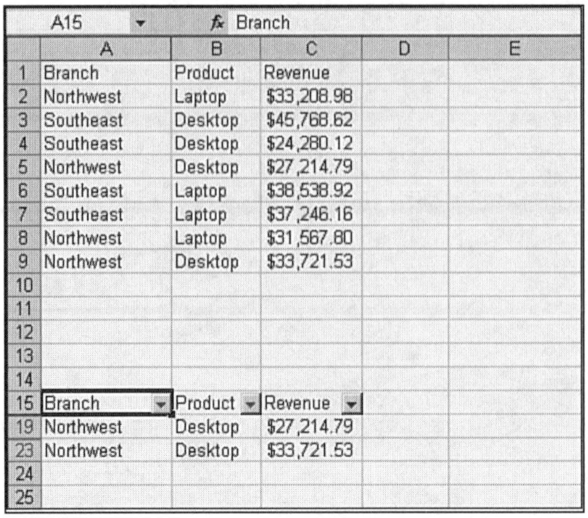

Figure 3.17
Only the sales of Desktops at the Northwest branch are shown.

You could get a similar effect by sorting the list on the Branch and Product columns. But you might find that approach to be less convenient if you then have to scroll down the worksheet to find the combination that you're interested in.

To reveal hidden records, but leave the dropdowns in place, choose **Data**, **Filter**, **Show All**. To remove the dropdowns, choose Data, Filter. You'll see a check mark by the AutoFilter menu item. Click AutoFilter again to remove the check mark from the menu and the dropdowns from the worksheet.

Using the AutoFilter with Other Criteria

Figure 3.16 shows that the AutoFilter has a Custom item in its dropdowns. Clicking it displays the window shown in Figure 3.18.

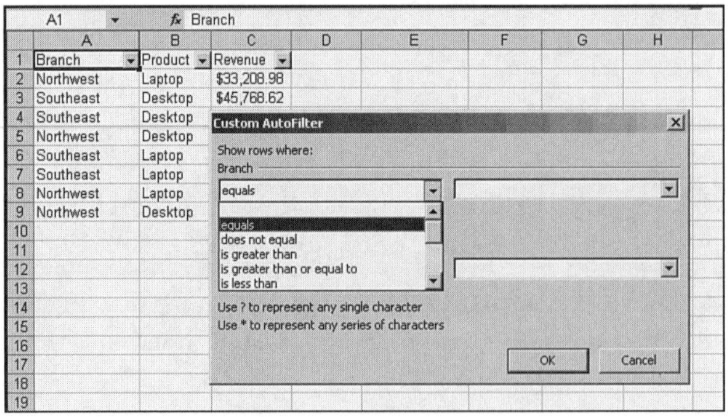

Figure 3.18
The AutoFilter enables you to specify two custom criteria for each column in your list.

The Custom AutoFilter window has two dropdowns with operators on the left and two value dropdowns on the right. You choose an operator and a value for it to operate on. For example, if you decided to view records from the Northwest branch only, you could select `equals` from the left dropdown, and `Northwest` from the right dropdown.

There are 12 operators available:

- Equals
- Does not equal
- Is greater than
- Is greater than or equal to
- Is less than
- Is less than or equal to
- Begins with
- Does not begin with
- Ends with
- Does not end with
- Contains
- Does not contain

> **NOTE**
> The Custom AutoFilter also supports wildcards. As usual, a question mark represents any single character and an asterisk represents any string of characters.

Using the Custom item makes it easy for you to arrange more complex analyses. Suppose that you wanted to filter records by a region that you just made up: North, for example, or East. In the Custom AutoFilter window, you could choose *equals* as the operator, and in the value dropdown, you could enter `North*`. Using the asterisk after North matches both Northwest and Northeast. You can see the result in Figure 3.19.

Keep in mind that the one or two custom criteria you set using the Custom AutoFilter apply to one column only. If you establish a custom criterion for Branch, and another custom criterion for Product, they act just as if you had selected simple criteria from the AutoFilter dropdowns; that is, they select records as if they were joined by an *and*.

Figure 3.19
You could create an *East* region instead, by entering ***east** in the value dropdown.

	A	B	C	D	E
	Branch	Product	Revenue		
1	Branch	Product	Revenue		
2	Northwest	Desktop	$33,721.53		
3	Northwest	Desktop	$27,214.79		
4	Northwest	Laptop	$33,208.98		
5	Northwest	Laptop	$31,567.80		
6	Southeast	Desktop	$45,768.62		
7	Southeast	Desktop	$24,280.12		
8	Southeast	Laptop	$38,538.92		
9	Southeast	Laptop	$37,246.16		
10	Northeast	Desktop	$79,998.88		
11	Northeast	Desktop	$97,444.60		
12	Northeast	Laptop	$36,477.68		
13	Northeast	Laptop	$66,185.68		
14	Southwest	Desktop	$67,751.96		
15	Southwest	Desktop	$77,383.85		
16	Southwest	Laptop	$30,852.08		
17	Southwest	Laptop	$24,926.69		
18					
19	Branch	Product	Revenue		
20	Northwest	Desktop	$33,721.53		
21	Northwest	Desktop	$27,214.79		
22	Northwest	Laptop	$33,208.98		
23	Northwest	Laptop	$31,567.80		
28	Northeast	Desktop	$79,998.88		
29	Northeast	Desktop	$97,444.60		
30	Northeast	Laptop	$36,477.68		
31	Northeast	Laptop	$66,185.68		

Using the Advanced Filter

The Advanced Filter used in Figure 3.20 provides three options that you can't get from AutoFilter:

- You can use it to create an entirely new, filtered list.
- You can obtain a list that contains unique records only—that is, only one instance of each possible combination of values.
- You have greater control over criteria. For example, you can establish more than two custom criteria that apply to a single column in the list.

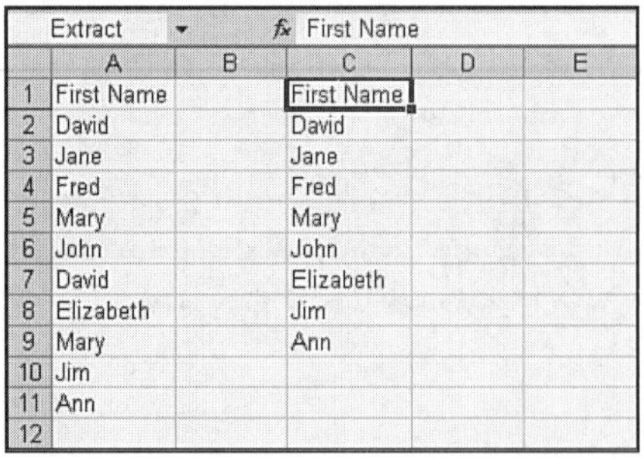

Figure 3.20
Filtering a list to a new location does not rely on hiding records.

	A	B	C	D	E
	First Name		First Name		
1	First Name		First Name		
2	David		David		
3	Jane		Jane		
4	Fred		Fred		
5	Mary		Mary		
6	John		John		
7	David		Elizabeth		
8	Elizabeth		Jim		
9	Mary		Ann		
10	Jim				
11	Ann				
12					

Column A of Figure 3.20 shows the original, unfiltered list. In column C, you see the new list that the user created with Advanced Filter: a list that consists only of unique names in column A. To get the result you see in column C, do this:

1. Click any cell in the original list.
2. Choose **Data**, **Filter**, **Advanced Filter**. The window shown in Figure 3.21 appears.

Figure 3.21
Filtering a list to a new location does not rely on hiding records.

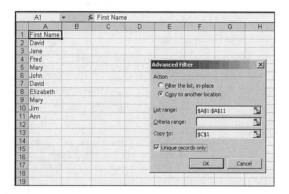

3. Click the **Copy to Another Location** option button. This enables the Copy To box.
4. Click in the **Copy To** box, and then in some cell on the worksheet to establish the copy-to location.
5. Fill the **Unique Records Only** check box.
6. Click **OK** to create the filtered list.

CAUTION

Be sure that there's no important data in the columns that the filtered list will occupy (in Figure 3.20, that's columns E through G). The Advanced Filter overwrites existing data in the copy-to columns, either with filtered data or, farther down, with blank cells. **Excel does not provide a warning, and there is no Undo command available to take back the filtering action**.

TIP

If you click the button (termed a *collapse dialog* button) on the right edge of any of the three boxes, the dialog box collapses to give you more room on the worksheet. Click the same button in the collapsed dialog box to restore it to the original size.

NOTE

You cannot copy to a location on a different worksheet. If the list you want to filter is on, say, Sheet2, you cannot cause the Advanced Filter to copy filtered records to Sheet3.

Using Criteria with the Advanced Filter

You can specify more criteria for the Advanced Filter than you can with the AutoFilter. Recall that for any column, you can choose one or two criteria using the Custom AutoFilter. For most purposes, this is plenty—especially when you consider that you can use wildcards in the criteria.

But suppose that you need more than two criteria per column, or that the filter you have in mind requires the Advanced Filter for some other reason. In that case, you'll need to specify in another worksheet location the criteria that the Advanced Filter will use. You might want to create a separate, filtered list that contains only records from the Northwest, Southeast, and Central branches. (Note that because this condition requires three criteria on the same field, AutoFilter won't do.) A separate list requires the Advanced Filter, so you would take these steps:

1. In some blank cell, enter Branch.

2. In the cell immediately below, enter Northwest. Below that enter Southeast, and below that enter Central.

3. Click in any cell in the existing list.

4. Choose **Data**, **Filter**, **Advanced Filter**. Click in the **Criteria Range** box, and then select the four cells you used in steps 1 and 2 (see Figure 3.22).

Figure 3.22
Any variable names in a criteria range must be identical to those in the list.

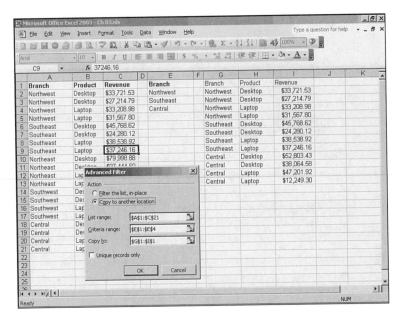

5. Continue as usual with the Advanced Filter, specifying a Copy To range, and Unique Values if you want.

The result appears in Figure 3.22, in cells G1:I13.

You can't specify a Copy To range on a different worksheet from the original list. But you can put the Criteria range on a different worksheet—even in a different workbook if you can think of a good reason to do so.

Using Formulas as Filter Criteria

With Advanced Filter, it's also possible to filter a list with the result of a formula as a criterion. Consider the list in A1:C22 of Figure 3.22. Suppose that you wanted to see only those records whose revenue value exceeded the average revenue of all the records. One way to arrange that is to use the Advanced Filter as before, but with a formula as the criterion. Your criteria range could occupy E1:E2, as shown in Figure 3.23.

Figure 3.23
The criterion in cell E2 actually evaluates to a string.

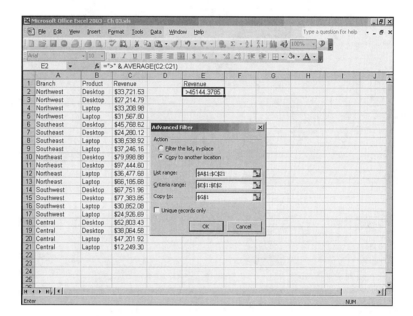

In E2, you enter `=">" & AVERAGE(C2:C21)`. This is the criterion that Advanced Filter will use: It is to return any value that is larger than the average of the Revenue values in C2:C21. Then take the usual steps:

1. Select any cell in the A1:C21 list.
2. Choose Data, **Filter**, **Advanced Filter**.
3. Select the **Copy to Another Location** option.
4. Click in the **Criteria Range** box, and drag through E1:E2.
5. Click in the **Copy To** box, and then click cell G1.
6. Click **OK**. The result appears in Figure 3.24.

Figure 3.24
Notice that the filtered list in G1:I9 contains only those records whose revenue exceeds $45,144.38.

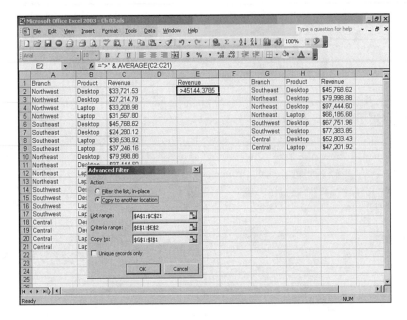

Looking Ahead

In Chapter 3, you've seen how to use three Excel techniques to manage data: lists, names, and filters. You've seen how to use them in conjunction with other Excel features such as the Data Form and the Sort command.

Because of the limitations of the printed page, the examples given in this chapter are necessarily brief and you've had to suspend your disbelief from time to time. (It would be unusual, for example, to apply a unique records filter to a list of 10 names.)

It's when you have hundreds and thousands of records in an Excel workbook that the techniques you learned in Chapter 3 start to become real timesavers. In Chapter 4, "Importing Data: An Overview," you'll start to see how you can quickly and automatically bring large amounts of data into an Excel worksheet from an external database.

Managing External Data from Inside Excel

III

Importing Data:
An Overview

4

Getting External Data into the Workbook

"Sorry. If you do that, you'll void the product warranty." That's what I was told by a software vendor when I asked him about pointing a query at the overpriced application he'd sold one of my clients.

No software publisher can possibly anticipate all the reasons that a customer might want his product. And that means that publishers can't possibly provide for all the ways that customers might want to view data. So, you'd think that a well-behaved publisher would offer an efficient means for users to get data out of one application and into another.

Some do. The same company that warned me about voiding the warranty later came out with a new, improved product that makes it easy to point queries at its tables.

But some don't, and then you need to work around the obstacles that the publishers put in your path. Fortunately, you can usually find a way. This chapter will help clarify for you that the search is worth the trouble.

One way to get data from some other application into Excel is to display the data in that other application, copy it, switch to Excel, and paste in the data. Although that method works, there are plenty of reasons to find another way—for example

- You're in a networked environment and not all users have access to an interface to the application that stores the data. In that case, not all users can display the data for a copy-and-paste operation.

- Again in a networked environment, you don't want to expose all the available data to every possible user. Maybe some of the data is confidential or sensitive.
- The way that the other application displays data is inconvenient. The application might display some fields that you don't care about. It might display subsets of records when you want to grab all of them. It might force you to display several different screens in order to get at all the data you're interested in.
- It's a pain.

Excel offers other ways to get data from other applications into a worksheet. Some involve Visual Basic for Applications (VBA) and some you can run from Excel's menus. Later chapters of this book, beginning in Part IV, "Managing Databases from Inside Excel," detail how to use VBA to get at external data. This chapter shows you how to get external data into a worksheet without writing a line of code. It also shows you how to update, or *refresh*, the external data to keep your worksheet current, both by setting options and by using VBA code.

Many applications, particularly database management systems, store data in *tables*. Tables usually arrange data in the same form as Excel's lists: different records occupy different rows, and different fields occupy different columns. Figure 4.1 shows an example from Microsoft Access.

4

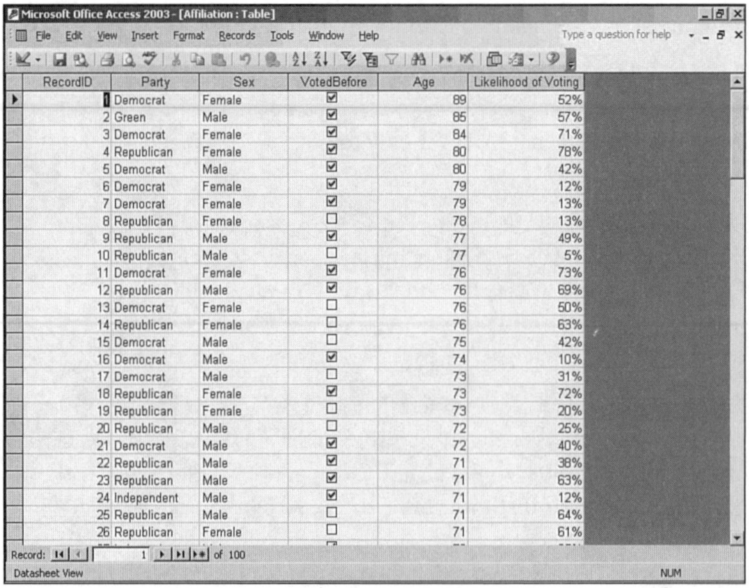

RecordID	Party	Sex	VotedBefore	Age	Likelihood of Voting
1	Democrat	Female	☑	89	52%
2	Green	Male	☑	85	57%
3	Democrat	Female	☑	84	71%
4	Republican	Female	☑	80	78%
5	Democrat	Male	☑	80	42%
6	Democrat	Female	☑	79	12%
7	Democrat	Female	☑	79	13%
8	Republican	Female	☐	78	13%
9	Republican	Male	☑	77	49%
10	Republican	Male	☐	77	5%
11	Democrat	Female	☑	76	73%
12	Republican	Male	☑	76	69%
13	Democrat	Female	☐	76	50%
14	Republican	Female	☐	76	63%
15	Democrat	Male	☐	75	42%
16	Democrat	Male	☑	74	10%
17	Democrat	Male	☐	73	31%
18	Republican	Female	☑	73	72%
19	Republican	Female	☐	73	20%
20	Republican	Male	☐	72	25%
21	Democrat	Male	☑	72	40%
22	Republican	Male	☑	71	38%
23	Republican	Male	☑	71	63%
24	Independent	Male	☑	71	12%
25	Republican	Male	☐	71	64%
26	Republican	Female	☐	71	61%

Figure 4.1
By default, Access tables show Boolean (also termed *Yes/No*) fields as check boxes—checked means TRUE.

After you get this data into Excel, you can summarize it with pivot tables, graph it with charts, analyze it with statistical tools, and so on. If you set it up right, you have to arrange the data acquisition only once. If more data is added to the original table later, your workbook can pull in all the new or changed data automatically each time someone opens it, or even every few minutes.

You begin the process by choosing Data, Get (or Import) External Data. Then Excel guides you through providing two basic sets of information:

- Where to find the data and how it's stored
- Which fields and which records you want to retrieve

The first set of information, the data's location and format, can be used repeatedly. This is useful if you want to import different sets of data into different worksheets or workbooks—for example, you might want to import data from January 2004 into one worksheet, from February 2004 into another, and so on.

CASE STUDY

You've volunteered to help out in a mayoral election—one of the candidates is your next door neighbor, so you suppress your distaste for the political process and offer your expertise in data management to your friend's election effort.

The campaign team has purchased a database containing voter rolls and it's up to you to help manage it. The first step is to get the data out of the database and into an Excel workbook where you can more easily analyze and summarize the information.

The data, shown in Figure 4.1, is in an Access database named Voters.mdb. The database is stored at C:\2005\CAMPAIGN.

Specifying the Data's Location and Format

You begin the first general step to importing data by choosing Data, Get External Data, New Database Query. The Choose Data Source dialog box shown in Figure 4.2 appears.

Figure 4.2
Starred data sources are Registry DSNs, either User DSNs or System DSNs. You can hide them by clicking Options.

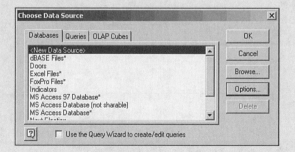

4

NOTE This is one of those annoying areas where Microsoft changes menu commands for no apparent reason other than sheer boredom. In Excel 97 and Excel 2000, the sequence starts with Data, Get External Data. In Excel 2002 and Excel 2003, it's Data, Import External Data. To add to the fun, Excel 97 has you continue with Create New Query, whereas in Excel 2000, 2002, and 2003 you continue with New Database Query.

TIP If you don't see the window shown in Figure 4.2, you'll probably instead see an error message to the effect that you haven't installed Microsoft Query. To install it, you'll have to run the Office installation procedure again, choosing to add a new feature. In Office 97, Microsoft Query is available from the Data Access option. In Office 2000, XP, and 2003, Microsoft Query is available under Office Tools.

As you'll see, each choice you make in the process of importing data has implications for what happens later, and this book deals with each of them. As a good starting place, select <New Data Source> from the list box shown in Figure 4.2. When you then click OK, the Create New Data Source dialog box shown in Figure 4.3 appears.

Figure 4.3
The controls in this dialog box become enabled in turn as you use each one.

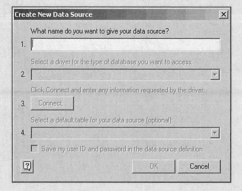

When you choose to create a new data source, you create a new file that contains information about the source of your data. For the purposes of your friend's run for the mayoralty, that file will specify an Access database named Voters.mdb, located in the C:\2005\CAMPAIGN path. Subsequently, you can use this new data source over and over—to pick up information about newly registered voters, perhaps, or because you're using another workbook to put together a different analysis.

The name of the new file you're creating is based on what you type into the What Name Do You Want to Give Your Data Source? box seen in Figure 4.3. Suppose that you type `Next Election` in that box. As soon as you begin typing, the box labeled Select a Driver for the Type of Database You Want to Access: becomes enabled. Use its dropdown to display a list of drivers that have been installed on your computer, as shown in Figure 4.4.

Figure 4.4
The name you give the data source is later used as the name of the Data Source Name (or *DSN*) file.

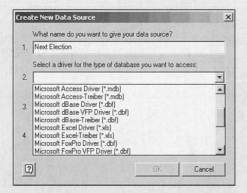

> **NOTE**
> If you know at the outset that you want to import data from Access, you can avoid having to make these choices by selecting MS Access Database in the Choose Data Source window (refer to Figure 4.2).

Because the data on voters is in an Access database, you would select *Microsoft Access Driver (*.mdb)*. When you click on a driver, the Connect button is enabled. Clicking it displays the ODBC Microsoft Access Setup dialog box shown in Figure 4.5.

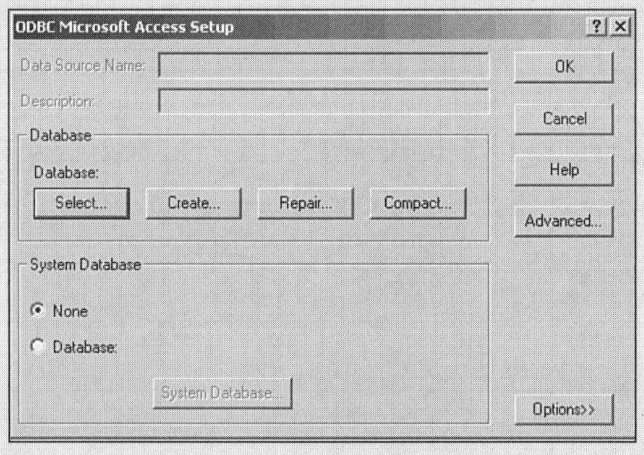

Figure 4.5
Use the Advanced button to supply a username and password, if one is needed to open the database.

From the ODBC Microsoft Access Setup dialog box, clicking Select displays the Select Database dialog box (see Figure 4.6).

At last, you're in a position to select the database that you want to use. From the Select Database window, use the Drives dropdown, if necessary, to choose the drive where your database is stored. Use the Directories list box to navigate to the folder on that drive that contains the database. In this example, you would choose C: from the Drives dropdown, and 2005\CAMPAIGN from the Directories list box. Click the Voters database in the Database Name list box, and click OK.

When you do so, you're returned to the ODBC Microsoft Access Setup window. The path to and name of the database are now shown on the window itself (see Figure 4.7).

Figure 4.6
Use the Network button to browse to a database that's stored on a network server.

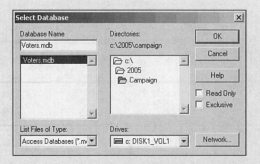

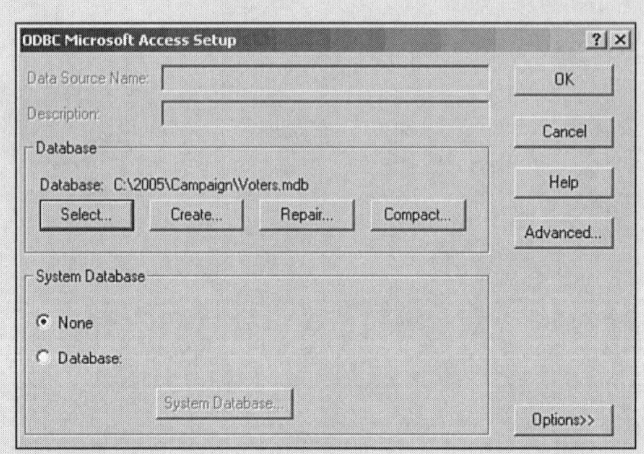

Figure 4.7
The path and database given on the Setup dialog box help you confirm that you have selected the correct database.

Click OK to return to the Create New Data Source dialog box, and click OK again to return to the Choose Data Source dialog box.

This case study continues later in the chapter on page 94. First, though, it's necessary to look more closely at the issue of multiple simultaneous users.

Using the Exclusive and Read Only Check Boxes

The Select Database dialog box shown in Figure 4.6 has two check boxes, Exclusive and Read Only, whose use is a little obscure.

Unlike Excel workbooks, databases are designed to be used by more than one person simultaneously. Yes, you can share an Excel workbook, but this feature came along relatively late in Excel's development and was tacked onto the application almost as an afterthought. It just does not work as well or as reliably as it does in an application such as Access or SQL Server that was designed from the ground up for multiple simultaneous usage.

Bearing in mind that databases can be opened in what's termed *shared mode*, you'd think that filling the Exclusive check box would prevent that. You might well have a situation in which you would want to prevent others from opening the database while your query is running. In that case, you would want to open the database in exclusive rather than shared mode.

But that doesn't happen here. If you fill the Exclusive check box *only* in the Select Database dialog box, when you return to the ODBC Microsoft Access Setup dialog box (see Figure 4.7) and click OK, you get an error message. The error states that Query `Could not use '(unknown)'; file already in use.`

Microsoft states that the reason for this behavior is that Microsoft Query attempts to make two connections to the database as it's creating the DSN. If you've specified exclusive mode in the Select Database dialog box, two connections can't be made and Microsoft Query reports an error.

The most straightforward way around this foolishness is as follows:

1. Create your data source as described in the prior section. Do not fill the Exclusive check box in the Select Database dialog box.
2. Start Notepad, or any other application that is able to open, edit, and save text files.
3. With Notepad active, choose **File**, **Open**. In the Files of Type dropdown, choose **All Files**.
4. Browse to the location where your DSN files are stored. The location depends on your version of Excel. For example, in Excel 97, it's C:\Program Files\Microsoft Office\Office; in Excel 2003, it's C:\Program Files\Common Files\ODBC\Data Sources.
5. Open the DSN file you created in step 1. You'll see statements much like those shown in Figure 4.8. Click at the end of any statement, including the final one, and press **Enter** to create a new, blank line.
6. Type this statement:
   ```
   Exclusive=1
   ```
7. Choose **File**, **Save** and then **File**, **Exit**.

Now when you use that DSN as the basis for a query, the database will be opened in exclusive mode.

As usual, there's a downside. If you try to use a DSN as the basis for a query, and the DSN specifies exclusive mode, *and* someone already has the database open, you'll get an error message. The message tells you which workstation has the database open. If you know who is using, for example, the workstation named WSMS256, you can ask that person to close the database. Or you can use Notepad to remove the `Exclusive=1` statement from the DSN file.

The Read Only check box in the Select Database dialog box might seem superfluous. After all, you can't write anything back to a data source using a worksheet's external data query.

But DSN files can be used for purposes other than importing data into an Excel worksheet. As you'll see in Chapter 8, "Opening Databases," you can use a DSN to establish a connection to a database for the purpose of updating, adding, or deleting records, and even modifying the database's structure.

4

So, one way of preventing that sort of access using your DSN is to fill the Read Only check box. That causes this statement to be put in the DSN file:

```
ReadOnly=1
```

That statement means that the DSN will not allow changes to be made to the data or structure of the database.

But as you saw earlier in this section, it's easy to modify a DSN. You can remove a `ReadOnly=1` statement as easily as you can add an `Exclusive=1` statement. If you're really concerned about preventing changes to a database, you're much better off using its security features.

Using DSN Files

After you've created a new data source, it's easy to use it as the basis for a new query. You can dispense with choosing a driver, naming the data source, and navigating to the location of the data—just select the source's name (instead of <New Data Source>) in the Choose Data Source window (refer to Figure 4.2). The information you supplied is stored in a file, known informally as a *DSN*. (The abbreviation *DSN* stands for *data source name*.) Excel displays it, along with other available data sources, in the Choose Data Source dialog box. Figure 4.8 shows the contents of a typical DSN file.

Figure 4.8
DSN files can be read by any application that can open a text file, including Notepad.

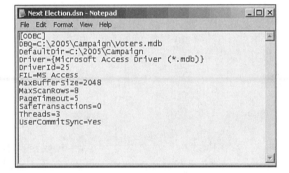

If you review Figure 4.2, notice the Browse button in the Choose Data Source dialog box. It enables you to navigate to other locations where you might have stored DSN files. In Office 2003, they are stored by default in C:\Program Files\Common Files\ODBC\Data Sources.

> **NOTE**
> You might have wondered about the other two tabs on the Choose Data Source dialog box, Queries and OLAP Cubes. Query files are similar to DSNs, except that in addition to information such as path, name, and type of database, they also include SQL that defines a query's tables, fields, filtering criteria, and so on. They can be more convenient but less flexible than DSNs. Queries usually have the file extension .dqy. Figure 4.9 shows a typical DQY file.
>
> OLAP Cubes tend to be very large, multidimensional data structures. (OLAP stands for *Online Analytic Processing*.) Because they are so large, some values are pre-calculated so as to save data retrieval time.

Figure 4.9
Note that the first part of the query file resembles a DSN, whereas the second part is standard SQL.

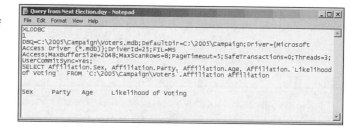

Suppose that someone has sent you a DSN file via email. You might have saved it on your desktop and in that case it won't show up in the Choose Data Source dialog box. To get to it, just click the Browse button and navigate to your desktop.

This is different from what you see if you click the Options button in Choose Data Source. Then the dialog box shown in Figure 4.10 appears.

Figure 4.10
This Browse button has a different effect than the Browse button on the Choose Data Source dialog box.

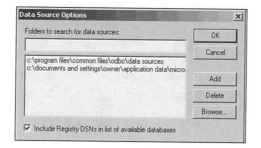

The Data Source Options dialog box enables you to make longer-lasting changes to the list of available data sources. If you click the Browse button shown in Figure 4.10, you can use the Select Directory dialog box to navigate to a folder where you store, or intend to store other DSN and query files (see Figure 4.11).

Figure 4.11
Files with *qy* in their extensions, such as .dqy and .oqy, usually contain SQL statements; that is, they are queries.

After you've navigated to a folder, clicking OK will add that folder to the list that Microsoft Query searches. Any data source files in that folder will appear in the list of available sources in the Choose Data Source dialog box. In brief

- Click the Browse button on the Choose Data Source dialog box to browse to a data source file that you want to use for this query. That file *will not* show up subsequently in the Choose Data Source dialog box.

■ Click the Options button on the Choose Data Source dialog box, and then the Browse button on the Data Source Options dialog box, to browse to a folder that you want to use now and in the future. Data source files in that folder *will* appear subsequently in the Choose Data Source dialog box.

> **NOTE**
> Of course, if at another time you want to use a different data source, you'll need to set it up as you did this one. If you want to use an Oracle database, for example, you need to create a DSN with a different driver; or, if you want to use a different Access database, you need a DSN that names it.

This completes the first of two general steps involved in creating a new data source: identifying the type and location of the data. We return you now to the mayor's race, where, with the data source identified, it's time to start creating a new query.

CASE STUDY

Building the Query

You have just finished creating a new data source (or, equivalently, you might have used an existing source by choosing Data, Import External Data, New Database Query). You now see the Choose Data Source dialog box shown previously in Figure 4.2.

With the Choose Data Source dialog box active, click the name of the data source you're interested in from the Databases list box, and click OK. The Microsoft Query window appears, as shown in Figure 4.12.

Figure 4.12
Use the Options button to choose between showing tables or views (*view* is sometimes used as another term for *query*).

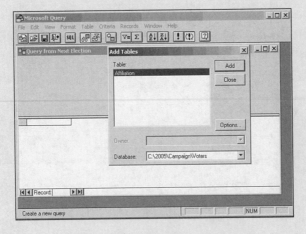

Although this is the first time in this sequence that the Microsoft Query window appears, Query's been running the show in the background, walking you through the creation of a new data source. The Add Tables dialog box also appears automatically when the Query window opens; all there is for you to do at this point is add one or more tables or existing queries from the database.

The next chapter goes into detail about various ways to use Microsoft Query to automatically get data out of databases and into Excel. If you're unfamiliar with true relational databases, just bear these points in mind for the present:

- A *table* closely resembles an Excel worksheet or list. It has records, and each record occupies a different row. It has fields, and each field occupies a different column. The current example shows how to bring data from a database table into an Excel worksheet.

- You can use this method to bring data into Excel from more than one table at once—even from more than one database.

- A *query* is a series of statements that acts on a table in some way. A query can use a table's data to do calculations (for example, "If the Sex field is 1, display 'Male' and otherwise display 'Female'"). It's often efficient to bring data into the worksheet directly from the query, and only indirectly from the table that the query uses.

The present example continues by getting data on voters directly from a single table into a worksheet.

1. In the Add Tables window shown in Figure 4.12, select the table named **Affiliation** and then click **Add**. When you do so, the table appears in the Microsoft Query window. If they exist, you can continue by adding more tables and queries. When you're through adding, click **Close**. The Microsoft Query window then appears as shown in Figure 4.13.

Figure 4.13
If you don't see the Criteria pane, choose Criteria from the View menu.

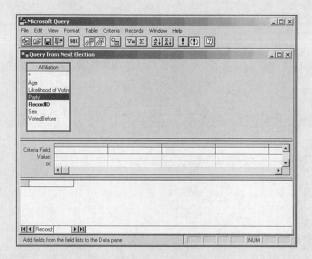

The Query window has three panes:

- The Table Pane—This is where tables that your query uses appear. As you can see in Figure 4.13, the individual fields in the table are also shown.

- The Criteria Pane—Here you can specify which records should be returned from the database table. Suppose that you want to return records of voters whose value on the Party field is either Republican or Independent. You could drag the Party field from its table into the first row of the criteria pane, labeled

Criteria Field. In the same column, you would enter "Republican" (with the quote marks) in the Value row. Again in the same column, you would enter "Independent" in the Or row.

- The Data Pane—This is where you specify which fields you want to return. You need not (although you can if you want) return all the fields in a table from the database. In the Table Pane, just click a field that you want and drag it into a column in the Data Pane (see Figure 4.14).

Figure 4.14
Double-clicking a field in the table copies it to the first available column in the Data Pane.

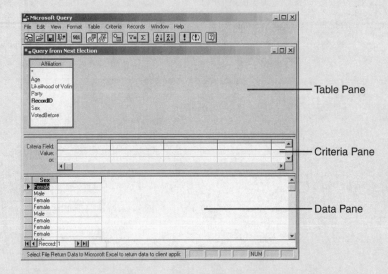

Table Pane

Criteria Pane

Data Pane

2. Double-click a field in the table to copy it to the Data Pane, or click on a field and drag it to a specific column in the Data Pane. When you have put as many fields as you want into the Data Pane, choose **File**, **Return Data to Microsoft Excel** (or just click the **Return Data** button). When you do, the Import Data dialog box shown in Figure 4.15 appears.

Figure 4.15
The exact appearance of this window depends on the version of Excel you're using.

3. Click **OK** to return the data to the active worksheet, beginning in the cell that was active when you began the process. Of course, if there is data that you want to avoid overwriting, you can supply a different cell address or even return the data to a new worksheet.

TIP Step 2 noted that you can either double-click a field or click and drag it to get it into the Data Pane. Double-clicking the field puts it in the rightmost available column of the Data Pane. If you drag a field, you can place it in any column you want in the Data Pane. If you drag the asterisk at the top of the field list into the Data Pane, you get all the fields.

Figure 4.16 shows the appearance of the worksheet after the data has been returned from the source.

Figure 4.16
Notice that the data comes to the worksheet in the form of a list, complete with field names.

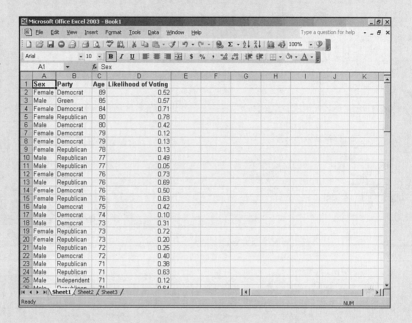

Your friend's campaign can now concentrate its advertising and the get-out-the-vote effort on the subgroups most likely to vote in the next election.

There are several useful properties about the range that contains the returned data—call it the *external data range*. Among other properties, you can

- Cause the range to refresh itself automatically whenever you open the workbook
- Specify how you want to manage an increase or a decrease in the number of records
- Copy down formulas that depend on the external data range to accommodate additional records

NOTE

Excel names the external data range automatically. The name depends in part on which version you're using. Excel 97 names it ExternalData1, and if you have other external data ranges on the same worksheet, it names them ExternalData2, ExternalData3, and so on. Subsequent versions name data ranges according to the data source name that you selected in the Choose Data Source dialog box; for example, *Query_from_Employee_DB*. Regardless of the version, the range names are sheet-level.

→ For a discussion of sheet-level versus book-level names, **see** Chapter 3, "Excel's Lists, Names, and Filters," **p. 55**.

To see what options are available to you, right-click in any cell in the external data range, and choose Properties (or, depending on your version, Data Range Properties) from the shortcut menu.

→ More information on the available options can be found in "Using Microsoft Query," **p. 113**.

Using the Query Wizard

As you accumulate more and more experience with Microsoft Query, you'll find that (within limits) it's a useful way of defining how you want to retrieve data from a database: which records, which fields, in which order.

Until you gain a measure of confidence, though, you might want to rely on an adjunct to Microsoft Query, called the Query Wizard. Have another look at Figure 4.2: There's a check box in the Choose Data Source window, labeled Use the Query Wizard to Create/Edit Queries.

If you fill this check box, Excel will present a series of windows—much like the Chart Wizard—that enables you to define your query, step by step. Figure 4.17 shows the first step of the Query Wizard, after you've finished defining the data source.

Figure 4.17
Using the Query Wizard, this window appears instead of the Microsoft Query window.

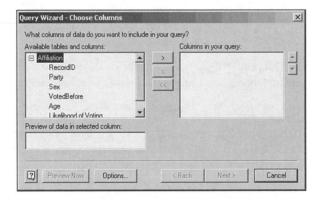

The Query Wizard's Choose Columns window combines the Add Tables window (refer to Figure 4.12) with the act of dragging fields to the Query window's Data Pane. In Figure 4.17, the user has expanded the Affiliation table by clicking the plus sign that's just left of the table's name. The list then expands to show the names of the fields in the table, and the plus sign by the table's name changes to a minus sign.

To continue, just click a field name and then click the button with the greater-than (>) sign. The field is moved into the Columns in Your Query list. If you change your mind, select a field name in that list and click the button with the less-than (<) sign (see Figure 4.18).

Figure 4.18
Click the double less-than (<<) sign to remove all previously selected fields.

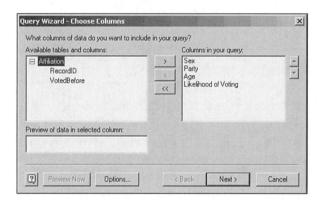

When you've finished selecting fields, click the Next button to move to the wizard's next step, shown in Figure 4.19.

Figure 4.19
The Query Wizard refers to fields as columns and to records as rows.

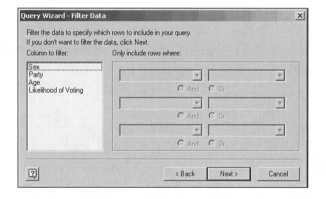

In this step, you identify which fields, if any, you want to use to restrict the records that are returned to the worksheet. To do so, take these steps:

1. Select a field in the **Column to Filter** list.

2. Click the first left-side dropdown and choose an appropriate operator: equals, is less than, begins with, and so on.

3. Click the first right-side dropdown and choose an appropriate criterion value (see Figure 4.20).

Figure 4.20
To add more criteria, you need to first select And or Or between the criteria sets—the And is the default choice.

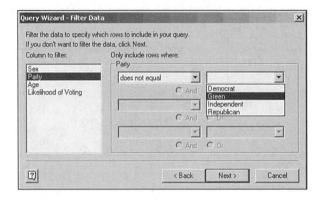

> **NOTE**
>
> You can also type a criterion value in the box instead of selecting one from a dropdown. If you do, make sure that you type a value that exists in the field. If the query cannot match the value you type, it will not return any records. These criteria are not case sensitive: "green" is treated in the same way as "Green".

4. If you want to add more operators and criteria, use the second and third pairs of drop-downs. If you establish three criteria, the dialog box displays a vertical scrollbar and another criteria set. You're not limited to the three criteria sets that are initially visible. When you're through, click **Next**.

Step 4 shows that the Query Wizard is both easier to use and less powerful than Query itself. The step enables you to choose among available operators, rather than relying on you to know what they are and how to specify them. It also displays the values that you can use as criteria, rather than relying on you to supply them.

On the other hand, you can filter on one field only. You could not, for example, specify that you want to return male Republicans; that would require you to use two fields: Sex and Party. Microsoft Query, on the other hand, enables you to filter on as many fields as you want.

When you click Next in step 4, the Sort Order window appears (see Figure 4.21).

Select one or more fields and specify whether you want an ascending or descending sort for each. The first field you specify becomes the primary sort key; the second field becomes the secondary sort key. That is, if you select Sex first and then Party, and specify an ascending sort for each, the records might come to Excel in this order (depending on the actual values for party affiliation): Female Democrat, Female Green, Female Independent, Female Republican, Male Democrat, Male Green, Male Independent, Male Republican.

Figure 4.21
The user has selected Age from the dropdown and clicked Descending. The default is an ascending sort.

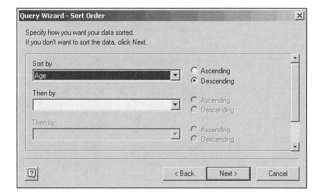

When you click Next, the Query Wizard's final step appears as shown in Figure 4.22.

Figure 4.22
Viewing the query in Microsoft Query is a good way to see how to build the same query without using the Query Wizard.

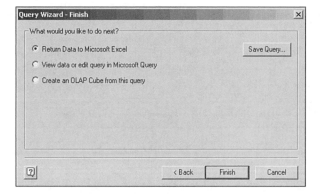

If you click Save Query, you'll save the query in a text-format data file. This can be useful, but it can also become a problem.

Suppose first that you click the Return Data to Microsoft Excel button and then click Finish. If you do, the query's definition is saved in the active workbook (in a hidden name, one that neither you nor anyone else has direct access to; this is very different from a readable DSN file). Subsequently, you can refresh the data in the external data range by re-executing the query.

> **TIP**
>
> You can refresh an external data range by right-clicking any cell in the range and choosing Refresh External Data from the shortcut menu (your version might instead say Refresh Data).

If you want to put the same query in another workbook, you'll either have to copy the external data range and paste it into that workbook, or you'll have to re-create the query with the other workbook active.

> **NOTE**
>
> It might seem too easy, but to copy the external data range *and* the query definition to another location, all you need to do is copy and paste the entire external data range. The query definition, as well as the name as defined, both follow along with the data.

On the other hand, suppose that you save the query instead of returning the data directly to the workbook. Then, with another workbook active, you could choose Data, Import External Data, and click Import Data. You would see your saved query as one of the available data sources. That makes it convenient to re-establish the query in a new workbook whenever you want, without copying and pasting it, and without re-creating it.

The hitch is that the query is stored in text format, and anyone might be able to use it. (The query is saved as a DQY file, of the type mentioned earlier in this chapter and shown in Figure 4.9.) Queries often need to have passwords saved with them, so if you're thinking of saving a query that gets data from a password-protected source, you might want to think twice.

You can choose View Data or Edit Query in Microsoft Query before clicking Finish. This choice is useful if you're learning how to use Microsoft Query, or if you simply find it convenient to begin by using the Query Wizard and then to fine-tune with Microsoft Query.

In most cases, though, you'll choose Return Data to Microsoft Excel. When you click Finish, the Import Data dialog box shown in Figure 4.15 appears. Click OK to finish the process. Figure 4.23 shows how your worksheet appears when you do so.

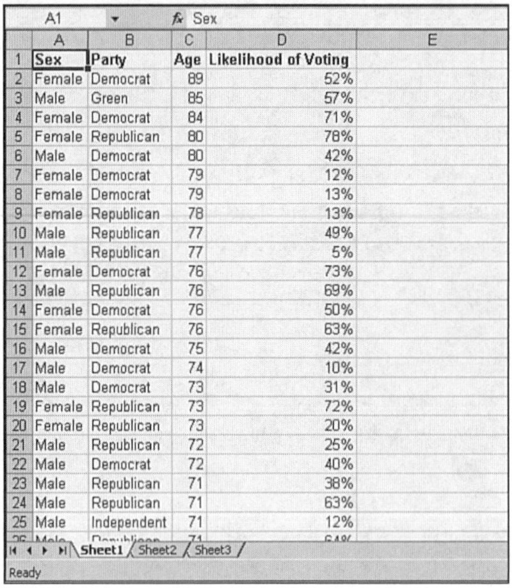

Figure 4.23

Notice that the order of the records conforms to the sort chosen in Figure 4.21.

	A	B	C	D	E
1	Sex	Party	Age	Likelihood of Voting	
2	Female	Democrat	89	52%	
3	Male	Green	85	57%	
4	Female	Democrat	84	71%	
5	Female	Republican	80	78%	
6	Male	Democrat	80	42%	
7	Female	Democrat	79	12%	
8	Female	Democrat	79	13%	
9	Female	Republican	78	13%	
10	Male	Republican	77	49%	
11	Male	Republican	77	5%	
12	Female	Democrat	76	73%	
13	Male	Republican	76	69%	
14	Female	Democrat	76	50%	
15	Female	Republican	76	63%	
16	Male	Democrat	75	42%	
17	Male	Democrat	74	10%	
18	Male	Democrat	73	31%	
19	Female	Republican	73	72%	
20	Female	Republican	73	20%	
21	Male	Republican	72	25%	
22	Male	Democrat	72	40%	
23	Male	Republican	71	38%	
24	Male	Republican	71	63%	
25	Male	Independent	71	12%	

A1 — Sex

Sheet1 / Sheet2 / Sheet3 /

Ready

This is a great situation for dynamic range names, which were introduced in Chapter 3, "Excel's Lists, Names, and Filters." When your external data range is refreshed with new data, its definition automatically changes.

Suppose that the range that contains the external data is named `Query_From_Next_Election`, and that it occupies the range A1:D100. You add five new records to the database—records that qualify to be returned by the query. When the data range is refreshed next, it will include those five new records and will extend an additional five rows in the worksheet, occupying A1:D105.

If you establish two dynamic range names that use `Query_From_Next_Election` as a basis, you can easily arrange other parts of your workbook to update along with the external data range. An XY (Scatter) chart is a good example: You might have one dynamic range that acts as the chart's x-axis values, and one that acts as the chart's y-axis values. For example, you might define the range name `AgesToChart` as

```
=OFFSET(Sheet1!Query_from_Next_Election,1,2, _
ROWS(Sheet1!Query_from_Next_Election),1)
```

and the range name `LikelihoodToChart` as

```
=OFFSET(AgesToChart,0,1)
```

Applied to the external data range shown in Figure 4.23, the dynamic range named `AgesToChart` is offset one row (so it starts in row 2), two columns (so it starts in column C), has as many rows as the external data range, and is one column wide. When the external data range gets more records, it has more rows, and so does `AgesToChart`.

The dynamic range named `LikelihoodToChart` is based on `AgesToChart`, but it is offset by zero rows and one column from `AgesToChart`. Because its definition does not specify the number of rows and columns in its range, it has by default the same number of rows and columns as its basis range.

The chart shown in Figure 4.24 has a single data series, defined as

```
=SERIES(,Sheet1!AgesToChart,Sheet1!LikelihoodToChart,1)
```

When the external data range is refreshed, new records enter the external data range. It occupies more rows, and the dynamic ranges that depend on it also grow. Because the chart's data series refers to the dynamic range names, it captures and displays the newly added records.

4

Figure 4.24
The chart updates automatically if it's based on dynamic range names.

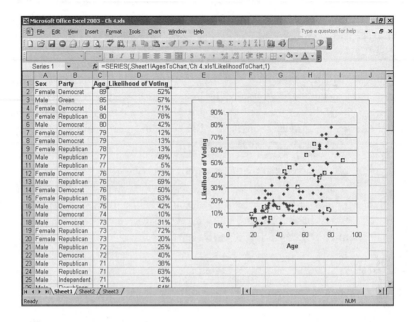

Importing Data to Pivot Tables

If you've worked much with Excel's pivot tables, you're surely familiar with a list as a pivot table's data source. And you could use the data as shown in Figure 4.23 as a pivot table source, without any further manipulation.

Refer to Figure 4.15, which shows the Import Data window, which appears when you're through defining a query with Microsoft Query or with the Query Wizard. You'll notice in that window there's an option to create a pivot table report (the exact wording depends on the version of Excel that you're using). If you select this option, you see the final step in the Pivot Table Wizard instead of the external data range with its records and fields.

There's nothing special about this capability. You get to the same place by taking these steps:

1. Start the Pivot Table Wizard by choosing **PivotTable and PivotChart Report** from the **Data** menu.

2. Select **External Data Source** in the wizard's first step.

3. Click **Get Data** in the wizard's second step.

You'll then see the Choose Data Source window, just as in Figure 4.2. You can now select an existing data source, or create a new one. Eventually you'll finish structuring the query with Microsoft Query (or, if you choose, with the Query Wizard) and when you return the data to Excel, you'll return to the PivotTable Wizard's final step.

The process and the end result are the same, no matter whether you start with the PivotTable Wizard or the Import External Data command.

Populating Pivot Tables

A pivot table stores its data in a special location, termed the *cache*. The cache makes it possible for a pivot table to carry out complex recalculations very quickly. But the cache has drawbacks.

You might have noticed that if a pivot table is based on data in an Excel list, and if the data in that list changes, the pivot table does not change in response. To get this to happen, you have to prompt it—by choosing Data, Refresh Data, or clicking the Refresh button on the pivot table toolbar, or one of at least two other methods.

The same is true if you base a pivot table on what Excel terms *external data*. Suppose that you use either the PivotTable Wizard or the Import External Data command to create a pivot table that summarizes records that are found in a database. Subsequently, the data in the database changes. Just as though the pivot table were based on an Excel list, you have to refresh the pivot table. Refreshing the pivot table updates the cache, and when the cache is updated, the pivot table itself is updated.

 TIP If you want, you can suppress the cache. One of the pivot table options is to Save Data with Table Layout. Unchecking this option means that the pivot table has no cache, on which a pivot table's functionality largely depends. You can save a little space and time by suppressing the cache. If you ever need a cache—to pivot the table, for example—you simply choose Data, Refresh External Data.

4

Refreshing the Cache

There's no really satisfactory solution to the problem described in the previous section. As of Excel 2003, the cache simply does not respond automatically to changes in its data source. The best you can do is set one or more pivot table options that cause the cache to be refreshed in response to an event. Events that can refresh the cache include opening the workbook that contains the pivot table and a specified amount of time passing.

Right-click a cell in the pivot table and choose Table Options. The dialog box shown in Figure 4.25 appears.

Use the PivotTable Options dialog box to do one or both of these:

- Fill the Refresh on Open check box and save the workbook. When you next open the workbook, the pivot table automatically refreshes its cache from the data source.

- If you want a more frequent refresh, fill the Refresh Every check box and use the spinner to specify the number of minutes to wait between automatic refreshes.

The problem, of course, is that it takes time and system resources to perform the refresh. If you have a lot of data underlying the pivot table, refreshing it every (say) 5 minutes can be wasteful. In a networked environment, where you're piping hundreds of thousands of bytes of data through the network during a refresh, consider the frequency of the refreshes very carefully.

Figure 4.25
It's a good idea to give the table a descriptive name, and not rely on the default name *PivotTable1*.

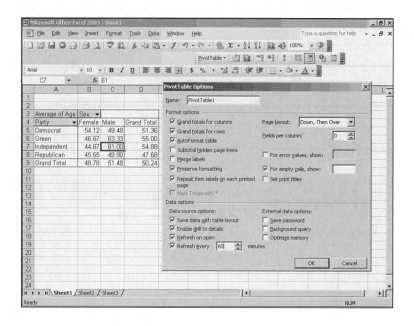

> **TIP**
>
> If your pivot table's data is in an external data source, you can create the pivot table without ever putting a list in the workbook. Subsequently, though, you might find that you want to look at the individual records and fields, just as if you had first imported the data into an external data range and then built the pivot table using that range. To create the list, double-click the pivot table's Grand Total cell. This inserts a new worksheet and puts the cache's data on it in list form.

Choosing Between Refresh on Open and the Workbook_Open Event

The previous section described how to make a pivot table automatically refresh its data: fill the Refresh on Open check box in the pivot table's options. You can also cause an external data range to refresh itself automatically: Right-click any cell in the data range, choose Data Range Properties from the shortcut menu, and fill the Refresh Data on File Open check box.

That's pretty straightforward, but things begin to get complicated when you have more than just one thing to do when a workbook opens. For example, opening the workbook might cause a VBA subroutine to run as part of the workbook's On Open event.

In that case, it can be important to know whether a pivot table, or an external data range, refreshes before or after the subroutine runs. I once spent eight nonbillable hours re-creating hundreds of pivot tables and charts that had accumulated over a five-month period, every one of them wrong, because I thought the refresh preceded the Open event. I promise you that it's important to keep in mind that the Open event precedes an automatic, on-open refresh.

Or you might have several pivot tables in a workbook, each of which should refresh when the workbook opens. This can present an annoyance. If a pivot table's structure changes as a result of an automatic refresh, Excel notifies you with a message box that says `Pivot table was changed during Refresh Data operation`. (Whether or not you see this message depends on the version of Excel that you're using.)

One alert message isn't a problem, but if you have, say, 10 or 15 pivot tables that are changing when they're refreshed, and you're getting an alert for each one, and you have to click OK to get to the next pivot table—that's annoying.

So, consider handling the pivot table refreshes with Visual Basic for Applications. For the purpose of refreshing pivot tables, this chapter provides an overview.

→ Chapter 7, "VBA Essentials Reviewed," goes into greater detail on VBA.

As mentioned previously, workbooks have Open events (among various others). The idea behind an event, in this context, is that Excel notices when the event occurs, and runs code in response to the event. This code is termed an *event handler*: It handles what happens when the event occurs. So, you can write VBA code that runs when the Open event occurs for its workbook, and that code can refresh your pivot tables.

The rationale is that in this way you can exert greater control over when the pivot tables refresh. And not incidentally, you can suppress those annoying alerts that the pivot table changed.

If you're using Excel 2003, there might be another reason yet. Excel 97 did not warn you that automatic refreshes could be based on harmful queries that could, for example, write data back to an external source. Beginning with Excel 2000, Service Release 1, you *are* alerted, and can choose to continue with the refresh, disable the refresh, or enable automatic query refresh for all workbooks and not see the warning again.

Excel 2003 does not provide the third option, which suppresses subsequent warnings. The only way to do so is to edit the system registry or to refresh pivot tables automatically with your own VBA code. As already noted, doing the refreshes with VBA code puts you in a position to exert greater control over the timing of the refreshes. To arrange to refresh all a workbook's pivot tables using its On Open event, take these steps:

1. Open the workbook that contains the pivot tables.
2. Right-click the Excel icon that appears directly to the left of the File menu to display a shortcut menu, and choose View Code.

> **TIP**
> You can also press Alt+F11 to open the Visual Basic Editor. Once there, right-click the This Workbook icon in the Project Explorer, and then choose View Code to open the workbook's code window.

You'll see a window similar to the one shown in Figure 4.26. For the purpose of building an Open event handler, it's not important that the Project Explorer or the Properties Window be visible, but if you want to, you can find them in the **View** menu.

Figure 4.26
The code that handles an event is associated with an Excel object, so it is not found in a Modules folder.

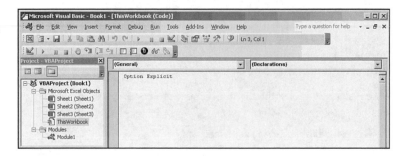

3. Notice in Figure 4.26 the code pane occupying the right portion of the window. It has two dropdowns at its top. The one on the left, which has (General) selected, is the Object dropdown. The one on the right, with (Declarations) selected, is the Procedure dropdown. Click the **Object** dropdown and choose **Workbook** from the list.

Two statements automatically appear in the code window: a Private Sub statement, naming the procedure (by default, Workbook_Open) and an End Sub statement, marking the end of the procedure. The Procedure dropdown also automatically selects Open (see Figure 4.27).

Figure 4.27
There are 28 procedures available as workbook events in the procedure dropdown, including Activate and NewSheet.

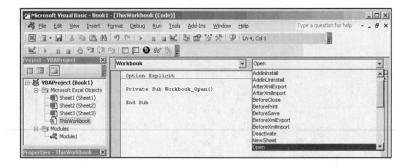

4. Type the code that you want to run between the Private Sub and the End Sub statements (see Figure 4.28).

5. Choose **File, Close and return to Microsoft Excel**, and then save the workbook.

→ To find out about Option Explicit, **see** "Establishing Subroutines," **p.168**.

Here's the code again, with some comments to explain it:

```
Private Sub Workbook_Open()
```

Establish a subroutine that will run when the workbook that contains the subroutine is opened.

Figure 4.28
Option Explicit requires that you declare variables before using them. It's good programming practice to do so.

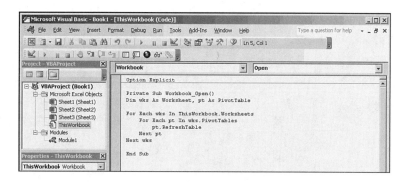

```
Dim wks As Worksheet, pt As PivotTable
```

Declare two objects variables: wks and pt. To *declare* the variables is merely to inform Visual Basic that they exist, that they have these names, and the type of objects that they represent. To declare (another term is *dimension*, which is the source of the keyword Dim) wks as Worksheet is to state that the variable wks can represent worksheets. Just as in algebra, the variable X might represent a value such as 1, 23, or 846; the variable wks can represent Sheet1, Sheet2, or any worksheet that has any name.

Similarly, to declare the variable pt as PivotTable is to state that it can represent any pivot table.

```
For Each wks In ThisWorkbook.Worksheets
```

This statement initiates a loop. The subsequent statements will execute once for each instance of the variable wks. Wks will represent each worksheet in the workbook—a different worksheet for each time the loop itself executes.

```
For Each pt In wks.PivotTables
```

Another loop is initiated. This one runs inside the outer loop, and it will run once for each pivot table on the worksheet currently represented by wks. Suppose that Sheet1 has two pivot tables and Sheet2 has three pivot tables. When wks represents Sheet1, pt will represent the first, and then the second of the two pivot tables on Sheet1. Then, when wks represents Sheet2, pt will represent the first, and then the second, and finally the third pivot table on that worksheet.

```
pt.RefreshTable
```

With wks representing a particular worksheet, and pt representing a particular pivot table on that worksheet, Visual Basic knows precisely which pivot table to refresh. The RefreshTable command does so, and it does so without making the user respond to any warning.

```
Next pt
```

Go to the next pivot table on the worksheet currently represented by wks.

```
Next wks
```

Go to the next worksheet in the workbook.

```
End Sub
```

End the subroutine.

> **TIP**
>
> Some commands that you give VBA to execute don't warn you when something happens that you might need to know about. The example shown here, RefreshTable, is one of them. Others do warn you. Changing the orientation of a pivot table field is one of them: Excel warns you if doing so will overwrite existing data.
>
> If you want to suppress warnings temporarily, use this command:
>
> ```
> Application.DisplayAlerts = False
> ```
>
> Handle this statement with care. Before you use it, make *certain* that you don't want your code to warn you of a possible problem. And reverse its effect as soon as possible with
>
> ```
> Application.DisplayAlerts = True
> ```

This subroutine is concise and exhaustive: In only eight statements, it refreshes every pivot table on every worksheet in the workbook. But it doesn't allow for much customized control. You need to micromanage the code to do that.

For example, suppose that you want to refresh only two specific pivot tables when a particular workbook opens. The code might look like this:

```
Private Sub Workbook_Open()
Dim wks As Worksheet, pt As PivotTable
ThisWorkbook.Worksheets("PartyStats") _
.PivotTables("Age By Party").RefreshTable
ThisWorkbook.Worksheets("StateStats") _
.PivotTables("Party By State").RefreshTable
End Sub
```

This code refreshes only two pivot tables: Age By Party and Party By State. Suppose that there were another pivot table, Hits By Date, that shows the number of hits on a Web site during each month. You might not want to update that pivot table each time the workbook is opened. A casual user could get the wrong impression if the entire month of September had 1,600 hits, and the entire month of October had 1,750 hits, and if he opened the workbook halfway through the current month, on November 15. The pivot table (and perhaps an associated chart) might show only half as many hits, month to date.

Probably, in contrast to Age By Party and Party By State, the interpretation of the Hits By Date pivot table depends on when during the month the user sees it. Therefore, you could put in code to refresh the Hits By Date pivot table on only the final day of each month.

Looking Ahead

In this chapter, you saw how to establish external data sources with DSN files. The DSN file contains information about the path to, and name and type of the external data source.

You saw how to refresh data ranges and pivot tables automatically, when the workbook opens, and by means of VBA code when you want to exert greater control over the refresh process.

And you saw how to use Microsoft Query to guide you through the process of pointing queries at the data source. This was necessarily a brief overview, but Chapter 5, "Using Microsoft Query," takes you through the process in considerably more detail.

4

Using Microsoft Query

Understanding "Query"

The previous chapter compared using the Query Wizard to using the Microsoft Query window. You saw that to choose the Query Wizard over Microsoft Query is to choose a friendlier, less powerful tool over a moderately demanding tool that offers greater functionality.

There's a similar choice involved between Microsoft Query and a database manager. Microsoft Query offers you a few ways to structure a query—the selection of fields and records and sort orders, for example—but does not provide the rich array of tools you have when you use a database directly.

Still, Microsoft Query is the only means available for bringing data into an Excel worksheet automatically and without programming. And one of the best ways to move data from a database into a worksheet is to use the database's tools to structure a query's data, and to use Microsoft Query to arrange the transfer of that data into the worksheet.

One difficulty in learning about queries is the word *query* itself. It's used, somewhat casually, to mean anything from the data returned by a query, to a set of instructions that define how to handle a set of data, to the application that helps create the query. It makes things more difficult that queries do more than simply return data from a data source: They can also add or remove data in tables, edit data, and even create new tables.

This book uses the term *query* to mean a set of instructions. For example, this is a simple query:

```
SELECT Tiles.TileID, Tiles.SpaceID,
Tiles.Floor, Tiles.SmokeZone
FROM Tiles;
```

5

It is written in Structured Query Language—SQL for short, and pronounced "sequel." It says to select the fields named `TileID`, `SpaceID`, `Floor`, and `SmokeZone` from something named `Tiles`, which could be a table or it could be another query. (You'll frequently find yourself constructing a query based on another query.) Most of the queries that this book discusses are *Select* queries; that is, queries that get data from a database and present it to another application. Here the application of interest is Excel, but the principles apply no matter what the receiving application might be.

If a Select query changes the data in any way (for instance, if Sex equals 1 show "Male" and if Sex equals 2 show "Female") that change takes place *after* the query has obtained the data. So, unless otherwise specified, you can assume that a query discussed in this book is a Select query. A Delete query (one that removes records from a table), an Append query (one that adds records), or an Update query (one that modifies a record's values) will be identified by its type.

> **NOTE**
>
> SQL is a *standard* language. A SQL statement that works in one database management system is very likely to work in the same way when used by a different one. That weaselly *very likely* is due to the fact that there are variations in SQL. Transact-SQL, for example, differs from SQL in important ways. But they are virtually identical in basic querying syntax.

It's very seldom necessary to write a query using SQL. Most popular applications that use SQL give the user a graphic interface to help design the query. The application then interprets the graphic information to write the query itself in SQL. Figure 5.1 shows an example. The table pane contains the table with its fields, the data pane shows the records and their field values, and the SQL window shows the structured query language statement.

Figure 5.1
This is how Microsoft Query visually represents the structured query language.

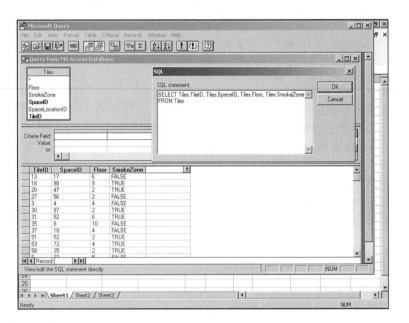

You can view the SQL of a query that you have built, or that you're building, by clicking Microsoft Query's SQL toolbar button.

 TIP Few applications that help you write SQL, such as Microsoft Query and Access, have a text search-and-replace capability. Suppose that you needed to change the table reference in the sample query shown earlier from `Tiles` to `Tiles2004`. You could add a table named `Tiles2004` to the table pane and change each field reference in the query from `Tiles` to `Tiles2004`. It's often quicker, though, to display the SQL window, copy its text, paste it into another application like Notepad or Word, replace `Tiles` with `Tiles2004`, and then copy and paste the result back into the SQL window.

The database management system, whether it's Access or Oracle or SQL Server or some other, sees the SQL statement, interprets it, and returns the data accordingly.

Querying Multiple Tables

A fundamental reason to build queries is to join together more than one table. There are several reasons that you might want to do that. The next two sections describe two typical reasons that were discussed briefly, and solely in the context of Excel, in Chapter 1, "Misusing Excel as a Database Management System."

CASE STUDY

5

You direct the facilities department at Ballou Realty. Ballou leases space in its several buildings to other companies in need of office space. Your staff has built several databases to help maintain information on the offices themselves, on building equipment such as air conditioners and PBXs, and on building components such as windows and doors.

One of your databases contains records that describe the doors in Ballou's office buildings: doors to offices, doors to closets, doors that separate halls, doors to the outside, and so on. For various reasons, including repair and warranty issues, you find that it's necessary to know the name of the maintenance technician who last inspected each door.

One way to set things up is to have a field, perhaps named `TechName`, in your `Doors` table. Then when a Ballou technician inspects a door, one of the items that's recorded is the technician's name.

But you want to be careful *not* to have to type the technician's name into each record. If you do that, a simple misspelling creates a new technician: "Smith" might have done the work, but if someone types "Smit" instead, any data summary involving the technicians will be wrong. It will show that a door has been inspected not by Smith, but by the nonexistent Smit.

Before you took your job with Ballou, the Facilities staff maintained data using Excel alone. They prevented the misspelling problem by setting up a validation list, by choosing Data, Validation and allowing a list (see Figure 5.2).

Figure 5.2
The validation list is yet another good opportunity to use a dynamic range name.

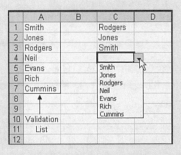

You have implemented a departmental policy to store information on facilities in a true database. The avoidance of keying errors by using Excel data validation has become irrelevant. To help ensure data integrity in a database, you create a table with (in this example) the names of the technicians who work for Ballou, and arrange for your main Doors table to display the available technician names in a dropdown. Selecting a name from that dropdown avoids typing errors.

You name the table Technicians, and store the technicians' names in a field named TechName. It's useful for that Technicians table to have a field with a unique record ID, perhaps TechID, and for your Doors table to have a field with the same name. Figure 5.3 shows how this might be set up in Microsoft Access.

Figure 5.3
Each table has a TechID field. This paves the way for a link between the two tables.

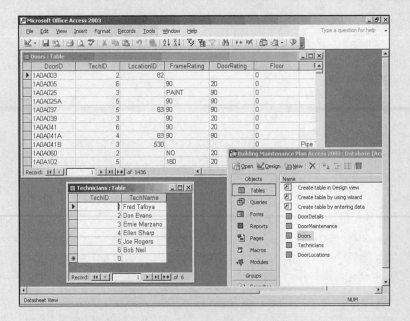

The Technicians table might have a record whose value for the field TechID is 1, and the value of TechName is Fred Tafoya. If Fred Tafoya was the last Ballou technician to inspect a particular door, that door's record would have the value 1 in the TechID field in the Doors table.

Given that setup, you return records to Excel via Microsoft Query by taking these steps:

1. With an Excel worksheet active, choose **Data, Import External Data**.

2. Create a New Data Source or use an existing source. The Microsoft Query window appears, along with the Add Tables box.

→ Creating a new data source is described in "Getting External Data into the Workbook," **p. 85**.

3. Click the Doors table in the Table list box to select it. Click the **Add** button to put the Doors table in the table pane.

4. Repeat step 3 for the Technicians table.

5. Click the **Close** button to dismiss the Add Tables box.

The table pane now appears as in Figure 5.4.

Figure 5.4
To return all the table's fields, double-click the asterisk at the top of a field list or just drag it to the data pane.

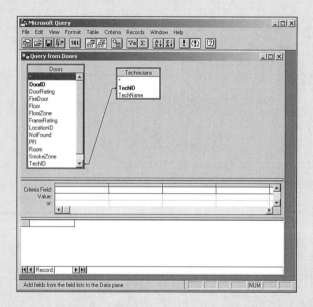

A line, termed a *join line*, appears between the two tables, connecting the TechID field in the Doors table to the TechID field in the Technicians table.

> **NOTE** Under some circumstances, the join line does not appear automatically. If it doesn't, just click one table's TechID field, drag to the other table's TechID field, and release the mouse button.

To return the ID of the door and the name of the technician who last inspected it, drag the DoorID field from the Doors table into the data pane. Then drag the TechName field from the Technicians table into the data pane. The result is shown in Figure 5.5.

5

Figure 5.5
You don't need to move either `TechID` field to the data pane in order to return the `TechName` field.

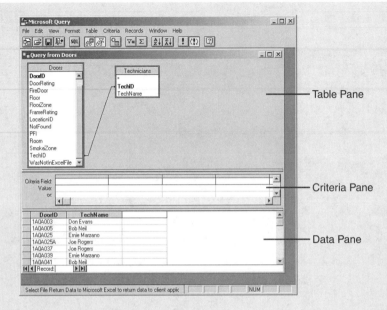

When you choose File, Return Data to Microsoft Excel, the Import Data dialog box appears. Click OK to accept its placement of the records on the worksheet as shown in Figure 5.6. You can now use Excel to review information about the ongoing maintenance of the doors in Ballou's office buildings using Excel's data analysis tools, such as pivot tables and charts.

Figure 5.6
The results of your query: records from two fields in different tables, joined by an unseen common field.

	A	B	C	D
		fx DoorID		
1	DoorID	TechName		
2	1A0A003	Don Evans		
3	1A0A005	Bob Neil		
4	1A0A025	Ernie Marzano		
5	1A0A025A	Joe Rogers		
6	1A0A037	Joe Rogers		
7	1A0A039	Ernie Marzano		
8	1A0A041	Bob Neil		
9	1A0A041A	Ellen Sharp		
10	1A0A041B	Ernie Marzano		
11	1A0A060	Don Evans		
12	1A0A102	Joe Rogers		
13	1A0A105	Joe Rogers		
14	1A0A109	Ellen Sharp		
15	1A0A115	Ellen Sharp		
16	1A0A117	Ellen Sharp		
17	1A0A121	Bob Neil		
18	1A0A122	Ellen Sharp		
19	1A0A209	Ernie Marzano		
20	1A0A233	Fred Tafoya		
21	1A0A233A	Fred Tafoya		
22	1A0A234	Joe Rogers		
23	1A0A300	Ernie Marzano		
24	1A0A309	Bob Neil		
25	1A0A321	Don Evans		
26	1A0A321A	Ellen Sharp		

Sheet1 \ **Sheet2** / Sheet3

Ready

Joining Parent and Child Records

The buildings discussed in the previous section are probably subject to municipal codes and other regulations that require the regular inspection of doors. Those regulations of course require you to correct any problems that are found. Outside doors need to work properly in emergencies. Doors separating hallways are often fire doors, and need to retard a fire's progress. Doors to closets often must be secure, especially if the closets might contain hazardous materials.

In turn, that means that each of those doors must be inspected regularly and a record made of its condition, including any maintenance action taken. Further, when an occupant of the building complains that, say, a bathroom door won't lock, that complaint needs to be recorded. So does the subsequent repair of the door. Complaints don't follow tidy schedules the way that regular maintenance does.

CASE STUDY

Choosing the Parent Record

Given this situation—a common one, by the way—how do you intend to store the information in the Doors database that you've set up for Ballou Realty? Does a door constitute a record? If so, how do you handle the fact that a door gets maintenance attention some indeterminate number of times during one calendar year?

How many fields should you allocate to record those maintenance actions? Bear in mind that each time a door receives maintenance, you need to store information about the technician, the date the work was done, what action was taken, whether it's covered by warranty, and so on. Your door-record is going to need a lot of fields. Figure 5.7 shows how your Facilities staff might have used a flat file structure to store the information.

Figure 5.7
A database designer who doesn't understand relational structures (or prefers not to use them) might employ this design.

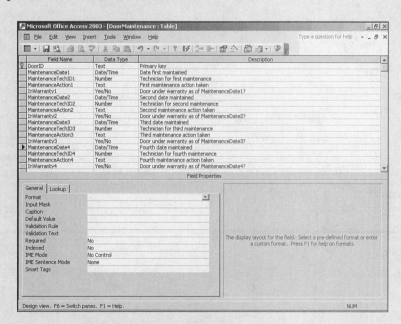

NOTE The term *flat file* means a data set that is not relational. An Excel list is a flat file: Different records occupy different rows, and different fields occupy different columns. It's two-dimensional or *flat*.

Sometimes the layout shown in Figure 5.7 makes good sense. If you know, for example, that a door will be maintained no more than four times during the time it's in service, you might opt for the simplicity of a flat file. Many designs that are wrong in theory are right in practice.

More often, though, this sort of layout creates problems for you. After all, each instance of maintenance really *is* a different record, and to treat it as a different field dismembers the reality of the situation. When it comes time to analyze all that data on maintenance, you'll need to convert it to individual records.

Suppose that you want to calculate the number of times that doors are repaired and the number of times that they're replaced. If you have each instance of maintenance stored as a separate record, it's easy: You just import, say, the `MaintenanceAction` field into Excel. Then use a pivot table (or an array formula) to count the number of records with "Repair" and the number of records with "Replace."

But if the maintenance records are stored in separate fields instead of separate records, you have a problem. It's solvable, yes, but it's still a problem. You have to import, for each record, the first, second, third, ... *N*th instance of maintenance, retrieving `MaintenanceAction1,MaintenanceAction2,MaintenanceAction3,...,` `MaintenanceActionN`. Then you have to convert all those values to list format before you can bring a pivot table to bear on the problem.

When you can't predict how many maintenance records you'll need to allow for, you need a different solution. Perhaps your record should instead represent each instance of a door's maintenance. That way, you wind up with an indeterminate number of *records*, not fields.

But then you need to repeat all the information about the door itself. You need to know which door was worked on, and there's quite a bit of information that gets dragged along with that. You'll need a field that uniquely identifies the door, one that shows its installation date, another for the name of the manufacturer, the warranty expiration date, whether it's a smoke door, whether the door is keyed, and so on. It's wasteful and unnecessary to repeat all that static information in every detail record that's intended to describe periodic maintenance.

Using Joins to Create Relational Structures

The solution to this problem, as to most similar problems, is to structure the database so that you have one table that contains information that doesn't change, and another that contains information that does. In this case, you would have one table with static information about the *door* (its ID, its installation date, and so on), and another table that contains information about *door maintenance* (the date that work was done, who did the work, and so on).

The `Doors` table stores information that either won't or is unlikely to change for a particular door: its unique ID, its manufacturer, its location, and so on. These are termed *parent* records.

The `Door Maintenance` table stores information that you expect to change from record to record: the action taken (inspection or repair, for example), a technician's name, the date when the action was taken, the action's outcome, and so on. These are termed *child* records. Each child record belongs to a particular parent record.

What's crucial in this setup is that the two tables each have a field that enables you to link, or *join*, them in such a way that if you focus on a particular parent record, you automatically get only those child records that belong to the parent.

In this case study, you want to make sure that when you call for information about the entrance door on the north side of the building's first floor, the only inspection and repair records that appear are the ones that belong to that door.

This relationship is shown graphically in the table pane, whether you're using Microsoft Query or a database manager such as Access (see Figure 5.8).

Figure 5.8
The line between the two tables is termed a *join*.

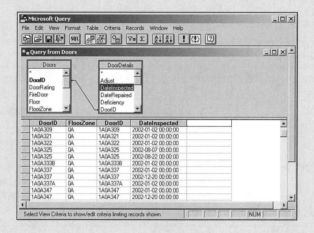

Notice in Figure 5.8 that the table named Doors stores relatively static information about a door: its rating, whether or not it's a fire door, its floor, and so on. The table named DoorDetails stores information that changes—in this case, the data changes over time: the date that a door was inspected, the date it was repaired, what the deficiency was, and so on.

In particular, notice in Figure 5.8 that both the Doors table and the DoorDetails table include a field named DoorID. It's this shared field that establishes a relationship between the two tables, and that establishes a *relational* structure. It is no longer simply a flat file.

> **NOTE** It is useful but not required that the two instances of the field have the same name. In the Doors table, it could have been named DoorID and in the DoorDetails table, it could have been named DoorIdentifier.

Understanding Inner Joins

When two or more tables are joined, as they are in Figure 5.8, your query can return records from one table and related records from the other table. Records are *related* if they have the same value on the fields that are on either end of the join. Figure 5.9 shows records returned from Microsoft Access into Microsoft Excel by this query.

5

Figure 5.9
It's not necessary to return the join fields from the query. They are shown here only for clarity.

	A	B	C	D
1	DoorID	FloorZone	DoorID	DateInspected
2	1A0A003	0A	1A0A003	8/22/2002 0:00
3	1A0A003	0A	1A0A003	2/26/2003 0:00
4	1A0A003	0A	1A0A003	8/7/2002 0:00
5	1A0A003	0A	1A0A003	2/2/2003 0:00
6	1A0A003	0A	1A0A003	2/26/2003 0:00
7	1A0A003	0A	1A0A003	12/5/2002 0:00
8	1A0A005	0A	1A0A005	12/20/2002 0:00
9	1A0A005	0A	1A0A005	1/2/2002 0:00
10	1A0A025	0A	1A0A025	12/20/2002 0:00
11	1A0A025	0A	1A0A025	1/2/2002 0:00
12	1A0A025A	0A	1A0A025A	1/2/2002 0:00
13	1A0A025A	0A	1A0A025A	12/20/2002 0:00
14	1A0A037	0A	1A0A037	1/2/2002 0:00
15	1A0A037	0A	1A0A037	4/26/2003 0:00
16	1A0A037	0A	1A0A037	8/7/2002 0:00
17	1A0A037	0A	1A0A037	2/26/2003 0:00
18	1A0A037	0A	1A0A037	12/20/2002 0:00
19	1A0A039	0A	1A0A039	12/20/2002 0:00
20	1A0A039	0A	1A0A039	1/2/2002 0:00
21	1A0A041	0A	1A0A041	12/20/2002 0:00
22	1A0A041	0A	1A0A041	1/2/2002 0:00
23	1A0A041A	0A	1A0A041A	8/22/2002 0:00
24	1A0A041A	0A	1A0A041A	8/7/2002 0:00
25	1A0A041B	0A	1A0A041B	1/7/2003 0:00

Notice that the value of `DoorID` from the table of parent records (door records) is always the same as the value of `DoorID` from the table of child records (door maintenance records).

Also notice in Figure 5.9 that the door with `DoorID 1A0A003` appears six times. The data in columns A and B comes from the `Doors` table, which contains only one instance of that particular door. That door appears six times in `DoorDetails`: once for each time that a Ballou technician has serviced the door. By relating the two tables, the query is able to display static information such as its floor and zone along with changing information such as the date the door was inspected.

The relational structure enables you to avoid the two problems discussed in the prior section: putting a large number of fields into a record when they might or might not be used, and unnecessarily repeating static information across many detail records.

In Figure 5.8, the join line connecting the `DoorID` fields in the two tables is the default join type: an inner join. An *inner join* returns a record only if the same value exists in both join fields. For example, Figure 5.8 shows a record with the value `1A0A321` in the `DoorID` field of the table `Doors`, and also in the `DoorID` field of the table `DoorDetails`. Given the join type, the query would not return that record if either table had no record with that value. Put another way, an inner join will not return a record unless it has the same value in both join fields.

There are a few aspects to keep in mind about the fields that are joined:

- The fields must be of the same data type; one can't be numeric and the other text, for example.
- If the fields have the same name and data type, and one of them is a table's primary key, both Microsoft Query and Microsoft Access are able to join the tables automatically.
- If the join is the default join type (an inner join), the query returns only those records with identical values on the join fields.

NOTE A *primary key* is a field in a table that uniquely identifies each record. For example, if a particular Social Security number is assigned to exactly one person, the Social Security Number field could be a table's primary key. In the Doors case study that this chapter has used, DoorID is the primary key of the Doors table: It uniquely identifies a door. It cannot be the primary key of the DoorDetails table because each door can appear more than once in that table; a primary key's values must all be unique. Primary keys have broad applicability in database design.

→ To find more information about primary and other keys, **see** "Establishing Keys," **p. 238**.

Understanding Outer Joins

There are two other join types: a *left outer join* and a *right outer join*. The meaning of these terms is not intuitively rich, and the only reason they're even mentioned here is so that you'll recognize them if you ever see them in a SQL statement.

In Figure 5.8, suppose that the Doors table contains a door whose DoorID is 1A0A321A, and that the DoorDetails table has no records with that DoorID (perhaps because no work has been done on that door this year). The query will return no record with DoorID 1A0A321A from DoorDetails because there are none in that table. And the record that does exist in the Doors table with DoorID 1A0A321A will not be returned: The inner join requires that a match exist if it is to return a record at all.

Figure 5.10 shows what happens if, in Microsoft Query, you choose Joins from the Table menu (or if you double-click the join line).

Figure 5.10
The first option specifies the default, an inner join. The second and third options specify outer joins.

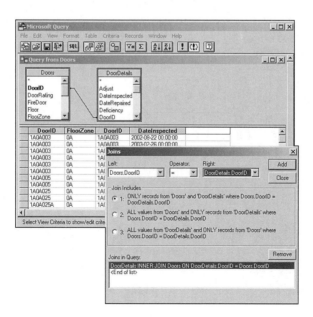

Suppose that you select the second option, All Values From 'Doors' and Only Records from 'DoorDetails' Where Doors.DoorID = DoorDetails.DoorID, and then click Add, and then click Close. Figure 5.11 shows what results in the Microsoft Query window.

Figure 5.11
Note the arrowhead at the end of the join line: It points to the table that might not match a join value.

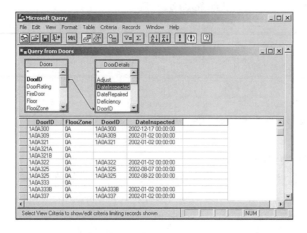

There are two main differences between Figures 5.8 and 5.11. One is the additional records in Figure 5.11's data pane. Those additional records have values in the DoorID field in the Doors table, but none for the DoorID field in the DoorDetails table. And that's what this join calls for: all values from Doors, and only records from DoorDetails with matching values on DoorID. In place of a DoorID and a DateInspected value from DoorDetails, the query returns null values—placeholders, in a sense.

Contrast this result with that shown in Figure 5.8. There the record with the DoorID value of, for example, 1A0A321A did not appear because there was no matching record in DoorDetails. In Figure 5.11, though, the join calls for *all* records from the Doors table, regardless of whether they have matching records in DoorDetails.

TIP

This type of join provides a convenient way of finding records in one table that are not matched by records in another table. In Figure 5.11, you could supply the criterion Is Null for the DoorID field in DoorDetails. Executing the query would return all the records (and *only* those records) with values of DoorID in the Doors table that were not matched by a value in the DoorID field of DoorDetails.

The other main difference between Figures 5.8 and 5.11 is the arrowhead at the end of the join line in Figure 5.11. In Microsoft Query and Microsoft Access, when you see the arrow head on a query's join line, you know that an outer join has been specified. You also know that the table that the arrow points to is the table that will return null values for those records that lack matching values on the join field.

The difference between a left outer join and a right outer join is trivial: It's merely a question of which table is mentioned before the join or after the join. These two joins are equivalent:

```
FROM Doors LEFT OUTER JOIN DoorsDetails ON Doors.DoorID = DoorsDetails.DoorID;
```

```
FROM DoorsDetails RIGHT OUTER JOIN Doors ON DoorsDetails.DoorID = Doors.DoorID;
```

In a left join, the table named to the left of the JOIN returns all its records; in a right join, the table named to the right of the JOIN returns all its records. (The word OUTER is optional in the SQL.)

Using Database Queries

In one way at least, after you've established an outer join using Microsoft Query, you have pushed that application to its limit. You're allowed no more than two tables in Microsoft Query's table pane if you've used an outer join (see Figure 5.12).

Figure 5.12
To establish an outer join with more than two tables, you need a more sophisticated query manager.

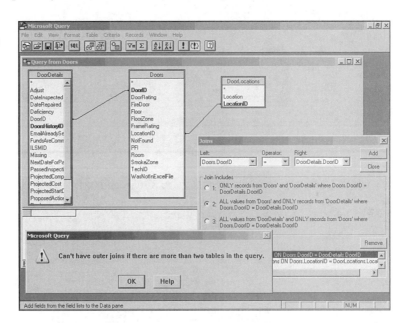

Therefore, if you have even a slightly more complicated situation, you need to involve a database management system directly. These applications, such as Access and SQL Server and Oracle, do not place such restrictive limits on designing queries.

Building a Query in Access

Because Access generally accompanies Excel in the Office software editions, it makes a convenient platform to discuss creating and managing queries in a database. But the concepts covered here extend well beyond Access and are employed in every relational database system.

5

> **NOTE**
> Later chapters show you how to use Excel to build queries that are executed by the database. This book is titled *Managing Data with Excel*, after all, not *Managing Data with Access*. But it's helpful to know how to build the query using the database before building it, one step removed, from the workbook.

Suppose that the data set that this chapter has discussed so far is found in an Access database. To extend the query on a building's doors beyond Microsoft Query's capabilities, you might use Access to build a more complicated query. Then, to get the data into an Excel external data range or pivot table, you use Microsoft Query to treat the Access query exactly as though it were a table.

You would begin by opening the database in Access. After the database has been opened, you see the main Access window, as shown in Figure 5.13.

Figure 5.13
The placement of the objects (tables, queries, forms, and so on) depends on the version of Access you're using.

You can see the tables named Doors, DoorLocations, and DoorDetails in the Database window. To build a query using these tables, begin by clicking the Queries button (or tab, in Access 97). Then click New to establish a new query. The New Query window shown in Figure 5.14 appears.

Figure 5.14
The wizards are occasionally useful, but you'll build most of your queries in Design view.

Make sure that Design View is selected in the list box, and click OK. The Show Table box appears: It's similar to the Add Tables box you saw earlier in Figure 4.12 of Chapter 4, "Importing Data: An Overview," which is part of Microsoft Query. The Show Table box remains open until you click the Close button. This enables you to continue adding tables and queries until you're finished.

If you have only a few tables and queries in the database, use the Both tab to show both tables and queries. If you have so many that you need to use the scrollbar to find them all, it's easier to select by using first the Tables tab and then the Queries tab.

After you've selected the tables and queries you want for your new query, click Close. Access's Query window appears as shown in Figure 5.15.

Figure 5.15
The tables appear in the table pane from left to right, in the order that you select them from the Show Table box.

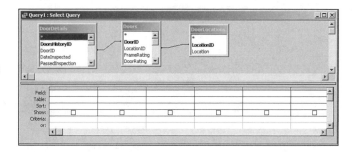

There are a few important differences between the Access query window and the Microsoft Query window (compare with, for example, Figure 5.11).

- The Access Query window has no data pane. To see what your query returns, you need to click the Run button, or click the View button and choose Datasheet View from the list. There's no difference between Run and View for Select queries. With other types of queries—Delete, Update or Append queries, for example—there's a reason to use the View instead of the Run button. The View button can present a preview of what the query will do, and the Run button actually carries out the action.

- You can add a field to the Design Grid and choose not to show it in the query's results. Suppose, for example, that you want to sort records on some field, but you don't want to return that field from the query. Put the field in the Design Grid, and choose Ascending or Descending in the grid's Sort row. Lastly, to prevent the query from displaying that field, clear the field's check box in the grid's Show row.

- Access does not limit you to two tables in a query when you're using an outer join. Figure 5.16 shows how you might structure a query involving the tables named Doors, DoorLocations, and DoorDetails. The query returns all records from Doors that are matched by records in DoorLocations, whether or not they're matched by records in DoorDetails, and uses the DoorLocations table to show a door's location. You would not be able to do this using Microsoft Query alone.

- You can summarize data in the query. For example, you might merely want to know the number of times that a door has been inspected. With the DoorID field in the query grid twice—once from the Doors table and once from the DoorDetails table, you would click the Totals button. In the new Totals row, choose Group By for the Doors table and Count for the DoorDetails table. The resulting design is shown in Figure 5.17. When you click the Run button, you get the result shown in Figure 5.18.

Figure 5.16
In Access, the Query window specifies which table a field comes from.

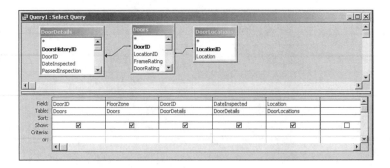

Totals button

Figure 5.17
Besides Count, other summary statistics available include average, sum, and standard deviation (shown as StDev).

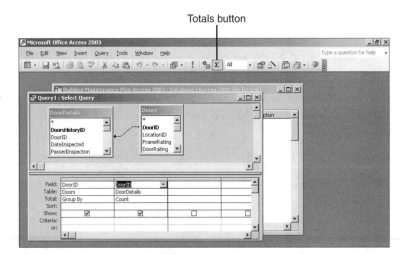

Figure 5.18
Note that DoorID 1A0A109 has no records in the DoorDetails table. Therefore this query uses an outer join (see Figure 5.17).

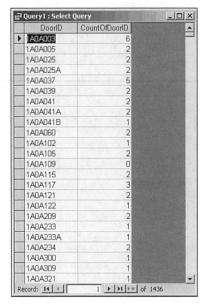

This list of features isn't even close to exhaustive: There are many ways to tailor a Select query in Access that are not available in Microsoft Query.

After you've designed the query, save it by choosing Save from the File menu or just close it. You'll be asked whether you want to save your changes, and you'll have a chance to give the query a name that's more useful than a default name such as Query1, Query2, and so on.

Using Microsoft Query to Return the Results of a Database Query

After the query has been saved, you get its results into an Excel worksheet or pivot table in the usual way via Microsoft Query, although in this case you work with the query instead of tables.

Suppose that you create a query shown in Figure 5.16, and named it Doors Query. You could return its data to Excel using these steps:

1. With an Excel worksheet active, choose **Data**, **Import External Data**. If you've already established the database as a data source, select it in the **Choose Data Source** window (bear in mind that adding a new query to a data source changes nothing about the data source itself). Otherwise, you'll need to create it by means of the New Data Source item.

2. Using the Add Tables window, add Doors Query to Microsoft Query's table pane. If you don't see Doors Query in the Tables list, click the **Options** button, fill the **Views** check box (and clear the Tables check box if you want), and click **OK** (see Figure 5.19).

Figure 5.19
A view is very similar to a Select query. In Access, the two terms are close to synonymous.

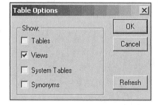

3. Drag each field that you want to return into the data pane. The Microsoft Query window now appears as shown in Figure 5.20.

4. Click the Return Data button, or choose File, Return Data to Microsoft Excel.

> **NOTE**
> As noted previously, views are very similar to Select queries. System tables are used by the database to keep track of information about tables, queries, and other structures you've defined in the database itself. *Synonymns* are the intersection of a table and the user of that table; you're unlikely to need to see them unless you're querying an Oracle data source.

Doors.DoorID	FloorZone	DoorDetails.DoorID	DateInspected	Location
1A5B456	5B	1A5B456	2003-03-20 00:00:00	Room 700
1A2C301	2C	1A2C301	2003-02-27 00:00:00	Room 700
1A4A242B	4A	1A4A242B	2003-03-26 00:00:00	Room 700
1A7B236	7B	1A7B236	2003-03-17 00:00:00	Room 700
1A7B421	7B	1A7B421	2003-03-17 00:00:00	Room 700
1A7B246	7B	1A7B246	2003-03-13 00:00:00	Room 700
1A7B423	7B	1A7B423	2003-03-17 00:00:00	Room 700
1A7B425	7B	1A7B425	2003-03-17 00:00:00	Room 700
1A7B253	7B	1A7B253	2003-03-14 00:00:00	Room 700
1A4A422	4B	1A4A422	2003-03-27 00:00:00	Room 700
1A3B443	3B	1A3B443	2003-02-27 00:00:00	Room 700
1A7B445	7B			Room 700
1A7B236A	7B	1A7B236A	2003-03-17 00:00:00	Room 700
1A7B236B	7B	1A7B236B	2003-03-17 00:00:00	Room 700
1A4A401A	4A	1A4A401A	2003-03-26 00:00:00	Room 700
1A7B263	7B	1A7B263	2003-03-14 00:00:00	Room 700
1A7B263	7B	1A7B263	2003-03-14 00:00:00	Room 700
1A7B266E	7B	1A7B266E	2003-03-17 00:00:00	Room 700
1A7B103	7B	1A7B103	2003-02-27 00:00:00	Room 700
1A1G051	1G	1A1G051	2003-02-26 00:00:00	Room 700
1A7B269	7B			Room 700
1A7B220	7B	1A7B220	2003-03-13 00:00:00	Room 700

Figure 5.20
When fields from two or more tables have the same name, they are qualified by the name of the table (for example, `Doors.DoorID`).

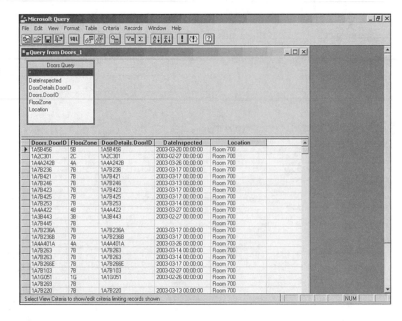

Figure 5.21 shows the data returned from Doors Query to the worksheet.

	A	B	C	D	E	F
1	DoorID	FloorZone	DoorID	DateInspected	Location	
252	1A5A043A	5A	1A5A043A	1/10/2003 0:00	Closet, Janitor	
253	1A5A043A	5A	1A5A043A	3/20/2003 0:00	Closet, Janitor	
254	1A3C127	3C			Closet, Janitor	
255	1A3B256	3B	1A3B256	1/7/2003 0:00	Closet, Janitor	
256	1A7B264	7B			Closet, Janitor	
257	1A5B264	5B	1A5B264	1/10/2003 0:00	Closet, Janitor	
258	1A5B264	5B	1A5B264	3/19/2003 0:00	Closet, Janitor	
259	1A3C321	3C	1A3C321	1/7/2003 0:00	Closet, Janitor	
260	1A7B453	7B	1A7B453	1/10/2003 0:00	CLOSET,COMMUNICATION	
261	1A4B453	4B	1A4B453	1/8/2003 0:00	CLOSET,COMMUNICATION	
262	1A4B453	4B	1A4B453	3/27/2003 0:00	CLOSET,COMMUNICATION	
263	1A7B217	7B	1A7B217	1/10/2003 0:00	CONF RM #725 PSY SRVC	
264	1A7B217	7B	1A7B217	3/13/2003 0:00	CONF RM #725 PSY SRVC	
265	1A2C706	2C	1A2C706	1/6/2003 0:00	CONF. LOUNGE ICCU	
266	1A3C713	3C			CONFERENCE "A" BRD RM	
267	1A2D305	2D	1A2D305	1/6/2003 0:00	CONFERENCE RM "K" EPA	
268	1A2D319	2D	1A2D319	1/6/2003 0:00	CONFERENCE RM "L"	
269	1A2D321	2D	1A2D321	1/6/2003 0:00	CONFERENCE RM "M"	
270	1A2D333	2D	1A2D333	1/6/2003 0:00	CONFERENCE RM "N"	
271	1A2D335	2D	1A2D335	1/6/2003 0:00	CONFERENCE RM "O"	
272	1A2D217	2D	1A2D217	1/6/2003 0:00	CONFERENCE RM "P"	
273	1A3C153	3C			CONFERENCE ROOM "B"	
274	1A3C145	3C			CONFERENCE ROOM "C"	
275	1A4A230	4A	1A4A230	3/26/2003 0:00	CONFERENCE ROOM "S"	

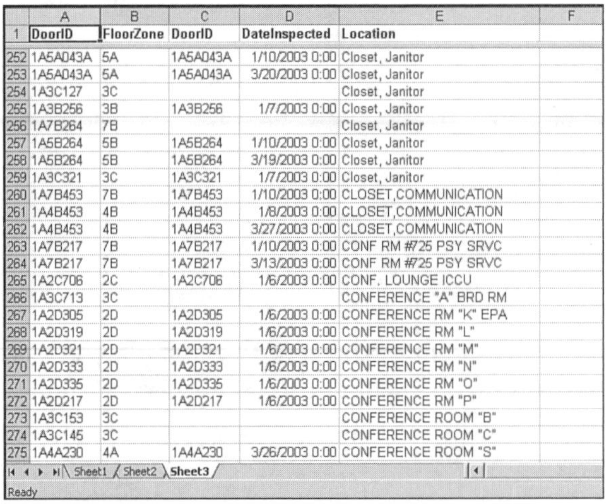

Figure 5.21
Note the empty cells in some records from `DoorDetails`: The outer join allows the query to return those records.

5

Handling the Data Range

After you've returned data to an external data range in an Excel worksheet, the range has some additional properties that you might want to work with.

NOTE Microsoft Office applications use the term *properties* to refer to aspects of objects. As just one of many, many examples, a range of cells has a Borders property that specifies which borders (top, bottom, left, right, diagonal, or none) that the range has. Until you become familiar with the notion of properties you may find it helpful to think of a property as an option.

Right-click any cell in an external data range, and choose Data Range Properties from the shortcut menu. The dialog box shown in Figure 5.22 appears.

Figure 5.22
If you don't see Data Range Properties in the shortcut menu, you haven't clicked inside an external data range.

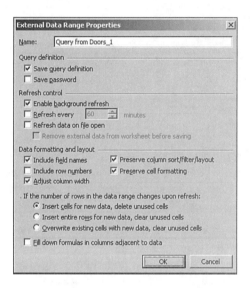

From the standpoint of managing the external data, the most important properties shown in Figure 5.22 are

- *Save Query Definition*. Don't clear this box unless you're certain of what you're doing. If you do clear it, you won't be able to refresh the query's data or even edit the query. If you clear the check box and then save the workbook, you've lost the query for good.

- *Save Password*. This is important mainly in a networked environment. (If you're in a standalone environment, who are you password protecting your data from? Yourself?) You can save the password in the DSN file that defines the data set—its path, its type, and so on—but that file is stored in ASCII format, so anyone with sufficient curiosity can get the password from it. In contrast, the query definition that's saved in the workbook is in a hidden name, something that's much more difficult to break into.

- *Enable Background Refresh*. Filling this check box means that refreshes can take place without interrupting your normal work in Excel. You can be entering formulas or pivoting tables while Excel updates the external data range. Clearing the check box means that you can't proceed until the query has finished executing. You'll probably have use for this property only if the data source itself is frequently updated and is large enough that queries take a long time to execute.

■ *Refresh Data on File Open*. When the workbook is opened, execute the query so that the most recent data is available from its source. The only cause for concern is the presence of an event handler that runs when the workbook is opened. Then you might need to know which occurs first (the Open event's handler executes first).

→ To find more information about refreshed data, **see** "Importing Data to Pivot Tables," **p. 104**.

For the next four properties listed in the External Data Range Properties dialog box, assume that the external data range occupies A1:B5 on the worksheet, as shown in Figure 5.23.

Figure 5.23
The original external data range is shaded.

In Figure 5.23, the boundaries of the original range are indicated by the row numbers in column C and the column letters in row 6. The data range is about to be refreshed. Each of the next six figures show the effect on the data shown in Figure 5.23 according to which property is selected, and whether the query returns more or fewer records than are shown in Figure 5.23.

■ *Insert Cells for New Data, Delete Unused Cells*. Starting with row 6, the cells in columns A and B will be pushed down as two new records are inserted. Columns from C through IV are not affected. The cells containing "Column A" and "Column B" are pushed down to accommodate the inserted cells, but nothing happens to the cells in column C (see Figure 5.24). If the data query loses records, cells below row 5 are pulled up as the lost records' cells are deleted. Again, only columns A and B are affected. The cells containing "Column A" and "Column B" are pulled up as cells are deleted, and nothing has happened to the cells in column C (see Figure 5.25).

Figure 5.24
The external data range has also been set to Preserve Cell Formatting.

Figure 5.25
The query has lost its original four records and added two new records.

■ *Insert Entire Rows for New Data, Clear Unused Cells*. Starting with row 5, all rows are pushed down by 2—and therefore cells C5:IV6 will be empty. Notice in Figure 5.26 that the cells in column C containing "Row 5," "Row 6," "Row 7," Column A," and "Column B" are pushed down by the insertion of two rows (although those rows are not inserted where you might expect). If the refresh returns only two records instead of the original four, cells A4:B5 are cleared. Figure 5.27 shows that the cells containing "Column A" and "Column B" remain in place because unused query cells are not deleted. Also notice that cells A4:B5 are cleared only of their contents, not their formats. Because neither cells nor rows are deleted, all other data outside the external data range remains where it was.

Figure 5.26
Notice that the row insertion indicated in column C does not match the record insertion indicated in A6:B7.

	A	B	C
1	DateInspected	Location	Row 1
2	1/2/2002	Emergency Department	Row 2
3	1/2/2002	Emergency Department	Row 3
4	1/2/2002	Emergency Department	Row 4
5	1/2/2002	Emergency Department	
6	1/2/2002	BY SWITCH	
7	1/2/2002	BY SWITCH	Row 5
8	Column A	Column B	Row 6
9			Row 7
10			

Figure 5.27
Unused cells in the external data range are cleared, not deleted, but the range is redefined to A1:B3.

	A	B	C
1	DateInspected	Location	Row 1
2	1/2/2002	BY SWITCH	Row 2
3	1/2/2002	BY SWITCH	Row 3
4			Row 4
5			Row 5
6	Column A	Column B	Row 6
7			Row 7
8			

■ *Overwrite Existing Cells with New Data, Clear Unused Cells*. No cells or rows are inserted to accommodate new records. If you have data *below* the external data range (and that's usually a worksheet design flaw), it will be overwritten *and you will not be warned*. Figure 5.28 shows that the values "Column A" and "Column B" have been overwritten by the new records, but nothing has happened to the data in column C because nothing has been inserted. Cells vacated by the query because there are fewer records are cleared, so no cells or rows are deleted and other data remains in place.

Figure 5.28
Beware of putting information below an external data range; it can be overwritten as shown here.

	A	B	C
1	DateInspected	Location	Row 1
2	1/2/2002	Emergency Department	Row 2
3	1/2/2002	Emergency Department	Row 3
4	1/2/2002	Emergency Department	Row 4
5	1/2/2002	Emergency Department	Row 5
6	1/2/2002	BY SWITCH	Row 6
7	1/2/2002	BY SWITCH	Row 7
8			
9			

5

■ *Fill Down Formulas in Columns Adjacent to Table.* This can be a handy way to avoid calculating fields in the query itself, using the database manager's formula syntax and built-in functions. Just create a formula on the worksheet in a column immediately to the left or the right of the external data range, and fill this check box. When new records arrive as you refresh the data, Excel automatically copies the existing adjacent formulas through the final row occupied by the external data range.

Managing Boolean Fields and Check Boxes

One annoyance involved in bringing data from a database to the worksheet is due to Boolean fields. *Booleans* are also termed *True/False fields*, and Access often refers to them as *Yes/No fields*.

Boolean fields take one of just two possible values: True and False. Difficulties arise when you return their values to the worksheet because databases don't necessarily store them as TRUE or FALSE, the values you normally see on an Excel worksheet. You need to account for this, either in the database or in Excel. And check boxes, which usually result in either a True value (checked) or a False value (unchecked) can have a third value, Null (shaded).

Returning Boolean Values to the Worksheet

Suppose that your database contains a table named `Patient_Restraints`, and that the field `Medical_Reason` is defined as Boolean. Figure 5.29 shows how that field might look with the table in Datasheet view.

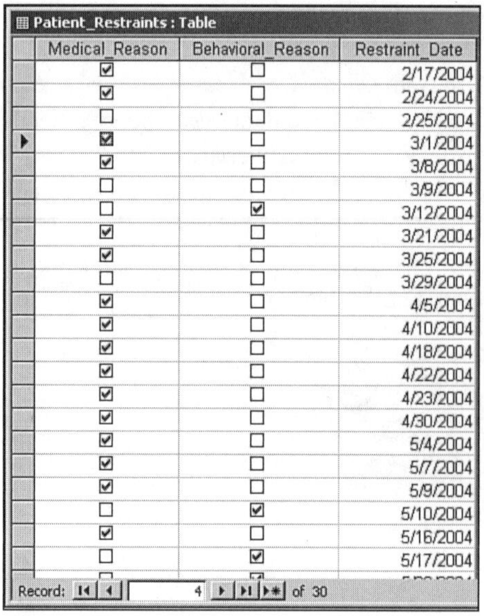

Figure 5.29
Access displays Boolean fields as check boxes in Datasheet view.

Figure 5.30 shows how `Medical_Reason` appears on an Excel worksheet, depending on how you put it there:

- If you select the field in the Access datasheet, copy it, and then switch to Excel and paste it to a worksheet, you'll see TRUE and FALSE values such as those shown in cells A1:A11 of Figure 5.30.

- If you bring the data into the worksheet by means of Import External Data, the TRUE values appear as 1's and the FALSE values appear as 0's. This is shown in cells C1:C11 of Figure 5.30.

Figure 5.30

Pasting an Access field into a worksheet provides the field name as a header and sets the header's fill to gray.

	A	B	C	D
1	Medical_Reason		Medical_Reason	
2	TRUE		1	
3	TRUE		1	
4	FALSE		0	
5	TRUE		1	
6	TRUE		1	
7	FALSE		0	
8	FALSE		0	
9	TRUE		1	
10	TRUE		1	
11	FALSE		0	
12				

If you want to deal with something other than the 1's and 0's in an external data range, consider refreshing the data using a VBA procedure such as this `Open` event handler:

```
Private Sub Workbook_Open()
Application.Goto Reference:="Query_from_MS_Access_Database"
Selection.QueryTable.Refresh BackgroundQuery:=False
Application.Goto Reference:="Query_from_MS_Access_Database"
With Selection
    .Replace What:="0", Replacement:="FALSE", LookAt:=xlWhole
    .Replace What:="1", Replacement:="TRUE", LookAt:=xlWhole
End With
End Sub
```

This code first selects the existing query range, and then refreshes its data. It then reselects the query range in case the number of records changed due to the refresh. Finally, it replaces 0's with FALSE and 1's with TRUE. It replaces a 0 or 1 only if it is the cell's whole value, to avoid, for example, replacing a header cell's value of `Medical_Reason1` with `Medical_ReasonTRUE`.

Managing Data from Check Boxes

When an Access form's check boxes are associated with Boolean fields, no new difficulties arise. But sometimes you need to provide for not just TRUE and FALSE values, but a Null value as well. This Null value might mean something such as Not Applicable.

Suppose that in the `Patient_Restraints` table, the `Medical_Reason` field needs to take on three values: TRUE when a patient was restrained for a medical reason, FALSE when there was some other reason, and Null when a restraint was not used. If the `Medical_Reason` field is defined as Boolean, it can't distinguish between FALSE and Null; in both cases, a record's field is not checked.

But if you define the `Medical_Reason` field as an Integer, it can take on many more values. And that opens the possibility of associating it with a check box on a data form that in Access has a `TripleState` property. With `TripleState` turned on, the form's check box can be checked (TRUE), unchecked (FALSE), or shaded (some other meaning, typically Not Applicable). Figure 5.31 shows how that data form might appear on the screen.

Figure 5.31
The shaded check box indicates a Null value.

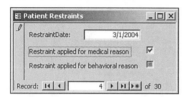

Whether or not you set the form's check box to take on one of three values, if the underlying field is numeric then TRUE is stored as –1 (instead of 1), whereas FALSE is still stored as 0. If the form's check box is set for `TripleState`, the field itself stores a Null as the value when the check box itself is shaded.

Figure 5.32 shows how external data ranges appear when a field is defined as numeric and its values are determined by a check box on a data form. Cells A1:A11 show 10 values. The five 1's mean that the form's check box was checked for those records. The five 0's mean that the form's check box was not checked.

Cells D1:D11 also show 10 values. The –1's mean that the check box was checked and the 0's mean that it was unchecked. The blank cells in rows 8 through 11 mean that the check box remained shaded.

Figure 5.32
To help distinguish between a Null value and no record, select the range's Include Row Numbers property.

	A	B	C	D	E
1	Medical_Reason			Medical_Reason	
2	1		0	-1	
3	1		1	-1	
4	1		2	-1	
5	1		3	0	
6	1		4	0	
7	0		5	0	
8	0		6		
9	0		7		
10	0		8		
11	0		9		
12					

If you replace 0's with FALSE and 1's with TRUE in the external data range, you should avoid replacing row numbers that are shown in column C. Therefore, alter the code shown previously to replace outside the column of row numbers:

```
Sub Workbook_Open()
Dim ExtRange As Range
Dim NCols As Integer, NRows As Integer

Set ExtRange = Worksheets("Sheet1") _
    .Names("Query_from_MS_Access_Database").RefersToRange
NCols = ExtRange.Columns.Count - 1
NRows = ExtRange.Rows.Count
Application.Goto Reference:="Query_from_MS_Access_Database"
Selection.QueryTable.Refresh BackgroundQuery:=False
ExtRange.Offset(0, 1).Resize(NRows, NCols).Select
With Selection
    .Replace What:="0", Replacement:="FALSE", LookAt:=xlWhole
    .Replace What:="-1", Replacement:="TRUE", LookAt:=xlWhole
    .Replace What:="", Replacement:="#N/A", LookAt:=xlWhole
End With
End Sub
```

This code counts the number of columns and rows in the external data range, and then selects the range of cells that's offset from that range by one column, with the same number of rows and one fewer column. In that selected range, it replaces 1's and 0's as before, and additionally replaces blank cells with the #N/A error value.

Looking Ahead

This chapter has extended the discussion, begun in Chapter 4, of using Microsoft Query to import data from an external data source into an Excel worksheet. The result is a focus on the New Database Query command.

But there are other options available to you in the main Data menu, including managing your data using pivot tables, grouping on continuous fields, and using Web queries. You'll find information on these in Chapter 6, "Importing Data: Further Considerations."

5

Importing Data: Further Considerations

6

Understanding Pivot Tables

Pivot tables are Excel's most powerful means of summarizing data. Whether you're interested in totaling expenses on a monthly basis, or finding the average income earned by people in various jobs, or getting a count of the number of items you've sold by product line, a pivot table is usually the way to do it in Excel.

Because of their summary capabilities, *pivot tables* are tools not only for data analysis but also for data management. If you haven't yet used pivot tables extensively, you'll find this section a useful introduction. If you're an experienced user, you might prefer to skip ahead to the next section, "Preparing Data for Pivot Tables."

Building a Pivot Table

Figure 6.1 shows a simple example of a pivot table and its underlying data.

It wouldn't be hard to build five array formulas that returned the total of units sold by region; for example

`=SUM(IF(B2:B39="South",D2:D39,0))`

But why bother? The pivot table gives you those totals very quickly and easily. Here are the steps to take, given that you have an Excel list like the one shown in columns A through D of Figure 6.1. Be sure that you're using a list as described in Chapter 2, "Excel's Data Management Features," with column headers that name the fields.

1. Choose **Data, PivotTable and PivotChart Report**. Step 1 of the PivotTable Wizard shown in Figure 6.2 appears.

Figure 6.1
Most pivot tables are based on either an Excel list or an external data source.

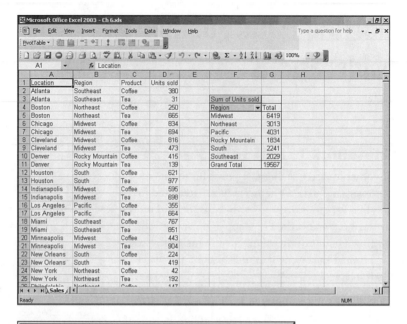

Figure 6.2
Basing a pivot table on another one means that they use the same data cache—an efficient use of memory.

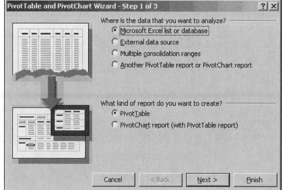

2. In this instance, you would select **Microsoft Excel List or Database**, and **PivotTable** as a report type. (An Excel *database* is a legacy term for a *list*.) Choose **Next**.

3. In step 2 of the PivotTable Wizard, shown in Figure 6.3, drag through the range of data in the worksheet so that its address, A1:D39 in Figure 6.1, appears in the Range box. Click **Next**.

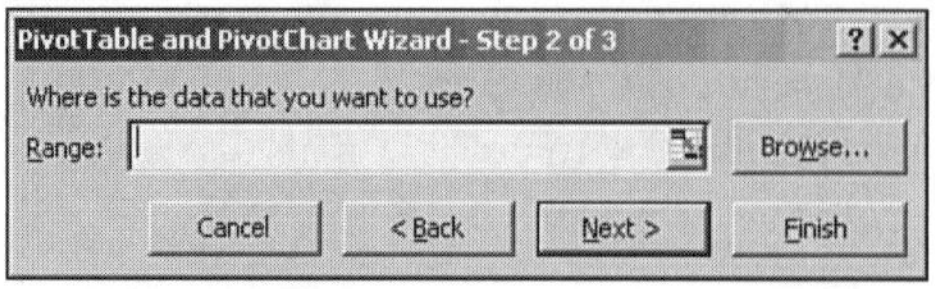

Figure 6.3
If the underlying data is in a different workbook, you can click the Browse button to locate it.

4. Step 3 of the PivotTable Wizard appears (see Figure 6.4). Select the location for the pivot table and click **Finish**.

Figure 6.4
A pivot table by default starts in row 3 to leave room for a Page field.

A schematic for the pivot table appears on the worksheet, along with the PivotTable Field List, as shown in Figure 6.5. To reproduce the pivot table shown in Figure 6.1, you would drag the Region field from the Field List into the Row Fields area, and drag the Units Sold field into the Data Items area. As soon as you put a field into the Data Items area, the pivot table replaces the schematic on the worksheet.

Figure 6.5
If you prefer, you can use the Add To dropdown in the PivotTable Field List instead of dragging and dropping fields onto the worksheet.

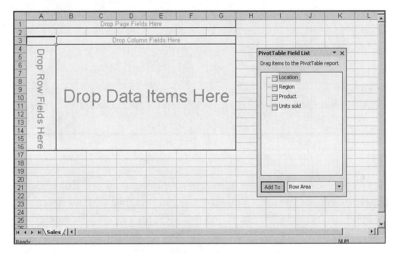

> **NOTE** In Excel 97, the PivotTable Wizard is somewhat different from the one shown in Figures 6.2 through 6.5. In particular, there's a layout step in which you can design the pivot table. In subsequent versions, you create the layout directly on the worksheet as just described. You can get to the layout step by clicking the Layout button in the wizard's third step.

6

Reconfiguring a Pivot Table

Why *pivot* table? Considering all that a pivot table is capable of, the reason for the term is relatively trivial. In Figure 6.1, if you click the button labeled Region, drag it into cell G3, and release the mouse button, the table *pivots*—that is, the Row field Region becomes Column field Region.

That's cute, but in nearly 10 years of using pivot tables to analyze and manage data, I've seldom had reason to pivot a table except to explain the term to people. Pivot tables are capable of much, much more than just pivoting.

Figure 6.1 shows the Sum of Units Sold. Apart from Sum, there are many more summaries that you can choose, including Count, Average, Maximum, and Minimum. A numeric Data field defaults to Sum, and a text Data field defaults to Count. To select a different summary statistic, right-click any cell in the Data field, choose Field Settings from the shortcut menu, and locate the summary you want in the Summarize By list box.

You can also have both a Row field and a Column field in a pivot table. This helps you assess the joint effect of the two fields. Figure 6.6 gives an example.

Figure 6.6

To add Product as the Column field, drag it from the Field List to the Column area in the schematic shown in Figure 6.5.

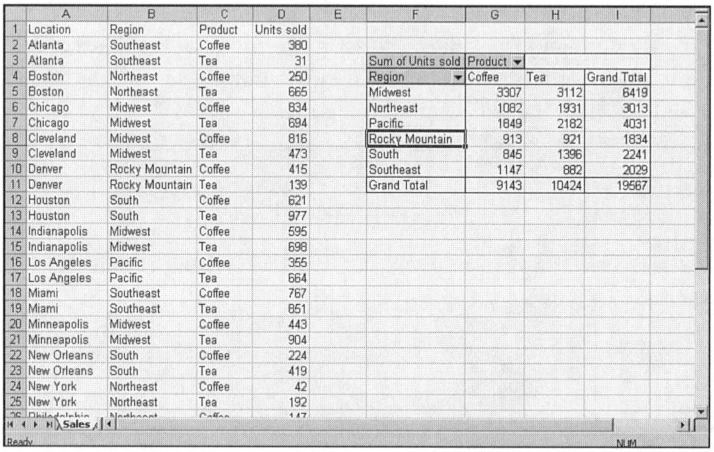

In addition, a pivot table can accommodate more than one Row field and Column field. Figure 6.7 shows the pivot table from Figure 6.6, but with an outer and an inner Row field and no Column field. To get two Row fields, for example, just drag them both into the schematic's Row area. Or, to revise the layout after the pivot table has been created, just drag the Region button directly to the right of the Product button.

Figure 6.7

To get Region subtotals, right-click Region, choose Field Settings, choose Custom subtotals, and select a subtotal such as Sum.

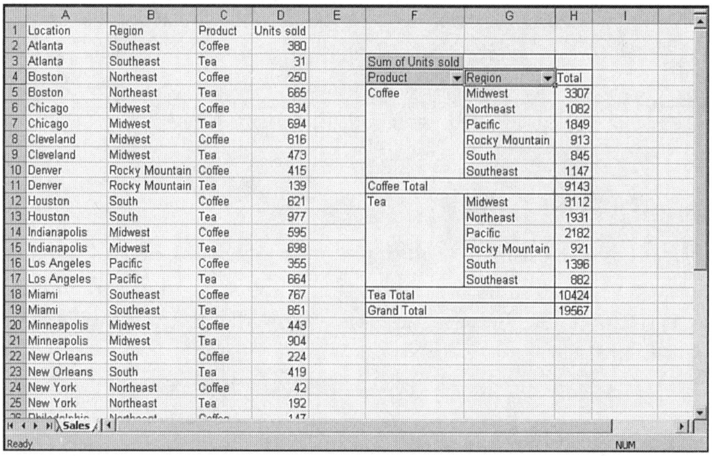

Besides Data, Row, and Column fields, pivot tables can also have Page fields. Page fields don't function in quite the same way as Row and Column fields. Their purpose is to enable you to select a subset of the underlying data and cause the pivot table to display only that subset.

Figure 6.8 shows the data from Figure 6.1 using Product as a Page field, and displaying information for the Coffee product only.

Figure 6.8
Your pivot table will include the records from each item in its Page field if you select All from its dropdown.

	A	B	C	D	E	F	G	H	I	J
1	Location	Region	Product	Units sold		Product	Coffee ▼			
2	Atlanta	Southeast	Coffee	380						
3	Atlanta	Southeast	Tea	31		Sum of Units sold				
4	Boston	Northeast	Coffee	250		Region ▼	Total			
5	Boston	Northeast	Tea	665		Midwest	3307			
6	Chicago	Midwest	Coffee	834		Northeast	1082			
7	Chicago	Midwest	Tea	694		Pacific	1849			
8	Cleveland	Midwest	Coffee	816		Rocky Mountain	913			
9	Cleveland	Midwest	Tea	473		South	845			
10	Denver	Rocky Mountain	Coffee	415		Southeast	1147			
11	Denver	Rocky Mountain	Tea	139		Grand Total	9143			
12	Houston	South	Coffee	621						
13	Houston	South	Tea	977						

If you want, you can use more than one Page field. If you do, they behave as though they were connected by Ands. For example, the pivot table shown in Figure 6.9 shows the Units Sold only for Coffee sales in the Northeast region.

Figure 6.9
Only the locations in the Northeast region are shown when you choose that item in a Page field.

	A	B	C	D	E	F	G	H	I
1	Location	Region	Product	Units sold		Product	Coffee ▼		
2	Atlanta	Southeast	Coffee	380		Region	Northeast ▼		
3	Atlanta	Southeast	Tea	31					
4	Boston	Northeast	Coffee	250		Sum of Units sold	Total		
5	Boston	Northeast	Tea	665		Total	1082		
6	Chicago	Midwest	Coffee	834					
7	Chicago	Midwest	Tea	694					
8	Cleveland	Midwest	Coffee	816					
9	Cleveland	Midwest	Tea	473					
10	Denver	Rocky Mountain	Coffee	415					
11	Denver	Rocky Mountain	Tea	139					
12	Houston	South	Coffee	621					
13	Houston	South	Tea	977					

You can set certain options in pivot tables. To do so, right-click a cell in the pivot table and choose Table Options from the shortcut menu. The dialog box shown in Figure 6.10 appears.

Figure 6.10
Giving the pivot table a descriptive name is particularly helpful if you want to base another pivot table on it later.

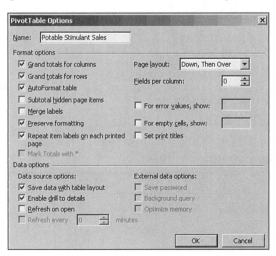

The more important of these options are as follows.

Grand Totals for Columns, Grand Totals for Rows

Refer to Figure 6.6, which shows a pivot table that includes both a Row field and a Column field. It shows Grand Totals in row 11 and in column I. If you clear the Grand Totals for Columns check box, the pivot table does not show the totals in row 11. If you clear the Grand Totals for Rows check box, the pivot table does not show the totals in column I.

AutoFormat Table

Excel offers 22 pivot table formats via the Format Report button on the PivotTable toolbar. If, having applied one of the formats, you want to remove the format from the pivot table, clear the AutoFormat Table check box.

> **NOTE**
> The format that's labeled None is *not* the same as the default format that's applied when you clear the AutoFormat Report check box.

Merge Labels

Figure 6.7 shows a pivot table with an outer Row field, Product, and an inner Row field, Region. If you fill the Merge Labels check box, cells F5:F10 and cells F12:F17 are merged (as though you had chosen Format, Cells, Alignment and filled the Merge Cells check box). This also centers the labels in the merged cells both horizontally and vertically.

Preserve Formatting

When you're working with a pivot table's Data field, it's usually best to format it by right-clicking one of its cells, choosing Field Settings from the shortcut menu, and then clicking the Number button. That way, the number format you select is preserved if you pivot or refresh the table.

But if you format the Data field's cells directly (or the cells in a Row or Column field) by selecting them and then choosing Cells from the Format menu, it's possible to lose the formatting (in particular, date formats). Filling the Preserve Formatting check box helps save direct cell formatting.

Repeat Item Labels on Each Printed Page

If you have a lengthy pivot table, it could span more than one printed page. And if you have only one Row field, the label that's in effect at the top of the second or subsequent printed page appears at the top of that page. But you might have more than one Row or Column field, as in Figure 6.7. In that case, the label of the outer Row or Column field is not repeated at the top of each page if this check box isn't filled.

Page Layout

Choose Down, Then Over to have multiple Page fields stacked vertically as in Figure 6.9, or choose Over, Then Down to have them appear side by side.

Fields Per Column or Fields Per Row

Depending on your choice for Page Layout, Page fields are either stacked in columns or side by side in rows. Suppose that you choose Down, Then Over. This option enables you to specify how many Page fields appear in a column before additional Page fields are placed in an adjacent column. If you choose Over, Then Down, you can specify how many page fields appear in a given row before additional ones are placed in the next row.

For Error Values, Show

If there are error values such as #DIV/0! or #REF! in the pivot table's data source, they appear in the pivot table itself. You might want a different value, such as Error, to appear in the pivot table. If so, fill this check box and type the value you want shown into the associated edit box.

For Empty Cells, Show

This check box and its associated edit box act in the same way as their counterparts do in For Error Values, Show, but for missing values instead of error values.

Save Data with Table Layout

A pivot table can store its underlying data in a *cache*. It's this cache that makes the pivot table so efficient at recalculating results when you pivot it or change it in some other way.

If you clear this check box, the pivot table will not save a cache. When you re-open its workbook, you'll have to refresh the pivot table's data before you can change the table's structure. You do save some storage space by omitting the cache.

Enable Drill to Details

If you've saved the cache along with the pivot table, you can get at the underlying data for any cell in the Data field. Just double-click that cell, and Excel inserts a new worksheet with a list. The list contains all the fields for all the records that belong to the cell you double-clicked. If you clear this check box, you won't be able to do that, and you might want to prevent other users of your pivot table from seeing detail records.

If you want to be able to drill to details, you must also have filled the Save Data with Table Layout check box.

Refresh on Open

This is a very useful option if the data that forms the basis for the pivot table changes from time to time. If the check box is filled, the pivot table automatically refreshes itself from the data source when you open the workbook.

6

> **TIP** Many of the workbooks I prepare for my clients have as many as 20 pivot tables that are based on external data sources such as Access databases. It can take a frustratingly long time for all the pivot tables in those workbooks to refresh. In such cases, I prefer to deselect this option and use the workbook's Open event to run VBA code that asks the user if he wants to refresh the pivot tables. If he does, the event runs more VBA code that refreshes all the pivot tables in the workbook.

The following options are available only if the pivot table is based on an external data source.

Refresh Every x Minutes

You can cause the pivot table to refresh itself from the data source by filling the check box and setting the number of minutes with the spinner.

Save Password

If the external data source is password-protected, you can cause Excel to save the password so that you (and other users of the workbook) won't have to supply it when the pivot table is refreshed later on. This is a more secure way of saving the data source's password than to save it with a DSN file, which can be read with something as ubiquitous and basic as Notepad.

Background Query

If your external data source supports asynchronous queries, you might want to use this option. If the check box is filled, you can continue doing other work in Excel as the query refreshes the pivot table. If the check box is cleared, you'll have to wait until the refresh is complete before you can do anything else in the workbook. This option is useful mainly in very slow networked environments.

Optimize Memory

If you fill this check box, Excel takes some preliminary steps before it refreshes a pivot table. In particular, Excel determines how many unique items there are in the pivot table's row and column fields. By doing so, it's able to manage its memory allocations more efficiently. You might notice a slight drop-off in performance as Excel makes these checks.

Preparing Data for Pivot Tables

There are some special considerations to keep in mind when you specify the records you want to use in pivot tables. These issues don't apply to external data ranges unless you then use the external data range as the source for a pivot table. The idea is to avoid putting records into the pivot table if they contain null values in a field that you want to use to group records.

Grouping on Date and Time Fields

It often happens that you want to analyze data in a pivot table using a date or time of day as a row, column, or page field. For example, you might want to know the average number of traffic accidents during each hour of the day or during each day of the week.

When the time and/or date that something occurs is important, it's typical to record the occurrence's exact time of day and, often, its specific date. But when you want to analyze the data, it's atypical to care about the exact minute when the event occurred. At least in the realm of descriptive statistics, you seldom pay attention to the fact that two traffic accidents occurred at 4:37 p.m. while one occurred at 4:38 p.m.

So, you would like to group your data according to broader categories than minutes—half-hour or one-hour brackets, perhaps. Other analyses, such as tracking a company's revenues, typically rely on even broader categories, such as months and quarters.

Excel pivot tables have a very useful capability that can help out here. If you establish a time or date field in a pivot table's row or column area, you can subsequently create groups based on that field, groups defined by hours, or days, or months, and so on. Figure 6.11 shows an example.

Figure 6.11
A pivot table based on date or time values seldom provides any useful information before you've grouped its dates or times.

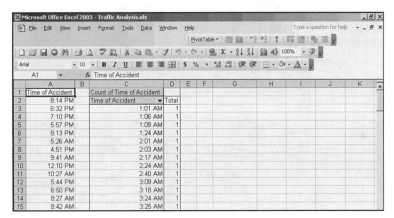

In Figure 6.11, the time at which traffic accidents were reported is shown in a worksheet range beginning in A1, adjacent to a pivot table based on that data range. The summary capabilities of pivot tables have not yet been brought to bear—the table just replicates the information in the underlying data range.

Now suppose that you'd like to see the number of accidents on an hourly basis. To do so, you take these steps:

1. Click any cell in the pivot table's row field, and choose **Data**, **Group and Outline**, **Group** (depending on your version, you can also right-click a cell in the row field and choose **Group and Show Detail**, **Group**). The Grouping dialog box shown in Figure 6.12 appears.

6

Figure 6.12
The starting and ending values are based on the smallest and largest values in the data source.

2. Because the Row field you selected is a date/time field, the dialog box offers by default to group the field into months. Click the **Months** item to deselect it, and then click the **Hours** item to select it, as shown in Figure 6.12.

3. Click **OK** to group the row field as shown in Figure 6.13.

Figure 6.13
The format of a grouped field in a pivot table is based on, but not necessarily identical to, the format of the underlying data source.

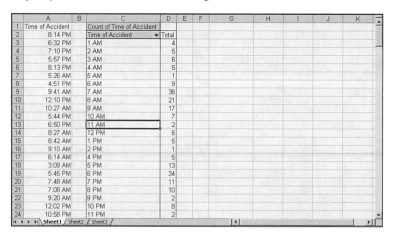

	A	B	C	D	E	F	G	H	I	J	K
1	Time of Accident		Count of Time of Accident								
2	8:14 PM		Time of Accident ▼	Total							
3	6:32 PM		1 AM	4							
4	7:10 PM		2 AM	5							
5	5:57 PM		3 AM	6							
6	8:13 AM		4 AM	5							
7	5:26 AM		5 AM	1							
8	4:51 PM		6 AM	9							
9	9:41 AM		7 AM	36							
10	12:10 PM		8 AM	21							
11	10:27 AM		9 AM	17							
12	5:44 PM		10 AM	7							
13	6:50 PM		11 AM	2							
14	8:27 AM		12 PM	6							
15	8:42 AM		1 PM	5							
16	9:10 AM		2 PM	1							
17	6:14 AM		4 PM	5							
18	3:09 AM		5 PM	13							
19	5:45 PM		6 PM	34							
20	7:48 AM		7 PM	11							
21	7:08 AM		8 PM	10							
22	9:20 AM		9 PM	2							
23	12:02 PM		10 PM	8							
24	10:58 PM		11 PM	2							

Now a pattern starts to emerge—one that was obscured by all the detail in the row field before you grouped it. It becomes apparent that most traffic accidents occur during rush hours. Just as you suspected.

> **NOTE**
> If you're using Excel 97, you can group in this way only if you make the field you want to group on a Row field—you can't do this with a Column or Page field in Excel 97. After you've created the groups, you can pivot the table to make the Row field either a Column or a Page field. In subsequent versions, you can begin by grouping on a Column field, but (as of Excel 2003) not a Page field. Nevertheless, the logic of the worksheet's dimensions mean that it's sensible to start it off as a Row field because you can accommodate many more ungrouped values that way.

6

Grouping on Other Numeric Fields

Figure 6.14 shows a similar situation. You have revenue data by date for the theatrical release of a movie that has been appearing in theaters for a few weeks. You couldn't care less about the specific day (or time of day, for that matter) on which the revenue was realized, but you're interested in the dollar amount that was realized by week.

Figure 6.14
Here you'll want to group by date instead of time.

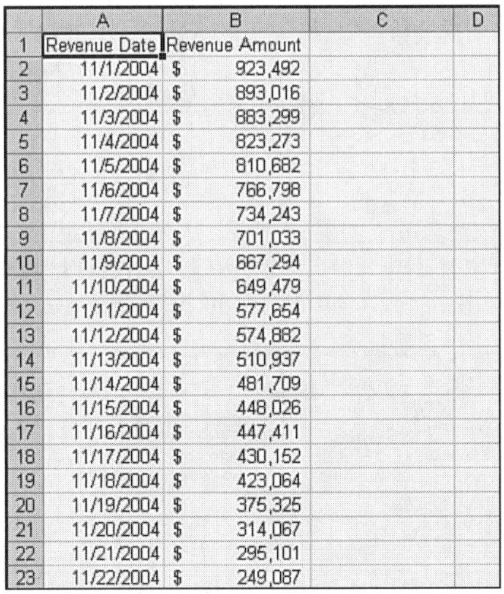

	A	B	C	D
1	Revenue Date	Revenue Amount		
2	11/1/2004	$ 923,492		
3	11/2/2004	$ 893,016		
4	11/3/2004	$ 883,299		
5	11/4/2004	$ 823,273		
6	11/5/2004	$ 810,682		
7	11/6/2004	$ 766,798		
8	11/7/2004	$ 734,243		
9	11/8/2004	$ 701,033		
10	11/9/2004	$ 667,294		
11	11/10/2004	$ 649,479		
12	11/11/2004	$ 577,654		
13	11/12/2004	$ 574,882		
14	11/13/2004	$ 510,937		
15	11/14/2004	$ 481,709		
16	11/15/2004	$ 448,026		
17	11/16/2004	$ 447,411		
18	11/17/2004	$ 430,152		
19	11/18/2004	$ 423,064		
20	11/19/2004	$ 375,325		
21	11/20/2004	$ 314,067		
22	11/21/2004	$ 295,101		
23	11/22/2004	$ 249,087		

You begin by creating a pivot table that uses Revenue Date as a Row field and Revenue Amount as a Data field. Then you select the Revenue Date field, choose Data, Group and Outline, clear Month by clicking it in the By list box, and select Days (refer to Figure 6.12). The Number of Days spinner becomes available and you use it to specify seven days. When you click OK, the pivot table is reconfigured to appear as in Figure 6.15.

Figure 6.15
Pivot tables' grouping options don't include Week—to group by week, you have to specify seven days.

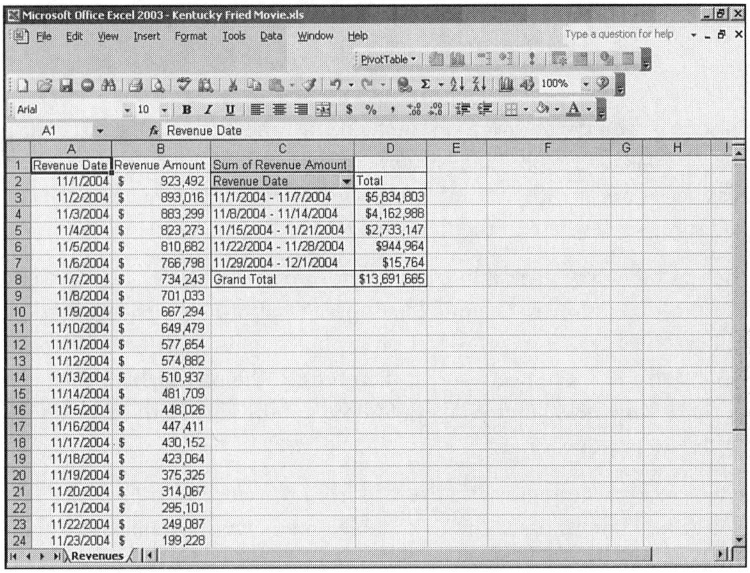

	A	B	C	D
1	Revenue Date	Revenue Amount	Sum of Revenue Amount	
2	11/1/2004	$ 923,492	Revenue Date	Total
3	11/2/2004	$ 893,016	11/1/2004 - 11/7/2004	$5,834,803
4	11/3/2004	$ 883,299	11/8/2004 - 11/14/2004	$4,162,988
5	11/4/2004	$ 823,273	11/15/2004 - 11/21/2004	$2,733,147
6	11/5/2004	$ 810,682	11/22/2004 - 11/28/2004	$944,964
7	11/6/2004	$ 766,798	11/29/2004 - 12/1/2004	$15,764
8	11/7/2004	$ 734,243	Grand Total	$13,691,665
9	11/8/2004	$ 701,033		
10	11/9/2004	$ 667,294		
11	11/10/2004	$ 649,479		
12	11/11/2004	$ 577,654		
13	11/12/2004	$ 574,882		
14	11/13/2004	$ 510,937		
15	11/14/2004	$ 481,709		
16	11/15/2004	$ 448,026		
17	11/16/2004	$ 447,411		
18	11/17/2004	$ 430,152		
19	11/18/2004	$ 423,064		
20	11/19/2004	$ 375,325		
21	11/20/2004	$ 314,067		
22	11/21/2004	$ 295,101		
23	11/22/2004	$ 249,087		
24	11/23/2004	$ 199,228		

This is a terrific feature in pivot tables—one that makes them so valuable in analyzing time-dependent events. Whether you use Excel 97 and base charts on pivot tables, or use a later version to create pivot charts, the time and date grouping capability is a great way to provide visual analyses.

> **TIP**
>
> You aren't restricted to just one grouping level. You could, for example, choose both Months and Years—and you should probably do so if you're analyzing data such as corporate revenues that span more than one year.

Avoiding Null Values

But there's a problem. Pivot tables are unable to group on fields that contain null values. For example, suppose that the underlying data sets shown in Figure 6.11 through 6.15 had an empty cell in, say, A207. The resulting pivot table would look like the one in Figure 6.16.

Figure 6.16
Notice the blank value in C210:D210.

	A	B	C	D	E	F
190	1:01 AM		8:09 PM	1		
191	10:40 AM		8:13 PM	1		
192	6:50 PM		8:14 PM	1		
193	6:41 PM		8:14 PM	1		
194	8:29 AM		8:16 PM	1		
195	8:09 AM		8:25 PM	1		
196	8:58 AM		8:34 PM	1		
197	6:17 AM		8:41 PM	1		
198	3:24 AM		8:50 PM	1		
199	6:46 PM		9:40 PM	1		
200	7:41 AM		9:49 PM	1		
201	7:37 AM		10:16 PM	1		
202	9:26 AM		10:16 PM	1		
203	12:02 PM		10:23 PM	1		
204	1:13 PM		10:23 PM	1		
205	7:19 AM		10:23 PM	1		
206	7:24 AM		10:29 PM	1		
207			10:58 PM	1		
208	4:46 PM		11:05 PM	1		
209	6:37 AM		11:05 PM	1		
210	3:55 AM	(blank)				
211	6:32 PM	Grand Total		209		
212						

As soon as you try to group on the field with the blank value, Excel displays the warning message `Cannot group that selection`, and you will not see the Grouping dialog box. Excel does not say why it can't group that selection, but the reason is usually that there's a null value somewhere in the field you're trying to group.

You can hide that blank value, either with Field Settings or by right-clicking it and selecting Hide from the shortcut menu. That doesn't help—if you try again to group the field, you still get the warning message instead of the Grouping dialog box. You can remove the null value from the worksheet list and then refresh the pivot table's data, again to no effect. With a date or time field, after you've admitted a null value to the pivot table, you're not going to be able to group on that field.

The solution is to remove that record from the worksheet list before you create the pivot table. Or, if you've based the pivot table on an external data source, you can use Microsoft

Query's Criteria pane to prevent any null values from entering the table in the first place (see Figure 6.17).

Figure 6.17
The criterion specifying Is Not Null prevents any records with a null value on that field from being returned to the workbook.

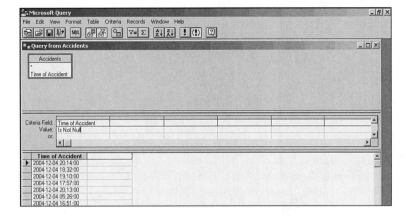

Therefore, if you need to group date or time values in a pivot table's field, it's a good idea to set up your data source so that it will provide no null values on that field.

→ Basing a pivot table on an external data source is covered in detail in "Importing Data to Pivot Tables," **p. 104**.

Avoiding Null Values in Other Grouped Fields

There are occasions on which you might want to group values other than dates and times. Suppose that you wanted to examine the ages of customers, or clients, or patients—in general, people you work with. Their age distribution appears in Figure 6.18.

Figure 6.18
Excel does not recognize the values in column A as dates or times.

	A	B	C	D	E
1	Patient Age		Count of Patient Age		
2	91		Patient Age ▼	Total	
3	12		2	1	
4	98		4	3	
5	80		5	1	
6	25		7	1	
7	77		9	1	
8	44		10	1	
9	89		11	1	
10	34		12	3	
11	30		13	1	
12	56		14	2	
13	40		15	1	
14	13		16	1	
15	43		17	1	
16	17		19	1	
17	21		20	2	
18	12		21	2	

When you click one of the cells in the pivot table and choose Data, Group and Outline, Group, the Grouping dialog box shown in Figure 6.19 appears.

Excel can recognize and divide a date or time field into standard categories such as year, month, day, and minute. In contrast, Excel has to rely on the user to provide brackets for an arbitrary scale, as in Figure 6.19. *You* know the numbers represent years, but Excel doesn't.

6

Figure 6.19
You can lump many records into one group at the top or bottom of the range by changing the Starting At or Ending At values.

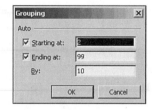

This sort of numeric grouping brings with it the same problem that accompanies dates and times: A null value in the data source causes Excel to say it can't group that field when you ask it to. So, it's wise to use the same sort of criterion, Is Not Null, as shown in Figure 6.17.

There is one difference, though. With a field such as the one shown in Figure 6.18, you don't need to start from scratch if you allow a null value into the pivot table. Just remove it from the table's data source—whether a worksheet list or an external data source—and refresh the pivot table's data. Now you'll be able to group on that field.

Using Criteria with Microsoft Query

The previous section showed how you can use criteria in Microsoft Query to resolve problems caused by null values in pivot tables. Microsoft Query provides more flexible criteria, termed *parameters*, in much the same way as does Microsoft Access.

When you tell Microsoft Query, or a database manager such as Microsoft Access or SQL Server, that you want it to return only certain records, you do so by means of a *criterion*. Perhaps you want to see only those birth records where the birth weight exceeds 2,000 grams. Then you would supply that weight as a criterion (see Figure 6.20).

Figure 6.20
You can supply more than one Criteria field. They will act as though they were connected by Ands.

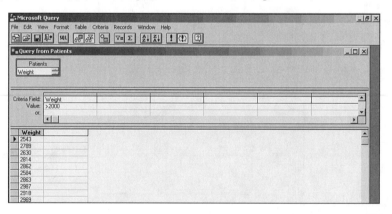

As shown in Figure 6.20, the person creating the query has entered the value >2000 in the Criteria pane. When he chooses File, Return Data to Microsoft Excel, only those records with a birth weight of more than 2,000 grams are returned.

If the user has based an external data range or a pivot table on this query, each time the data range or the table is refreshed it will get only those records with a value greater than 2,000 on the birth weight field.

But if the user puts a special sort of criterion, a *parameter*, in the Criteria pane, he can change the value of the criterion each time the query runs. A parameterized query is shown in Figure 6.21.

Figure 6.21
Notice the use of the comparison operator > before the parameter. Operators are frequently useful, but are not required in parameter-ized queries.

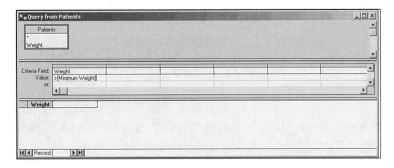

By enclosing the criterion in square brackets, the user has established it as a parameter. Both Microsoft Query and Microsoft Access recognize the square brackets as signaling a parameter. When the query is executed, the user is prompted to supply a value that will be used as a criterion. Executing the query shown in Figure 6.21 first displays the dialog box shown in Figure 6.22.

Figure 6.22
The dialog box prompt-ing for a value appears if you refresh a worksheet data range that gets its data from this query.

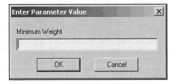

Why is this useful? Because each time the query executes, it prompts the user for the value to use as a criterion. That means that the user can supply a different value each time. In this example, the user could specify 2000 as a criterion one time and the query would return only those records with a birth weight greater than 2,000; the next time, the user could specify 2500 and the query would return only those records with a birth weight greater than 2,500.

You can arrange to supply a range of criteria by using the keyword Between. Suppose that you wanted to return only those records with a value in birth weight greater than or equal to one value and less than or equal to another value. You can use the parameter Between [Lower Weight] And [Higher Weight]. When the query runs, it will prompt the user first for a value for Lower Weight and then for a value for Higher Weight. After the second of the two criteria has been supplied, the query will return only those records that satisfy the two criteria. The Between...And... usage also works well with date and time data—for example, Between [Starting Date] And [Ending Date].

→ You'll find information on using parameters with queries by means of VBA, in "Bringing Data Back from a Parameterized Query," **p. 293**.

6

Querying Web Sites

Web sites can be a rich source of information for your workbooks—particularly financial sites and sites that offer products for sale. By building a query to such a site, you can refresh the results whenever you want without having to use your browser.

CASE STUDY

Getting Financial Data

Suppose that you want to keep an eye on both the levels and volume of major financial market indices. Doing so can be a good way to tell whether the markets are starting to turn, whether up or down.

1. Begin by selecting a worksheet cell that is not part of an existing external data range. If the active cell is part of such a range, the Import Data, the New Web Query, and the New Database Query menu items are disabled.

2. Choose **Data, Import External Data, New Web Query**. The dialog box shown in Figure 6.23 appears.

Figure 6.23
The actual page that appears depends on the location of your browser's home page.

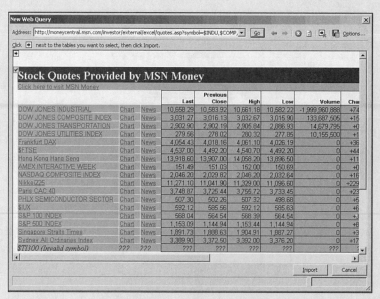

3. In the dialog box's Address box, enter the URL of the page you want to use, and click the **Go** button to reach the page. After the page has loaded, you'll see yellow boxes with black arrows scattered across the page. Each one indicates the presence of a table that can be queried.

4. These square icons are by default turned off: That is, their associated tables are not selected. To select a table, click its icon. The icon turns green and the arrow is replaced by a checkmark. To make it easier to see what you're selecting, a table is outlined when you move your mouse pointer over its associated icon.

5. When you've selected the table you want, click the **Import** button in the lower-right corner of the dialog box. The dialog box closes and the Import Data dialog box appears. You can set data range properties at this point, or do so later by right-clicking a cell in the data range and choosing Properties from the shortcut menu.

➔ The Import dialog box is discussed in "Handling the Data Range," **p. 130**.

6. Click **OK** and the data is returned to an external data range in your workbook. Graphic images, if there were any in the table you selected, are not returned (see Figure 6.24).

Figure 6.24
This query used no data formatting.

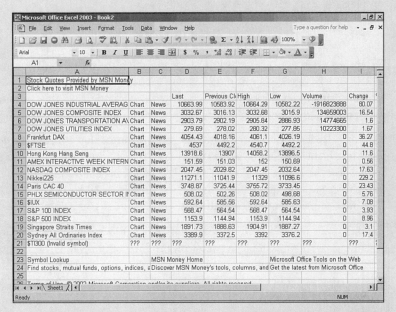

Now, you can update the information in your data range whenever you want. Just right-click a cell in the data range and choose Refresh External Data from the shortcut menu.

> T I P
>
> It's a good idea to use the Properties button on the Import Data dialog box to check the name that will be assigned to the data range. Some sites return meaningful names. Others return only the URL, which often isn't a good choice for a range name.

Using Web Query Options

In Figure 6.23, if you click the Options button in the dialog box's upper-right corner, the dialog box shown in Figure 6.25 appears.

You can choose None to get no formatting. If you choose Rich Text Formatting Only, you'll get the fonts used in the table: boldface, colors, italics, and so on. If you choose Full HTML Formatting, you'll get the fancy fonts, and if the table contains any hyperlinks, those hyperlinks become part of the external data range. This can be a useful way to get further information on an element in a table.

Figure 6.25
You can reset these options by right-clicking in the data range and choosing Edit Query from the shortcut menu.

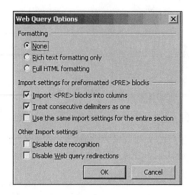

Web pages often use <PRE> blocks to format sections of the page. If you select the Import <PRE> Blocks Into Columns option, those sections are returned to the worksheet in columns using the delimiters on the Web page. If you deselect this option, the remaining two options in this section of the dialog box are disabled.

Choosing Treat Consecutive Delimiters As One means that consecutive delimiters won't result in a blank cell. If you select this option, the option labeled Use the Same Import Settings for the Entire Section is enabled. If you choose not to use the same import settings, your choices will be applied only to the first preformatted block that the query encounters. The query will attempt to select the best choices for any remaining preformatted blocks.

You might encounter a Web page that contains numbers that look like dates but are really something else. For example, a page with product numbers might use a pattern such as 11-5-98. Excel would typically recognize this as a date and convert it to its standard date serial number representation. You can keep this from happening by choosing the Disable Date Recognition option.

Finally, some Web pages have automatic redirection to other sites. When you refresh the query later on, you might be redirected and your data might not be refreshed properly. To prevent this from happening, choose the Disable Web Query Redirections option.

Looking Ahead

Queries are powerful tools for use in bringing data into an Excel workbook, and they become more powerful yet when you apply parameters to them.

The techniques discussed in Chapter 5, "Using Microsoft Query," and in this chapter are fine for interactive work—when you're doing something once only, or when you're early in the development process for something that you expect to grow. Those techniques are still used, and used heavily, in more complex situations.

The greater complexity of a solution often depends on the use of coding, and in Office applications that usually starts with VBA. It progresses from there to the use of object libraries that enable VBA to create and execute queries of the sort discussed in Chapters 5 and 6.

To get to that point, you need to know something about VBA. In the next chapter, this book departs briefly from its main theme of data management so as to familiarize you, or perhaps remind you, of some of the fundamental aspects of VBA that you'll need to automate a workbook's relationship with external data sources.

6

Managing Databases from Inside Excel

IV

VBA Essentials Reviewed

Using VBA to Manage Data

This is supposed to be a book about managing data using Excel, so what's a chapter about Visual Basic for Applications (VBA) doing here?

As it happens, the remainder of this book is all about working with VBA. The first six chapters were concerned with the use of Excel's built-in data management capabilities. For example

- The worksheet functions that help you manage data

- The tools that help you filter and sort data

- The ways to populate pivot tables and data ranges

- The methods of importing data from sources such as databases, text files, and the Web

These are powerful techniques and they have broad applicability. For standard situations, they'll serve you very well. You'll have to do some tweaking here and there to get the results exactly as you want them, but in many cases that's all that's needed.

Those standard situations include managing data that's already in an Excel workbook, and bringing data from other sources into a workbook where you can take advantage of Excel's worksheet functions, pivot tables, and its charting capabilities.

Adding Objects to VBA

So far, though, this book has not discussed moving data the *other* direction: in particular, moving it from Excel to a database. For that you really need VBA. You also need a set of tools such as those provided by *ActiveX Data Objects (ADO)*, or its predecessor, *Data Access Objects (DAO)*. These toolsets are also both well suited and necessary for other tasks such as manipulating a database directly from the Excel platform.

You'll see much more on ADO and DAO in Chapters 8 through 12, but here's a brief overview.

Both ADO and DAO are *object libraries*—that is, collections of objects that you can use in VBA code. You use either ADO or DAO, not both simultaneously. The objects that are in the libraries are database objects. They define for VBA the objects that you find in databases: tables, queries, records, fields, and so on.

By making one of these libraries, either ADO or DAO, available to your VBA code, you make it possible to manipulate data stored in a database just as you can use VBA to manipulate data stored in an Excel workbook.

ADO and DAO differ from one another in various ways, and these differences are also discussed in later chapters. For now it's enough to know that ADO is newer than DAO, that you can use it with a broader range of databases than DAO, and that many developers regard it as easier to use than DAO.

As you'll see, both ADO and DAO are well suited to moving data from Excel to a database, but they go well beyond that role. They're also valuable in moving data from a database to Excel, in situations where the techniques discussed in the preceding chapters won't do what you need. And you'll need one or the other when you want to modify a database's records while you're working in Excel.

If you are to use ADO or DAO, you need to use it in the context of VBA. Neither behaves like an add-in such as the Solver, which is installed as an option and is then callable from the worksheet. ADO and DAO are both collections of objects, methods, and properties that extend the reach of VBA.

It's important to keep in mind that you need to use VBA to take advantage of the database object model as provided by ADO or DAO. VBA is a necessary part of this interface between Excel and databases, and you need a working knowledge at least of VBA basics to manage the interface. That's what this chapter is doing here.

Putting VBA in Historical Perspective

In 1995, Microsoft took a step that significantly increased the power of the applications in the Office suite: It *exposed the object model*. That meant that Microsoft enabled users of Excel and other Office applications to write programs in BASIC that could directly manipulate an application's objects.

Before VBA and the exposure of the object model, an Excel user who wanted to automate certain tasks was severely limited by the available programming language. There was an arcane macro language that you could use in Excel, but to use it was nothing like coding with popular programming languages of the time such as C, BASIC, and FORTRAN. You put your macro code on a sheet that looked much like a worksheet, and you placed a statement or function in one cell and its arguments into an adjacent cell.

But VBA and the object model made things much more straightforward. Suddenly your code looked normal: Other programmers could understand and maintain it. Your code could directly manipulate Excel objects such as worksheets, ranges, names, and charts. It could bring methods to bear on objects—for example, your code could invoke a range's `Clear` method to clear that range of its contents. It could manipulate properties, such as setting a font's `Color` property to Red.

This is what was meant by exposing the object model. At last you had access to the hierarchy of objects: the Excel application at the top, to which belong workbooks, to which belong chart sheets and worksheets, to which belong axes and data series and cells and ranges and columns and rows, and so on. Each of those is an *object*.

Using the Object Model

Objects have *methods*. A worksheet range, for example, has methods such as `AutoFilter`, `Clear`, `Copy`, `Delete`, `Select`, and `Sort` (there are many others). By invoking a range's `Copy` method, I can put its contents on the clipboard, ready to paste elsewhere.

Objects have *properties*. A worksheet range, for example, has properties such as `Borders`, `Columns`, `Formula`, `Offset`, and `RowHeight` (there are many others). By setting a range's Resize property, I can work with a range that is taller or shorter, wider or narrower.

You can get at all Excel's objects, and their associated methods and properties, by using VBA in Excel. Excel's *Visual Basic Editor (VBE)* automatically makes them available to your code because the object model has been exposed.

Databases have objects, too, as well as methods and properties that belong to the objects. Databases' objects include tables, queries, parameters, and so on. But they don't belong to the Excel object model: There's not just one overarching object model that contains, for example, Excel worksheets, Access tables, PowerPoint slides, and Word paragraphs. There's a different object model for each application.

Using Other Applications' Object Models

Those other object models are not automatically available to VBA in Excel. If you start the VBE from, say, Access, you'll find that all the Access database objects are automatically available to you. But they are not if you start the VBE from Excel.

To use a database object in your Excel VBA code, you need to establish a reference to an object model that's compatible with the database. By establishing the reference, you let VBA know where to look for information about the objects it uses. There are several such object models, and each is stored in a library—in particular, a *dynamic link library*, or DLL. You establish the reference by means of a simple menu command. From the VBE, choose Tools, References and fill the check box for the library you want (see Figure 7.1).

7

Figure 7.1
When you have a choice of versions, it's usually best to choose the one with the highest version number.

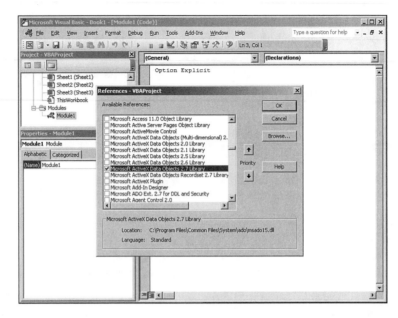

NOTE The version of DAO or ADO that's available to you depends on the version of Office (and therefore on the operating system) that you have installed on your computer. They have the same purpose: to give your code access to database objects. From the user's perspective, DAO and ADO are identical in some ways but very different in important respects. At the time this book was being written, Microsoft was focusing development efforts on ADO and regarded DAO as a legacy technology. This book highlights differences between the two where your VBA code would be affected. Elsewhere, you can regard discussion of ADO as applying to DAO as well.

After you've established the reference, you'll find that your VBA code recognizes the database objects.

TIP When you compile or run your VBA code, if you get the compiler error message User-defined type not defined, it almost certainly means that you have miskeyed the name of a variable type or that you haven't yet established a reference to the type's library.

For example, with a library reference established properly, your VBA code can do each of the following, all without ever opening the database's window:

- Return records and fields from a table or query directly to the worksheet
- Filter the records returned by a query by supplying a parameter value to the query before executing it

- Add records to or delete records from a table
- Edit records
- Create and execute a query, and either cause the query to be saved in the database or to vanish as soon as you're through with it

The previous list is only a small sample of the tasks you can accomplish when you make the database object model available to your Excel VBA code.

Managing the Database from Excel

Why would you *want* to manipulate a database from within Excel? As it turns out, there's a variety of reasons, not all of them self-evident.

Accommodating the User

If people other than you ever use systems that you develop, you need to take into account the user interfaces that they're comfortable with. Most computer users feel comfortable in a worksheet context. They're used to the notion of rows and columns, and how they intersect to make cells. Their experience with worksheets might go all the way back to 1-2-3, whereas database managers such as dBASE came along later (and were never as popular as the spreadsheet applications).

Most users appreciate the flexibility of the worksheet—for example, that one can make a row stand for anything and a column stand for anything—and are often put off by the prickliness of the database where a row *must* represent a record and a column *must* represent a field.

Any time you can help a user feel more comfortable using your product, you're ahead of the game.

Taking Advantage of Excel's Features

Excel offers capabilities that are simply not available in databases, or that are not implemented as well as they are in Excel. Charts, for example, are implemented in Access, but they have to be embedded in forms or reports. Pivot tables are similarly available, but only in datasheets and forms.

More serious is the limited function set. Although Access offers a reasonably good function list, given that it's a database manager, the list is nowhere near as extensive as Excel's. As basic a function as Median is unavailable in Access—you have to create your own using VBA in Access.

But if you make database records and fields available to your Excel VBA code, you can use Excel's worksheet functions to analyze the data.

> TIP
>
> Whether or not you ever use Excel VBA in direct conjunction with a database, bear in mind that Excel's worksheet functions are available in VBA. For example, to get the median value of an array, you might use something like this:
> ```
> MyMedian = Application.WorksheetFunction.Median(MyArray)
> ```

Maintaining Flexibility

Earlier in this chapter, the generalized nature of Excel's worksheet layout was mentioned: that rows and columns aren't relegated to any specific role as they are in a database's datasheet view. This fact has applicability that goes beyond that of user comfort.

Sometimes you encounter a situation that calls for a matrix, or an array, or a table, or a range of cells; the term matters less than the fact that you need to use rows that intersect columns. And the situation is such that you cannot regard the rows as records and the columns as fields, as demanded by the database.

An example is a resource calendar. For your users to employ the calendar effectively, you'd like them to be able to reserve a resource for a particular period of time on a particular day. Excel's structure is ideal for this. You can arrange things as follows:

- Assign each worksheet row to represent a specific resource (a meeting room, for example, or a workstation-compatible overhead projector or a high-definition screen)
- Assign each worksheet column to represent a half-hour increment, so that column C might represent 0600 to 0630, column D 0630 to 0700, and so on
- Assign each worksheet to represent a different day

With this sort of structure, a user can quickly see that Room K has already been reserved starting at 10:30 on October 14, so that his meeting will have to use Room O. See Figure 7.2.

This is the sort of thing that Excel's worksheets are so well suited to. The Western eye likes to see time progress from left to right, not up and down (and definitely not right to left), so time slots are best placed so that they occupy different columns. For the user's convenience, it makes sense to put available resources adjacent to one another, so that if Room K is unavailable at a particular time, it's easy to see if some other room is available. If different columns are in use to represent different time slots, that leaves different rows to represent different resources.

But it's difficult to see how you would manage that in a database. You would need first to define a field as a time slot. So, each record would have perhaps 48 fields that represent whether it's in use during a particular half-hour.

Each record would have to represent a particular resource on a particular day. And each record would need child records to store data such as who made the reservation, which accounts are to be charged for any expenses incurred, what refreshments are to be supplied, whether the reservation is to recur on subsequent dates, and so on.

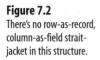

Figure 7.2
There's no row-as-record, column-as-field strait-jacket in this structure.

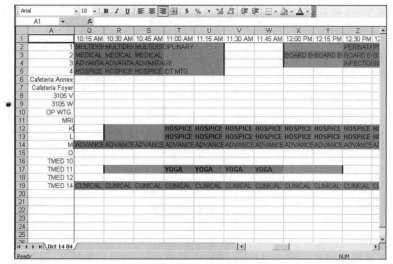

All in all, the user interface is difficult to handle with a database alone. But it's easy to do using a workbook. And it gets easier yet when you bring a database to bear on the problem, but in such a way that its use is transparent to the user.

For example, you could decide that in the database a reservation is a record. It has a field that identifies the reservation's date, another to identify the start time and another for the stop time, another for the resource that's been reserved, and so forth.

So doing means that you can use the workbook to *display* the information and the database to *store* the information. This approach leverages the strengths of both applications: the worksheet's capability to represent information in a visually informative and intuitive way, and the database's capability to store, locate, and retrieve large amounts of data very quickly.

Notice that although the scenario as described here involves a one-way data flow only, you could not accomplish it by importing external data, whether to an external data range or to a pivot table: The layouts they use are just too restrictive. (This is, by the way, a real-world application that has been used daily by a mid-sized corporation for several years.)

Reviewing the Rationale

Really, the main point raised in the prior section—using the strength of each application—is the rationale for using Excel VBA in conjunction with a database object model such as ADO or DAO.

Excel has been built and refined over several years and several releases principally as an application that analyzes, synthesizes, and displays data, and it's very good indeed at those tasks.

7

In response to user requests, Microsoft has added certain capabilities to Excel that were not part of the original design. For example, Excel was not originally intended as a multiuser application with all the features needed to ensure data integrity when several users have a given workbook open at the same time. You can arrange for the workbook to be shared, but that feature came along relatively late in Excel's development and just doesn't work as well as it does in applications that have it built into their basic design.

Similarly, databases such as Access have been developed as engines that store large amounts of data reliably and retrieve records very quickly, even from quite large data sets. They also have sophisticated methods of resolving conflicts when more than one user at a time is attempting to modify a particular record.

If you have relatively few records to deal with, you're usually better off using Excel's native worksheet functions and features to manage them, as discussed in Chapters 2, "Excel's Data Management Features," and 3, "Excel's Lists, Names, and Filters." And if you have a relatively large data set, you *might* be better off using a database manager alone.

But if you have a large data set and need a flexible user interface, or a large function set, or a strong charting capability, you need both a database and a workbook. And the best way to manage two-way communication between them is by means of VBA as enhanced with ADO.

With the foregoing as rationale, you should head for the next chapter if you're already a VBA maven. Otherwise, the rest of this chapter will give you a quick introduction to the aspects of VBA most frequently used in the contexts of data management and database management.

Establishing Subroutines

A *subroutine* is a collection of VBA statements that, taken together, accomplish something. The term is a little unfortunate, implying that it is subordinate to something. The meaning is broader than that, though: A subroutine can be the main, top-level code in your project, or it can be a set of code that accomplishes some smaller task on behalf of the main code.

Providing the Subroutine's Basic Elements

In VBA, subroutines are stored in *modules*, and establishing a module is where it all starts. To establish a module you need to start the VBE.

From the main Excel window, one way to get to the VBE is by choosing Macro from the Tools menu, and then selecting Visual Basic Editor from the shortcut menu. As you become more experienced with the VBE, you'll find yourself using the keyboard shortcut (Alt+F11) so consistently, that you're liable to forget there's another way to get there. When you start the VBE, the window shown in Figure 7.3 appears.

7

Figure 7.3
The VBE looks much the same in other Office applications such as Word and Access.

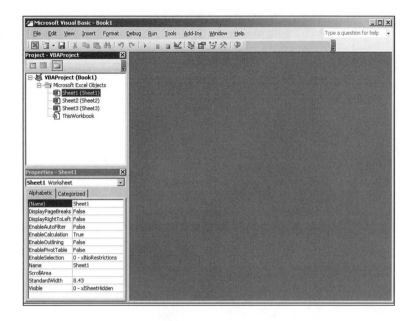

The two windows on the left in Figure 7.3 aren't necessary if you're establishing a subroutine, but they can be useful. The VBE refers to the whole collection of sheets, modules, and user forms in an Excel file as a *project*. When you have several modules in a project, the Project Explorer is the most convenient way to switch among them.

The Properties Window is not as routinely useful as the Project Explorer, and you might decide to close it if only to get it out of your way. I like having it there because I frequently have hidden worksheets in my workbooks. The Properties window is a convenient way to hide and unhide worksheets, by changing its `Visible` property.

> **TIP**
> You can set a worksheet's `Visible` property to `xlSheetVisible`: This is its normal state. Or you can set it to `xlSheetHidden`: This is the same as choosing Format, Sheet, Hide. There are at least two problems with a hidden worksheet. Unless the workbook is protected, the user can tell that the sheet exists because the Unhide menu item is enabled, and the user can unhide the sheet. By using the Properties Window (or VBA code) to set a worksheet's `Visible` property to `xlSheetVeryHidden`, you solve both problems. Even if the workbook itself is not protected, the Unhide menu item remains disabled—and, therefore, the user can neither unhide from the Format menu nor infer that a hidden sheet exists.

After you have the VBE open, there are several ways to establish modules, depending on what you mean to accomplish. The most basic, straightforward method is to choose Module from the Insert menu. Figure 7.4 shows the result.

7

Figure 7.4
The active object is the one whose properties appear in the Properties window. Standard modules have only one property.

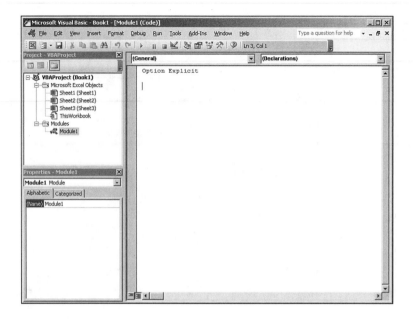

TIP

> Notice the `Option Explicit` statement at the start of the module in Figure 7.4. It's good programming practice to use that statement because it forces you to explicitly declare all variables in your code (the importance of explicit declaration is discussed in the next section). In case you forget to use it, you can choose Options from the VBE's Tools menu, click the Editor tab, and make sure that the Require Variable Declaration check box is filled. Then all new modules automatically include the `Option Explicit` statement.

Now, all that's necessary is to type a statement such as the following somewhere below the `Option Explicit` statement:

`Sub MoveListToDatabase`

The string `MoveListToDatabase` becomes the name of the subroutine, by virtue of being the first string of characters following the keyword `Sub`. When you have finished typing the name of the subroutine, press Enter. When you do, two things immediately happen:

- An empty pair of parentheses is automatically provided following the name of the subroutine (unless you've typed the parentheses yourself).
- An End Sub statement is provided, with an empty line between the Sub and the End Sub where you can begin entering your code.

Both of these have already happened in Figure 7.5.

At this point, you've established a subroutine: You've provided a beginning statement (`Sub`) and an ending statement (`End Sub`), and there is a pair of parentheses at the end of the `Sub` statement (see Figure 7.5). You could now switch back to the workbook window, choose Tools, Macro, Macros, select the `MoveListToDatabase` macro, and click the Run button. The subroutine would run, although it wouldn't do anything because you have not yet supplied the subroutine with any instructions—statements that indicate where to find data and what to do with it.

Figure 7.5
The subroutine's basic elements are now complete.

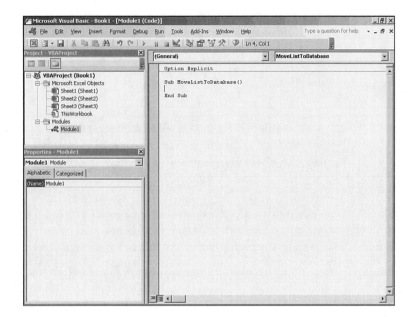

Declaring Variables

The previous section urged you to use `Option Explicit`, and to use the Require Variable Declaration option to provide that statement automatically. The following paragraph provides the reason.

In the bad old days—roughly, the 1950s through the 1980s—coding followed a go-as-you-please approach (*coding* is just another term for *programming*). When you needed a new variable, all you had to do was use it. For example, this would have been not only syntactically legal, but part of established practice even if the program had never mentioned the existence of a `NumberOfRows` variable prior to that statement:

```
NumberOfRows = Rows(MyMatrix)
```

This sort of thing led to code that was very difficult to understand and document, much less troubleshoot. Especially in a lengthy program, it was all too possible for the coder to forget that he had already used a `NumberOfRows` variable to store the number of rows in the range named `MyMatrix`. Then he might create yet another variable to carry the same information, just by using a new one on the fly. Imagine the difficulty faced by the programmer months or even years later, trying to remember what he had in mind with two variables for a single purpose.

7

Worse yet, the unfortunate coder might remember that he was already using a variable named `NumberOfRows`, but err typographically when using it later. Suppose that he wanted to start creating a square range by putting the value of `NumberOfRows` into a variable named `NumberOfColumns`:

```
NumberOfColumns = NumberOfRow
```

But look what he's done: He has miskeyed `NumberOfRows` by leaving off the final *s*. In so doing, he's created a new variable—remember, they can be created just by using them. And a new variable would have the special value of Empty, indicating that the variable is as yet uninitialized. So, the variable `NumberOfColumns`, instead of taking as its value the number of rows in `MyMatrix`, takes the value 0 from `NumberOfRow`.

> **NOTE** A variable declared in this way (thus, in the absence of `Option Explicit`) using VBA would be of a special type, Variant. Variant variables start life with a special value: `Empty`. Numeric variables begin as zero, and string variables begin as zero-length strings ("").

Things are not going to work as the programmer had anticipated. It's going to be tough for him to figure out what's gone wrong because he'll be looking for problems with `NumberOfColumns` when the source of the problem is `NumberOfRow`.

One good way to protect yourself against this sort of nonsense is to require variable declaration. That means that before you can use a variable, you have to *declare* it. In VBA, you do that with a `Dim` statement such as this one, which declares two variables:

```
Dim NumberOfRows As Integer, NumberOfColumns As Integer
```

`Dim`, like `Sub`, is a little misleading. It is short for *dimension*, which traditionally meant to specify the structure of a memory array. In VBA syntax, when you *dim* a variable, you declare to the VBE that the variable exists, and you usually also declare what sorts of values the variable can take on. In this example, the variables `NumberOfRows` and `NumberOfColumns` can take on integer values only: Neither one of them can equal 5.3 or 5/4/2009 or "Fred."

In this example, then, the effect of `Option Explicit` is to prevent you from using a variable named `NumberOfRow` (again, note the missing final *s*) when you haven't already declared it. So, if you miskey a variable's name, you won't have automatically created a new variable. The VBE will note that you're trying to use an undeclared variable and will warn you with an error message.

The effect of declaring your variables in one or more `Dim` statements is that you can look back to see what variables you have declared. It's a lot easier to find them in `Dim` statements than it is to scan an entire program looking for first instances of a variable. This helps you avoid declaring multiple variables to accomplish the same purpose.

> **NOTE**
> It's also considered good programming practice to declare your variables at the beginning of a sub-routine or the beginning of a module, and *not* defer any declarations until farther down in the code. It is, however, legal to do so.

If you *don't* use `Option Explicit`, the VBE will not complain when you suddenly refer to a new variable—whether or not you mean to. It will let you use that new variable and, by the way, it will give that variable the most flexible (and resource-intensive) type: Variant. A variable whose type is Variant can take on nearly any sort of value: integers, decimal numbers, strings, dates, and so on.

The Variant type is the default in a `Dim` statement such as this:

```
Dim NumberOfRows, NumberOfColumns
```

If you don't specify the type of a variable, it defaults to Variant. This is better than not declaring variables at all in the absence of `Option Explicit`, but it's much better to declare a variable's type. Among other reasons, you protect yourself against assigning, say, "Fred" to a variable declared as Integer.

> **NOTE**
> It's in the `Dim` statement that you'll declare variables that represent database objects. You must first establish a reference to the object library, as discussed earlier in this chapter. But after that reference has been established, you can use statements such as these:
> ```
> Dim dbMyDatabase As Database
> Dim tdfDoors As TableDef
> Dim qdfDoors As QueryDef
> ```

> **TIP**
> To start the name of a variable with a clue to what it represents is a matter of personal style, but it can't hurt and can sometimes help. In the example from the previous note, the variable `qdfDoors` is declared to be a query definition (QueryDef). The 3-letter string *qdf* can help you or someone else remember, later in the code, that `qdfDoors` represents a query definition.

Understanding Dot Notation

This chapter's first section mentioned that the Excel object model is a hierarchy. For example, one object near the top of the hierarchy is the *workbook*. Workbooks have worksheets that belong to them. In turn, worksheets have rows and columns and cells. (Worksheets have many other objects as well. This book focuses on objects that are important for data management, and the Comment object, for example, isn't critical to managing data.)

In the course of moving data to a database from a worksheet, or to a worksheet from a database, you always need to direct attention to the particular column, row, or cell from which you want to get data or to which you want to write it. And that requirement implies that you need to specify the worksheet where the column, row, or cell is found. Furthermore, if more than one workbook is open when your code runs, you need to specify which workbook you're interested in.

VBA handles all this by means of items and dot notation:

- When you're dealing with a collection of objects, such as a collection of worksheets in a workbook, you identify a particular object as an item. For example,

```
Worksheets("Sheet1")
```

refers to the worksheet named Sheet1. You can also use an object's number instead of its name:

```
Worksheets(1)
```

but this can be tricky unless you're absolutely certain that you know which worksheet the number 1 refers to; it's often Sheet1 but it can easily be some other worksheet. Typically you specify an object by means of its name. Sometimes you specify it by its number, especially in the context of loops (see "Using Loops," later in this chapter).

- You refer to an object that belongs to another object by connecting them with dots. Here's an example:

```
Worksheets("Sheet2").ChartObjects("Chart 1")
```

This statement uses dot notation to refer to the embedded chart named Chart 1 on the worksheet named Sheet2: Notice the dot between the first closing parenthesis and the keyword `ChartObjects`. If you didn't specify where to look for Chart 1, on Sheet2, you'd get an error message. In general, whatever follows a dot belongs to whatever precedes that dot.

In the object model, objects "have" other objects: A workbook has worksheets, a worksheet has cells, cells have borders. But objects also have properties and methods. In your code, you also use dot notation to connect properties and methods to the objects that have them.

For example, you might want to activate Chart 1 on Sheet2. This statement would do that:

```
Worksheets("Sheet2").ChartObjects("Chart 1").Activate
```

The statement says to activate something. Lots of things can be activated: workbooks, worksheets, charts, and so on. This statement refers to the `Activate` method as it applies to the chart object named Chart 1 that's found on the worksheet that's named Sheet2.

After your code has activated the chart, you might want it to change the chart's type from whatever it started out as—a column chart, perhaps—to a line chart with markers. You could use this statement to do that:

```
ActiveChart.ChartType = xlLineMarkers
```

Here, you begin by referencing the active chart (it's up to you to make sure that there is an active chart at the point that VBA executes the statement). Charts have properties, and one of those properties is the chart's type: column, bar, line, XY (Scatter), and so on. Therefore, the statement determines the chart's type by assigning a particular value, xlLineMarkers, to the ChartType property.

It can help to think of methods and properties in concrete terms. One homely example might be a car. You could consider that a car has several methods, and one of them is the LeftTurn method. You would execute that method to make the car turn left. You could consider that a car has several properties, and one of them is the Color property. You might set its Color property to Red, Blue, Beige—whatever color you want that's available.

If you're new to VBA, the distinction between a method and a property might seem a little obscure. Don't worry about it: Over time and with experience, it gets clearer.

> **TIP**
>
> One great way to become familiar with VBA in general and dot notation in particular is to use the macro recorder. Choose Tools, Macro, Record New Macro, and click OK. Then do something relevant to Excel: Open a workbook or delete a row or enter a value or insert a name. Then click the Stop Recording button, switch to the VBE, and examine the code that has been recorded for you. You'll see one way that VBA would automate whatever you just did manually. See "Understanding the Macro Recorder's Code," later in this chapter.

> **NOTE**
>
> Formally, your reference to a collection of objects is to a property. So, in this statement
>
>   Worksheets("Sheet1").Rows(2)
>
> the reference to Rows is to a property of the worksheet: The collection of the 65,536 rows on that worksheet, and a collection is not an object. But as soon as you specify which row you're referring to (here, that's *2*), you've made reference to an object. That's why, when you examine the object model in the VBA Help documentation, you see that Rows is a *property* of the Worksheet object.

Using Loops

It often happens in VBA code—particularly code that is intended to add, edit, copy, move, or delete data values—that you want to make reference to many values or cells or rows, one at a time. You might want to add recently obtained records to a set that already exists, or to edit many values by concatenating onto each a string such as @mydomain.com, or to add new records to a database table and assign them values from your worksheet.

By designing loops correctly, you can carry out actions a huge number of times and get your results with great speed and accuracy.

Using For-Next Loops

A For-Next loop is a fundamental structure in VBA code. It's a basic way of taking an action or set of actions a specified number of times. Here's a straightforward example:

```
For RowCounter = 1 To 10
        Cells(RowCounter, 1) = RowCounter
Next RowCounter
```

The statement inside the loop, between the `For` statement and the `Next` statement, assigns a value to a cell. This fragment

```
Cells(RowCounter, 1)
```

refers to a cell in the `RowCounter` row and in column 1. After the `Cells` keyword, the first number in parenthesis specifies the row, and the second number specifies the column.

This loop runs 10 times:

1. The `For` statement specifies that `RowCounter` starts with a value of 1.

2. Any statements between the `For` and the `Next` are executed. In this example, the current value of `RowCounter` is put into the cell defined by the `RowCounter` row and the first column.

3. The `Next` statement increments `RowCounter` by 1, and control of the program returns to the top of the loop.

4. The loop executes again, with `RowCounter` equal to 2. Then it executes again, with `RowCounter` equal to 3. Each time, it executes any statements found between the `For` statement and the `Next` statement.

After 10 circuits through the loop, the value of `RowCounter` is incremented to 11. But this is one more than the final value specified by the `For` statement, so the loop terminates before it can run an eleventh time. The result is that on the active sheet, cell A1 contains 1, cell A2 contains 2,..., cell A10 contains 10.

This is nearly a trivial use of a `For-Next` loop, of course, but it illustrates the basic idea and some of the aspects of a `For-Next` loop. And simple as it is, it has its uses. Suppose that you're using the loop to return records, one by one, from a table in a database and into a worksheet. You want the worksheet to associate the records' values on a specific field with their record numbers. One good way to show record numbers is to put the record number in column A, as in this example, and the record's value on a field such as Age in column B. Using the counter's value on each circuit through the loop is a handy way to provide a record number.

Looping with Item Numbers

Earlier this chapter cautioned you about using an item number to refer to a particular object. When you first write a statement, `Worksheets(2)` might well refer to the worksheet named Sheet2. But if later another worksheet is inserted before Sheet2, there's no telling which worksheet that `Worksheets(2)` refers to.

But it's a different situation when you want to refer, in turn, to each object in a collection. In that case, you're not interested so much in a particular worksheet, say, as you are in addressing all the worksheets, one by one. Then an item number used in conjunction with a loop makes good sense. Here's an example:

```
Option Explicit

Sub RefreshAllPivotTables()

Dim i As Integer, j As Integer
Dim SheetCount As Integer, PivotTableCount As Integer
```

The code begins by declaring four variables. The first two, i and j, will be used as counters in For-Next loops. The second two, SheetCount and PTCount, will be used to determine how many times the loops execute.

```
SheetCount = ActiveWorkbook.Worksheets.Count
```

This statement sets the variable SheetCount to a particular value: the number of worksheets in the active workbook. The dot notation begins with the active workbook, and moves from there to the collection of worksheets in the active workbook.

The collection of worksheets, as is true of all collections, has the Count property. In this case, the Count property returns the number of worksheets in the active workbook. That number is assigned to the variable SheetCount.

```
For i = 1 To SheetCount
```

The code enters a For-Next loop. It will execute once for every worksheet in the active workbook. The counter i starts at 1 the first time through, increments to 2 the next time, 3 the next time, and so on until it's greater than the value of SheetCount.

```
ActiveWorkbook.Worksheets(i).Activate
```

This statement activates a worksheet in the active workbook. Which worksheet is activated depends on the current value of i: the first, the second, the third, and so on.

```
PivotTableCount = ActiveSheet.PivotTables.Count
```

The active sheet might have any number of pivot tables: zero, one, five—you don't know and for the purposes of this code you don't care. Just as the variable SheetCount was set to the number of worksheets in the active workbook, the variable PivotTableCount is set to the number of pivot tables in the active sheet.

Notice, though, that the value of SheetCount is set only once, before any loops are entered. The value of PivotTableCount is reset once again, *each time a new worksheet is activated*. VBA does all the counting on your behalf: It counts the number of worksheets to activate, and on each worksheet it counts the number of pivot tables to refresh.

Next an *inner* For-Next loop starts. The counter j begins at 1 and increments by 1 as it loops through all the pivot tables on the active worksheet, as determined by the current value of PivotTableCount.

```
For j = 1 To PivotTableCount
    ActiveSheet.PivotTables(j).PivotCache.Refresh
Next j
```

The inner `For-Next` loop refreshes the cache of each pivot table on the active sheet. There are three points about this loop to note in particular:

- It's an inner loop; that is, it exists inside another loop. This sort of structure is often termed a *nested loop*, and it's a useful technique any time you're dealing with a collection (here, pivot tables) that's subordinate to another collection (here, worksheets).

- The inner loop is controlled by a different counter than the outer loop. It would be syntactically illegal (as well as logically senseless) to use `i` for both the inner and outer loop.

- No harm is done if the active worksheet has no pivot tables. In that case, `PivotTableCount` has been set equal to zero, and the `For` statement runs the counter from 1 to 0—that is to say, not at all, so it doesn't try to refresh any pivot tables.

 TIP   A `For` counter *can* run from 1 to 0, but you have to arrange for that by adding something like `Step -1` to the `For` statement: `For j = 1 to 0 Step -1`. The default is to increase the counter by 1 each time the loop executes.

Finally,

```
Next i
```

causes the outer loop to continue to the next value of its loop counter.

```
End Sub
```

End the subroutine after the outer loop terminates.

Notice the way that the subroutine is designed: It activates every worksheet in the workbook, one by one. When a given worksheet has been activated, it refreshes every pivot table on that worksheet, one by one. So, you're not setting yourself up for a problem as you might by referring to a *specific* item number such as `Worksheets(2)` or `Worksheets("Sheet1").PivotTables(3)`.

Looping with `Do While`

`For-Next` loops give your code *structure*; that is, they execute a given number of times. Even if you don't know beforehand how many times a loop will execute, you're forced to provide an endpoint for the loop. In the last example, the endpoints were `SheetCount` for the outer loop and `PivotTableCount` for the inner loop. VBA evaluates those endpoints before the loop begins to run, and therefore has determined exactly how many times it will execute.

A different situation calls for a different sort of approach. You often find that you need to loop through subsets of records, and each subset can have a different number of records. That situation is discussed in the following case study.

CASE STUDY

You have in an Excel worksheet a list of vendors and the amounts that you have paid each one during the prior fiscal year. In the process of closing the books for that year, you want to store the total amount paid to each vendor in an external database. Your data is laid out as shown in Figure 7.6.

Figure 7.6
Data sets that have varying numbers of records in different groups, as here, often call for Do While loops.

You would like to get a total dollar amount for each vendor shown in Figure 7.6. Notice that different vendors have different numbers of records, and that the records have already been sorted by vendor name. You'd rather not get a count of records for each vendor—which would be necessary if you were to use a For-Next loop to total the purchase amounts from a vendor.

If you didn't intend to move the information to a database, this would be an obvious and ideal setup for a pivot table. You could cause the PivotTable Wizard to use the data in columns A and B as its source, and construct a table with Vendor as its row field and Sum of Amount as its data field. But because you want to automatically update a database with vendor totals, a pivot table won't help you: A pivot table can import external data but it can't export it. Instead, you use the following code in preparation to update the database. You begin by setting a reference to the DAO object library, as discussed earlier in this chapter in "Using Other Applications' Object Models." You then declare the subroutine and the variables it needs:

```
Sub TotalVendorPurchases()

Dim InputRow As Long, OutputRow As Long, FinalRow As Long
Dim PurchasesFromVendor As Currency
```

7

```
Dim CurrentVendor As String
Dim VendorBuys As DAO.Recordset
Dim Vendors2004 As DAO.Database
```

Excel worksheets can have as many as 65,536 rows. The variables `InputRow`, `OutputRow`, and `FinalRow` will each contain a row number and it is conceivable that the row numbers will be greater than 32,767—the maximum legal value for an integer variable. Therefore, you declare the variables as Long—a numeric type that is an integer but can take on values (much) larger than 65,536.

You also declare two object variables, one to represent the database and one to represent a set of records, or *recordset*, in the database. Your code then sets the two object variables. It sets the `Vendors2004` object variable equal to an existing Access database, found in the same path as your workbook. The code then sets the `VendorBuys` object variable equal to a table, `TotalByVendor`, in that database.

```
Set Vendors2004 = OpenDatabase(ThisWorkbook.Path & "\2004 Finals.mdb")
Set VendorBuys = Vendors2004.OpenRecordset("TotalByVendor", dbOpenDynaset)
```

Next, you need to find out how far down into the worksheet your data extends:

```
FinalRow = Worksheets("Purchases").Cells(65536, 1).End(xlUp).Row
```

The `End(xlUp)` usage is a valuable one. You use it here to determine how far down the worksheet the code should look in its search for more records. Suppose that you activate cell A65536 (the final cell in Column A), that it is an empty cell, and that you hold down the Ctrl key and then press the Up Arrow button. Excel would make the active cell the first one above A65536 that is *not* empty. That's what this statement does: It starts in Cells(65536,1) and travels to the end, going up until it locates a non-empty cell. Whatever that end cell is, its row number is assigned to the `FinalRow` variable. (You can also use `xlDown`, `xlToRight`, and `xlToLeft`, depending on what you want to accomplish.)

```
OutputRow = 1
InputRow = 2
```

The output will begin in row 1 and the input begins in row 2, because of the row headers Vendor and Amount.

```
CurrentVendor = Worksheets("Purchases").Cells(InputRow, 1)
```

You store the current value of the vendor name in the variable `CurrentVendor`. As the code proceeds through the rows of input, the vendor name changes. When that occurs, the total purchases for that vendor are written to an output sheet and to the database, and variables are re-initialized.

```
Do While InputRow <= FinalRow
```

The outer loop will run as long as the row from which input is taken is less than or equal to the final row of input data.

```
Do While CurrentVendor = Worksheets("Purchases").Cells(InputRow, 1)
```

The inner loop runs as long as the vendor name in the current row of input equals the value of `CurrentVendor`.

```
PurchasesFromVendor = PurchasesFromVendor + _
Worksheets("Purchases").Cells(InputRow, 2)
```

Until the inner loop terminates (when the vendor name changes) continue to increment the total purchases for that vendor by the value found in the current input row, second column.

```
InputRow = InputRow + 1
```

And increment the value of `InputRow`, so that the next time through the loop will look at the next row down the worksheet.

```
Loop
```

The `Loop` statement marks the end of the inner loop. When the vendor name changes, the inner loop terminates and the following code executes:

```
Worksheets("TotalByVendor").Cells(OutputRow, 1) = CurrentVendor
Worksheets("TotalByVendor").Cells(OutputRow, 2) = PurchasesFromVendor
With VendorBuys
    .AddNew
    .Fields("VendorName") = CurrentVendor
    .Fields("PurchaseTotal") = PurchasesFromVendor
    .Update
End With
OutputRow = OutputRow + 1
CurrentVendor = Worksheets("Purchases").Cells(InputRow, 1)
PurchasesFromVendor = 0
```

In English (not in the BASIC programming language): Write the name of the current vendor to column 1 of the `TotalByVendor` worksheet, in the row identified by `OutputRow`. Write the total purchases from that vendor in column 2 of the same row. Add a new record to the database table and set that record's two fields equal to the name of the current vendor and the total of the purchases from that vendor. Establish the new record by calling the table's Update method. Increment `OutputRow` by 1. Get the next vendor name from the `Purchases` worksheet and store it in `CurrentVendor`. Reset `PurchasesFromVendor` to zero.

```
Loop
End Sub
```

Terminate the outer loop when `InputRow` has become greater than `FinalRow`, and terminate the subroutine.

Figure 7.7 shows what the output looks like when the code has completed.

7

Figure 7.7
These records appear the same in the database table as they do in the worksheet range.

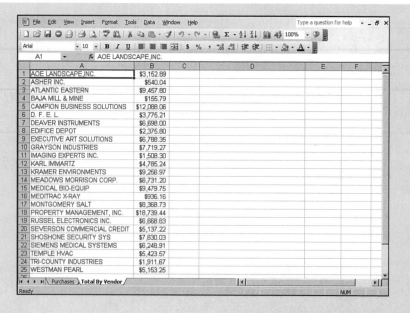

Using With **Blocks**

A handy and useful way of using dot notation concerns what are termed With-End With blocks, or simply With blocks. You use the keyword With, teamed with an object of some sort, to indicate that one or more subsequent statements pertain to other objects (or properties or methods) that belong to the object named in the With. Everything from the With statement through the accompanying End With statement is considered part of the With block.

It's a lot easier to understand With blocks by looking at them than by reading about them. Here's an example, first with no With block and then using one:

```
ActiveSheet.Rows(2).Font.ColorIndex = 3
ActiveSheet.Rows(2).Font.Bold = True
```

These two statements, when executed, turn the font color of the active sheet's second row to red, and its style to bold.

```
With ActiveSheet.Rows(2)
    .Font.ColorIndex = 3
    .Font.Bold = True
End With
```

These four statements do the same thing as the prior two. Inside the block—that is, after the With statement—whatever begins with a dot is deemed to belong to the object that's cited in the With statement. In the prior example, the font, its color index, and its style are taken to belong to the second row of the active sheet.

You can extend the reach of the With statement beyond what was shown earlier. Because the Font property starts both the statements after the With statement, it could be moved up to the outer With:

```
With ActiveSheet.Rows(2).Font
    .ColorIndex = 3
    .Bold = True
End With
```

Nested With Blocks

With statements can be nested within other With statements. The requirement, of course, is that the element used in the inner With must belong to the element used in the outer With. Here's an example that doesn't use a nested With, but could:

```
With ActiveSheet.Cells(10, 12)
    .VerticalAlignment = xlTop
    .WrapText = True
    .Font.Name = "Times New Roman"
    .Font.Size = 12
End With
```

This code sets four properties for cell L10 on the active sheet: Its value is displayed beginning at the top of the cell, lengthy text is wrapped, its font is Times New Roman, and its font size is 12. Because the cell's Font property is used twice within the block, it makes sense to revise it as a nested With, as follows:

```
With ActiveSheet.Cells(10, 12)
    .VerticalAlignment = xlTop
    .WrapText = True
    With .Font
        .Name = "Times New Roman"
        .Size = 12
    End With
End With
```

Notice the second inner With block. The fact that its element, .Font, begins with a dot means that it belongs to a prior With—here, cell L10 on the active sheet.

Understanding the Rationale for With Blocks

With blocks are touted as a way to speed up processing. The notion is that it takes more time to interpret these two statements

```
ActiveSheet.Rows(2).Font.ColorIndex = 3
ActiveSheet.Rows(2).Font.Bold = True
```

than to interpret this With block, even though it has two additional statements:

```
With ActiveSheet.Rows(2).Font
    .ColorIndex = 3
    .Bold = True
End With
```

Although it's true that there's an increase in speed, for most purposes, the increase is imperceptible. The following two subroutines were run on a 1.8GHz Pentium 4. The first one has no With block and took 17 seconds to run to conclusion on a fresh worksheet:

```
Sub NoWith()
Dim i As Integer
For i = 1 To 10000
ActiveSheet.Cells(i, 1).VerticalAlignment = xlTop
ActiveSheet.Cells(i, 1).WrapText = True
ActiveSheet.Cells(i, 1).Font.Name = "Times New Roman"
ActiveSheet.Cells(i, 1).Font.Size = 12
Next i
End Sub
```

The second one uses nested With blocks and took 14 seconds, again on a fresh worksheet:

```
Sub WithWiths()
Dim i As Integer
For i = 1 To 10000
With ActiveSheet.Cells(i, 1)
    .VerticalAlignment = xlTop
    .WrapText = True
    With .Font
        .Name = "Times New Roman"
        .Size = 12
    End With
End With
Next i
End Sub
```

Fourteen seconds versus 17 seconds is an 18% increase in speed. But if you format 100 rows instead of 10,000 you're unlikely to notice that 18%. And some tasks are not sped up at all by using With blocks.

With blocks are better thought of as a way to encourage you to structure your code more tightly. They save you keystrokes, even though they always add two statements to the code (the With and the End With). Because you don't need to repeatedly type, or to copy and paste, the element in the With statement, you find yourself using With blocks as a timesaver.

One consequence is better structure in your code. For example, it's not at all unusual to enter a VBA statement that sets some object's property: a cell's font size, or the maximum value shown on a chart axis, or the number format property of a pivot table's data field.

Subsequently, 10 statements farther down in your code, you decide to set some other property belonging to the same object: the cell's height or the chart axis's text alignment, or the data field's summary statistic. It's tempting to just type the statement that would set the property.

But if you have in mind your later problems—maintaining the code, or debugging it, or walking someone else through it—you'll go back and put that statement along with the earlier statement in a With block. When you can rationally do so, it's best to keep statements that operate on the same object together. As a bonus, you'll find yourself doing less typing after you've established the With block—and the less typing you do, the better.

Understanding the Macro Recorder's Code

You very likely know that you can record VBA code that, when run, repeats any actions that you took while the recorder was running. The rationale for this is not so much to record a utility that saves you having to take the same keyboard or mouse pointer sequence over and over, although this does happen. The real benefit of recording macros is to learn more about VBA.

If you're not familiar with the macro recorder, try it out. Choose Tools, Macro, Record New Macro. Click OK in the Record Macro dialog box (see Figure 7.8).

Figure 7.8
For something you use frequently, you can store the recorded macro in a personal macro workbook.

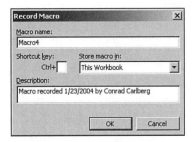

Now do something relevant to Excel—enter a value in a cell, or sort a range of values, or copy and paste something. Click the Stop Recording button or choose Tools, Macro, Stop Recording (see Figure 7.9).

Figure 7.9
Click the Stop Recording button when you're through taking actions that you want recorded in VBA.

Stop Recording button

Press Alt+F11 to switch to the VBE. You'll see something similar to what is shown in Figure 7.10.

The code you see in Figure 7.10 was created by the macro recorder in response to these actions:

1. Set the active cell's number format to Currency.
2. Set the active cell's horizontal alignment to Right (Indent).
3. Set the active cell's font to Courier.
4. Give the active cell a thin left border.

The macro recorder attempts to provide code that's comprehensive, and so doesn't limit itself strictly to the results of actions taken by the user. For example, it uses a With block to set nine formatting aspects of the selected cell: number format, horizontal alignment, vertical alignment, text wrapping, and so on. It does this even though the only properties belonging directly to the selection that were changed were its number format, horizontal alignment, its font and its left border.

Figure 7.10
The macro recorder usually records much more than actually took place.

> **NOTE**
> Although the macro recorder attempts to be comprehensive, there are actions you might take while recording that don't get recorded, or that don't record as you might expect them to. For example, if you switch to another application, or even to the VBE, while recording a macro, this action goes unrecorded. If you take an action repeatedly, the recorder does not put a For-Next or a Do While loop in the code; it just records each action separately. The recorder does not declare variables for you. If you can't do it on the worksheet, the recorder ignores it.

The recorder responds not to changes in worksheet elements, but to their properties following some action taken by the user. After setting the horizontal alignment to Right (Indent), the other properties (vertical alignment, text wrapping, and so on through cell merging) were as shown in the recorded code. They were left alone, but the recorder doesn't know that.

Working directly with the code created by the recorder has several benefits. Two of the most important are discussed in the next two sections.

Learning the Names in the Object Model

The Excel object model is so large that it's not feasible, nor even sensible, to learn all its objects, methods, and properties. Even if you did, you'd still need the names of the values that the properties can take on.

For example, using the Range object's End property can take you up or down from a selection—you can use xlUp or xlDown. But to go left or right, you have to specify xlToLeft or xlToRight. It's pointless to remember that. Stuck for a name, use the macro recorder to provide it for you.

On the other hand, there are some objects and constructions that you use so frequently while developing your code that you really have to know their names. Otherwise, you'll spend your time ineffectively. Suppose that you frequently format cells, as Currency, or Date, or Percentage. In that case, it's important to know what string you use to call for a particular number format. And the fastest way to find that out is seldom by means of the Help documentation, but by recording a macro that assigns a format to a cell and then examining the code that results.

Adapting the Code to Another Purpose

It often happens that you're coding some task when you're brought up short: You realize that you've taken the next step many times on the worksheet but never in code. You've inserted a new name for a range, for example, or sorted a range of cells into ascending order. Now you want to do something similar in your VBA code, but you have no idea how to go about it.

The macro recorder is an ideal solution here. Suppose that you want to know how to call for VBA to sort the data in a range of cells. You happen to have data in cells A1:B17, and cells A1 and B1 contain row headers (in other words, you have an Excel list in A1:B17). So, click in some cell inside A1:B17—say, A7—and choose Tools, Macro, Record New Macro to find out how to sort it using VBA.

Then sort the list. Assume that you sort first on the values found in Column B, and then on the values found in Column A, and that you want an ascending sort on both columns. In the Sort dialog box, if necessary, you identify Row 1 as a header row. You click OK, stop the macro recorder, switch to the VBE, and see the following:

```
Range("A7").Select
Range("A1:B17").Sort Key1:=Range("B2"), Order1:=xlAscending, Key2:=Range( _
    "A2"), Order2:=xlAscending, Header:=xlGuess, OrderCustom:=1, MatchCase _
    :=False, Orientation:=xlTopToBottom, DataOption1:=xlSortNormal, _
    DataOption2:=xlSortNormal
```

The first statement just shows that you started out by selecting cell A7, a cell inside the range you want to sort.

The next statement shows you that in general you get VBA to sort a range of cells by calling that range's Sort method. In the code for the more generalized task that you're coding, you might use something like this:

```
Dim SortRange As Range
Set SortRange = ActiveSheet.Range(Cells(1, 1), Cells(17, 2))

SortRange.Sort Key1:=SortRange.Offset(1, 1).Resize(1, 1), _
    Order1:=xlAscending, Key2:=SortRange.Offset(1, 0).Resize(1, 1), _
    Order2:=xlAscending, Header:=xlYes
```

7

There are several aspects to this code that are worth noting:

- The address of the sort range is not specified in the statement that performs the Sort method. Instead, an *object variable* (see this chapter's next section, "Using Object Variables") that represents a range is assigned to a range of cells (here, A1:B17). That object variable, standing in for the actual range, is sorted.

- The sort keys are still B2 and A2 (in that order), but they're referred to as offsets from the upper-left cell of the range. The cell B2 is offset from A1 by one row and one column; the cell A2 is offset from A1 by one row and zero columns. This way, the sort statement does not use the cell references "B2" and "A2" that are provided by the macro recorder. That makes it possible to use the sort statement elsewhere in your code when you want to sort a range that does *not* include B2 or A2.

- The Header specification in the code provided by the macro recorder uses xlGuess; that is, Excel is required to determine whether or not the range has a header row. The revised code specifies xlYes because the programmer knows that the range has a header row.

- The code has been shorn of extraneous specifications, such as DataOption1 and MatchCase. When you adapt something you get from the macro recorder, you spend some time getting rid of unnecessary code that the recorder, in its effort to be comprehensive, insists on providing.

You'll notice that the code generated by the macro recorder frequently uses Select, sets the properties of selections, and carries out methods that apply to the selections. For example

```
Range("A2").Select
Selection.Font.ColorIndex = 3
```

If you use this as a building block for a different subroutine, you could and should change that to something such as

```
Range("A2").Font.ColorIndex = 3
```

There's no requirement that you select an object before you set one of its properties; to do so slows down your code needlessly and makes it that much more difficult to maintain.

Using Object Variables

Object variables occupy an important place in VBA for Excel, and later in this book when database structures are discussed, they assume even greater importance. It's possible to use VBA effectively without knowing how to use object variables, but it isn't easy.

Understanding Object Variables

Consider the notion of age as a variable. It's something you measure when you're dealing with information about people. If you're issuing them driver's licenses, you measure their age. If you hire them, you put their age—at least, their date of birth—in a file. If you're meeting them socially, you make a mental note with a rough estimate of their age.

Age is a variable. It varies from person to person. Each person has *an* age: 75 years, 52 years, 16 months, 25 days, and so on. A single age is a value that the variable Age can assume.

In VBA, if you're dealing with information about people, you might well declare a variable named Age:

```
Dim Age As Single
```

Declaring Age in this way, as a single-precision number, means first that it *is* a number and not, say, a text string such as "Tom"; second it means that Age can have fractional values, such as 75.083 and 1.3. Having declared it, you can use it in statements such as this one:

```
Age = 52.5
```

VBA knows nothing about ordinary variables such as Age, except that as declared here it's a number and it can have fractional values. It doesn't know that, in people, age values usually run from 0 to the 80s, or that it has to be at least 18 for its owner to vote in state and federal elections, or that society attaches certain attitudes to certain ranges of age.

In contrast, an object variable in VBA is a special kind, and VBA knows quite a lot about it. An object variable can represent an Excel worksheet range, for example. I have to declare it as such; for example,

```
Dim TheRange As Range
```

but after I've done so, VBA knows that

- TheRange can take on values such as A1:B17, or C4:C65536, or even D4 (yes, a single cell is a range as far as the object model is concerned). TheRange can take on any set of cells as its value.
- TheRange has some number of columns, some number of rows, possibly a font, the capability to be sorted, and all the other properties and methods that belong to ranges, no matter which cells they comprise.

In the prior section, you saw this code used:

```
Dim SortRange As Range
Set SortRange = ActiveSheet.Range(Cells(1, 1), Cells(17, 2))
```

It uses SortRange as an object variable, first declaring to VBA that it will represent range values (which are sets of cells) and then assigning a particular set of cells, A1:B17, to the object variable SortRange. By assigning the cell addresses to the object variable, and then using the Sort method on the range that the variable represents, the programmer keeps specific cell addresses out of the sort statement. In turn, that enables the programmer to use the sort statement over and over, on different sets of cells, just by assigning different ranges to the SortRange object variable.

Setting Object Variables

Notice how the range of cells—the value—is assigned to SortRange—the variable. When you assign some value to a simple variable such as Age, all you need to do is mention the variable's name, enter an equal sign, and then enter the value you want the variable to have.

In contrast, when you're working with an object variable, you have to use the special keyword `Set`. Then continue as with a simple variable: mention its name, provide an equal sign, and then enter the value you want the object variable to have. Here are a few more examples:

```
Dim WS As Worksheet
Set WS = ThisWorkbook.Worksheets("Sheet1")
WS.Move Before:=Sheets(1)

Dim TheName As Name
Set TheName = ActiveWorkbook.Names("Revenues")
TheName.RefersTo = "=Purchases!$A$1:$B$19"

Dim TheChart As Chart
Set TheChart = Workbooks("Quarter2.xls").Charts("Costs")
TheChart.ChartType = xlLine
```

Declaring Object Variables

Object variables can represent many Excel objects beside ranges. A person who writes VBA code for Excel often uses object variables to represent columns, rows, toolbars, charts, chart components such as axes and data series, worksheets, and so on. It's even possible to assign a module with VBA code to an object variable.

In general, you can use VBA to declare an object variable representing anything in an Excel workbook that is in the object model. By doing so, you declare that it *is* an object variable. After you've declared an object variable, you cannot assign to it anything that's a different type. For example, if you have declared `TheAxis` to represent a chart axis

```
Dim TheAxis As Axis
```

you cannot assign a value such as 2 to it. That is, this statement

```
Set TheAxis = 2
```

would result in the compile error `Type Mismatch`.

Objects in `For Each` Loops

This chapter has already discussed `For-Next` loops and `Do While` loops in the section "Using Loops." Another sort of loop, the `For Each` loop, is handy when you're working with object variables.

Like a `For-Next` loop, a `For Each` loop executes a specific number of times, once for each instance of a variable. In a `For-Next` loop, the variable is a simple one, often an Integer or Long Integer, that runs from a starting value to an ending value. In a `For Each` loop, that variable is an object variable that takes on each available instance of its object type.

Suppose that you wanted to assign a name representing a year (2003, 2004, 2005, and so on) to each worksheet in a workbook named Annual Results. The following code shows one way to do that:

```
Dim WS As Worksheet
Dim WhichYear As Integer
WhichYear = 2003
For Each WS In Workbooks("Annual Results").Worksheets
    WS.Name = WhichYear
    WhichYear = WhichYear + 1
Next WS
```

Two variables are declared: one object variable, `WS`, to represent worksheets and one simple variable, `WhichYear`, to represent integer numbers. `WhichYear` is initialized to 2003 and a `For Each` loop starts.

The `For Each` statement, coupled with the `Next` statement, causes the object variable `WS` to take on, in turn, each worksheet in the collection of worksheets that belongs to the work-book named Annual Results. Each time through the loop, the object variable `WS` represents a different worksheet, and the name of that worksheet is set to the current value of `WhichYear`. Then `WhichYear` is incremented, the `Next WS` assigns the next worksheet to `WS`, and the loop repeats. When the final worksheet in the collection has been processed, the loop terminates.

These elements are necessary for a `For Each` loop to work properly:

- The name of an object variable must follow the `For Each` keywords.
- The object variable must be followed by a collection, and the collection must be of the same type as the object variable. In the example given earlier, the object variable `WS` is declared with the Worksheet type. The collection of worksheets in a workbook are also of type Worksheet.
- It's usually necessary to specify what the collection belongs to. In the example, the collection of worksheets belongs to the workbook named Annual Results.

Looking Ahead

This chapter reviewed the aspects of VBA that help you get to data existing on a worksheet. VBA is often the best way to automate moving data from a database into a worksheet, and it's always the best way to automate the export of data from Excel to a database. But you have to provide guidance to VBA, and techniques such as For-Next loops, `Do While` loops, and `For Each` loops are key to helping VBA locate and move through existing data. Other VBA tools such as `With` structures and object variables are vital for keeping your code manageable.

Chapter 8, "Opening Databases," complements the material you have read about in this chapter. Here you saw how to use VBA to reach and manipulate data in the worksheet. In Chapter 8, you'll see how to use VBA to reach and manipulate tables in external databases. Chapters 9 through 12 combine this information to show you how to automate two-way communication between Excel workbooks and external databases.

7

Opening Databases

8

Connecting to a Database

Chapter 7, "VBA Essentials Reviewed," mentioned that there are differences between Data Access Objects (DAO) and ActiveX Data Objects (ADO). In some areas, the two are identical—at least from the perspective of writing the code that uses the objects. For example, one way to move from one record to the next is

```
EmployeeRecords.MoveNext
```

You can use that command whether you've established your connection to the database with DAO or with ADO.

In other areas, the two object libraries couldn't be more different. The older DAO approach involves a strict hierarchy and your code has to observe it. A typical DAO sequence of events is as follows:

1. Set an object variable, such as `TheDB`, that represents a database.
2. Set another object variable, such as `TheQuery`, that represents a query or table in `TheDB`.
3. Set yet another object variable, such as `TheRecords`, that represents the records and fields in `TheQuery`. (Both DAO and ADO term this a *recordset*.)

Even if you didn't set each of these explicitly as an object variable, DAO would insist that you conform to its hierarchy: refer first to the database, and then to a table or query in the database, and then to the records in the table or query.

You might take the same approach using ADO, but ADO is much more flexible. Objects in ADO still belong to other objects, but ADO is comparatively lenient as to when and where objects, properties, and methods are used. For example, using ADO, you could declare and create a recordset, complete with fields and records, before even mentioning a database to contain the recordset.

The act of connecting to a database, the topic of this chapter, is one area where the differences between ADO and DAO are most pronounced. ADO is discussed next in "Connecting Using ADO"; if you do not have access to ADO, or prefer to use DAO, you'll find the information you need in "Opening a Database Using DAO."

Connecting Using ADO

There are three objects for you to use in establishing a connection to a database using ADO. They will be largely unfamiliar to you if you're used to DAO. Which object you use depends in part on what you want to accomplish. One object, the Connection object, is discussed here. The remaining two, the Command object and the Recordset object, are discussed in Chapters 10, "Defining Fields and Records in DAO," and 11, "Getting Data from Access and into Excel with ADO and DAO."

Establishing a Reference to the ADO Library

Before you can use ADO at all, you need to establish a reference to the ADO library. If necessary, switch to the VBE and choose References from the Tools menu. Scroll down until you find the reference you want and fill its check box (see Figure 8.1). If you want to establish more than one reference, continue locating them and filling their check boxes. When you're through, click OK.

Figure 8.1
The ADO library shown in the list box provides references to ADODB objects.

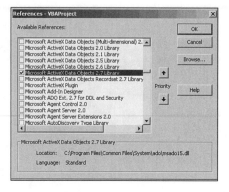

Although the object library's contents are commonly referred to as *ADO*, or *ActiveX Data Objects*, ADO is not a single library but a set of libraries. The one you're actually making reference to by checking, say, Microsoft ActiveX Data Objects 2.7 Library, is ADODB. When you make reference to the library in your VBA code by declaring an object variable, you often should qualify the reference with ADODB.

It's usually best to choose the highest release level available. If you find that a higher (the term is equivalent to *newer*, but alas, not always to *better*) release level doesn't work as you expect, you can step back down to a lower level.

> **NOTE**
>
> As shown in Figure 8.1, the References dialog box has a list box containing available libraries. Of the libraries that are checked, the higher in the list box, the higher the library's priority for resolving naming conflicts. For example, both the Excel object library and the ADO object library have a Parameter object. VBA will use the Excel Parameter object if the Excel library is higher in the list box, and the ADO Parameter object if the ADO library is higher. Still, it's better to make things explicit. If you want to declare an object variable to represent an ADO object, qualify it with ADODB, an Excel object with Excel, and so on:
>
> ```
> Dim rsRevenues As ADODB.Recordset
> Dim dbFinancials As DAO.Database
> Dim prmYear As Excel.Parameter
> ```

> **TIP**
>
> There's something about the structure of the Available References list box that tends to mislead users. It's easy to click a library so that it's highlighted, and then click OK to dismiss the dialog box. If you do that, you might think that you've established a reference to a library when in fact you haven't. Of course, you have to fill the library's check box before you close the dialog box. But I've seen many users just click on a library's name and immediately click OK—then they're mystified when their code doesn't recognize a library. I've done it myself more times than I care to admit. If your code doesn't recognize a library that you think you've selected, double-check the references list.

Preparing a Connection Object

You declare a Connection object in much the same way that you declare any object variable in VBA. For example

```
Dim cnConnectToLedger As ADODB.Connection
```

If you're certain that you have not set a reference to any other library that has a Connection object, you could instead declare it this way:

```
Dim cnConnectToLedger As Connection
```

As noted earlier, however, you might have also referenced another library that has a Connection object, and that library might be higher up in the priority pecking order than is the ADO library. It's partly a matter of how sure you are of yourself and partly of programming style, but you should at least consider preceding the Connection class with the ADODB qualifier.

> **NOTE**
>
> A *class* is an object's definition. It contains all the information that VBA needs to create a new instance of the object: what properties apply to it and what values they can take on, methods that can be used with the object, and so on. It is a sort of template for its object.

After you've declared an object variable as a Connection, you can create a new instance of it:

```
Set cnConnectToLedger = New ADODB.Connection
```

The `Dim` statement probably looked reasonably familiar to you, but this `Set` statement might not. The `Set` statements that were discussed in Chapter 7 all set an object variable equal to a particular worksheet, or chart axis, or range of cells—whatever the object variable represented, *the object already existed*. So, it was possible to set an object variable to represent Sheet1, or the chart's vertical axis, or the range A3:D15.

When you're first setting a Connection object, however, it doesn't yet exist. So, your `Set` statement uses the keyword `New` to inform VBA that it needs to create a new instance of an `ADODB.Connection`.

At this point, you haven't pointed the connection, `cnConnectToLedger`, at any database. You haven't opened the connection. You haven't stated that the connection will use the Jet database engine, or SQL Server, or some other provider. It's just out there.

Using the Keyword New

The example given in the prior section was

```
Dim cnConnectToLedger As ADODB.Connection
Set cnConnectToLedger = New ADODB.Connection
```

and the keyword `New` was used in the `Set` statement. It could instead have been used in the `Dim` statement:

```
Dim cnConnectToLedger As New ADODB.Connection
```

There's a difference between the two usages. When you use the keyword `New` in the `Set` statement, as was done in the prior section, you're allowing for the possibility that the object variable might already have been representing another object. In that case, when you set the object variable to some other object, the first reference is released and VBA creates a new instance of the class.

In contrast, suppose that you declare the object variable as a `New ADODB.Connection`, as in this example. If you do so, you do *not* use `Set` to create a new instance of the class. You just use the object variable. For example

```
Dim cnConnectToLedger As New ADODB.Connection
With cnConnectToLedger
    .Provider = "Microsoft.Jet.OLEDB.4.0"
    .ConnectionString = "C:\GeneralLedger.mdb"
End With
```

Notice that a `Set` statement is not used.

Opening the ADO Connection

After you've established the connection, you need to refine it. There are several properties that you can set and methods that you'll want to invoke. Because of the great flexibility of ADO, you'll find that you have different ways to do so.

If you've used DAO in the past and are just now learning about ADO, you might legitimately wonder why you should change horses. One reason is that the Jet engine won't be around forever.

Microsoft Access is modular. It's partly a development toolkit, providing the user means of designing tables, queries, forms, reports, and VBA code. Wrapped in with all those tools is a database engine that actually manages the storage, modification, and retrieval of the data. The Access database engine is termed the *Jet* engine, and DAO is optimized to work with Jet databases.

If you were never going to deal with databases other than those that use Jet, there would be little reason to use any object library other than DAO. DAO is optimized for Jet, and is more efficient for working with Jet than are other models such as ADO.

But Microsoft has been distancing itself from Jet—*not*, though, from Access—starting at least with the 2000 release of Office. Microsoft has developed a newer product, SQL Server, which is intended to provide a more robust engine and to handle much more user traffic than does Jet.

Access itself is capable of using other database engines. For example, you can use Access as a front end into a SQL Server back end. You continue to design your tables, queries, forms, reports, and code in Access, which then turns over the data management to SQL Server instead of Jet.

But DAO is comparatively ineffective for working with SQL Server or, for that matter, data sources other than those managed by Jet. ADO, on the other hand, effectively handles a wide variety of data sources, including SQL Server.

This is not intended to be an argument for using ADO or against using DAO. It is intended as background to the fact that when you use ADO, you should specify a provider for the connection. Here's an example:

```
Dim cnConnectToLedger As New ADODB.Connection
cnConnectToLedger.Provider = "Microsoft.Jet.OLEDB.4.0"
```

You could use this syntax to specify that the connection is to use an Access database that manages its data with Jet. If you're connecting to SQL Server, you'd use something like this:

```
Dim cnConnectToLedger As New ADODB.Connection
cnConnectToLedger.Provider = "SQLOLEDB.1"
```

The actual specification of the provider would depend on the provider version you have installed.

Specifying the Data Source

The Connection object has a property, ConnectionString, which you can use to inform ADO where to find the data source, as well as information about opening it. Here's a simple example:

```
Dim cnConnectToLedger As New ADODB.Connection
With cnConnectToLedger
    .Provider = "Microsoft.Jet.OLEDB.4.0"
    .ConnectionString = _
    "Data Source=C:\Documents and Settings\GL.mdb"
End With
```

Building More Complicated Connections

The ConnectionString is a wide-ranging property and typifies the flexibility of ADO: You can use it to specify aspects of the connection that can also be specified elsewhere. The example given earlier specified the provider using the Provider property. It could also have been managed this way:

```
Dim cnConnectToLedger As New ADODB.Connection
With cnConnectToLedger
    .ConnectionString = _
    "Provider = Microsoft.Jet.OLEDB.4.0;" & _
    "Data Source=C:\Documents and Settings\GL.mdb"
End With
```

Notice that the provider is specified within the connection string instead of in its own property.

Building Connection Strings with UDL Files

If you want, you can get help building a connection string. The approach relies on creating a universal data link, or *UDL*, file. The file is saved as text, so you can open and view it with Notepad, Word, or any application that can read text files.

You begin by creating a blank data link file and then opening it by double-clicking it. The Data Link Properties dialog box appears and assists you in building the link. When you're through, the information is saved as text, much like a DSN file.

When you've opened the data link file with a text reader, you'll see the connection string and you can copy and paste it into the VBA code where you're using a connection string. More explicitly, take these steps:

1. Start Notepad. Without typing anything, choose Save As from the File menu. In the File Name box, type something such as New Data Link.udl. The filename is irrelevant (although it helps to make it a meaningful one); what's important is that the file have the extension *.udl*. Quit Notepad.

2. Using Windows Explorer or My Computer, browse to the location where you saved the file in step 1. Locate the file and double-click its icon. The Data Link window opens. Click the Providers tab, shown in Figure 8.2.

Figure 8.2
All providers available to
your workstation appear
in the list box.

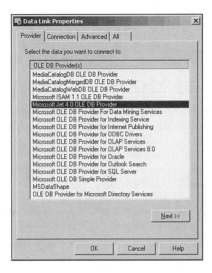

3. Select the provider you want from the OLE DB Providers list box. For an Access database, select Microsoft Jet 4.0 OLE DB Provider or (for more options) select Microsoft OLE DB Provider for ODBC Drivers. For a SQL Server database, select Microsoft OLE DB Provider for SQL Server. For an Excel workbook, select Microsoft OLE DB Provider for ODBC Drivers. When you've selected a provider, click the Connection tab or the Next button. The Connection tab appears (see Figure 8.3).

Figure 8.3
This Connection tab is
based on selecting
Microsoft Jet 4.0 OLE DB
Provider on the Provider
tab.

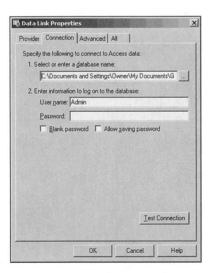

4. Click the button to the right of the box in step 1. This enables you to browse to the location of an Access database.

> **NOTE**
> The contents of the Connection tab vary, depending on the provider you selected on the Provider tab. The ODBC Drivers provider, for example, lets you supply a DSN.

> **NOTE**
> The username that's supplied by default in step 2 is Admin. This is also the default username for opening an Access database. The normal state of affairs is for the Admin user to have no password. When the Admin user has a password, Access requires the user to supply a recognized username and password.

5. Supply a username and password if the database has been secured and the Admin user has a password. If you do not supply a password, or if you fill the Blank Password check box, the resulting text file will show, among other things, `Password=""`. If you supply a password *and* fill the Allow Saving Password check box, the password will be saved in the text file, easily read by anyone who cares to point Notepad at it. (You'll get a warning if you try this.)

6. Click the Test Connection button. If the data source can be opened with the information you've supplied, you'll see a message box that says `Test connection succeeded`. If for some reason the connection failed, you'll see a message to that effect, along with some brief information about the reason for the failure.

7. Click the Advanced tab. For Jet databases and some other providers, such as ODBC, you can check permission levels that will apply to this connection (see Figure 8.4).

Figure 8.4
An additional access permission, Write, is hidden in the list box until you scroll down to it.

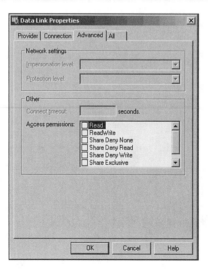

8. Fill the check box of one or more permissions. If the database has been secured, make sure that the permissions you assign to this connection do not conflict with those assigned in the database to the user named on the Connection tab.

9. If you want, click the All tab on the Data Link Properties dialog box. There, as shown in Figure 8.5, you'll see all the properties that can be set for the provider you chose: The components of that list depend on which provider you chose. You shouldn't normally find it necessary to edit a property. If you do, though, you can edit each of them from this tab by selecting it and clicking the Edit Value button.

10. Click the OK button whenever you're through.

Figure 8.5

Any of these properties, including those farther down the list, can be set in the connection string.

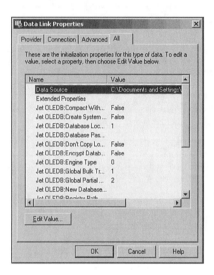

11. Now restart Notepad or whatever other application you used to create the UDL file in the first place. Choose Open from the File menu, browse to the location where you saved it, set its Files of Type dropdown to All Files, and open the UDL file. You'll see something like this:

```
[oledb]
; Everything after this line is an OLE DB initstring
Provider=Microsoft.Jet.OLEDB.4.0;Password=""; _
Data Source=C:\Documents and Settings\Owner\My Documents\GL.mdb; _
Persist Security Info=True
```

Using the Code

The code developed in the prior section needs some comments:

- You can name the UDL file in a connection string, much as you do with a DSN. Your connection string might look like this:

```
Dim cnConnectToLedger As New ADODB.Connection
With cnConnectToLedger
    .ConnectionString = "File Name=C:\Documents and Settings\_
    Owner\My Documents\MyUDL.udl"
End With
```

8

- The first line of the UDL file, [OLE DB], is a section declaration. The second line, beginning with the semicolon, is a comment. If you use the UDL file directly, by naming it in a connection string, make sure that both the section declaration and the comment line are in place—if either is not, you'll get an error message that The file is not a valid compound file.

- You can use the UDL file's connection string indirectly, by putting its contents in your connection string. Then, your connection string might look like this:

```
Dim cnConnectToLedger As New ADODB.Connection
With cnConnectToLedger
    .ConnectionString="Provider=Microsoft.Jet.OLEDB.4.0;" & _
    "Data Source=C:\Documents and Settings\Owner\My Documents\GL.mdb;" & _
    "Persist Security Info=False"
End With
```

- If you paste the connection string from the UDL file into an actual connection string in your VBA code, be sure to replace this

```
Password="";
```

with this

```
Password=;
```

or delete the Password argument completely to avoid confusing the interpreter as to where the connection string ends.

Opening the Connection

With the connection declared, you can open it wherever it makes sense to do so in your VBA code. After it's open, you can begin to move data back and forth across the connection.

This is another area that highlights the flexibility in ADO: As you'll see, it's even possible to establish the connection and open it simultaneously. Depending on your preferences, you can provide the connection string to the Connection object directly, as shown in the prior section. Or you can provide it as an argument to the Connection object's Open method, as shown in the following sections.

Using the Open Method with No Arguments

If you've already supplied the necessary connection information to the Connection object, you can simply invoke the Connection object's Open method. For example

```
Dim cnConnectToLedger As New ADODB.Connection
Dim strConnectToLedger As String

strConnectToLedger = "Provider=Microsoft.Jet.OLEDB.4.0;" & _
    "Data Source=C:\Documents and Settings\Owner\My Documents\GL.mdb;" & _
    "Persist Security Info=False"

With cnConnectToLedger
    .ConnectionString = strConnectToLedger
    .Open
End With
```

This approach is handy when it's part of a subroutine that you call repeatedly, using another subroutine to send the connection string as an argument:

```
Sub GetConnectionStrings
Dim strConnectData As String
Dim i as integer
For i = 1 to 10
    strConnectData = Sheets("LedgerAccounts").Cells(i,1)
    MakeTheConnection (strConnectData)
Next i
End Sub

Sub MakeTheConnection(strConnectData As String)
Dim cnConnectToLedger As New ADODB.Connection

With cnConnectToLedger
    .ConnectionString = strConnectData
    .Open
End With

'Statements using the connection go here

End sub
```

Passing an argument from one subroutine to another is a common practice in all programming languages, including VBA. In the preceding example, the subroutine named `GetConnectionStrings` picks up a series of 10 strings from the worksheet named LedgerAccounts by means of a `For-Next` loop.

After the loop has obtained a string from the worksheet, it passes the string to the subroutine named `MakeTheConnection`. That subroutine uses the string that it receives as the value assigned to the Connection object's connection string.

In this way, the main subroutine `GetConnectionStrings` can obtain a series of strings, each containing different connection information, and use them to direct the connection to different data sources. For example, if the ledger data is stored in different databases, the source locations in the worksheet might appear as shown in Figure 8.6.

The first time the loop executes, information in cell A1 is picked up and passed to `MakeTheConnection`. The second time through the loop, the information in A2 is picked up and passed. Each time, `MakeTheConnection` sets a different connection based on the connection string it receives from `GetConnectionStrings`.

Specifying the Connect String in the Open Method

If you prefer, you can specify the connect string as part of the Open method itself. The Open method can take from zero to four arguments. The prior section showed how you can use it without arguments; of course, in that case, the Connection object itself must already have information about where the data is located.

The Open method's syntax is

```
Connection.Open ConnectionString, UserID, Password, Options
```

Figure 8.6
By resetting its connection string, you can use the same Connection object repeatedly.

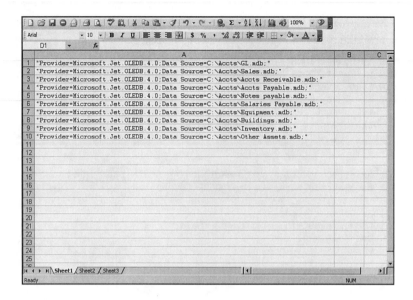

Each of its arguments is optional.

Suppose that you need to open the databases with a different user ID. You might put the user ID in the connect string itself or in some other location—perhaps next to the connect string in the worksheet, as shown in Figure 8.7.

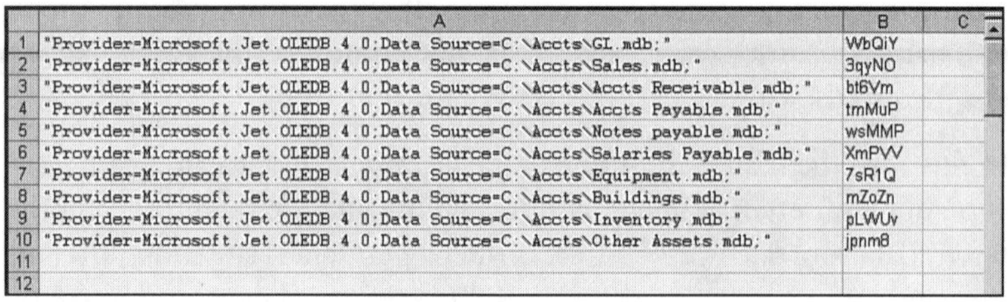

Figure 8.7
If you are confident enough of your security arrangements, you could specify passwords along with user IDs.

With this sort of setup, your VBA code might be as follows:

```
Sub GetConnectionStrings
Dim strConnectData As String, strPassword as String
Dim i as integer
For i = 1 to 10
    strConnectData = Sheets("LedgerAccounts").Cells(i,1)
    strPassword = Sheets("LedgerAccounts").Cells(i,2)
    MakeTheConnection strConnectData, strPassword
Next i
End Sub

Sub MakeTheConnection(strConnectData As String, strPassword As String)
Dim cnConnectToLedger As New ADODB.Connection
cnConnectToLedger.Open strConnectToLedger, strPassword
```

```
'Statements using the connection go here

End sub
```

Here the code picks up not one but two strings from the worksheet: a connection string and a password. They are both passed to the `MakeTheConnection` subroutine and used as arguments to the Connection object's Open method.

There are two aspects of this code to bear in mind:

- When you supply the connection string as part of the Open method, you don't need to do anything special with the Connection object other than to open it.

- Recall that you can supply a user ID as part of the connection string itself. Using the UserID and (if necessary) the Password arguments to the Open method, you don't need to supply them with the connect string. If you do both, however, the values supplied as Open method arguments supersede any values supplied within the connection string.

> **NOTE**
> Besides the Connection object, ADO has two other major objects, the Recordset and the Command object. They can both be used to establish connections, and they have other properties than are supplied by the Connection object. The Recordset and the Command objects are covered in Chapters 10 and 11.

Opening a Database Using DAO

So far, this chapter has focused on opening a database using ADO. If you don't have access to ADO, or if you're opening a database that uses the Jet database engine (as a practical matter, this means Microsoft Access databases), you should consider using DAO instead.

As mentioned earlier in this chapter, DAO is optimized for Jet and you'll get better performance using DAO on Jet databases than using ADO. (Admittedly, the delta isn't large.) And DAO syntax is identical to ADO syntax in many ways, so when it comes time to shift your code from using DAO to using ADO, the change will not be as painful as it might have been to shift from, say, Lotus 1-2-3 to Excel.

Declaring a DAO Database

You begin using DAO to access a Jet database by establishing a reference to DAO, just as you did for ADO. With the VBE active, select References from the Tools menu. Scroll down until you locate the DAO object library, fill its check box, and click OK (see Figure 8.8).

With the reference established, you declare an object variable to represent the database. For example

```
Dim dbGLDatabase As Database
```

Figure 8.8
The latest version of DAO depends on which version of Office you have installed.

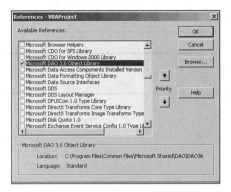

You would not normally use the New keyword in the declaration, as you often would when declaring an ADO connection. The reason is that in ADO, a connection really does start out as a new one: It doesn't exist before your code begins to run (although its data source usually does).

In DAO, there is no object that directly corresponds to an ADO connection. (A DAO Connection object is a reference to a database; in other words, it's a Database object.) You point your code at an existing database and open it. Here's a typical example:

```
Dim dbGLDatabase As DAO.Database
Dim strDBPath As String
strDBPath = "C:\Documents and Settings\Owner\My Documents\GL.mdb"
Set dbGLDatabase = OpenDatabase (strDBPath)
```

The full syntax of the statement that sets the database object is

```
Set dbObject = Workspace.OpenDatabase (Name, Options, ReadOnly, Connect)
```

where

- dbObject is an object variable declared as a DAO Database.

- Workspace is an object that defines how your code interacts with the data source. It uses either the Jet database engine or ODBC Direct—a method of interacting with ODBC data sources that bypasses the Jet engine. In general, if you're using DAO, it's because you want to use an Access database, and the Workspace object will therefore use Jet. Workspace is an optional argument and in most cases you won't need to use it.

- The Name argument to the OpenDatabase method specifies the path to, and name of, the database that's being opened.

- The Options argument, for Jet workspaces, is either True (which means that the database is opened in exclusive mode) or False (the default, meaning that the database is opened in shared mode). In exclusive mode, no other user can subsequently open the database. If you want to modify, say, a table's structure, you won't get a message that you can't because another user has already opened it: No one else can get in. But if another user has the database open *before* you attempt to open it in exclusive mode, you'll get a runtime error message to that effect.

- The `ReadOnly` argument also takes a True or False value. If False, the database is opened for read-write access. If True, it is opened read-only. Opening a database as read-only is occasionally useful in special circumstances. However, setting permissions for databases or password-protecting Excel projects and workbooks is usually a better strategy.

- The `Connect` argument is almost always used in conjunction with non-Jet, ODBC data sources.

Letting the User Locate the Database

At times, you don't know which database your code should open. This happens most often when your code is intended to support a user whose familiarity with database usage and data management is limited to knowing where the database is stored.

VBA provides a method, `GetOpenFilename`, that enables you to let the user browse to the database that he wants to open. The method is a member of the Application object.

> **NOTE** The `GetOpenFilename` method is not limited to use with databases—you can use it in your VBA code to let the user identify Excel workbooks, Word documents, PowerPoint presentations, even executables—any file whose path and name your code needs access to. Furthermore, you can use it in VBA code regardless of the host application; for example, you can use it in VBA code that you're writing for Access or Word.

In its simplest form, the `GetOpenFilename` usage is merely

```
Dim strFileToOpen As String
strFileToOpen = Application.GetOpenFilename
```

Figure 8.9 shows what the user sees when the second statement runs.

Figure 8.9
The user sees the contents of the folder from which he last opened a file.

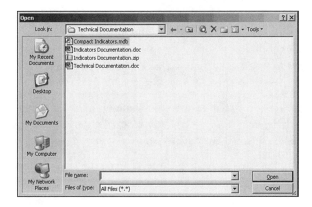

If, in Figure 8.9, the user chose to select the Access database named Compact Indicators.mdb and then clicked OK, the variable strFileToOpen would take something like this value:

```
C:\Technical Documentation\Compact Indicators.mdb
```

The value returned by the GetOpenFilename method includes its path.

Bear in mind that when your code confronts the user with a GetOpenFilename dialog box, no file is actually opened when he clicks OK. All that happens is that the name of and path to the file selected by the user are captured and stored in a variable. If the file is to be opened, it's up to your code to do it.

What if the user clicks the Cancel button instead? In that case, the variable that the method's result is assigned to takes on the value False. To keep your code from trying to open a file named False, you need to provide a way for it to recover.

Looking Out for Your User

If you want, you can exert more control over what the GetOpenFilename method displays to the user. Suppose that you know the user will always want to open one of the databases found in a particular folder. In that case, you can save the user some steps by means of code like this:

```
Dim strFileToOpen As String
Dim strOldFolder As String
Dim dbGLDatabase As Database
strOldFolder = CurDir
ChDir "C:\"
strFileToOpen = Application.GetOpenFilename
If strFileToOpen = "False" Then
    MsgBox "No file was selected."
    Exit Sub
End If
Set dbGLDatabase = OpenDatabase (strFileToOpen)
ChDir strOldFolder
```

Two string variables are declared: one to store the path to and name of the file to open, and one to store the current directory's path. The CurDir function is used to store the current directory. Then, because you know that the user will want to open a file in the C: drive's root, you use the ChDir statement to change the default directory to C:\.

The GetOpenFilename method then returns the name of the file the user wants to open. Should the user click the Cancel button, the If block is entered: The user sees a message to confirm that no file was selected, and the subroutine is exited.

If the user clicks OK, the path and name of the selected file are stored in strFileToOpen, which is used by the OpenDatabase method to assign the file to the object variable dbGLDatabase.

Finally, the default directory is reset to the location in use before it was changed to C:\. This is just a matter of good coding manners.

T I P It's a good idea to put this sort of code in its own subroutine or function. If a function, you could then set its value either to the name of the file selected or to `False` if the user cancelled. If a subroutine, it could accept a string variable as an argument; the code assigns the filename or `False` to the variable, which is then (by default) returned to the calling procedure. Either way, the calling procedure knows what to do: continue normally in response to a valid path and filename, or tie up loose ends and stop processing in response to `False`.

Filtering File Types for Your User

You can tidy things up even more if you want, by specifying the type of file that the user can select in the GetOpenFilename dialog box.

```
strFileToOpen = Application.GetOpenFilename _
➡("Access databases (*.mdb), *.mdb")
```

This statement uses the `FileFilter` argument of the `GetOpenFilename` method. It limits the files shown in the main window of the GetOpenFilename dialog box. As used earlier, it shows only those files with the `.mdb` extension. It also restricts to MDB files the file types shown in the Files of Type dropdown.

If you want to direct the user's attention to MDB files, but to allow for the possibility that the user might want to specify another type of file, you can put two (or more) file types in the `FileFilter` argument. The following example gives the user access to MDB files, and secondarily to any type of file, through use of the Files of Type dropdown.

```
strFileToOpen = Application.GetOpenFilename _
("Access databases (*.mdb), *.mdb,All files (*.*),*.*")
```

Figure 8.10 shows the effect of this specification of the `FileFilter` argument.

Figure 8.10
Notice that only MDB files are visible. All files become visible when the user chooses All Files (*.*).

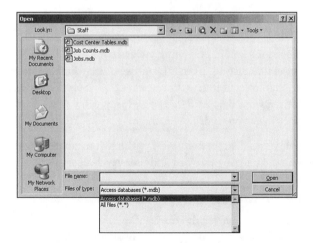

The `GetOpenFilename` method has three other arguments that you might find useful:

- `FilterIndex`. If you've specified more than one filter in the `FileFilter` argument, `FilterIndex` identifies the one to use. The default is 1, meaning the first filter is used. A value of 2 would use the second filter first; the user can still select the first filter from the Files of Type dropdown:

```
strFileToOpen = Application.GetOpenFilename _
("Access databases (*.mdb), *.mdb,All files (*.*),*.*",2)
```

- `Title`. Use this argument to provide text to display in the dialog box's title bar. The following shows MDB files by default, and puts `Select a database` in the title bar:

```
strFileToOpen = Application.GetOpenFilename _
("Access databases (*.mdb), *.mdb,All files (*.*),*.*",1, _
"Select a database")
```

- `MultiSelect`. This argument enables the user to select more than one file. The variable to which the result is assigned *must* be declared as Variant because `GetOpenFilename` will return an array (even if the array contains only one element). You can then loop through the array to get the filenames:

```
Dim varFileArray As Variant, i As Integer
varFileArray = Application.GetOpenFilename _
("Access databases (*.mdb), *.mdb,All files (*.*),*.*",1, _
"Select one or more databases", ,True)
For i = 1 To Ubound(varFileArray)
    ActiveSheet.Cells(i,1) = varFileArray(i)
Next i
```

Dealing with Secured Jet Databases

This chapter has already discussed dealing with user IDs and passwords in non-Jet, ODBC Direct data sources. This is usually managed in a connection string, whether that string is supplied as the value of the Connection object's `ConnectString` property or as an argument to its Open method.

As mentioned in the prior section, "Opening a Database Using DAO," DAO does not offer a Connection object that is distinct from a Database object. Furthermore, Jet databases are secured in a fashion that's very different from, say, a SQL Server database. This section provides an overview of the ways that Jet databases—specifically, Access databases—are secured, as well as code that enables you to deal with them.

An Access database has two distinct methods by which you can deter a user from taking unauthorized actions: a database password and user-level security.

Using Access Database Passwords

Setting a database password is by far the easier of the two methods, and also the most easily defeated. To secure an Access database by means of a password, you take these steps:

1. At the outset, the database that you want to secure should be closed.

2. Begin by starting **Access**. Do *not* begin by double-clicking the icon of the database you want to open. Instead, start Access from the Start menu or from some other shortcut that targets the Access application.

3. If Access displays a window that enables you to open a blank database, or to create a new database, or to open an existing file, dismiss the window.

4. Choose **File**, **Open**. In Access's Open dialog box, navigate to the location of the database you want to secure. When you find the database, select it.

5. In the lower-right corner of the Open dialog box, click the **arrow** on the right edge of the Open button to display the drop-down list shown in Figure 8.11.

Figure 8.11
It's also necessary to open a secured database in exclusive mode if you want to *unset* a database password.

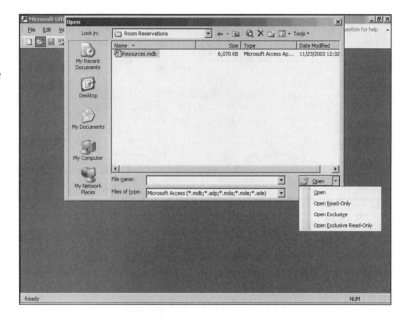

6. Click **Open Exclusive** to open the database in exclusive mode.

7. From the **Tools** menu, select **Security**. Then select **Set Database Password** from the cascading menu.

8. Enter and verify a password in the Set Database Password dialog box, as shown in Figure 8.12. Then click **OK**.

If you need to use DAO to open a database that's been secured in this way, you have to use syntax similar to the following:

```
Dim dbGLDatabase As DAO.Database
Dim strDBPath As String
strDBPath = "C:\Documents and Settings\Owner\My Documents\GL.mdb"
Set dbGLDatabase = OpenDatabase (strDBPath, False, False, _
"MS Access;PWD=Dismal")
```

Figure 8.12
As usual, it's best to choose a password consisting of a mix of letters, numbers, and special characters.

To accomplish the same thing with ADO, you would use code like this:

```
Dim cnGeneralLedger As New ADODB.Connection
Dim rsGL As New ADODB.Recordset
Dim strDBPath As String
strDBPath = "C:\Documents and Settings\Owner\My Documents\GL.mdb"
With cnGeneralLedger
    .Provider = "Microsoft.Jet.OLEDB.4.0"
    .Properties("Data Source") = strDBPath
    .Properties("Jet OLEDB:Database Password") = "Dismal"
    .Open
End With
```

This illustrates a convenient aspect of ADO connections. After you've established the connection's provider, the connection's Properties collection is populated with properties that the Provider supplies. Here, the Jet engine provides a `Data Source` property (so does SQLOLEDB.1) and a `Jet OLEDB:Database Password` property (SQLOLEDB.1 does not supply a database password property that is qualified by `Jet OLEDB`). Although these properties are not members of the VBA or ADO libraries, they're automatically supplied by the provider.

Using Databases Secured with User-Level Security

A method of securing an Access database that's much stronger (although hardly bulletproof) than a database password is by means of user-level security. Before you're in a position to understand DAO or ADO code that opens Access databases that have user-level security in place, you need to understand how that security is arranged.

When you install Microsoft Access on a computer, one of the files that's installed is named System.mdw. Its location depends on the version of Office that you're using, so you might need to search for it. System.mdw is termed a *workgroup information* file, and its purpose is to store information about

- The names of users who can open a Jet database, and the passwords that authenticate them
- The names of groups of users who can open a Jet database
- Which users belong to which groups

If no one has modified the System.mdw file (and you would know if *you* had done so), there is only one user in the workgroup information file, and that user is named *Admin.*

Admin is the default user of an Access database. Any time you open an Access database, Access assumes that you are Admin, unless you say differently.

> **NOTE**
>
> Don't be misled by the term *Admin.* Although the name connotes the possession of overarching privileges, the Admin user in a secured Access database usually has relatively few privileges. When an actual user opens a secured database, that user is deemed to be the default Admin user. Because a secured database has been protected for one reason or another, it's typical to prevent the random user from deleting tables or renaming queries or taking other actions that would harm the database's functionality. Therefore, Admin is often restricted from doing much more than reading data.

After you've secured a database with user-level security, the process of opening it depends on whether the default Admin user has been assigned a password. If Admin has a password, Access displays the dialog box shown in Figure 8.13 when anyone tries to open the secured database.

Figure 8.13
Access shows the name of the most recent user to supply one. Type over the default name if necessary.

Unless you're armed with a profound sense of determination, some experience, and some tools, you're not going to get past the dialog box shown in Figure 8.13 without a recognized name and password. That means that if you want to open the database by means of DAO (or even ADO), you'll need to supply that name and password in your code. This chapter will discuss doing so presently, but first some more information about setting up user-level security.

Implementing User-Level Security in an Access Database

As you'll see when you begin using SQL Server—if you haven't already—security in SQL Server can be both tighter and easier to administer than is the case in Access. Nevertheless, you're likely to encounter Access databases that require maintenance for some years yet, and even to have need for new, secured Access databases.

> **NOTE**
>
> Much of the information in this and subsequent sections can also be found in a white paper in the Microsoft Knowledge Base. It is titled SECFAQ.doc, is authored by Mary Chipman, Andy Baron, et al., and includes a considerable amount of good information and advice about securing Access databases.

Establishing a Workgroup Information File

Before you can initiate user-level security, you'll need a workgroup information file. If, as is probably the case, you're using Microsoft Office in a networked context, you'll need to establish that file in a share folder that users of the database can open.

To establish a workgroup information file, you need to run either Wrkgadm.exe or the Workgroup Administrator. Which you use depends on the version of Office installed on your computer. In Office 97 and Office 2000, you run Wrkgadm.exe, an executable file usually found in the System subfolder of the Windows folder appropriate to the operating system you're using. Locate that file and double-click it to start.

In Office 2002 and Office 2003, the workgroup administrator is part of the Access menu itself. You'll find it by selecting Security from the Tools menu, and then clicking Workgroup Administrator in the cascading menu.

Whether you use Wrkgadm.exe or the Workgroup Administrator menu item, when you start it you'll see the dialog box shown in Figure 8.14. Click Create.

Figure 8.14
The dialog box shows the path and name of the workgroup information file you're currently using.

> **TIP**
> One workgroup information file can manage information about multiple groups and users that use different databases. Even if you're managing several databases with user-level security, it's a good idea to keep all that data in one workgroup information file. So doing helps to minimize the administrative headaches.

When you've clicked Create, the Workgroup Owner Information dialog box shown in Figure 8.15 appears.

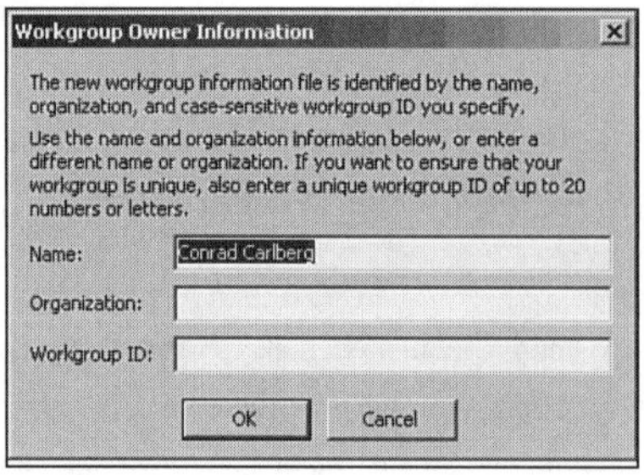

Figure 8.15
You should specify a workgroup ID. This ID is not a password, but helps re-create the file if it is damaged.

Be sure to make a separate note of the name, organization, and workgroup ID that you specify, and put it away where you and you alone can get at it later. Although many networks now perform comprehensive backups daily, it can take some time to restore a file from backup. You might want to re-create the file quickly from scratch, and to do that you'll need the information shown on Figure 8.15.

When you click OK, the Workgroup Information File dialog box appears (see Figure 8.16).

Figure 8.16
If you type the path and name yourself, don't forget to give the file an extension of .mdw.

After you click OK on the Workgroup Information File dialog box, you'll see a Confirm Workgroup Information dialog box, summarizing the data you've just entered. If it's correct, click OK to return to the Workgroup Administrator, and then click OK again to return to the Access interface. If anything is incorrect, click the Change button to return to the Workgroup Owner Information dialog box, where you can correct any errors.

Making Access Request a Password

If it was running, quit Access, restart it, and open any database (including a new one). Because the default Admin user does not have a password, you won't be prompted to supply one.

Choose Security from the Tools menu, and then click User and Group Accounts. This is the route to managing users and groups: their names, passwords, and membership. The User and Group Accounts dialog box appears (see Figure 8.17).

Figure 8.17
The new workgroup file starts out with three default accounts: the Admin user and the Admins and Users groups.

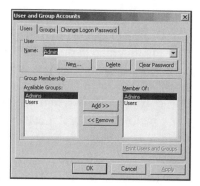

Verify that the default Admin user appears in the Name dropdown. Your next step is to temporarily assign a password for the Admin user, so click the Change Logon Password tab, which is shown in Figure 8.18.

Figure 8.18
The Admin account generally has no password, so you usually skip right to the New Password box.

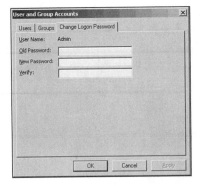

Enter and verify a password for the Admin account, and click OK.

> I set and remove the Admin account's password so frequently that I give it just a single character, and I use the same one every time. I am unrepentant: I do this solely to get Access to prompt me for *my* name and password. I can get through this process more quickly if I never have to think up a new password for Admin, and if it's only one character. There's no real exposure involved because Admin has a minimum of privileges anyway, and they are the same ones that a random user would have when he opens a database secured by this workgroup file, and after I'm in, I immediately clear the Admin user's password.

Establishing Yourself as a User

Once again, choose Tools, Security, User and Group Accounts. On the Users tab (refer to Figure 8.17), click the New button to establish yourself as a user. The dialog box shown in Figure 8.19 appears.

After entering your name and a personal ID, click OK to return to the Users tab. With your name in the Name box, click on the Admins group in the Available Groups box, and click the Add button. This makes you a member of the Admins group. Put your name and personal ID in the same location where earlier you stored the workgroup name, organization, and workgroup ID information. Again: If you need to restore the workgroup information file, you might be able to do so from a tape backup, but it might be quicker to do so from scratch.

Also, if at a later time you delete a user and subsequently want to restore him to membership in the workgroup information file, you'll need his personal ID (*not* his password).

Quit Access again and restart it. Because you've given the Admin account a password, you'll be prompted for a name and password. Supply *your* name, not the Admin name. Your account does not yet have a password, so leave the Password box blank.

Figure 8.19
The personal ID that you supply is not the password. It must contain between 4 and 20 characters.

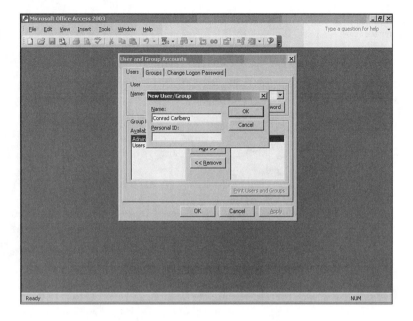

But do give yourself a password at some point, just as you gave the Admin account a password. Making sure that you've started Access using your account, choose Tools, Security, User and Group Accounts, and click the Change Logon Password tab. Your username should appear near the top. (If it does not, because you did not log in on your account, quit Access and restart it, using your name to log in.) Supply a password, verify it, and then click OK.

Restricting Admin's Permissions

It's now time to restrict the permissions that belong to the Admin account. That's easy: just remove the Admin user from the Admins group. Choose Tools, Security, User and Group Accounts. If necessary, use the dropdown on the Users tab to select the Admin user. In the Member Of list, click Admins. Then click the Remove button. The Admins group disappears from the Member Of list, and the Users tab should appear as in Figure 8.20.

Reviewing and Summarizing the Process

This probably seems like a lengthy, complicated process, and it is—and you're not nearly through yet because you haven't yet applied the security you've been arranging to any database. This is a good point to review what you've done so far. You've done the following:

1. Created a new workgroup information file to contain the names, IDs, and passwords of database users, the name and ID of the workgroup itself, names of groups, and user membership in groups.

2. Assigned a password to the default Admin user. This forces Access to ask who you are when next you start Access.

Figure 8.20
You can't remove Admin (or any user) from the Users group. To do so, you have to delete the user's account entirely.

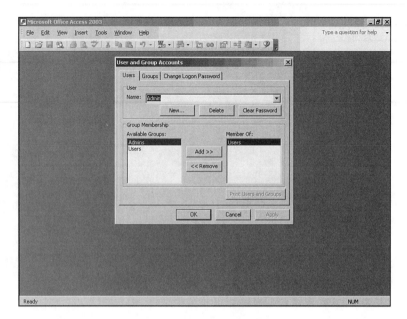

3. Established yourself as a user and joined the Admins group.

4. Quit and restarted Access to get Access to ask who you are, and you identified yourself. As a member of the Admins group, you're able to remove the Admin user from the Admins group, and you did so.

The net effect of all this is to establish a workgroup information file that has you and only you as a member of the Admins group, and that has both you and the default Admin user as the members of the Users group.

A note in a prior section suggested that you not read too much into the default username *Admin*. The same is not true of the group named *Admins*. It starts out with extensive privileges. For example, it's only as a member of Admins that you are able to remove the user Admin from the Admins group.

This highlights a fundamental aspect of users and groups. The idea (and it's one used by SQL Server's Enterprise Manager and other database managers) is that the database is likely to have many users. Each user might have slightly different requirements, but most users share many requirements. For example, most users need to be able to see information in the database. Fewer users need to be able to add records and edit information in fields. Even fewer need to add, delete, and modify fields, tables, and queries. And so on.

Because there are so many shared requirements, it's a good idea to set up *groups*: one that can read data but do nothing else, one that can both read and modify data, another that can modify both data and the structures that contain it, and so on.

Given that approach, it's much easier to administer permissions. Instead of assigning permissions individually to each and every user, you assign permissions to groups and then arrange to have individual users enter the groups that give them the permissions they need. (A user can belong to more than one group.) If a user needs a slightly different permission structure than your groups supply, you can add or remove specific permissions for that user.

So, by this point, you've laid the foundation: You've established yourself as the sole administrator, and now it's time to apply the foundation to a database.

Securing the Database

In this part of the process, you need to make sure that you are the user of record. You've done that if you're still running an instance of Access in which you identified yourself as the user at startup. If not, start Access and identify yourself as the user in response to Access's Logon prompt, supplying a password if you've already given yourself one.

Now open a database that you want to make secure. (At the end of this process, you'll wind up with two databases: the original, unsecured version and a new, secured version.) Choose Tools, Security, User-Level Security Wizard. You'll see the wizard's first step, shown in Figure 8.21.

Figure 8.21
The current user must be a member of the Admins group in order to use the Security Wizard.

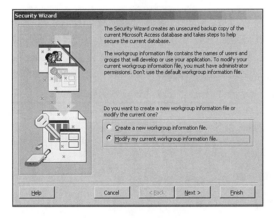

You might see some differences between the wizard on your computer and the figures in this section. Different Access versions have minor differences in the wizard's appearance.

You've already established a workgroup information file, with your user account as a member of Admins and with the Admin account a member only of Users. Therefore, choose Modify My Current Workgroup Information File and click Next. (You might not actually modify the workgroup information file, but you want to avoid creating yet another one.) Figure 8.22 shows the wizard's second step.

Figure 8.22
The Select All and Deselect All buttons refer only to objects on the active tab.

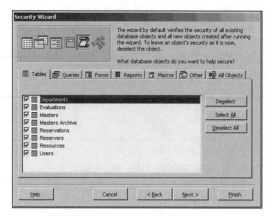

By default, all the check boxes for all the objects in the database are filled, meaning that they'll be secured. Only unusual circumstances would make you decide not to secure all the objects in the database, so you'll usually leave things as they are and click the Next button.

> **TIP**
>
> If you want the wizard to skip one or more objects, just click the appropriate tab and clear the appropriate check box.

After you click Next, the wizard appears as shown in Figure 8.23.

Figure 8.23
You can accept the proposed group IDs or modify them to other values.

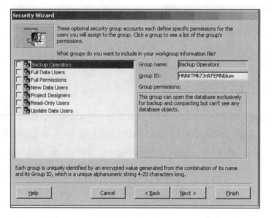

In this step, you reject (the default) or accept the creation of new groups in your workgroup information file. These groups have pre-set permissions and are handy to have in place. For example, if your workgroup information file has the wizard-supplied group named New Data Users, a member of that group will be able to view data and insert new records. Unless a member also belongs to a group with broader permissions, though, he won't be able to modify or delete existing records, or change the design of any table, query, form, or other database object.

It's useful to have such a group already defined because you're likely to want to give various users (Admin, for example) precisely those permissions.

You can always delete one or more of these groups at a later time, so it doesn't hurt to have them. Fill their check boxes and click the Next button to view the next step in the wizard, shown in Figure 8.24.

> **NOTE** The proposed group IDs are regenerated each time you start the Security Wizard, so you needn't worry overmuch about another user obtaining and using them by rerunning the wizard.

Figure 8.24
Any permissions you assign to the Users group will be available to anyone who opens the database.

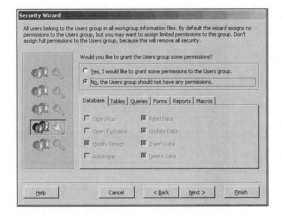

You can assign some permissions to the Users group in this step, but it's not recommended. Anyone who opens the database as the default Admin user is automatically a member of the Users group and so will have any permission you assign to Users. For example, you might assign a Read permission for tables. This may seem benign enough, but so doing also assigns a Read Design permission, which you might not regard as quite so harmless.

When you click Next, the wizard's next step appears (see Figure 8.25).

The User and Group Accounts dialog box is a little more powerful than is this step of the wizard, but if you want to add other users here you can do so, and assign them to one or more default groups as shown in Figure 8.26.

Your basic choices in this step concern ease of assignment, not functionality. If as yet you've added just a few users, perhaps only one or two (Admin is not counted), it's easier to choose Select a User and assign the user to groups. If you've added several users and have only one or two groups, it's easier to choose Select a Group and assign users to the group.

In any other case it doesn't much matter, and in fact you don't need to make any assignments at this point: You can do that later by choosing Tools, Security, User and Group Accounts.

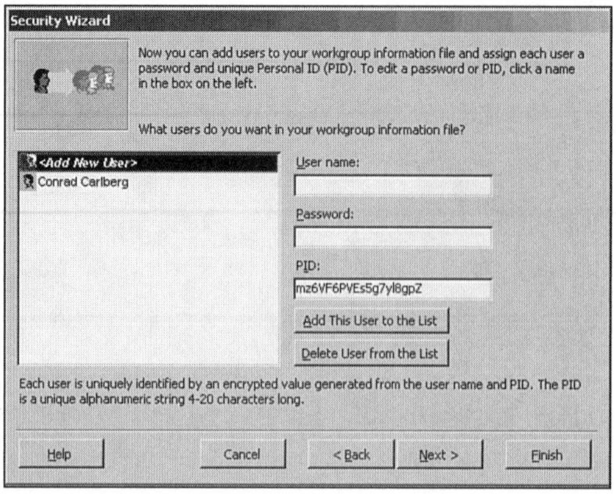

8

Figure 8.25
If you prefer not to do it, a user can set his own password by logging on with a username and going to User and Group Accounts.

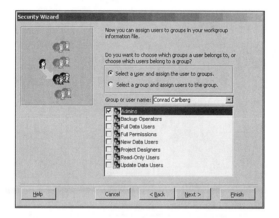

Figure 8.26
Because this user was already a member of Admins, you cannot remove him from that group in this step.

After you're finished making assignments, click Next to reach the wizard's final step (see Figure 8.27).

Figure 8.27
By default, the unsecured version of the file has an extension of .bak.

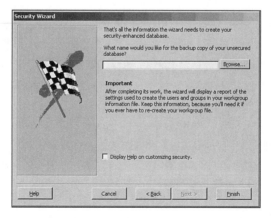

It's a good idea to store the unsecured version of the database in a path where users cannot get at it. A folder to which only you and your network's system administrators have access would be a good choice. Browse to that location to get its path in the box, edit its name if you want, and click Finish.

When you do so, the wizard creates a summary report of the information you have entered, as shown in Figure 8.28. You can print it if you want. If you simply close the report, Access offers to save it as a snapshot (.snp) file that you can open and print later. You normally should do one or the other, so that you'll have a paper trail of the changes you've made.

Figure 8.28
If you save the report as a snapshot file, you can find it later in the same folder as the secured database.

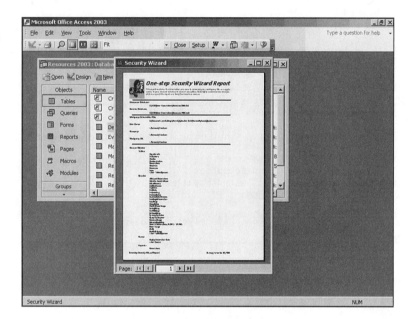

Your database has now been secured. See the next section for information about how to open it using ADO.

Opening a Secured Access Database

After you've secured the database, you can open it as usual if Admin has no password. If Admin has a password, you can still open the database, but you'll need to supply your user-name and password in the Logon dialog box.

You might also need to know how to get the database open using VBA code. To open the database using DAO, you would use code similar to this (don't forget to set a reference to the DAO object library first):

```
Dim wkspTempWorkspace As Workspace
Dim strSecuredDB As String
Dim strUserName As String
Dim strPassword As String
```

```
Dim dbSecureDB As DAO.Database
Dim rsTableToOpen As DAO.Recordset
```

After declaring the necessary variables, tell VBA where to find the workgroup information file:

```
DBEngine.SystemDB = _
"C:\Documents and Settings\Resources.mdw"
```

You'll want to be very careful with this code because it exposes a username and password. The username should be for a user identified in the workgroup file:

```
strUserName = "Conrad Carlberg"
strPassword = "KeepThisSecret"
```

Create a new, temporary workspace and append it to the existing workspaces collection. It contains the username and password:

```
Set wkspTempWorkspace = DBEngine.CreateWorkspace _
("New", strUserName, strPassword)
DBEngine.Workspaces.Append wkspTempWorkspace
```

Now provide the path to and name of the secured database, and open it:

```
strSecuredDB = _
"C:\NCS\Room Reservations\Resources 2003.mdb"
Set dbSecureDB = DBEngine.Workspaces("New") _
.OpenDatabase(strSecuredDB)

'Code to manipulate the database given the user's _
permissions goes here.
```

And close the database:

```
dbSecureDB.Close
```

The code that is not shown—that you would use to manipulate data and objects in the database—will run a little more efficiently if you use the DAO approach to opening the secured database. If you prefer, though, you can use ADO. It's not quite as efficient because ADO is not optimized specifically for Jet databases. But it's a *lot* shorter. The admonition about the exposed username and password still applies (and don't forget to set a reference to the ADO object library first):

```
Dim cnResourceConnection As New ADODB.Connection
With cnResourceConnection
    .Provider = "Microsoft.Jet.OLEDB.4.0"
    .Properties("Data Source") = _
"C:\NCS\Room Reservations\Resources 2003.mdb"
    .Properties("Jet OLEDB:System database") = _
"C:\Documents and Settings\Resources.mdw"
    .Open UserId:="Conrad Carlberg", Password:="KeepThisSecret"
End With

'Code to manipulate the database given the user's _
permissions goes here.

cnResourceConnection.Close
```

Looking Ahead

This chapter builds on a foundation begun in Chapter 7. That foundation puts you in a position to use VBA in conjunction with Excel to connect to external databases.

VBA and Excel can't connect to databases without help, though. You need to provide them with an object library, one that contains information about the objects, properties, and methods found in a database. ADO and DAO are two such object libraries, and this chapter has shown you how to integrate them with your VBA code, and how to open databases by applying references to the libraries.

You have also read about the theory and practice of making Access databases secure. This material was supplied because as data networks have become more and more accessible, shared databases have become the rule—and it's important to secure a shared database. If you're to successfully integrate Excel, VBA, and ADO/DAO in the management of a shared database, you need to know how the database's security works. This chapter concluded with some examples of the use of VBA with DAO or ADO to legitimately open a secured database (not, that is, to break into it illicitly).

Chapter 9, "Managing Database Objects," continues by showing you how to use VBA and an object library to manage database tables and queries, and their components, from the context of an Excel workbook.

Managing Database Objects

Creating Tables

Before exploring how to use Excel to manage a database, it's useful to look inside one for a tour of its fundamental objects: tables, joins, and queries. This chapter discusses those topics. With that discussion as a basis, Chapter 10, "Defining Fields and Records with ActiveX Data Objects and Data Access Objects," shows you how to create and manage these objects from Excel.

Using Access, begin with the main database window. You create a new table by clicking the Tables tab or button (depending on your version) if necessary, and then clicking the New button. The dialog box shown in Figure 9.1 appears.

Select Design View, and then click OK to open the window where you'll design the table (see Figure 9.2).

When you have the table design window on your screen, it's time to define the fields that make up the table.

Figure 9.1
You have more tools available to you in Design view than in the other views.

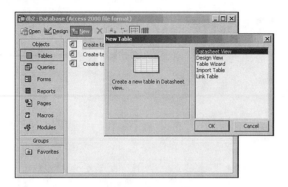

Figure 9.2
The properties on the General tab don't appear until you've named the field.

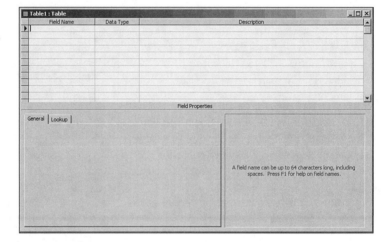

Defining Fields

You must name a field before you can specify any of its other characteristics. There are a few general principles to keep in mind when you choose a field's name.

Using Meaningful Names

A meaningful name is important, even more so than when you're choosing a name for an Excel list. Whether by means of the Access interface or via Excel, much of your work with the table will require you to supply the names of the table's fields.

Whether you're putting a field onto a screen form where a user can supply a value, or adding a field to a query, or making reference to a field in VBA code, your task will be much easier if you've given the field a name such as SocSecNum or FICA_Rate. Your task is that much harder if you've used a name such as Field1 or VariableB.

Excel is different. With an Excel list, you can often just glance at its values to know what it represents. When you see a value such as 800-555-1212 or Republican, it's usually pretty clear what the field represents. (But not always: Is that 800-number a voice line or a fax line?)

In contrast, it's unusual to be looking at a field's values when you're doing design work in a database, or managing a database from the Excel platform. There's no good contextual clue, and you'll save yourself hours in the long run by spending a few seconds at the outset in the selection of a meaningful name.

Living with Your Choices

At one time or another, we've all thought, "I just need to get the table built right now. I'll come back and fix the field names later."

But "later" never comes soon enough. Shortly after you've built the table, you're creating queries that depend on the presence of a field named `Field1` and `VariableA`. Those queries are meant to pass data along to a user form, so the form itself comes to depend on those names. And shortly you find that your VBA code, whether it's in Access or Excel, has those names scattered throughout.

These misnomers create a problem, but you can solve it by changing every instance of the field's name—in the table, in any query that refers to the field, in any form that refers to those queries, and so on. It can be a major and error-prone project, but it's feasible because you can put your hands directly on the field's name no matter where it appears.

The problem is worse if you have an external data range in an Excel worksheet. To change the field's name then, you'll have to edit the query that populates the data range. If you start by changing the field's name in the database, Microsoft Query won't be able to find it; if you start by changing the reference in Microsoft Query, you'll be told that the field doesn't exist. The least obnoxious solution is to change the field's name in the database, and then rebuild the external data range from scratch.

Name AutoCorrect

Access 2000 introduced a feature termed Name AutoCorrect. The idea is that you can change the name of a database object, such as a field name, and Access will automatically correct other objects' references. So, if in a table you change a field's name from Profit to NetProfit, a query that uses the field will be corrected automatically to refer to NetProfit. Access keeps a log of such changes. To invoke Name AutoCorrect, choose Options from the Tools menu, click the General tab, and fill the appropriate check boxes.

But this feature brings with it its own problems. It slows processing, particularly in a database with user-level security enabled. It does not change names in macros or VBA procedures. And messages in Usenet newsgroups (not a uniformly reliable source of information) have blamed other problems on Name AutoCorrect—problems that just seem to go away when the user turns it off.

I admit that I have some databases still in use that have fields with meaningless names. By the time I was ready to bite the bullet and change the names wherever they appeared, they had spread like mold, through queries, forms, linked tables, VBA code, documentation, and so on. At this point, it's more effective to live with the problem than to fix it. At least these databases are a constant reminder to me to get my field names right at the outset.

Using Spaces in Names

You can use spaces in field names; for example, `Retained Earnings`.

> **NOTE**
> You can't start the name of a field with a space, or include a period, an exclamation point, an accent grave (that's the character below the tilde), square brackets, or the control characters represented by ASCII 0 through 31.

Suppose that you embed a blank space in a field name, and later drag the field onto a user form to create a control. Access replaces the space with an underscore in any VBA references (see Figure 9.3).

Figure 9.3
Access inserts an underscore in place of the embedded blank space.

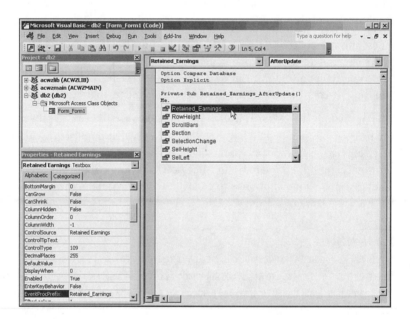

> **NOTE**
> There are other ways to create controls on forms. For example, you could drag a text box control from the Toolbox onto the form. By default it would be named `Text12` or `Text25`, depending on how many controls were already on the form. Later, you can associate that text box with a field in a table, and (until you rename the control itself) it would retain its original, default name.

The field named `Retained Earnings` is represented in the form's VBA code as a control named `Retained_Earnings`. The field's name itself does not change. If you open the table, you'll note that it's still `Retained Earnings`. And if you examine the control's properties, you'll find that on the form it's still termed `Retained Earnings`. But in any VBA code that's saved with the user form, such as the code for its After Update event, the control is referred to by the name `Retained_Earnings`.

It's very convenient for VBA code referring to controls on forms to use the same name as the field they represent. Suppose that you're writing VBA code that runs in response to a user clicking an OK button on a form named `FinancialForm`. You want to perform a calculation based on the value that the user typed in the form. You're calculating the average quarterly earnings, given the annual earnings figure supplied by the user. If the control in question is named `Text18`, your code might look like this:

```
MeanQuarterlyEarnings = FinancialForm.Text18 / 4
```

9

Subsequently, while reviewing the code, you realize that you don't know what kind of earnings the control named `Text18` stores: retained earnings, earnings per share, diluted earnings, or something else.

So, it's handy for the code to refer to `Retained_Earnings` instead of `Text18`, but there's still a source of confusion. Your field's name has an embedded blank, but the control's VBA reference has an embedded underscore. That causes problems when you're writing code, especially if you're writing code in Excel to manage the database. Then you're a whole application away from the field names.

All that really matters is to arrange things so that names are consistent. In the long run, you'll save yourself headaches by taking one of these two approaches:

- Avoid using separators in field names. A field named `RetainedEarnings`, dragged onto a form named MyForm to create a control, is referred to as `MyForm.RetainedEarnings`. The VBA reference is the same as the field's name.

- If you want to use a separator in a field name, use an underscore. A field named `Retained_Earnings`, dragged onto a form named MyForm to create a control, is referred to as `MyForm.Retained_Earnings`. Again, the VBA reference is the same as the field's name.

After you've settled on an approach—even if you choose to use embedded spaces in names— use that approach consistently. You'll spend a lot less time reopening databases and tables to check how you named something.

Setting Field Types

When you create a new field in a table, it is given a default *type*. The type determines what sort of data the field can contain. You can, of course, change a field's default type to another, more appropriate one.

Text is the default type that Access assigns unless you change the default. You do so by choosing Tools, Options and clicking the Tables/Queries tab (see Figure 9.4).

Figure 9.4
Use the Text and the Number boxes to set the size of the default field type; for example, 50 for Text or Byte for Number.

If you want each new field that you establish to automatically be a Number type, choose Number from the Default Field Type dropdown. Then choose one of the Number field sizes from the Number dropdown. These sizes are available for the Number data type:

- Byte
- Integer
- Long Integer
- Single (single precision; supports 38 digits to the right of the decimal point)
- Double (double precision; supports 308 digits to the right of the decimal point)
- Decimal (supports 28 digits to the right of the decimal point)
- Replication ID (a 16-byte field normally used in replicas of databases)

> **NOTE**
> Single- and double-precision variables can contain numbers in the ranges from about $-3.4 * 10^{38}$ to $3.4 * 10^{38}$, and about $-1.7 * 10^{308}$ to $1.7 * 10^{308}$, respectively. This doesn't mean that they can do so *precisely*, however. A double-precision variable, for example, is precise to 15 digits. A number that requires more than 15 digits of accuracy cannot be stored precisely in a double-precision variable.

Access offers these data types:

- Text
- Memo (Access 2000, 2002, and 2003 support indexing on Memo fields)
- Number
- Date/Time
- Currency

- AutoNumber (a Long Integer that increments itself automatically as new records are added to a table)
- Yes/No
- OLE Object
- Hyperlink

Your choice of data type for a given field is usually dictated by the values you want it to store. If it can have letters—for example, a person's name—you'll choose Text (limited to 255 characters) or Memo (not limited). If the field will store numbers only, your choice depends on whether the numbers are always integers, such as number of family members, or possibly floating point, such as area in square feet.

Given a choice between two or more data types, you usually choose the more parsimonious. Where possible, choose Byte over Integer, Integer over Long Integer, Single Precision over Double, and so on. (Memo is the most roomy data type.)

But there's another consideration, one that's raised by joins. When you join two tables in a query, the joined fields must be compatible, and that means that you must plan ahead.

There are three field types that cannot be used in a join: Memo, OLE Object, and Hyperlink. So, if you know that you're going to join, say, a Hospitals table with a HospitalTypes table, don't give either field that will comprise the join a type of Memo, OLE Object, or Hyperlink—not even if *both* fields have the same type.

> **NOTE**
>
> Note that although you can now index on Memo and Hyperlink fields, it doesn't mean that you can join tables using them.

A join can be successfully created using two Text fields, regardless of their length. For example, if the field `UnitName` is a Text field with a maximum length of 50, and `UnitTypeID` is a Text field with a maximum length of 2, you can create a join with those two fields.

But you cannot create a join using a Text field and a numeric field of any type. (Bear in mind that Date/Time and Yes/No fields qualify as numeric types.) So, an easy rule of thumb is to type fields that might be used for joins as either both Text or both Number.

Preparing Table Joins

Access provides a Relationships window, which enables you to define joins between tables. Either click the Relationships button or choose View, Relationships. When you do so, the Relationships window opens. If you open it before any relationships have been defined, a Show Table dialog box also appears; if at least one relationship already exists, you can display the Show Table dialog box by choosing Relationships, Show Table.

To add a table to the Relationships window, click the table in the Show Table dialog box and then click the Add button or simply double-click the table. When you've finished adding tables, click Close to dismiss the Show Table dialog box. You now see the tables in the Relationship window (see Figure 9.5).

Figure 9.5
The line between the two fields is the default, inner join.

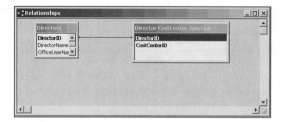

In the Relationships window, you can define the joins that you want between the tables in your database. With at least two tables showing, click on a field in one table and drag the mouse pointer to a field in another table. When you release the mouse button, the join between the two tables appears.

There is an advantage to creating the join in the Relationships window instead of in a query window. Access will create a join automatically for you in a query if there are two tables with identically named fields, and if one of those fields is a primary key.

But if those two conditions are not met, Access won't create the join for you. The Relationships window can help here. If you create a join in the Relationships window, that join automatically appears when you subsequently design a query based on the joined tables—regardless of whether the fields have the same name, and regardless of whether one of them is a table's primary key.

> **NOTE** Neither the Relationships window nor the Query Design window warns you if you're creating an illegal join, such as between a Text and an Integer field. You won't get an error message until you try to use the join, as you would if you tried to open the query.

Choosing Join Types

Table joins can represent either one-to-one or one-to-many relationships. In a one-to-one relationship, each table has only one instance of a value in its join field. In a one-to-many relationship, one table has only one instance of a value whereas the other table can have multiple instances of the same value.

→ Another type of join, many-to-many, is really two instances of a one-to-many join; see "Using Multiple Field Indexes" later in this chapter for more information.

Understanding One-to-Many Relationships

One-to-many relationships are by far the most common type. A typical example consists of a table, Voters, with data on many people, some of whom are registered Democrats and others who are registered Republicans. A record gets a value of 1 on the `PartyID` field if the person is a Democrat and a 2 if a Republican. There are many instances of each value in the Voters table.

Another table, Parties, contains two fields: `PartyID` and `PartyName`. One record has a 1 on `PartyID` and the label Democrat on `PartyName`. The other record has a 2 on `PartyID` and the label Republican on `PartyName`.

You join the Voters table and the Parties table in a query using `PartyID` as the common field. Instead of displaying either instance of `PartyID`, you show `PartyName`. In this way, you can see which party each person identifies with. It's a one-to-many relationship: There's one instance of each `PartyID` value in Parties, and many instances of each `PartyID` value in Voters.

Understanding One-to-One Relationships

One-to-one relationships are much less common. They occur when each table has only one instance of each value on the fields that establish the join. They are less common because you would usually put all the fields in one table, rather than in separate tables joined by a common field.

One reason to use a one-to-one relationship is security. In a networked, human resources application, you might want to show all users the full name, department, and telephone extension of each employee. At the same time, you might want to hide from most users the employee's salary and Social Security number.

One way to handle that is to split the data into two tables: one that has information for public consumption and one for HR purposes only. You can set database permissions so that all users can open one table, but only certain users can open both tables. By linking the two tables in a one-to-one relationship, by means of some field such as `EmployeeID`, you can tie together all the data for a particular employee, while maintaining security for the confidential information.

Defining and Identifying Relationships

In Access, a one-to-one relationship is shown with a 1 on both ends of the join line. A one-to-many relationship is denoted by a 1 at the end near the one-table, and an infinity symbol at the end near the many-table (see Figure 9.6).

Figure 9.6
`DirectorID` is the primary key of the Directors table, so it's the one side of the one-to-many relationship.

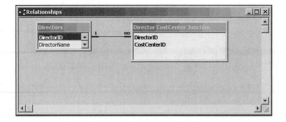

There are a few requirements that you must meet before you can define a relationship as one-to-many or one-to-one.

- You need to use the Relationships window. You cannot define a one-to-many or one-to-one relationship in a query's design view.

- In a one-to-many relationship, the join field in one of the tables must be its primary key or the basis for a unique index. This ensures that there really *is* just one instance of each value on the one-side of the relationship.

- In a one-to-one relationship, the join field must be the primary key (or the basis for a unique index) in *both* tables.

- Referential integrity must be enforced.

Referential integrity is a highfalutin' term for a fairly simple concept: You have to preserve matching values in joined tables. The next section discusses this notion in greater detail.

Preserving Referential Integrity

You've taken some trouble to create a relationship between two tables: Voters and Parties. Both tables have a Byte field, `PartyID`, which is the primary key of the Parties table (in this context, the Parties table is termed the *primary table*). The Parties table has just two records: one for Democrats and one for Republicans.

You add both tables to the Relationships window, and join them by clicking on `PartyID` in one table and dragging to `PartyID` in the other table. Figure 9.7 shows the result.

Figure 9.7
Choose Relationships, Show Direct to hide indirect relationships and tidy up a window cluttered by tables.

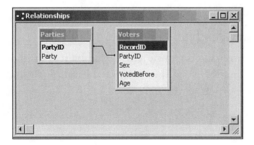

Subsequently you fine-tune the join by right-clicking on the join line and choosing Edit Relationship from the shortcut menu. The Edit Relationships dialog box appears as shown in Figure 9.8.

> **NOTE** The Edit Relationships dialog box appears by default if you've just created the join. If you're editing the relationship at a later time, you get to the dialog box by right-clicking the join or by choosing Relationships, Edit Relationship.

Figure 9.8
The Cascade check boxes are enabled only after you fill the Enforce Referential Integrity check box.

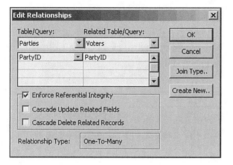

On the Edit Relationships dialog box, fill the Enforce Referential Integrity check box and click OK. You have now prevented yourself, and other users of these tables, from taking three actions. These actions are as follows:

- *You can't add unmatched records on the many side.* Access won't let you add a record to the Voters table with a value of 3, perhaps representing Whigs, on the PartyID field. The idea here is that you should prepare the ground by adding a new record in the primary table before you use its value in the related table. If you begin by adding a record to the Parties table, one with 3 on PartyID and Whig on PartyName, you can subsequently add a record to the Voters table with 3 on PartyID.

- *You can't delete a record from the primary table.* Access won't let you delete either the Democrat or the Republican record from the Parties table if there is at least one matching record in the Voters table. More generally, under referential integrity, you can't delete a record from the primary table if it has a matching record in the related table. But if you had a Whig record in the Parties table and no Whig record in the Voters table, you could delete it from Parties.

- *You can't change a value in the primary key.* Suppose that you decide you don't like using the value 1 on PartyID to represent Democrats—you'd rather use 18. If you try to change the 1 in Parties to 18, Access won't let you. To do so would leave you with a bunch of orphaned Democrats in the Voters table.

And that's what referential integrity means: You can't add a record to the related table if it isn't matched in the primary table; you can't delete a record from the primary table if it's matched in the related table; and you can't modify a value in the key of the primary table.

Actually, you *can* do two of those things if you want. Refer to Figure 9.8 and notice that there are two additional check boxes. If you fill the Cascade Update Related Fields check box, you *can* change a key value in the primary table. Using the Voters example, you could change the Democrat record in the Parties table to have a value of 18 instead of 1. Then a cascade update would change the value 1 to 18 in all matching records of the Voters table.

If you fill the Cascade Delete Related Records check box, you can delete a record from the primary table, even if it's matched by records in the related table. However, the related records are also deleted (you're warned first, and have a chance to stop the procedure from going forward).

Establishing Keys

The term *key* usually means a *primary key*. A primary key is a field (or fields) in a table that uniquely identifies each record in that table.

If each of these is true

- You are represented in a record in a table named ExcelUsers.
- Your record has the value 3 on the field named UserID in the table named ExcelUsers.
- The field named UserID is the primary key of the table named ExcelUsers.

then no other record in ExcelUsers can have the value 3 in the field named UserID. Furthermore, no record can have a null value in the field named UserID.

When you read about database design, you often find that you're advised to establish a primary key for each table in your database. That's frequently good advice. But it's more important to understand *why* you should do something than it is to know you're supposed to do it.

There are only a few reasons to use primary keys. The most important ones are discussed in the following sections.

Finding a Specific Record

You'll see more about indexes in the next section, but for now be aware that a unique index associates a position in a table with a value on the table's primary key. As a result, a database is able to locate a particular record much faster than if it had to look through all the table's records, one by one.

> **NOTE**
> When you establish a field as a table's primary key, Access automatically indexes the table on that field. If in addition you want to index a table on a different field, you must do it manually or by means of the AutoIndex feature (see the following section).

Suppose that a table used by a human resources department has employee's Social Security number (SSN) as its primary key. You want to search for the record of the employee whose SSN is 987-65-4321 which, although you don't yet know it, is the 32,767th record in the table.

The database management system (DBMS) uses a very fast search algorithm to find that SSN in the index. Once it finds in the index the SSN you're after, the database engine has also found the SSN's location in the table. That's what the index does: It pairs the SSN (in this case, 987-65-4321) with the table location of the record that has the SSN (in this case, 32,767).

Knowing the record's location enables the DBMS to display the full record to the user: the employee's name, date of hire, SSN, rate of pay, W-4 deductions, and so on.

Establishing Indexes

As you saw in the previous section of this chapter, "Finding a Specific Record," indexes can help a DBMS find a record very fast. It's a homely old analogy, but a good one: A table's index is like a book's index. With a book's index, you look up a word you're interested in and find a page where the word exists. With a table's index, the DBMS looks up a value that you're interested in and finds the record where that value exists.

DBMS use a very fast search strategy to locate an entry in an index. The strategy is termed *b-tree*, and it involves drilling down through a series of either-or choices. Continuing the book index analogy (which starts to break down about here), you might look in the first half of the index to find a word beginning with *c*, and then in the second quarter to find a word beginning with *ch*, and then in the third eighth to find a word beginning with *cha*, and so on until you locate the word *chasm*. Similarly, DBMS continuously divide the entries in the index into balanced (hence the *b* in *b-tree*) groupings until they locate the field value being sought.

In Access, when you have identified a field as a table's primary key, Access automatically creates an index for that field. There are two general ways, other than establishing a primary key, by which you can create an index for a field.

Establishing an Index Automatically

Suppose that it's your practice to provide a particular prefix or suffix for names of fields that you want to index. For example, you might use the suffix *CD*, short for *code*. Then your indexed fields might be named `PhysicianCD`, `AccountCD`, `ProgramCD`, and so on. If you use CD as a prefix instead, you might name fields `CDPhysician`, `CDAccount`, and `CDProgram`.

If you want Access to automatically index a field based on a prefix or suffix, begin with a database active and then choose Tools, Options. Click the Tables/Queries tab (see Figure 9.9).

Figure 9.9
Separate prefixes or suffixes by semicolons, not commas.

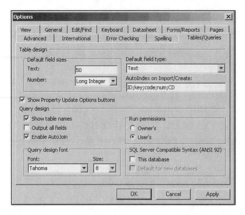

Following the existing list of prefixes and suffixes, enter **;CD**. This establishes CD as a string which, affixed to a field's name, causes Access to automatically index the field when it's created.

Creating an Index Manually

There are several ways to create an index other than automatically. Two of them use a table's Design view, as shown in Figure 9.10.

Figure 9.10
The Field Properties pane enables you to set various field properties.

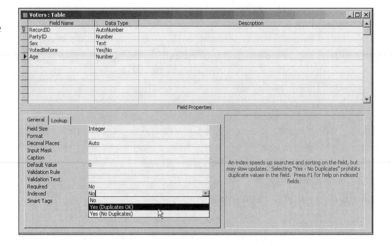

In Figure 9.10, the field named Age is selected. To set an index on this field using the Field Properties pane, take these steps:

1. In the General tab, click in the box to the right of the Indexed caption.
2. A drop-down arrow appears. Click it to display the drop-down list.
3. Click either **Yes (Duplicates OK)** or **Yes (No Duplicates)**.
4. Save the table.

To use the other method, choose View, Indexes (or click the Indexes button). The dialog box shown in Figure 9.11 appears.

Figure 9.11
You can give the index a meaningful name if you use the Indexes dialog box.

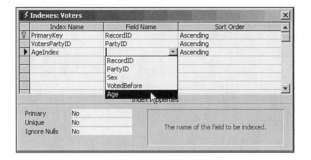

Take these steps:

1. Type a name, which could be the name of the field itself, in the **Index Name** column.

2. Click in the **Field Name** column, and select the field you want to index from the drop-down list.

3. Indicate whether you want the index to put the records in ascending or descending order according to their value on the indexed field.

4. Set the **Primary**, **Unique**, and **Ignore Nulls** options to either Yes or No.

5. Click the **X** button to close the dialog box.

Setting the Primary option to Yes means that the field used by the index becomes the table's primary key. Because you can reset this option to Yes on a different index, it's clear that a table can have more than one primary key—although it can use only one index at a time as its primary key.

In some rare cases, you'll want to index a field that might contain null values. If you set Ignore Nulls to Yes, records that contain null values on that field will not enter the index. (A primary key cannot contain null values; therefore, the Ignore Nulls setting is not used for primary key indexes.)

The Unique option, if set to No, allows more than one instance of the same value in the indexed field. This raises the question of which fields to index.

Indexes are a mixed blessing. They do usually make data retrieval quicker, although you won't perceive an increase in speed unless you have many, many records to search. On the other side of the medal, you have to keep indexes updated. When you add a record, for example, the DBMS must account for that record's value on the index's field. It needs to add to the index the record's value and its position in the table. The situation is similar when you delete a record. The DBMS must remove that record's instance, its field value as well as its position in the table, from the index.

That by no means exhausts the jobs that the DBMS must perform to keep the index current. If you delete a record, for example, that alters the position in the table of all the subsequent records. Their position values in the index have to be updated. The reverse occurs, of course, when you add a new record.

Only experience can tell you whether establishing an index for a field will result in a net gain or net loss—whether the gain in retrieval speed outweighs the loss due to index maintenance. The more sophisticated DBMS assist you in making this judgment with statistical sampling techniques, and tools that you can use to fine-tune your choice of indexes.

Using Multiple Field Indexes

You're not limited to a single field in an index. It can sometimes pay to index a table on two, and rarely more than two, fields.

You can find an example of a multiple field index in the Northwind database that accompanies Microsoft Access. The Order Details table provides a junction between the Products table and the Orders table.

In the Northwind database, any given product can appear on many different orders; for example, Johnson's Ketchup could be part of orders number 1, 10, and 25. But any given order can contain many different products: Roger's Clams, Neal's Wine, and Garlic By Fred might all appear on order number 31. This is an example of a *many-to-many* relationship.

Northwind's Order Details table associates many products with many orders. Each record in the table represents one product on one order. The Northwind database uses the junction table to relate the Products table and the Orders table. Figure 9.12 shows the design of a query that joins the two tables.

Figure 9.12
In Query Design view, referential integrity assigns the junction table the many side of one-to-many relationships.

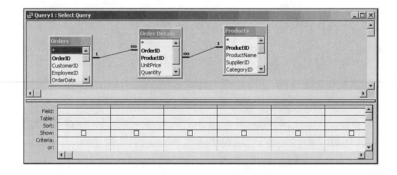

To maximize the junction table's efficiency, its primary key should consist of *both* a product field and an order field. To establish this multiple field key, take these steps:

1. With the table in Design view, click the box to the left of the name of the first of the two fields. The entire row is selected.

2. Hold down the **Ctrl** key and click the box to the left of the name of the second of the two fields. Both rows are now selected.

3. Click the **Primary Key** button. The key icon appears next to both fields in the design grid (see Figure 9.13).

4. Save the table.

Figure 9.13
It's the *combination* of the two fields that must be unique in the junction table. Either field can by itself assume duplicate values.

If you prefer, you can establish a multiple field index via the Indexes dialog box. Take these steps:

1. Choose **View**, **Indexes**.

2. Enter a name for the index in the **Index Name** column of the first blank row.

3. In the same row, select the first field from the dropdown list in the **Field Name** column.

4. Set the Primary dropdown to **Yes**.

5. In the next row down, leave the Index Name column blank, but select the second field from the dropdown list in the **Field Name** column (see Figure 9.14).

6. Click the **X** box to close the dialog box.

Figure 9.14
Notice that both fields have the key icon, indicating that they are combined to form the table's primary key.

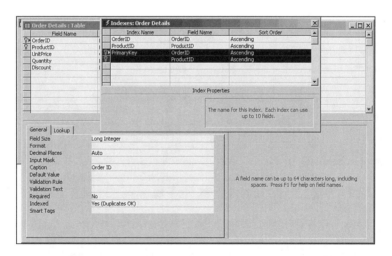

When I first started designing databases, I had the idea that many-to-many relationships of the sort discussed here were rare and exotic. It wasn't until I kept running into them in real-world situations that I saw how commonplace they are, and how using them made many of my queries much more efficient.

Creating Queries

You saw in Chapter 5, "Using Microsoft Query," how to create a simple Select query in Access. The Select query was used as a data source for Microsoft Query, in situations that were too complex for Microsoft Query to manage.

Prior sections in this chapter have discussed joins in greater detail, as well as the implications of choosing names and data types for the fields in the database's tables. The present section builds on those concepts to deal with action queries and criteria in select queries.

The Select query that you saw in Chapter 5 is doubtless the most frequently used type of query. It fulfills several objectives, among them

- Returning data from one or more tables that are joined by common fields
- Returning data summaries, such as averages and counts of one field according to different values of another field
- Calculating new, temporary fields by building expressions based on existing fields

In general, you should use queries in preference to other methods of retrieving or manipulating records in a database because queries' SQL make more efficient use of resources than do other approaches (such as DAO and ADO recordsets).

There are many occasions when you need to resort to recordsets because SQL doesn't meet your needs. For example, you might need to modify the appearance of a form based on the value of a record in a table. But when possible, you should use queries—and that includes the action queries: Update, Append, Delete, and Make Table.

Using Update Queries

Use an Update when you want to change the value of a field in some or all of a field's records.

CASE STUDY

You're responsible for a database that maintains records on a hospital's employees. One of the requirements for the hospital to maintain its accreditation is that all employees pass an annual examination on safety procedures: what to do if an infant is abducted, where to find material safety data sheets, how to report a hazmat spill, and so on.

The test is administered online using the hospital's data network, and one of the database's tables is keyed on the employee's unique ID number. It also stores the date he took the test, his response to each of 30 test questions, and the number of questions he answered correctly.

The hospital's human resources department maintains another table that contains other information such as the employee's Social Security number, the department he works for, his hire date, and all the other personal information needed on an employee of a highly regulated industry. The HR table is also keyed on the employee's unique ID.

From time to time, the hospital wants to analyze two critical summary variables: the average percent correct on the safety test for each department, and the percent of current employees who have taken the test, again by department. A department with an unusually low mean score on the test receives additional training. A department that is lagging in completion rate is targeted for unwelcome attention from the hospital's administration. You use a Select query to join the Safety Test table to the Employees table, and use that query (see Figure 9.15) as the data source for an external data range on an Excel worksheet (see Figure 9.16).

Figure 9.15
The query returns for each department a count of employees and of test completions to calculate a percent.

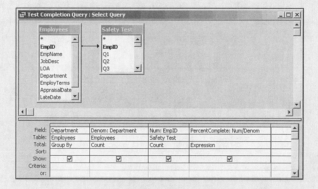

TIP

To get the query shown in Figure 9.15 to display the `PercentComplete` field in percent format, first click any row in the column in Query Design view to select a cell in the design grid. Then right-click the cell (you can't start by right-clicking in the design grid; Access assumes you're right-clicking the query, not the cell). Choose Properties from the shortcut menu and in the Field Properties window choose Percent for the field's format. This controls the display of the field in Access only—if you want to show the field as a percent in Excel, you'll need to format it on the worksheet too.

Figure 9.16
An analysis of percents should usually include the percent's denominator (here, the employee count per department).

	A	B	C	D
1	Department	PercentComplete	Denom	
2	6010	93%	86	
3	6015	96%	25	
4	6070	92%	24	
5	6075	89%	19	
6	6091	100%	7	
7	6110	94%	18	
8	6150	95%	63	
9	6155	98%	42	
10	6170	97%	62	
11	6173	92%	53	
12	6176	92%	12	
13	6177	93%	60	

One day you learn that HR will no longer maintain data on ex-employees in its Employees table, but will archive the data in a Terminations table. Once monthly, the records of employees who have left the hospital are removed from the Employees table and placed in the Terminations table.

This causes you some minor heartburn. The hospital wants to see departmental results both for current employees only, *and* for all employees since it started administering the test. The query shown in Figure 9.15 relies on the Employees table to provide each employee's department, but if ex-employees are no longer to be kept in that table, you'll have to look elsewhere for department membership.

There are various solutions, but you decide that the most straightforward is to begin storing the employee's department in the Safety Test table. Before the HR department archives records on ex-employees for the first time, you duplicate the Department field from the Employees table in the Safety Test table. Then you create the Update query shown in Figure 9.17.

Figure 9.17

Note that an inner join is used: It returns only records where the joined fields from both tables are equal.

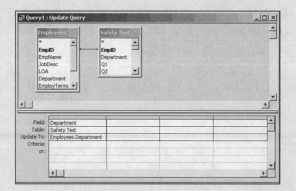

To create the query shown in Figure 9.17, take these steps:

1. From the main Access window, click the **Queries** tab.

2. Click the **New** button, choose **Design View** in the New Query dialog box, and click **OK**.

3. Add the **Employees** table and the **Safety Test** table to the query's design pane and then click **Close** in the Show Table dialog box. If, as here, the tables' primary key fields have the same name, Access automatically creates a default join between the two tables. (If not, you would create the join yourself by clicking one field and dragging to the other.)

4. Choose **Query, Update Query**. This changes the active query from the default Select query type to an Update query type. Notice that the Sort row and the Show row are removed and replaced by an Update To row.

5. Drag the `Department` field from the Safety Test table to the query design grid's first column. Or, click in the Field row and select **Safety Test.Department** from the drop-down list.

6. In the **Update To** row under Department, enter `[Employees].[Department]`. Because there are two Department fields in the query—one from each table—you need to qualify the one that you want to update from.

7. Choose **Query**, **Run** or click the Run button on the toolbar. Click **Yes** in response to Access's confirmation message.

9

> **NOTE**
>
> The query uses an inner join: It returns only those records that exist in *both* tables, and therefore does not try to update a record found in the Safety Test table that is not found in the Employees table. It could also use an outer join that returns all records from the Safety Test table and only those records from the Employees table with a matching value on `EmpID`.
>
> Suppose that instead you use an outer join that returns all records from the Employees table and only those records from the Safety Test table with a matching value on `EmpID`. Then the update query will attempt to update nonexistent records in the Safety Test table. If you're running the query manually, you'll get a warning message that some records were not updated due to key violations. You can bypass the warning, but it's an annoyance you don't need. Unless you're sure of your ground, use inner joins in multi-table Update queries.

→ For more information about inner and outer joins, **see** "Joining Parent and Child Records," **p. 119**.

Using Delete and Append Queries

It's not too difficult to delete a record from a table in a database: just open the table, find the record, select it, and then press the Delete key.

But when you have many records to delete, and when for one reason or another you need to delete the same records over and over, you don't want to do it manually. Apart from the time you waste, there's always the nagging little doubt that you might have deleted the wrong records. Delete queries can come in handy here. They're faster than deleting records manually, and you can rely on them to act the same way time after time—just make sure that you set them up correctly to begin with.

Chapter 4, "Importing Data: An Overview," mentioned the difficulty you encounter when an application stores data internally but does not offer you a straightforward way to access it. Fortunately, such applications generally provide the user with a report writing capability, which exports data in either a formatted report layout or a comma-separated values (CSV) format.

In some cases you must access and reuse this data frequently. Then you'll want to use Delete queries in conjunction with Append queries. When you have this sort of situation, it usually helps to use VBA code to run the queries. It's a more effective use of your time to run a single VBA procedure that executes several queries in turn than to execute each query in turn by hand.

Human resources isn't through with you yet. You've been asked to create a form that directors can use to view information about employees in their departments: people whose annual performance appraisals are due during the next month, dates that annual physicals are required, employees returning from leaves of absence, and so on.

Creating the form is not the real problem. The problem is to get the data for the form out of HR's secure employee database and into a database that can be more broadly accessed by various users—here, the department directors.

Normally this would be a simple task: just point a Select query at the appropriate table in HR's database and use it as the data source for a user form. The problem is that you can't point a Select query at the HR database: It stores its data in a proprietary format that isn't compliant with today's standards.

The program that HR uses is an old one. But it does have a report writer that you use periodically to create a CSV file. With the CSV file created, you can use it to populate a database table.

There's one further wrinkle: You need to create a new field as part of the process. The HR application will provide you with the date that an employee's next appraisal is due. But the directors have a grace period for filing the annual appraisal. The grace period extends from the appraisal's due date to four weeks following the due date. That is, if Ms. Smith's appraisal is due on August 9, her appraisal is not regarded as overdue until after September 6.

So, your project will have to calculate that overdue date in addition to updating the basic employee data. The sequence of events will be as follows:

1. Use HR's report writer to create a new CSV file.
2. Import the text data from the CSV file into a database table.
3. Delete the old employee records from their table.
4. Append the new employee records to the table. At the same time, you can calculate the appraisal overdue date from the appraisal due date.

Each of these items is discussed in detail in the following sections.

Importing the Text Data

The first task is to arrange to import the data. Suppose that the HR report writer outputs its text data to a file named Employees.csv. You'll want to import the data into an Access table in such a way that subsequent imports can be automated. You do that by taking these steps.

1. With the Access database window active, choose **File**, **Get External Data**, **Import**. The Import window appears.

2. From the Files of Type dropdown, choose **Text Files (*.txt;*.csv;*.tab;*.asc)**.

3. Using the **Look In** dropdown if necessary, browse to the location of the Employees.csv file.

4. Click the **Employees.csv** file to highlight it and click the **Import** button. The Import window closes and is replaced by the first step of the Import Text Wizard (see Figure 9.18).

Figure 9.18
Notice that the first row of the data file includes field names.

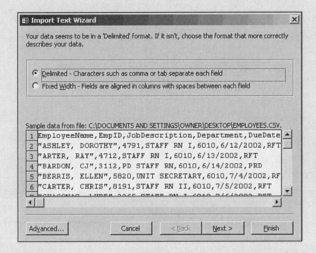

5. No options need changing in the wizard's first step, so click **Next** to go to the second step (see Figure 9.19).

Figure 9.19
Access notes the location of the commas and separates the fields into columns accordingly.

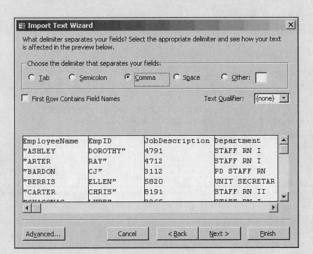

6. Your file separates fields with commas, so you can leave the choice of delimiter alone. As shown, field names occupy the first row, so you should fill the First Row Contains Field Names check box. So doing prevents Access from treating a row of field names as a record. Also, the file uses double quotes to set off text values, so use the Text Qualifier dropdown to choose the double quote mark. Click **Next** to go to the next step (see Figure 9.20).

Figure 9.20
Specifying First Row Contains Field Names in the prior step makes column headers of the field names.

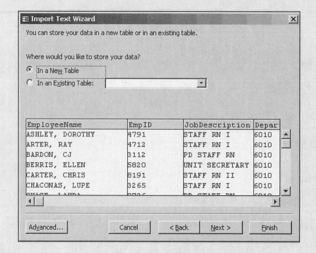

7. Make sure that **In a New Table** is selected and click the **Next** button (see Figure 9.21).

Figure 9.21
If necessary, select a field by clicking in its column and change its properties as needed—for example, its Name.

8. If your data file did *not* have field names in its first row, Access proposes default names (Field1, Field2, and so on). Use this step to change those names to something more descriptive, because the names will become the field names in the new table. This is

also the right place to indicate a particular data type for each field (Date/Time in particular, because Access won't automatically recognize some date/time formats). Click **Next** to go to the next step (see Figure 9.22).

Figure 9.22
If your data has a unique record ID, consider using that as the table's primary key.

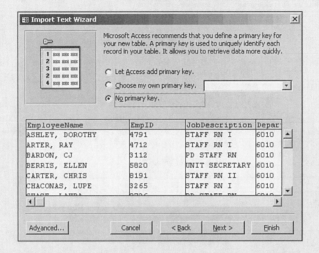

9. In this example, the table that the data is imported into does not need a primary key, so you would choose No Primary Key. In a different situation, you might either let Access add a primary key (which would usually be named ID and be typed as a Long Integer increment), or choose your own primary key from the dropdown. Click **Next** (see Figure 9.23).

Figure 9.23
Click the Advanced button to avoid losing all the information you supplied to the wizard.

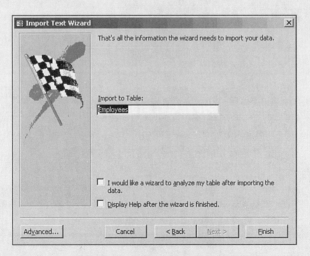

10. Figure 9.23 shows that you can supply a different name for the new table; otherwise, it will be named according to the name given to the CSV file. In this case, it's

important to save the information you have supplied, and you do so by clicking the **Advanced** button (see Figure 9.24).

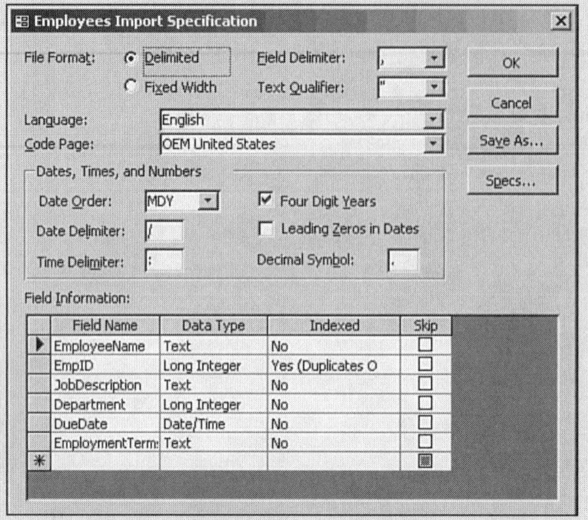

Figure 9.24
The ID suffix is set via Options to call for an index, so the wizard proposes a duplicate-value index for the EmpID field.

11. Make any changes you might require using the controls in the Import Specification window. Then be sure to click the **Save As** button. This will save your specification so that it can be reused later, and you won't have to supply field names, field types, indexing information, and so on. The Save Import/Export Specification window appears (see Figure 9.25).

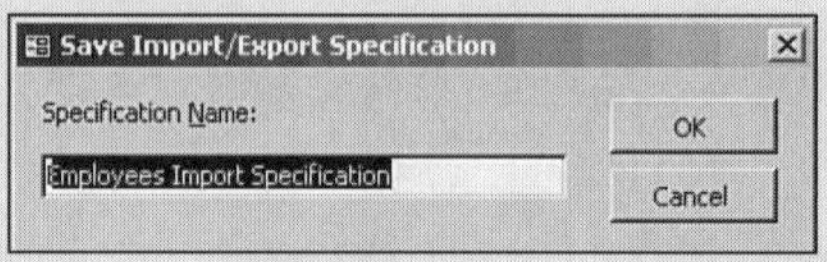

Figure 9.25
There's seldom a reason to change the default specification name supplied by Access.

12. If necessary, change the specification name that Access supplies and click **OK**. You are returned to the Import Specification window.

13. Click **OK** to return to the final step of the Import Text Wizard, and click **Finish**. Access informs you that it has imported the data into the table.

Now, so long as you don't change the structure of the data file—deleting and adding fields, putting Text data where the specification expects Date/Time, using a space instead of a comma as the field delimiter—you'll be able to reuse the import specification that you saved in step 11. As you'll see, you can refer to it in VBA code to automate the process of bringing new data into the database.

Deleting the Old Records

The next task is to prepare to delete the existing records. Then you can replace them with the newly imported records.

Of course, the solution is to run a Delete query followed by an Append query. The first step is to create the queries. The completed Delete query is shown in Figure 9.26.

Figure 9.26
In another situation, you could selectively delete records by supplying a value for a particular field in the Criteria row.

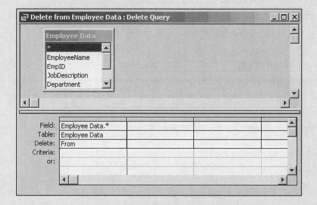

To create the query shown in Figure 9.26, take these steps:

1. With the Access database window active, click the **Queries** tab. Then click the **New** button. With **Design View** selected in the New Query list box, click **OK**.

2. The New Query window disappears and the Show Table window appears. Click the **Tables** tab if necessary.

3. Click the **EmployeeData** table in the **Show Table** list box, and then click **Add** to add the table to the query design. This is the only table involved in the query, so you can click **Close** to remove the Show Table window.

4. Choose **Query, Delete Query**. This changes the new query from a default Select query to a Delete query.

5. Click on the **asterisk** in the **EmployeeData** table shown in the query's Table Pane. This asterisk is a sort of wild card, standing in for all the table's fields. Drag it to the **Field** row of the design grid's first column. The query window now appears as in Figure 9.26.

6. Choose **File, Save**. Access prompts you to replace the default name (Query1, Query2, and so on) with a more descriptive one. This example saves the query as **Delete From Employee Data**.

You'll run the Delete From Employee Data query to remove existing records from the table in preparation for adding new records obtained from the HR application. You'll also want to create a Delete query to dispose of the old records in the Employees table, perhaps named Delete From Employees.

Appending the New Records

You can add the records most efficiently by means of an Append query, shown in Figure 9.27.

Figure 9.27
An Append query can also calculate new field values to append to the target table.

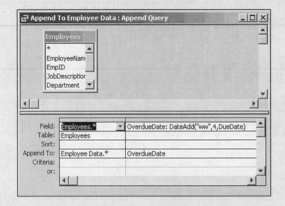

To create the query shown in Figure 9.27, take these steps:

1. With the Access database window active, click the **Queries** tab. Then click the **New** button. With **Design View** selected in the New Query list box, click **OK**.

2. The New Query window disappears and the Show Table window appears. Click the **Tables** tab if necessary.

3. Click the **Employees** table in the **Show Table** list box, and then click **Add** to add the table to the query design. Click **Close** to remove the Show Table window.

4. Choose **Query, Append Query**. The Append window appears (see Figure 9.28). Choose **Employee Data** from the Table Name dropdown, and click **OK**. This changes the new query from a default Select query to an Append query that will obtain records from Employees table and append them to the Employee Data table. You're returned to the query design window.

Figure 9.28
When designing an Append query, start with the source table and specify the target table in the Append window.

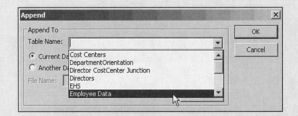

5. Click on the **asterisk** in the **Employees** table shown in the query's Table Pane. Drag it to the **Field** row of the design grid's first column.

6. In the second column of the design grid, enter in the expression **OverdueDate: DateAdd("ww",4,DueDate)**. This uses the Access function **DateAdd** to calculate a field

named `OverdueDate`. In this case, it adds four weeks (the `ww` argument) to the `DueDate` field. The query window now appears as in Figure 9.27.

7. Choose **File**, **Save**. Replace the default name with a more descriptive one. This example saves the query as **Append To EmployeeData**.

Executing the Queries

With these two queries in the database, you can run VBA code similar to the following listing:

```
Sub UpdateEmployeeData()
Dim PathName As String

CurrentDb.QueryDefs("Delete From Employee Data").Execute
CurrentDb.QueryDefs("Delete From Employees").Execute

PathName = "C:\Documents and Settings\Owner\Desktop\Employees.csv"
DoCmd.TransferText acImportDelim, "Employees Import Specification", _
"Employees", PathName, True
CurrentDb.QueryDefs("Append To Employee Data").Execute

End Sub
```

There are some aspects to this code that deserve a mention:

- The `TransferText` method of the `DoCmd` object is used to import the data from the CSV file. Its `acImportDelim` argument indicates that Access is to import a delimited file. The import specification, Employees Import Specification, is identified, as is the Employees table into which the data will be inserted.

- The path to and the name of the CSV file is stored in a `PathName` variable and passed to the `TransferText` method. This approach isn't necessary, but it does make it easier to change the path or filename when necessary.

- You can execute a query, just as the code shown earlier executes three queries, simply by naming the query and calling the `Execute` method. The query can be of any type—a Select or an action query.

- By attaching this code to a command button on a user form in the database, you make it very easy to update a table when necessary.

- You can run this code directly in an Access VBA module. You can also run it (with some adjustments, such as identifying the database) using an Excel VBA module. You would first need to set a reference to a DAO or ADO object library, by choosing References from the VBE Tools menu and filling the appropriate library's check box.

You really don't want to have to jump through such hoops just to get data into a database. It's much more sensible to make direct use of the database or other application that's used to maintain the original data set.

But there are times when that isn't feasible. It's often the case, for example, that the data maintenance package can be used on only a few workstations, for licensing reasons.

Even then, you would hope that the application supported a linkage from a more widely available application, such as Access or Excel. But many applications don't provide that degree of compatibility or convenience. Then you have to resort to methods discussed in this chapter, as kludgy as they seem. In my own experience, they turn out to be necessary more often than not.

Looking Ahead

This chapter has concerned itself mostly with structures and activities more appropriate for use with a database manager, such as Access or SQL Server, than for a data analysis application such as Excel. The reason is that if you are to manage data in a database from the Excel platform, it's useful to understand what effect your actions have in the database.

The next chapter returns to Excel, and the methods you use there to do what this chapter discussed in the context of Access: defining tables and fields, managing table joins, and creating and executing queries, all without ever using the database management system.

Defining Fields and Records with ActiveX Data Objects and Data Access Objects

10

Creating Databases from Excel

In a sense, creating a database from the platform that Excel provides is very simple. With a reference to Data Access Objects (DAO) established in a VBA module (as described in Chapter 8, "Opening Databases"), you just execute the following statement:

```
CreateDatabase Name:= "NewDB.mdb", _
Locale:=dbLangGeneral
```

That's all there is to it. Executing that statement in VBA creates a new Access database named NewDB.mdb in the default directory. It has no tables or queries or any of the other structures that you normally find in an Access database, but it's there and ready to store them for you.

Of course, that's disingenuous. You need to prepare the ground first. You would want to check that there's not already a file named NewDB.mdb in the default directory, and if there is, you need to decide whether to delete it before creating a new one. You also need to decide what to do if the file exists and another user has it open.

This chapter shows you how to go about doing that. It does so using DAO as the toolkit, rather than ActiveX Data Objects (ADO). ADO wasn't initially designed to provide all the functionality needed to create a new database. An extension of ADO—ADOX, short for *ADO Extensions*—supports the creation of new tables and fields in an existing database, and it's discussed later in this chapter.

It's a little unusual to create a new database from Excel, but by no means unheard of. In particular, if you develop Office-based applications for your company or clients, you often have users who want to create their own Excel workbooks to store data. For data backup reasons, as well as for more effective storage and retrieval, these users often want to store data they put in their workbook in a true database.

You can meet their needs by providing an Excel template. The template is a workbook on which new workbooks are based. The template can include VBA code that establishes a new Access database, complete with tables and fields that enable it to shadow data that the user places in the new workbook, as shown in the following case study.

Creating a New Database Using DAO

Suppose that you want to automate the creation of a new Access database. With a new Excel workbook open, begin by establishing a VBA module. Choose Tools, Macro, Visual Basic Editor. With the VBE active, create a new module by choosing Insert, Module.

To create a database using DAO, you need to establish a reference to the DAO object library. Choose Tools, References and scroll down until you see a Microsoft DAO Object Library. The highest-numbered version is the one to use, and the versions available on your system depend on which version of Office you have installed. For Office 2003, that's Microsoft DAO 3.6 Object Library; for Office 1997, it's DAO 3.5. Fill its check box and click OK.

Providing the Code to Create the Database

After establishing the necessary reference, enter this code into the new module:

```
Sub CreateDatabaseWithDAO(DatabaseName As String)
Dim GoAhead As Boolean

GoAhead = True

If Dir(DatabaseName) <> "" Then
    If MsgBox(Prompt:="Delete existing " & DatabaseName & "?", _
        Buttons:=vbYesNo, Title:="Naming conflict.") = vbYes Then
        Kill DatabaseName
        GoAhead = True
    Else
        MsgBox Prompt:="Okay, leaving existing " & DatabaseName _
            & " alone.", Title:="Taking no action."
        GoAhead = False
    End If
End If

If GoAhead Then
    CreateDatabase Name:=DatabaseName, Locale:=dbLangGeneral
End If

End Sub
```

You would call this subroutine by means of another statement, one that both invokes the subroutine and that passes the database name to it. For example, if you wanted the database to be named `Crash Carts.mdb`, the statement might be

```
CreateDatabaseWithDAO "Crash Carts.mdb"
```

The subroutine's logic is as follows:

1. Check to see whether a database with the name that's been passed already exists in the default path. That's the purpose of the `Dir` function.

2. If that database already exists, display a message box to inform the user and ask whether to delete the existing version.

3. If the user says yes by clicking the message box's Yes button, delete the existing version and set a Boolean, `GoAhead`, to TRUE.

4. If the user says no by *not* clicking the message box's Yes button, don't delete the database. Just display a message box saying that the existing version will be left as is and set the Boolean `GoAhead` to FALSE.

5. If `GoAhead` is TRUE, create the database.

The critical part of the subroutine is the statement that actually creates the database. Its full syntax is

```
Set DatabaseVariable = Workspace.CreateDatabase _
(Name, Locale, Options)
```

You would need the `Set DatabaseVariable` portion only if you had already declared `DatabaseVariable` as an object variable; for example:

```
Dim DatabaseVariable As DAO.Database
```

The subroutine `CreateDatabaseWithDAO` makes no further use of the database beyond creating it, so the subroutine doesn't assign it to an object variable.

You would specify a workspace in the `CreateDatabase` statement if you had already invoked a new one and wanted to use it. By omitting that specification the statement uses the default, active workspace.

The `CreateDatabase` method itself takes three arguments:

- `Name`—This establishes the name and the extension of the database. You can, optionally, supply a path: `Name:="C:\NewDatabase.mdb"`. If you don't supply a path, the Excel workbook's default path is used. This argument is required.

- `Locale`—This specifies the order in which text strings are to be sorted. You'll almost always use `dbLangGeneral`, which subsumes most European languages including English. This argument is required.

- `Options`—This argument is optional. Omit it to create a new database that is based on your current Office version. You can create a database that's based on an earlier version if you want. For example, suppose that you're running Access 2003 but most of your users are running Access 97. You could use `Option:=dbVersion30` to create a database compatible with Jet 3.5, and thus compatible with Access 97.

Creating a Table Using DAO

After they've used your code to create a new database, your users will surely need to put one or more tables in it. The approach shown in this section works for any existing Access database, whether or not you've just created it.

> **NOTE**
> As you'll see, you can't save a new table in an existing database without putting at least one field in the table. However, you can save a new database without putting any tables in it. This is consistent with the process of creating a database using the Access interface: An empty database is perfectly legal, but a table devoid of any fields isn't.

As usual, you'll need a module that has a reference set for a DAO library. With the reference set, you enter the following code in a module. The code shown here is the minimum code needed to create a table in an existing database using DAO:

```
Sub MakeNewTableWithDAO(DatabaseName As String, _
TableName As String, FieldName As String)

Dim dbBackupData As DAO.Database
Dim tdBackupTable As DAO.TableDef
Dim fldBackupField As DAO.Field

Set dbBackupData = OpenDatabase(DatabaseName)
Set tdBackupTable = dbBackupData.CreateTableDef(TableName)
Set fldBackupField = tdBackupTable.CreateField(FieldName, _
dbText, 45)

tdBackupTable.Fields.Append fldBackupField

dbBackupData.TableDefs.Append tdBackupTable
End Sub
```

You might well want to integrate this code with the code that creates the database itself. For example

```
DatabaseName="SalesBackup.mdb"
TableName="GiftShopSales"
FieldName="SalesAmount"

CreateDatabaseWithDAO DatabaseName
MakeNewTableWithDAO DatabaseName, TableName, FieldName
```

This code passes the same database name to both procedures, ensuring that when the tables are created and the fields appended, they go into the database that was created with the `CreateDatabaseWithDAO` subroutine.

> **NOTE**
>
> Suppose that your Access database is open when you run the code that creates a new table, and that the Tables tab is active. If you now switch to Access, you might not see the name of the new table. This is because you need to refresh the list of tables in the database. Click another tab, such as Queries, and then return to the Tables tab to see the new table.

Getting Names from the User

Of course, you avoid the static-name approach in the workbook you have under development. It's seldom wise to assign static values to string variables (or to variables of any other data type, for that matter) in the code itself. But the code shown earlier does just that to the names of the database, the table, and the table's field.

One good alternative, which allows the user some realistic flexibility in naming the objects, is to pick up the names from the user's workbook. You could obtain the name of the database from the name of the workbook, the table name from the name of the active worksheet, and the name of the field from a column header.

Eventually the user will enter data on a worksheet in the workbook you're developing. Suppose that the worksheet appears as shown in Figure 10.1.

Figure 10.1

Notice that the maximum length of a value in A2:A20 is 6, and compare with the table design in Figure 10.2.

	A	B	C	D	E	F
1	MedRecNumber	Date	Doctor	AdmitTime	DischargeTime	
2	118146	6/12/2004	French	5:47	12:32	
3	804931	6/12/2004	Taylor	6:15	9:17	
4	821491	6/12/2004	Connaugh	6:43	12:58	
5	234005	6/12/2004	Taylor	7:09	12:50	
6	282764	6/12/2004	French	8:01	12:16	
7	109941	6/12/2004	Taylor	8:09	12:09	
8	295187	6/12/2004	French	8:36	13:54	
9	837044	6/12/2004	Connaugh	8:42	11:34	
10	319247	6/12/2004	Nussbaum	8:58	14:04	
11	199883	6/12/2004	Astin	9:00	17:37	
12	705593	6/12/2004	Nussbaum	10:06	13:24	
13	535328	6/12/2004	Connaugh	10:46	14:38	
14	274627	6/12/2004	McIntyre	11:22	17:19	
15	600438	6/12/2004	McIntyre	12:01	18:03	
16	672363	6/12/2004	Nussbaum	12:16	16:10	
17	280800	6/12/2004	Astin	12:24	20:38	
18	931057	6/12/2004	Astin	13:39	18:36	
19	876317	6/12/2004	Edwin	13:56	18:24	
20	445583	6/12/2004	McIntyre	14:20	17:51	
21						

Now you could use code like this to tailor the database to the way that the user has structured the worksheet:

```
Option Explicit
Option Base 1
```

`Option Base 1` is one way to ensure that VBA arrays refer to their first element as 1. The default is 0, so unless you arrange otherwise, the first element of an array is its zero-th. If you use `Option Base 1` at the top of a VBA module, all arrays declared in that module will refer to their first element as element number 1.

```
Type FieldType
    FieldName As String
    FieldLength As Integer
End Type
```

VBA supports *user-defined data types*. That is, you can declare a variable as something other than String, Integer, Date, or Variant. If you've already defined your own type, you can subsequently declare a variable to be of that type.

In many cases, this comes about because you want to mix two incompatible data types in an array. In the current example, it will be useful to have an array that contains information about the names of fields (text data) and about the length of each field (numeric data).

An alternative is to declare a variable of type Variant, which can store any mix of data types. But that's usually a lazy approach and it denies you one of the benefits of declaring a type: named elements.

By declaring a type—here, FieldType—at the outset, the code can later declare an array of type FieldType. There are several advantages to doing so. In this case, the two most important reasons are

- It's possible to have a single array that consists of one column of text data and one column of numeric data.

- It's easy and self-documenting to refer to an element called FieldName and to one called FieldLength. In contrast, if you declared the array as Variant, you'd have to refer to the first column and to the second column by number instead of by name, and you'd have to remember which is which. A year or two from now, someone else might have to maintain this code. Considering the difficulty you'd be saddling him with, you'd do well to stay out of dark alleys.

After declaring the options that are in effect and a user-defined data type, you continue by developing the subroutines themselves. You use a subroutine named Driver to initiate the processing. Its code follows:

```
Sub Driver()

Dim DatabaseName As String
Dim LockFileName As String
Dim TableName As String
Dim FieldCount As Integer
Dim i As Integer
Dim GoAhead As Boolean
Dim FieldArray() As FieldType
```

Note that FieldArray is dimensioned with a pair of empty parentheses, and declared as FieldType. The implications of this, along with ReDim, are discussed later in this section.

After declaring several variables, you arrange to store the names picked up from the Excel workbook in those variables. This approach avoids the problems created by working with static, constant names.

```
DatabaseName = Left(ThisWorkbook.Name, Len(ThisWorkbook.Name) - 4)
DatabaseName = ThisWorkbook.Path & "\" & DatabaseName & ".mdb"
LockFileName = ThisWorkbook.Path & "\" & DatabaseName & ".ldb"
```

You store the name of the workbook in the `DatabaseName` variable. Notice that the `Left` function is used in conjunction with the `Len` function to strip off the four rightmost characters in the workbook's name, and the remaining characters are stored in `DatabaseName`. So, if the workbook's name is DBTemplate.xls, the characters ".xls" are removed and the remaining string, `DBTemplate`, is stored in `DatabaseName`.

Also, the path of the workbook that contains the code, as well as a backslash, are prepended to the database name. This ensures that whatever path Excel currently considers to be the default, the database will be created in the same path as the workbook.

Then `LockFileName` is assigned the value of `DatabaseName` plus the characters ".ldb" and the characters ".mdb" are appended to the end of `DatabaseName`. A later procedure uses these values to test for the existence of a database with the current name (for example, `DBTemplate.mdb`).

```
TableName = ActiveSheet.Name
```

You assign the name of the active sheet to the variable `TableName`. If the active sheet's name is `Sheet1`, the database table created by the code will also be `Sheet1`.

Counting Fields

You now need to determine the number of fields to put in the table. Begin with the following statement:

```
FieldCount = ActiveSheet.Cells(1, 256).End(xlToLeft).Column
```

The number of fields that will be put in the database table is determined by the number of the rightmost column in row 1 that has a value.

> **NOTE** This statement isn't quite true. The `End(xlToLeft)` method emulates what happens when you select a cell, hold down the Ctrl key, and press the left arrow. Suppose that you start with cell IV1. If IV1 is empty, Excel goes left until it finds a nonempty cell and stops there. If IV1 isn't empty but IU1 is empty, Excel heads left until it finds a nonempty cell. If IV1 isn't empty and neither is IU1, Excel heads left until it finds the last contiguous nonempty cell. The code makes the assumption (a valid one in most real-life situations) that cell IV1 is empty; therefore, Excel heads left until it finds the first nonempty cell—assumed here to be in the rightmost column of a list.

Note the assignment statement for `FieldCount`. It instructs VBA to start in the first row, 256th column of the active sheet and go left until it finds a used cell. The assumption is that the number of the column containing that cell gives the number of fields to create.

Ideally, the user has created a list that occupies, say, columns A through G and an indeterminate number of rows. Then the code finds that cell G1 isn't empty. Because G is the seventh column, `FieldCount` is assigned the value 7.

Maintaining Flexibility with ReDim

The next statement redimensions FieldArray according to the value of FieldCount:

```
ReDim FieldArray(FieldCount)
```

ReDim is an interesting and useful command in VBA. Its value stems in part from the fact that you cannot use a variable as an argument to a Dim statement.

For example, suppose—as is the case—that the code has by this point determined the value of FieldCount, the number of fields to put in the database table. The next task is to put the names of those fields into the memory array FieldArray. But it has not yet dimensioned FieldArray; that is, the code has not yet stated that FieldArray contains three rows, or six rows, or some other number of rows.

If the code now dimensioned FieldArray with this statement:

```
Dim FieldArray(FieldCount)
```

the code would fail with an error: Constant expression required. In other words, a constant value is needed in place of the variable FieldCount.

But ReDim is intended specifically for this sort of situation. This statement

```
ReDim FieldArray(FieldCount)
```

assigns as many columns to the array FieldArray as the value of FieldCount.

> **TIP**
> Before you can redimension an array with ReDim, you must have already declared the array with Dim. Furthermore, in the Dim statement, the array's name must be followed by a pair of empty parentheses.

```
For i = 1 To FieldCount
    FieldArray(i).FieldName = ActiveSheet.Cells(1, i)
Next i
```

This loop puts each value in the worksheet list's header row into the FieldName element of FieldArray. (Recall that the first row of a list in a worksheet contains the names of the variables, or fields, that when taken together make a list.)

Completing the Field Definitions

The next task is to determine the length of each field in the database. This implies that each field is a Text field. It would be possible to include tests to determine whether a field in the list is numeric, and if so, whether it is single or double precision, a date, currency, and so on. So doing would introduce considerable complications, and you decide to assume that all the user's fields will contain text. (A Text field in an Access table can contain numeric types and subtypes, although it stores them *as* text. This is analogous to typing '4 in an Excel cell: It looks like a number, but it's stored as text.)

The following loop checks for the maximum length of each field in the Excel list and stores it in the FieldLength element of FieldArray, where it's associated directly with the name of the field.

```
For i = 1 To FieldCount
    RecordCount = ActiveSheet.Cells(65536, i).End(xlUp).Row
    For j = 2 To RecordCount
        If Len(ActiveSheet.Cells(j, i)) > FieldArray(i).FieldLength Then
            FieldArray(i).FieldLength = Len(ActiveSheet.Cells(j, i))
        End If
    Next j
Next i
```

You use this nested loop to get the number of records in each field of the worksheet list. Suppose that the final record (or even the final two or three records) in the list is missing a value on one or more fields. In that case, checking the number of rows used in only one column might result in an undercount of the number of records in another column. Therefore, you arrange for the loop to check the number of rows used in each column and store that value in RecordCount.

The inner loop uses the current value of RecordCount to determine how many cells to check in the current column. The length of each cell is checked by means of the Len function. If the result is larger than the current value of that field's FieldLength element, it replaces that current value. By the time the loop has looked at the final cell in the current column, it has determined the length of the longest value in the column and stored it in the FieldLength element of FieldArray.

```
CreateDatabaseWithDAO DatabaseName, LockFileName, GoAhead
```

Now the main Driver subroutine calls the subroutine named CreateDatabaseWithDAO, discussed in the next section. Notice the use of the Boolean variable GoAhead as an argument that's passed to the subroutine. Thus far, your Driver subroutine has done nothing with the variable. But it's passed to CreateDatabaseWithDAO, which might modify its value. When control returns to the Driver subroutine, GoAhead can be used to determine whether to continue by adding a table to a database.

The point to bear in mind is that the value of a variable can be modified by a called subroutine. It is that modified value that is subsequently available to the calling subroutine.

> **NOTE** This behavior is the default, and is termed *passing by reference*. When, as here, a variable is passed by reference, its value may be modified by a called procedure. The modified value is returned to the calling procedure. If you override the default behavior and pass the variable *by value*, the called procedure might modify the variable's value but the changed value is not returned to the calling procedure.

After the new database has been created, the `Driver` subroutine concludes with the following statements:

```
If GoAhead Then
  MakeNewTableWithDAO DatabaseName, TableName, FieldName()
End If

End Sub
```

Your code first checks the value of `GoAhead`. If it's TRUE, that means a new database has been created and the code can continue by putting a new table into it. After that's accomplished, you end the main `Driver` subroutine and processing has finished.

The `Driver` subroutine is a lengthy one. It's shown here in its entirety to make it easier to follow its structure by viewing it all at once, instead of broken up by explanations.

```
Sub Driver()

Dim DatabaseName As String x
Dim LockFileName As String x
Dim TableName As String x
Dim FieldArray() As FieldType x
Dim FieldCount As Integer x
Dim RecordCount As Long x
Dim i As Integer x
Dim j As Integer x
Dim GoAhead As Boolean x

DatabaseName = Left(ThisWorkbook.Name, Len(ThisWorkbook.Name) - 4)
LockFileName = ThisWorkbook.Path & "\" & DatabaseName & ".ldb"
DatabaseName = ThisWorkbook.Path & "\" & DatabaseName & ".mdb"

TableName = ActiveSheet.Name

FieldCount = ActiveSheet.Cells(1, 256).End(xlToLeft).Column
ReDim FieldArray(FieldCount)

For i = 1 To FieldCount
    FieldArray(i).FieldName = ActiveSheet.Cells(1, i)
Next i

For i = 1 To FieldCount
    RecordCount = ActiveSheet.Cells(65536, i).End(xlUp).Row
    For j = 2 To RecordCount
        If Len(ActiveSheet.Cells(j, i)) > FieldArray(i).FieldLength Then
            FieldArray(i).FieldLength = Len(ActiveSheet.Cells(j, i))
        End If
    Next j
Next i

CreateDatabaseWithDAO DatabaseName, LockFileName, GoAhead

If GoAhead Then
    MakeNewTableWithDAO DatabaseName, TableName, FieldArray()
End If

End Sub
```

Checking for a Preexisting Database

Your `Driver` subroutine calls another subroutine named `CreateDatabaseWithDAO`.

```
Sub CreateDatabaseWithDAO(DatabaseName As String, _
LockFileName As String, GoAhead As Boolean)
```

It calls this subroutine with three arguments:

- `DatabaseName`—This is the name with which the database will be saved, including the `.mdb` extension. As you've seen in the `Driver` subroutine, `DatabaseName` is based on the name of the active Excel workbook.

- `LockFileName`—This is the name of the database with the extension `.ldb` instead of `.mdb`. Under most circumstances, when an Access database is open, a lock file also exists. The lock file's name is the name of the database and the extension `.ldb`. This subroutine checks for the existence of a lock file before it attempts to erase an existing database.

- `GoAhead`—This Boolean variable is used to determine whether it's okay to create the new database. If `GoAhead` is FALSE, the database won't be created. The user can set `GoAhead` to FALSE by declining to allow the subroutine to create the database; the code can set it to FALSE if the database already exists and is open.

> **NOTE**
> The sole instance in which Access opens an Access database without also creating a lock file (or using an existing lock file) is when a user has opened the database as read only and in Exclusive mode.
>
> There is a situation in which no one is using an Access database, and yet the lock file still exists. That occurs when the final user has closed the database, and that user doesn't have Delete permission for files in its folder. In that case, the lock file remains in place until some other user, one who does have Delete permission, is the final user to close the database.

The next several lines of code determine what to do if a file with a name identical to that stored in the variable `DatabaseName` already exists. Begin by setting the `GoAhead` Boolean variable to TRUE. Unless the code changes its value to FALSE, the database will be created at the end of the subroutine.

```
GoAhead = True
```

The `Dir` function checks to see whether a file matching its argument's value already exists in the current directory. If such a file does exist, `Dir` returns the filename; if one does not exist, `Dir` returns a null string (represented in code as an empty pair of quote marks). So, if the value that `Dir` returns is something other than a null string, the file already exists and further handling is necessary.

```
If Dir(DatabaseName) <> "" Then
  If MsgBox(Prompt:="Delete existing " & DatabaseName & "?", _
    Buttons:=vbYesNo, Title:="Naming conflict.") = vbYes Then
```

If the Dir function finds a file named DatabaseName in the current directory—that is, if it returns a value other than a null string—then the code displays a message box asking the user whether to delete the existing file. A message box can return a value. In this case, the buttons displayed in the message box are a Yes button and a No button. If the user clicks the Yes button, the value returned by the message box is vbYes; if the user clicks the No button, the message box returns vbNo.

If the user does click the Yes button, the code continues by checking for the existence of a lock file. The reason is that if the existing file named DatabaseName is an Access database, and if it's open, the code will terminate with an error if it tries to delete the file. By checking for the existence of a file named LockFileName, it's very likely that the file named DatabaseName can be deleted without causing an error.

"Very likely" isn't quite good enough, though, and the code includes an error handler.

```
If Dir(LockFileName) <> "" Then
  MsgBox Prompt:=DatabaseName & " is already open and " _
    & "cannot be erased. Taking no action.", _
    Title:="File already open."
  GoAhead = False
```

The code finds that the lock file exists and therefore the database not only exists but is open. It notifies the user and sets GoAhead to FALSE.

```
Else
  On Error GoTo Recover
  Kill DatabaseName
  On Error GoTo 0
  GoAhead = True
End If
```

If the code does not find the lock file, it prepares to delete the file named DatabaseName. However, as noted earlier, it's possible that the database is open even if no lock file is found. Therefore, an error handler is established.

The code is instructed, by means of the On Error GoTo statement, to transfer control to the code following the Recover label if an error occurs. This would come about if the code should attempt in vain to delete the file DatabaseName in the Kill statement. In that event, the code shown at the end of the subroutine executes.

Notice the On Error GoTo 0 statement. This cancels the directive of the preceding On Error statement. The error handler following the Recover label is intended only for an error caused by the Kill statement. If the code gets past that statement without an error, the handler is irrelevant and so error handling is returned to its normal status.

```
  Else
    MsgBox Prompt:="Okay, leaving existing " & DatabaseName _
      & " alone.", Title:="Taking no action."
    GoAhead = False
  End If
End If
```

The prior six statements complete the logic of the first `If` block, which asks the user what to do if an instance of `DatabaseName` already exists. If your user clicks the No button in the first message box, it means to leave the file alone, and the `GoAhead` variable is set to FALSE.

```
If GoAhead Then
  CreateDatabase Name:=DatabaseName, Locale:=dbLangGeneral
End If

Exit Sub
```

The code checks the value of `GoAhead`. If it's still TRUE, a database is created with the name `DatabaseName`. It is as yet empty. Note the `Exit Sub` statement following the `End If`. If this statement is reached, control returns immediately to the procedure that called the subroutine (as you've seen, that procedure is the `Driver` subroutine).

The reason for departing the subroutine via the `Exit Sub` statement is that the remaining code is the error handler. It shouldn't run unless an error has occurred, so in the normal course of events, control returns to `Driver` before the error handler executes. But if an error did occur, the following code runs:

```
Recover:
    MsgBox Prompt:="Could not delete " & DatabaseName & _
        ". It's likely that a user has opened it in exclusive " _
        & "mode and read only. Taking no action.", Title:= _
        "File already open."
    GoAhead = False

End Sub
```

The error handler simply informs the user that the code could not delete the existing instance of the file named DatabaseName, and then sets `GoAhead` to FALSE. It's worth noting that `Recover:` isn't an executable statement, but is merely a line label. As such, it must begin in the first column (labels cannot be indented), must be the only instance of that particular label in the procedure, and must end with a colon.

Here's the full procedure:

```
Sub CreateDatabaseWithDAO(DatabaseName As String, _
LockFileName As String, GoAhead As Boolean)

GoAhead = True

If Dir(DatabaseName) <> "" Then
    If MsgBox(Prompt:="Delete existing " & DatabaseName & "?", _
        Buttons:=vbYesNo, Title:="Naming conflict.") = vbYes Then
        If Dir(LockFileName) <> "" Then
            MsgBox Prompt:=DatabaseName & " is already open and " _
                & "cannot be erased. Taking no action.", _
                Title:="File already open."
            GoAhead = False
        Else
            On Error GoTo Recover
            Kill DatabaseName
            On Error GoTo 0
            GoAhead = True
```

```
            End If
        Else
            MsgBox Prompt:="Okay, leaving existing " & DatabaseName _
                & " alone.", Title:="Taking no action."
            GoAhead = False
        End If
    End If

    If GoAhead Then
        CreateDatabase Name:=DatabaseName, Locale:=dbLangGeneral
    End If
    Exit Sub

Recover:
    MsgBox Prompt:="Could not delete " & DatabaseName & _
        ". It's likely that a user has opened it in exclusive " _
        & "mode and read only. Taking no action.", Title:= _
        "File already open."
    GoAhead = False

End Sub
```

Creating a New Table in the Database with DAO

By now your code has created the new database using the `CreateDatabaseWithDAO` subroutine. Your `Driver` subroutine has collected information about the table the database will contain and the fields the table will contain. It's time to actually create the table and append the new fields.

As you saw at the end of the "Completing the Field Definitions" section, when the `CreateDatabaseWithDAO` subroutine has completed, control returns to the `Driver` subroutine. `Driver` then checks the value of `GoAhead` and if it's TRUE, calls the subroutine that follows:

```
Sub MakeNewTableWithDAO(DatabaseName As String, _
    TableName As String, FieldArray() As FieldType)
```

This procedure accepts three arguments: a string that provides the name of the database, the name of the table to be inserted in the database, and an array of field names to be inserted in the table.

```
Dim dbDataFile As DAO.Database
Dim tdDataTable As DAO.TableDef
Dim fldDataField As DAO.Field
Dim FieldCount As Integer
Dim i As Integer
```

In contrast to the `CreateDatabaseWithDAO` subroutine, the `MakeNewTableWithDAO` subroutine makes use of several object variables. They're declared in the `Dim` statements. Notice that the first three variables are declared as objects whose type (`Database`, `TableDef`, and `Field`) are qualified as DAO objects. This is to protect against the possibility of another object library, referenced by the module, with its own `Database`, `TableDef` or `Field` type.

```
Set dbDataFile = OpenDatabase(DatabaseName)
Set tdDataTable = dbDataFile.CreateTableDef(TableName)
```

The database was created by the `CreateDatabaseWithDAO` subroutine, but it wasn't opened. By opening it using `OpenDatabase`, it's established as an object and is assigned to the `dbDataFile` object variable. Then the `CreateTableDef` method is used in conjunction with the string variable `TableName` to create the table and assign it to the object variable `tdDataTable`.

With the table established, it's time to insert the fields. Begin by determining how many field names the `Driver` subroutine put in the array. The code determines that by using the `UBound` function on the array. `UBound` returns the number of the final element in an array. It is for this reason that `Option Base 1` was used at the head of the module. Otherwise, the developer would have had to remember to add 1 to whatever number `UBound` returned.

```
FieldCount = UBound(FieldArray)

For i = 1 To FieldCount
    Set fldDataField = tdDataTable.CreateField(FieldArray(i).FieldName, _
        dbText, FieldArray(i).FieldLength)
    tdDataTable.Fields.Append fldDataField
Next i
```

A loop runs from 1 to `FieldCount`. For each record in `FieldArray`, the `CreateField` method is used to create a new field in the data table. Each field is named according to the value in the `FieldName` element. The field is typed as `Text` by means of the `dbText` argument. The field's length is set according to the value in the `FieldLength` element.

Note that it's necessary to explicitly append each field to the table using the `Append` method of the `Fields` collection. Simply creating the field is not enough.

```
dbDataFile.TableDefs.Append tdDataTable

End Sub
```

When all the fields have been created, named, and given a type and length, your code appends the table itself to the collection of tables in the database. Again, the `Append` method is used, but this time on the `TableDefs` collection instead of the `Fields` collection.

The full procedure is as follows:

```
Sub MakeNewTableWithDAO(DatabaseName As String, _
    TableName As String, FieldArray() As FieldType)

Dim dbDataFile As DAO.Database
Dim tdDataTable As DAO.TableDef
Dim fldDataField As DAO.Field
Dim FieldCount As Integer
Dim i As Integer

Set dbDataFile = OpenDatabase(DatabaseName)
Set tdDataTable = dbDataFile.CreateTableDef(TableName)

FieldCount = UBound(FieldArray)

For i = 1 To FieldCount
    Set fldDataField = tdDataTable.CreateField _
```

10

```
      (FieldArray(i).FieldName, _
         dbText, FieldArray(i).FieldLength)
      tdDataTable.Fields.Append fldDataField
   Next i

   dbDataFile.TableDefs.Append tdDataTable

   End Sub
```

If the database created by the code discussed in this section were based on the worksheet shown in Figure 10.1, it would look like the one shown in Figure 10.2.

Figure 10.2
Notice that the field length for the first field is 6 and compare it with Figure 10.1.

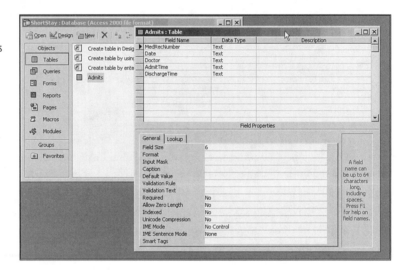

It remains to populate the table with the records on the Excel worksheet. That process is taken up in the section "Declaring and Using Recordsets." First, though, it's useful to examine a slightly different approach to creating the tables and fields in an existing database.

Creating a Table and Fields Using ADO

This chapter noted at the outset that ADO isn't well suited to creating new databases; its strength lies in moving data back and forth between a database and some other application such as Excel.

Therefore, if you're using Access and its Jet database engine as the database, it makes good sense to create your databases either using DAO (as shown in this chapter's prior sections) or directly with the database's user interface. If you're using another DBMS, such as SQL Server, it's far easier to use its interface to create the database.

However, after the database exists, ADO offers tools that are entirely appropriate for creating new tables, fields, and other structures. What follows is an example of how to set up a table using ADO.

CASE STUDY

You've been asked to prepare a database named ShortStay, which will contain information about hospital patients who spend only a brief period of time as inpatients. The database needs to maintain information about the patients, the medical and surgical procedures used for each, the cost of supplies, the hospital staff involved, and so on.

Having set up the ShortStay database using DAO, at a later point you find that you want to create a table that contains a field with the names of medical procedures and one that contains a procedure's ID, which will be the table's primary key. You'll use the table subsequently as a lookup table: You'll store a procedure's ID in the main data table and display its name when you bring a record back to Excel from the database.

You begin by inserting a new module into your workbook and setting references to these libraries:

- Microsoft ActiveX Data Objects 2.x Library
- Microsoft ADO Ext. 2.x for DDL and Security
- The standard references to VBA, the Excel object library, OLE Automation, and the Office object library

> **NOTE** In both cases, 2.x refers to the highest level version on your system. (If you're running Office 97, you probably have version 2.1; if you're running Office 2003, you probably have version 2.7.)

You enter the following code into the module:

```
Sub NewShortStayTable()

Dim cnConnectToShortStay As ADODB.Connection
Dim SourceName As String
Dim rsProcs As ADODB.Recordset
Dim i As Integer
Dim LastProc As Long
Dim catDatabaseFile As ADOX.Catalog
Dim tdfProcs As ADOX.Table
```

There are two new items in this list of declarations: an ADOX catalog and an ADOX table. Both belong to the ADO extensions mentioned at the beginning of the chapter. A *catalog*, as used here, is much the same as a database. ADO uses it as a container for the objects you normally find in a database: tables, queries, and so on. The ADOX table is no different from the tables that have been discussed and used so far in this book.

```
Set cnConnectToShortStay = New ADODB.Connection
Set catDatabaseFile = New ADOX.Catalog
Set tdfProcs = New ADOX.Table
```

Three object variables are set: a connection variable that will be pointed at the ShortStay database, a catalog variable that will represent the database itself, and a table variable that will represent the new table to be created.

```
SourceName = ThisWorkbook.Path & "\ShortStay.mdb"
cnConnectToShortStay.Open "Provider=Microsoft.Jet.OLEDB.4.0;Data Source=" &
SourceName
```

The `SourceName` variable is used to store the path to and name of the database. The connection specifies the provider and the path and name, just as shown in Chapter 8.

```
Set catDatabaseFile.ActiveConnection = cnConnectToShortStay
```

The code connects to the database by way of the connection.

```
tdfProcs.Name = "Procedures"
```

The new table is named Procedures. Then two new fields are appended to the table. Notice the difference from DAO, where a new field is first established and then appended to the table's collection of fields. In ADO, you name the field, specify its type, and append it to the table in one step, as shown in the next two statements:

```
tdfProcs.Columns.Append "ProcedureID", adInteger
tdfProcs.Columns.Append "ProcedureName", adVarWChar, 50
```

The first statement appends a new field named `ProcedureID` to the Procedures table. The second statement appends a new field named `ProcedureName`. The `adVarWChar` type results in a `Text` field in Access. The final argument, `50`, specifies a maximum length of 50 characters for the field.

```
tdfProcs.Keys.Append "PrimaryKey", adKeyPrimary, "ProcedureID"
```

A primary key is established for the table. Recall from Chapter 9, "Managing Database Objects," that a table can have more than one index. If the table has a primary key, that's just one particular index, distinguished by the facts that it doesn't allow duplicate values, and that only one index at a time can be designated as the table's primary key.

The primary key is established here by simply appending a key to the table's collection of keys (ADO uses the term *keys* whereas Access uses the term *indexes*; they're largely synonymous). The key is named `PrimaryKey`, its type is `adKeyPrimary` (other options are `adKeyUnique` to create a unique index that is not the primary key, and `adKeyForeign` to link to another table's primary key). The statement specifies `ProcedureID` as the key's basis.

```
catDatabaseFile.Tables.Append tdfProcs
```

The newly created table is appended to the catalog's collection of tables, and it's time to put records in the table. Your code begins by counting the number of records on the worksheet (see Figure 10.3).

```
LastProc = ThisWorkbook.Worksheets("Procedures") _
.Cells(65536, 1).End(xlUp).Row
```

Then establish and open a new recordset based on the Procedures table.

Figure 10.3
If the procedures will be used later in a drop-down, it's useful to begin by sorting them alphabetically.

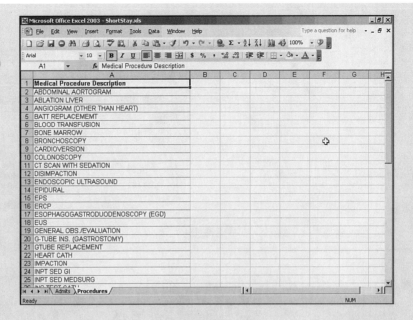

```
Set rsProcs = New ADODB.Recordset
rsProcs.Open "Procedures", cnConnectToShortStay, _
adOpenStatic, adLockOptimistic, adCmdTable
```

Establish a With block and run a For-Next loop to populate the Procedures table. During each cycle through the loop, its counter i is used to provide a unique value to the primary key field, and the procedure name is placed in its field.

```
With rsProcs
  For i = 2 To LastProc
    .AddNew
    .Fields("ProcedureID") = i - 1
    .Fields("ProcedureName") = ThisWorkbook.Sheets("Procedures").Cells(i, 1)
    .Update
  Next i
End With
```

Clean up by setting the object variables to Nothing (thus releasing the variables) and closing the connection.

```
Set tdfProcs = Nothing
Set catDatabaseFile = Nothing
cnConnectToShortStay.Close
Set cnConnectToShortStay = Nothing

End Sub
```

You now have a new table in the database, with a primary key and a text field, as shown in Figure 10.4.

Figure 10.4
It can be convenient, but it's not descriptive to name a table's primary key as `PrimaryKey`.

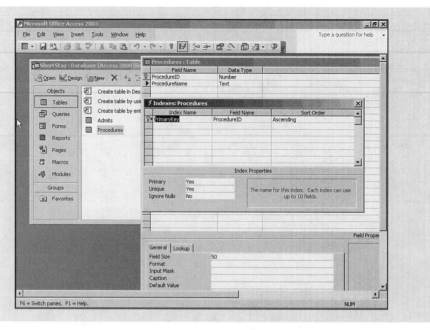

Here's the full subroutine:

```
Sub NewShortStayTable()
Dim cnConnectToShortStay As ADODB.Connection
Dim catDatabaseFile As ADOX.Catalog
Dim tdfProcs As ADOX.Table
Dim SourceName As String
Dim rsProcs As ADODB.Recordset
Dim i As Integer
Dim LastProc As Long

Set cnConnectToShortStay = New ADODB.Connection
Set catDatabaseFile = New ADOX.Catalog
Set tdfProcs = New ADOX.Table

SourceName = ThisWorkbook.Path & "\ShortStay.mdb"
cnConnectToShortStay.Open _
"Provider=Microsoft.Jet.OLEDB.4.0;Data Source=" & SourceName

Set catDatabaseFile.ActiveConnection = cnConnectToShortStay

tdfProcs.Name = "Procedures"

tdfProcs.Columns.Append "ProcedureID", adInteger
tdfProcs.Columns.Append "ProcedureName", adVarWChar, 50

tdfProcs.Keys.Append "PrimaryKey", adKeyPrimary, "ProcedureID"
catDatabaseFile.Tables.Append tdfProcs

Set rsProcs = New ADODB.Recordset
LastProc = ThisWorkbook.Worksheets("Procedures") _
```

```
    .Cells(65536, 1).End(xlUp).Row
    rsProcs.Open "Procedures", cnConnectToShortStay, _
    adOpenForwardOnly, adLockOptimistic

With rsProcs
    For i = 2 To LastProc
        .AddNew
        .Fields("ProcedureID") = i - 1
        .Fields("ProcedureName") = ThisWorkbook _
        .Sheets("Procedures").Cells(i, 1)
        .Update
    Next i
End With

Set tdfProcs = Nothing
Set catDatabaseFile = Nothing
cnConnectToShortStay.Close
Set cnConnectToShortStay = Nothing

End Sub
```

Declaring and Using Recordsets

It's when you begin using recordsets that you start making significant claims on your system's resources. As Chapter 9 mentioned, SQL queries both are powerful and make relatively efficient use of processors and memory. Whenever you reasonably can use a SQL query to append data, or to update data, or to select and display data, by all means do so.

But queries are bludgeons. They don't do well in situations that call for branching and looping, for example. The more complicated the logic that you must bring to bear on the data, the less attractive a SQL query looks.

Recordsets, on the other hand, enable you to use more delicate tools. You can use the extensive capabilities of VBA when you work with recordsets—and that includes the rich set of worksheet functions that accompanies Excel. For example, if you wanted to add records to a table depending on where they fall relative to some median value, you'd almost certainly opt for VBA in conjunction with a recordset, rather than a SQL query. SQL doesn't typically offer a function that returns a median. (It's not hard to write your own, but why bother when it's already available?)

A recordset is analogous to an Excel list or a database table. It's also analogous to the array named `FieldArray` that was used in the section named "Creating a New Table in the Database with DAO": an array of records with elements that can have different types.

A recordset consists of one or more records and one or more fields. You declare a recordset in VBA after you've established a reference to a DAO or an ADO library. Then you can declare that a recordset exists, give it a name, and assign it to a database table or query.

After the recordset has been established, you use VBA commands to manipulate its data by adding to it, deleting from it, modifying the values in its fields, importing its records into another location such as an Excel worksheet or a Word document, and so on.

As an introduction to recordsets, consider the following code, which establishes a recordset using DAO. You might use it in conjunction with the code discussed in the prior section that created a new database, a table to hold records, and fields in that table to contain the actual values. A good place to put it would be at the end of the Driver subroutine, in the final If block:

```
If GoAhead Then
  MakeNewTableWithDAO DatabaseName, TableName, FieldName()
  AddRecordsWithDAO DatabaseName, TableName, FieldCount
End If
```

Here's the code. It establishes a recordset based on the new database table and adds records to it. The records are taken from the worksheet.

```
Sub AddRecordsWithDAO(DatabaseName As String, _
TableName As String, FieldCount As Integer)
Dim i As Integer, j As Integer
Dim RecordCount As Long, LastRowInColumn As Long
Dim dbDataFile As DAO.Database
Dim rsDataRecords As DAO.Recordset
```

After declaring some variables, the code goes on to set the database using the DatabaseName variable (recall that DatabaseName includes the path to the database). Then the recordset named rsDataRecords is established.

```
Set dbDataFile = OpenDatabase(DatabaseName)
Set rsDataRecords = dbDataFile.OpenRecordset(TableName, _
➥ dbOpenTable)
```

The assignment of the recordset needs a little explanation. The object variable rsDataRecords is assigned to the result of the OpenRecordset method. That method as used here takes two arguments:

- Source—The source of the recordset is the name of a table or query in which the records are found, or into which the records will be placed. The source can also be a SQL query in text form, although this usage is rare in practice. In the current example, the recordset's source is the value of TableName.

- Type—In DAO, there are various types of recordsets, such as dynaset, table type, and snapshot. The different types and the implication of choosing a particular type are discussed later in this chapter, in "Understanding DAO Recordset Types." The current example specifies a table type.

```
For i = 1 To FieldCount
    LastRowInColumn = ActiveSheet.Cells(65536, 1). _
    End(xlUp).Row
    If RecordCount < LastRowInColumn Then
        RecordCount = LastRowInColumn
    End If
Next i
```

After the recordset has been established, the code determines the number of records to be taken from the worksheet and placed into the database table. It does this by looping through the number of columns (determined earlier, in the Driver subroutine) and finding the final used cell in each of them. The `RecordCount` variable is used to determine the largest number of records in any column.

The heart of the subroutine is in the following nine statements. They're enclosed in a `With` block, which takes the recordset as its object.

```
With rsDataRecords
```

By using the `With` block, the code avoids repetitively naming the recordset and causing the code to navigate through the recordset to its methods and properties.

The code then enters a nested loop. The outer loop cycles through the records. Notice that it begins at 2, not 1, because on the worksheet the records begin in row 2, using row 1 for the headers.

```
For j = 2 To RecordCount
```

The first statement in the outer loop adds a new record to the recordset. One of the effects of adding a new record is to make it the current record; any record operations that take place do so on the current record, until another one becomes current. Notice the use of the dot before the `AddNew` keyword. The dot means that `AddNew` belongs to the `With` statement's object; in this case, the recordset. The code is adding a new record to the recordset.

```
.AddNew
```

With a new record current, and at the outset empty, the inner loop runs. It cycles through the fields in the recordset. Its purpose is to put the value of each column in the worksheet's current row into the corresponding field in the current record. While the inner loop is executing, the code remains on the same worksheet row and puts a value in a field in the same record.

```
For i = 1 To FieldCount
    .Fields(i - 1) = ActiveSheet.Cells(j, i)
Next i
```

There are three items of note about this inner loop. First, the counter `j` remains constant. There's nothing in the loop that changes it, and therefore the `Cells` reference points to the same row as long as the loop executes. It's the outer loop, the one that cycles through the list's rows, that increments `j`.

Second, notice the use of the dot before the `Fields` keyword. This means that the fields belong to the object named in the `With`—again, that's the recordset. In the example, just like the `AddNew` method, the `Fields` collection belongs to `rsDataRecords`.

Also notice that the recordset's fields are indexed by `i-1` instead of by `i`. The first field in a recordset is field number 0, the second field is field number 1, and so on. This is a little disconcerting until you get used to it. (`Option Base 1` has no effect on field indexes, by the way, just on memory arrays.) But you're likely to get used to it fairly quickly because by far the most common use of loops and field indexes in VBA is to move data back and forth between recordsets and worksheets—and worksheets have no column numbered zero.

```
.Update
```

10

When you add a new record, as here, you edit it. In this example, the editing process takes place in the inner loop, where contents of the worksheet cells are placed in the active record of the recordset.

The editing doesn't take place on the recordset itself, but in a copy buffer. That is, as the code picks up values from the worksheet and apparently places them in fields in the recordset, it actually and temporarily places the values in the copy buffer, a memory location that Access manages. It isn't until the code executes an Update statement that the values are moved from the copy buffer and placed in the recordset.

Anytime your code uses a statement with AddNew (or, if you're editing a record that already exists, a statement with Edit) you have to follow it with an Update. Otherwise the values in the copy buffer are lost.

> **NOTE**
> The Update requirement is true only of code using DAO. An Update statement is not required if you're using ADO. But see Chapter 12, in the section titled "Using ADO to Add Records," for reasons that you should use it anyway.

```
    Next j
End With

rsDataRecords.Close
dbDataFile.Close

End Sub
```

Here's the full code for AddRecordsWithDAO:

```
Sub AddRecordsWithDAO(DatabaseName As String, _
TableName As String, FieldCount As Integer)
Dim i As Integer, j As Integer
Dim RecordCount As Long, LastRowInColumn As Long
Dim dbDataFile As DAO.Database
Dim rsDataRecords As DAO.Recordset

Set dbDataFile = OpenDatabase(DatabaseName)
Set rsDataRecords = dbDataFile.OpenRecordset(TableName, dbOpenTable)

For i = 1 To FieldCount
    LastRowInColumn = ActiveSheet.Cells(65536, 1).End(xlUp).Row
    If RecordCount < LastRowInColumn Then
        RecordCount = LastRowInColumn
    End If
Next i

With rsDataRecords
    For j = 2 To RecordCount
        .AddNew
        For i = 1 To FieldCount
            .Fields(i - 1) = ActiveSheet.Cells(j, i)
        Next i
```

```
        .Update
    Next j
End With

rsDataRecords.Close
dbDataFile.Close

End Sub
```

Figure 10.5 shows the appearance of the Admits table in datasheet view after this code has put the records in the worksheet into the table.

Figure 10.5
The times shown on the worksheet have been saved as date/time serial numbers.

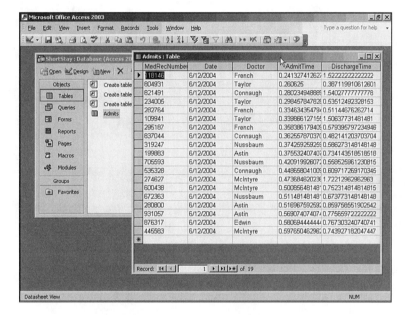

The times from the worksheet have been saved in an inconvenient format. Perhaps the most straightforward way of handling this is after the fact. As noted earlier in this chapter, it would be possible to determine data types by writing code to examine the worksheet data, but if you don't do that, you can convert the data using an update query. Figure 10.6 shows the query in design view.

As shown in Figure 10.6, two new fields have been added to the Admits table: `ConvertedAdmitTime` and `ConvertedDischargeTime`. The update query uses the `CDate` function to convert the times, typed as `String`, from the worksheet to times, typed as `Date/Time`, in the database. The result of running the query is shown in Figure 10.7.

Notice that the converted times shown in Figure 10.7 match the original times as shown on the worksheet in Figure 10.1.

Figure 10.6
The CDate function in Access converts a serial number to a date/time representation.

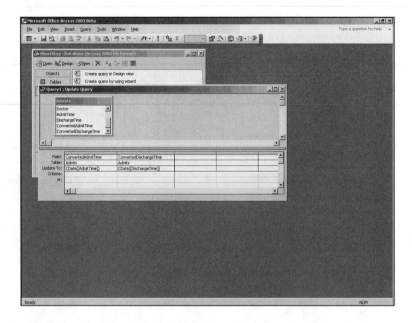

Figure 10.7
The fractional portion of a serial number specifies the time of day; the integer portion specifies a date.

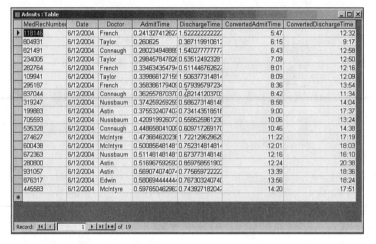

Understanding DAO Recordset Types

The DAO library offers several different *types* of recordsets. When you assign a table or a query to a recordset by means of a Set statement, you specify the type of recordset that you want to use. Your choice has implications for the demands on system resources that your code will make, as well as for the ways that your code can use the recordset.

Your Set statement can take any of several forms. In each case, the OpenRecordset method is used, and it takes several arguments:

- `Source`—This is the only required argument. It's a string, and is the name of the object that contains the records. The source is usually a table or an existing query, but it could also be a SQL statement that defines a query.

- `Type`—There are five types of DAO recordsets. The requirements for each type are set out in the sections that follow. This is an optional argument. If you don't specify a type, a table-type recordset is opened.

- `Options`—This is an optional argument. There are 11 options available. They're largely concerned with permitting or denying read and write permissions, or are provided for backward compatibility with earlier versions. As a practical matter, you don't normally need to set these options in your code, and this book won't discuss them. They're described in Access's Help documentation of the `OpenRecordset` method.

- `LockEdits`—This is an optional argument. The possible settings include specifying optimistic or pessimistic updates. When a recordset is locked *pessimistically*, a record that one user is editing is unavailable for editing by any other user as soon as the recordset's `Edit` method executes, and made available again after the `Update` method executes. If *optimistic* locking is in place, the record is locked only while the `Update` method is executing. The default is pessimistic locking. Again, your code does not usually need to specify `LockEdits`.

You can execute the `OpenRecordset` method against a database or a connection to a database, using either of these two forms:

```
Set Recordset = Database.OpenRecordset _
(Source, Type, Options, LockEdits)

Set Recordset = Connection.OpenRecordset _
(Source, Type, Options, LockEdits)
```

You can also execute the `OpenRecordset` method against a table, a query, or another recordset. In that case, you would use this form:

```
Set Recordset = Object.OpenRecordset (type, options, lockedits)
```

where `Object` is a table, query, or recordset. For example

```
Set rsProcedures = dbDataFile.TableDefs("Procedures") _
.OpenRecordset (dbOpenDynaset)
```

or

```
Set tblProcedures = dbDataFile.TableDefs("Procedures")
Set rsProcedures = tblProcedures.OpenRecordset (dbOpenDynaset)
```

The most commonly used DAO recordset types are discussed in the next three sections.

Setting a Table-Type Recordset

You set a table-type recordset with a statement such as the next one:

```
Set rsProcedures = dbDataFile.OpenRecordset("Procedures", dbOpenTable)
```

In this statement, `Procedures` is the *source* of the recordset and `dbOpenTable` is its *type*.

`Procedures` must be a table, not a query, and the table must be physically within the database, not a link to a table in another database. A table-type recordset is the default, so if `Procedures` is a table, this is an equivalent statement:

```
Set rsProcedures = dbDataFile.OpenRecordset("Procedures")
```

If `Procedures` is instead a query or a linked table, `rsProcedures` is by default a dynaset recordset.

If the table is a very large one, you might be able to make your code more efficient by accessing records using the `Seek` method. For example

```
Sub SeekARecord()

Dim dbDatabaseFile As DAO.Database
Dim rsProcs As DAO.Recordset
Dim SourceName As String
Dim WhichID As Integer

WhichID = InputBox("Enter a procedure ID")

SourceName = ThisWorkbook.Path & "\ShortStay.mdb"
Set dbDatabaseFile = OpenDatabase(SourceName)

Set rsProcs = dbDatabaseFile.OpenRecordset _
("Procedures", dbOpenTable)
rsProcs.Index = "PrimaryKey"
rsProcs.Seek "=", WhichID

MsgBox rsProcs.Fields("ProcedureName")

End Sub
```

This subroutine prompts the user for the value of a table's primary key. It then opens the database, and establishes a recordset based on the database's Procedures table.

It sets the table's index to the index named *PrimaryKey*. Then it executes the recordset's `Seek` method. This is how, using DAO, you access a record very rapidly. VBA can use a b-tree search to locate the ID supplied by the user in the table's index, and return the record's value on the `ProcedureName` field.

This can speed up processing with very large tables. But there's a tradeoff: Before you can use the `Seek` method, you must set the table's current index. With smaller recordsets, it might take longer to set the index and execute the seek than to look directly for the record, as in the following code:

```
Sub FindARecord()

Dim dbDatabaseFile As DAO.Database
Dim rsProcs As DAO.Recordset
Dim SourceName As String
Dim WhichID As Integer

WhichID = InputBox("Enter a procedure ID")
```

```
SourceName = ThisWorkbook.Path & "\ShortStay.mdb"
Set dbDatabaseFile = OpenDatabase(SourceName)

Set rsProcs = dbDatabaseFile.OpenRecordset("Procedures", dbOpenSnapshot)

rsProcs.FindFirst "ProcedureID = " & WhichID

MsgBox rsProcs.Fields("ProcedureName")

End Sub
```

The subroutine named `FindARecord` doesn't involve the table's index. It just looks through the Procedure table's `ProcedureID` field until it finds the ID that the user supplies. Then it reports that record's value on the `ProcedureName` field.

Notice that the recordset is declared not as `dbOpenTable` but as `dbOpenSnapshot`, a DAO recordset type discussed next. To use the `FindFirst` method, the recordset must be `dbOpenSnapshot` or `dbOpenDynaset`.

> **NOTE** You cannot use DAO's `Seek` method with a *linked* table. It's available only with recordsets typed as `dbOpenTable`, and as noted at the beginning of this section, a linked table cannot be typed as `dbOpenTable`.

Setting a Snapshot-Type Recordset

You set a snapshot recordset with the `dbOpenSnapshot` type:

```
Set rsProcs = dbDatabaseFile.OpenRecordset _
("Procedures", dbOpenSnapshot)
```

A snapshot recordset, unlike other recordset types, is read only. This is because all the records in its source are brought into memory when the `Set` statement is executed. Any changes to the source's records that subsequently occur will *not* be reflected in the recordset. Furthermore, you cannot edit, add, or delete records from the recordset.

A snapshot recordset can be useful if you're just accessing fields and records and your code is not intended to modify them. Because it's less flexible than other recordset types, it can make more efficient use of system resources than other types.

However, it can run slightly more slowly than other types because it brings all the source's records and fields into memory. This is in contrast to, for example, the dynaset type of recordset, which brings only bookmarks into memory when the recordset is established.

The term *snapshot* can be a source of confusion. This section discusses DAO recordsets, and a DAO snapshot recordset is not *updatable* (another term for editable). There is a type of ADO recordset, a *static* recordset, that Access projects refer to as a snapshot. But an ADO snapshot recordset *can* be made updatable.

10

Setting a Dynaset-Type Recordset

A dynaset recordset is the most flexible of the DAO recordset types. It can be based on a table or a query, and it allows the code to edit, append, or delete the source's records. You call for a dynaset, as usual, in the recordset's Set statement.

```
Set rsProcs = dbDatabaseFile.OpenRecordset _
("Procedures", dbOpenDynaset)
```

When this statement runs, records are brought into memory, but only their bookmarks. (A *bookmark* is a property of the recordset. It's analogous to a primary key in that it uniquely identifies each of a recordset's records.) It's only when the code modifies records that the fields are made available. This is the reason that dynasets can initially open more quickly than other recordset types.

Understanding ADO Recordset Types

ADO also uses different sorts of recordsets, but they're defined differently than DAO recordset types. The two principal ways to specify an ADO recordset's properties are by setting them directly or as part of the recordset's Open method. For example

```
Set rsProcs = New ADODB.Recordset
With rsProcs
  .Source = "Procedures"
  .ActiveConnection = "Provider=Microsoft.Jet.OLEDB.4.0;" & _
  "Data Source=" & SourceFile
  .CursorType = adOpenDynamic
  .LockType = adLockOptimistic
  .CursorLocation = adUserServer
End With
```

Using the recordset's Open method, you could use this statement:

```
rsProcs.Open rsProcs.Open "Procedures", strConnectToShortStay, _
adOpenStatic, adLockOptimistic, adCmdTable
```

This example passes recordset parameters to the recordset's Open method; in order, its source, a string defining the connection, the cursor type, the lock type, and the cursor location. (See the following sections for discussions of the latter three parameters.)

With an ADO recordset, you don't need to worry as you do with DAO about the recordset's source. You can use a table, a query, a SQL statement, and other sources without having to make sure that you've chosen the right type of recordset.

The connection string is a parameter we've met before in ADO structures. It typically specifies a provider such as Microsoft.Jet.OLEDB.4.0 for an Access Jet database or SQLOLEDB.1 for SQL Server. It also provides information about the path to and name of a database, or the name of a server and a catalog for SQL Server.

Other parameters are introduced in the next three sections.

Using the `CursorType` **Property**

The `CursorType` property is in one way similar to a DAO recordset's `Type` property: It determines whether changes that other users might make to the source's records show up in your recordset, and whether all the fields and records are brought into the recordset when it's opened. The values that the `CursorType` property can assume are as follows:

- `adOpenDynamic`—This cursor type initially retrieves key values only. When you edit a record or otherwise access its fields, the remaining data for that record is retrieved. Changes made by other users to the source are reflected in the recordset, including adding and deleting records. This cursor type makes a greater demand on resources than do other types.

- `adOpenForwardOnly`—This is the default setting. You don't have access to changes that other users might make after opening the recordset. You should use it only to move forward in the recordset; depending on conditions, you might encounter errors if you try to move, for example, from the final record to the first. It makes more efficient use of system resources than other cursor types.

- `adOpenKeyset`—Like `adOpenDynamic`, the keyset type initially retrieves keys only. If other users edit field values in records, those modifications show up when you retrieve a full record. Records that are newly added to the source by other users are not added to the recordset.

- `adOpenStatic`—Changes made by other users do not show up in the recordset. Access terms this cursor type a *snapshot*, but it's not the same as a DAO snapshot because you can make it updatable by setting its lock type (see the next section).

Using the `LockType` **Property**

The `LockType` property enables you to control whether and how it's possible for your code to change the data in the recordset's source. There are four values:

- `adLockBatchOptimistic`—All edits your code might make to the recordset are saved until an `UpdateBatch` method is encountered. At that point, the edits are saved to the source of the recordset. This isn't necessarily on a record-by-record basis: You could, for example, edit each record in the recordset before an update caused the changes to be saved.

- `adLockOptimistic`—This is similar to setting an optimistic lock on a DAO recordset. During the editing process, the record isn't locked and can be edited by other users. It's locked during the recordset update and then released again.

- `adLockPessimistic`—This is similar to a DAO pessimistic lock. Another user cannot edit a record that you've already begun to edit until after you've updated the recordset.

- `adLockReadOnly`—This is the default setting. You cannot update the recordset. This setting does not, however, prevent another user from editing the source's records while you have it open. If you're doing nothing but viewing data or copying it to a target such as a worksheet, this is the most efficient choice.

Using the CursorLocation **Property**

You might expect a cursor location to refer to the current record, but it actually refers either to the server or the client.

If the database engine, such as Jet or SQL Server, manages the cursor, and thus manages the recordset, this property has been set to adUseServer. That's the default setting, and it means that the same engine that is managing all the other users is taking care of you. When there are many users, that can slow things down.

You can take it easy on the database engine and let ADO manage the cursor by setting the CursorLocation property to adUseClient. You cannot set this property by way of the record-set's Open method. Instead, use a statement of the following type before invoking Open:

```
rsProcs.CursorLocation = adUseClient
```

Looking Ahead

This chapter has discussed ways to use the two main data object libraries, DAO and ADO, to manipulate objects in databases. You've seen how to use DAO to create an Access database from scratch. You've also seen how to use both DAO and ADO to create tables and fields. The latter part of this chapter has described how you create and type both DAO and ADO recordsets.

This is necessary groundwork for the real crux of managing data from the Excel platform. Chapter 11, "Getting Data from Access and into Excel with ADO and DAO," goes into the detail of moving data into database tables, and retrieving it to Excel from recordsets based both on tables and queries.

Getting Data from Access and into Excel with ADO and DAO

11

Using `CopyFromRecordset`

This chapter focuses on using the ADO and DAO object libraries to bring data from a database into an Excel workbook. Most of the material concerns fine-tuned activities, such as using VBA code to find the exact location that data needs to occupy on a worksheet. Often, though, you're less interested in picking and choosing among records and putting a field value in a particular location, and more interested in copying a lot of data very rapidly.

You could use an external data range, if you wanted to, as described in Chapters 4, "Importing Data: An Overview," and 5, "Using Microsoft Query." Refreshing an existing data source is a speedy process. But you usually set up an external data range manually, starting with Data, Import External Data. (You can set one up using VBA, of course. To see how this is accomplished, just turn on the macro recorder before you start the process.)

No matter how you set up an external data range, a named range is needed. You might not want to add a named range to the workbook. In that case, consider using Excel's `CopyFromRecordset` method. Note that `CopyFromRecordset` isn't part of the DAO or ADO object libraries. It's a method that belongs to Excel worksheet ranges. Nevertheless, you must establish a reference to either ADO or DAO in your code because the principal argument used by `CopyFromRecordset` is the recordset object to be copied into the worksheet.

Here's an example that uses a DAO recordset. (An example using an ADO recordset follows.) Of course, before you could run it, you would need to establish a reference to a DAO library using Tools, References from the VBE.

→ For more information on establishing library references **see** "Connecting Using ADO," **p. 194**.

```
Sub CopyFromRecordsetWithDAO()
Dim dbNorthWind As DAO.Database
Dim tdfOrders As DAO.TableDef
Dim rsOrders As DAO.Recordset
Dim i As Integer

Set dbNorthWind = OpenDatabase("C:\Documents and Settings" & _
"\Owner\My Documents\Northwind.mdb")
Set tdfOrders = dbNorthWind.TableDefs("Orders")
Set rsOrders = tdfOrders.OpenRecordset(dbOpenTable)

With ActiveSheet
    For i = 0 To rsOrders.Fields.Count - 1
        .Cells(1, i + 1) = rsOrders.Fields(i).Name
    Next i
    .Cells(2, 1).CopyFromRecordset rsOrders
End With

End Sub
```

The code establishes a recordset, rsOrders, that represents the Orders table in the Access example database, Northwind.mdb. When it executes the CopyFromRecordset method, the contents of that table are copied to the active worksheet. The copy occurs very quickly. In this example, 830 records with 14 fields each were copied to a worksheet in less than one second, using a Pentium 4 1.80GHz processor.

Notice that the code loops through the list of fields that belong to the recordset, and writes the name of each field to the first row of the active worksheet. The CopyFromRecordset method does not supply field names. In contrast, if you establish an external data range, you get the field names by default. Because the first row contains the field names, the recordset's records and fields are copied to the active worksheet beginning in row 2, column A.

The following code passes an ADO recordset to the CopyFromRecordset method. Notice the use of ADO's Recordset object, and also its use of a SQL Server file instead of a Jet database.

```
Sub CopyFromRecordsetWithADO()

Dim rsOrders As ADODB.Recordset
Dim i As Integer
Dim cnnConnectSpec As String

cnnConnectSpec = "Provider=SQLOLEDB.1;Data Source=(local);" & _
    "Initial Catalog=NorthwindCS;Integrated Security=SSPI"

Set rsOrders = New ADODB.Recordset
rsOrders.Open "Orders", cnnConnectSpec, adOpenStatic, _
adLockReadOnly, adCmdTable
```

```
With ActiveSheet
    For i = 0 To rsOrders.Fields.Count - 1
        .Cells(1, i + 1) = rsOrders.Fields(i).Name
    Next i
    .Cells(2, 1).CopyFromRecordset rsOrders
End With

End Sub
```

The logic of returning field names and values to the worksheet is identical whether you're using DAO or ADO. Notice the string that contains the connection information for the ADO recordset. It specifies SQLOLEDB.1 as the provider and (local) as the data source. In a networked environment, you would use the name of the server storing the catalog as the data source. The use of (local) indicates that a server has been installed on the local work-station.

Microsoft has offered a desktop version of SQL Server since Office 2000, termed the *Microsoft Data Engine*, or *MSDE*. (SQL Server refers to this version as the *SQL Server Desktop Engine*.) The steps to install it depend on the version that you're running. In Office 2000 Premium, for example, you install Microsoft Office Server Extensions from Disk 3 of the Office 2000 product. In Office 2003, one way is to locate a folder named MSDE2000 on the installation disks. That folder contains an executable installation file; double-click its icon to run it.

With the server installed, you can use the SQL Server–compatible version of the Northwind sample database. Again, getting to it depends on the Office version you're running. In Access 2000, you use File, Open and browse to the Samples subfolder within the Office folder. In Access 2003, choose Sample Databases from the Help menu.

If all you're doing is bringing a set of data—based on a query or on a table—from a database to an Excel worksheet, the CopyFromRecordset method might be all you need. When the data is on the worksheet, you can use the full array of Excel tools, such as charts and pivot tables and worksheet functions, to analyze the data.

If you need to return the data in a specific format, however, you'll need recourse to the techniques discussed in the remainder of this chapter.

Building an Application

Not so long ago, a company came to me with a problem. The company needed a better sys-tem to enable its employees to reserve rooms for meetings, conferences, and other func-tions. The company had about 2,200 employees in four buildings, and it had barely enough meeting rooms, so a room reservation system that operated accurately and smoothly was essential.

For some time, if you wanted to reserve a room, you phoned administration and told them when your meeting was scheduled and where you wanted to hold it. An administrative assis-tant checked a wall calendar to see whether the room was available on your hoped for date and time, and if it was, you gave the rest of the particulars—what refreshments should be served, whether A/V equipment was needed, what account should be charged, and so on.

Once a week, that same assistant would gather the information together and re-enter it into a two-page form, showing each day for the following week and listing each scheduled meeting on each day. Each meeting also showed the assigned room and the scheduled start time. A typical day had about 20 meetings. The form was duplicated and posted in various locations throughout the building each Friday evening.

There were problems with this system. The paper-and-pencil approach to gathering, storing, and retrieving information about meetings caused the standard problems of incomplete and illegible information, overbooking of rooms, lost reservations, and so on—to say nothing of one entire person-day each week devoted to compiling the information and typing the form.

So, when a campuswide data network was installed, the company thought it was time to bring its room reservation system up to date. By putting it on the network, it would be easier for staff to check the status of rooms that they had reserved, and possibly decentralize the entry of reservations. They purchased a shrink-wrap room scheduler for $6,000. One of their more technically savvy staff, who understood both their existing problems and the nature of the new software, installed it.

But the company had not taken into account that its employees were used to the forms that for years had been posted outside the meeting rooms. The staff liked them, even though they were notoriously inaccurate, and they liked the way the form was laid out. They were used to it.

The new software, although it included a report writer, proved incapable of mimicking the layout of the old familiar scheduling form. And it had some other wrinkles that the company didn't care for. So, its representatives came to my company and asked for a custom system.

We came to terms, so we thought, and started on the design work. But every time we got close to freezing the model, our client's representative would show up like Columbo, wearing a tattered old raincoat, smoking a foul old stogie, waving one hand in the air, and calling "Just one more thing …."

By the time we were through, our client had spent four times as much as it had on the off-the-shelf software. But it had a nearly bulletproof system (*no* system is completely bulletproof) that did a lot more than we'd originally anticipated.

The system relied on the Excel interface for user input because of the flexibility of the worksheet and the wealth of ways that it can be formatted. To store the data, it relied on an external database. To attempt to keep upward of 7,000 reservations per year, with 55 fields each, in an Excel workbook would get us right back to one of the situations that was discussed in Chapter 1, "Misusing Excel as a Database Management Tool."

So, we have an application that relies on an object library, VBA-driven interface between Excel and a database. Information about a new reservation is entered into Excel and stored in the database. A full day's worth of reservations are visible on an Excel worksheet, making it easy for the user to see what rooms are available at what times on any given calendar date. If information about a reservation needs to be changed, it's easily recalled from the database into the Excel workbook for modification, and the changes stored back to the database. And of course the report, the one that gets posted on all the meeting room doors, is generated automatically every Friday afternoon, in the old layout that's so favored by the company's staff.

You're invited to look over the developer's shoulder in the following case study to see exactly how information that's stored in the database is returned to the Excel workbook in some very particular ways—ways that make it necessary to tailor the process by way of recordsets, rather than by way of SQL. You'll also see how the data is used to populate a user form, so that the user can edit existing data. In Chapter 12, "Getting Data from Excel and into Access with ADO," you'll see how data is automatically moved from a workbook to a database.

Bringing Data Back from a Parameterized Query

This section walks you through the process of populating a worksheet with data returned from a database using a parameterized query.

Setting the Layout Requirements

The layout and appearance of the worksheet are important for the room scheduling purposes described earlier. The data must be put in specific cell ranges. That's the reason that the code resorts to recordsets: It's insufficient to merely return records from the database by choosing, for example, Import External Data from the Data menu. That approach imports data as a list, but the layout that's required is as shown in Figure 11.1.

Figure 11.1
Names of meeting rooms are shown in column A, and times are shown in row 1 in 15-minute increments.

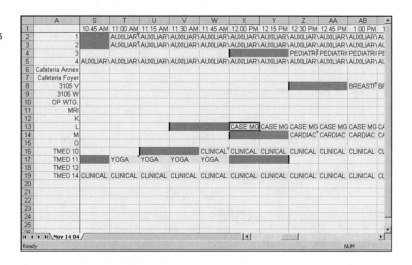

The worksheet shown in Figure 11.1 has several aspects that the code must attend to:

- The caption on the worksheet tab is the date for the meetings shown on the worksheet.

- Each meeting occupies multiple columns and usually just one row. It spans as many columns as needed to capture its start time and stop time, and it occupies the row that represents a particular meeting room. (In one case shown in Figure 11.1, a meeting occupies rooms 1 and 2, which appear in rows 2 and 3.)

- The purpose of a meeting is shown in each cell that represents the meeting. So, YOGA appears in cells T17:W17.

- Before a meeting, a crew must set the room up: see to tables and chairs, set out refreshments, and so on. After a meeting, a crew must clean up: empty wastebaskets, remove coffee urns, and so on. It usually takes half an hour for setup and cleanup, so there is a period before and after each meeting time reserved for setup and cleanup. These periods are shown in a different color on the worksheet. Examples in Figure 11.1 are cells V13:W13 (setup for the CASE MGMT TRAINING meeting) and X17:Y17 (cleanup after YOGA).

- Notice cells V13 and Y17 in Figure 11.1. V13 has a dark black border on its left edge and Y17 has one on its right edge. These borders help distinguish the cleanup period for one meeting from the setup period for another, should the two periods abut one another.

To get the room reservations for a particular date onto the worksheet, the user chooses Jump to a Date from the custom Calendar menu. He selects a date and that date is written to the worksheet tab's caption. Then the following subroutine is called:

```
Option Base 1
Option Explicit
```

The two option statements, placed at the top of the module, apply to all procedures located in the module. `Option Explicit` is included as good programming practice. `Option Base 1` is included because it simplifies the array handling, discussed later in this section.

```
Sub GetSingleDayFromDB()
```

```
Dim dbReservation As DAO.Database
Dim qdfRetrieveCurrent As DAO.QueryDef
Dim rsRecordsToRetrieve As DAO.Recordset
```

A reference to the DAO library has been set for the subroutine's module. With that reference set, it's possible to declare three object variables: one to represent the database that contains information on room reservations, one to represent a query definition in that database, and one to represent a recordset that will contain the records returned by the query.

```
Dim StartCol As Integer, StopCol As Integer, _
WhichRow As Integer
Dim ReservationRange As Range
```

The `StartCol`, `StopCol`, and `WhichRow` variables are used to locate the column in which a reservation begins, the column where it ends, and its row. Together, these are used to define a worksheet range, `ReservationRange`.

```
Dim SetupPeriods As Integer, CleanupPeriods As Integer
```

As mentioned earlier, a reservation needs to allow time to set the room up before the meeting, and to clean it up afterward. The variable `SetupPeriods` stores the number of 15-minute periods needed for setup and `CleanupPeriods` does the same for cleanup.

```
Dim TimeAsText As String
```

Microsoft Office applications store time as a serial number, with the integer portion representing a date and the decimal portion representing time. Excel has various ways to display date and time information. It can show time as hours and minutes, as hours, minutes, and seconds, on a 24-hour clock or using AM/PM notation, and so on. It's possible to store time information as text. For example, the time that's represented numerically as .4688 can be displayed, using a time format, as `11:15 AM`. This is the format, `h:mm AM/PM`, used in the first row on the worksheet. In order to compare a reservation time with those row 1 values, it's useful to store the time as a text value instead of as a serial number. The variable `TimeAsText` is used for that purpose.

```
Dim TimeArray(71) As String, RoomArray() As String
```

Two arrays are declared. `TimeArray` will store all the times in row 1 of the worksheet. That array has exactly 71 elements. The 15-minute periods are on the worksheet in the range B1:BT1. They range from 6:30 a.m. through 12:00 a.m., inclusive, and that's 71 periods.

The array `RoomArray` is declared as a dynamic array, one whose number of elements can be changed in the code as it runs. From time to time, the number of rooms available for meetings changes. By making the array dynamic instead of static, the code can count the number of rooms on the worksheet and redimension `RoomArray` accordingly.

```
Dim i As Integer
Dim ResourceCount As Integer
```

Two integer variables are declared. The variable `i` is used as a counter in a `For-Next` loop, and `ResourceCount` is used both to redimension `RoomArray` and to help define a range on the worksheet.

```
Application.ScreenUpdating = False
DatabaseName = ThisWorkbook.Sheets("UserNames").Cells(1, 3)
```

To speed up processing because the active worksheet will be completely refreshed, screen updating is turned off (this "freezes" the monitor momentarily).

The path to and name of the database that stores reservation information is kept in cell C1 of a worksheet named `UserNames`. Storing it there makes it unnecessary to store it somewhere in the VBA code, where it can be hard to locate, given that the project includes seven modules. The value in that cell is assigned to `DatabaseName`.

```
Set dbReservation = OpenDatabase _
(DatabaseName, False, False, "MS Access")
```

The database is opened and assigned to the `dbReservation` object variable.

```
Set qdfRetrieveCurrent = _
dbReservation.QueryDefs("RetrieveSingleDay")
```

11

The object variable `qdfRetrieveCurrent` is set to the query, found in the Resources database, named `RetrieveSingleDay`.

```
qdfRetrieveCurrent.Parameters("ThisDate") = ActiveSheet.Name
```

The query named `RetrieveSingleDay`, which is represented in this code by the object variable `qdfRetrieveCurrent`, has a *parameter*. The DAO and ADO libraries both include this object. It's a type of *criterion*, one that you reset each time the query executes. See Figure 11.2, which shows the query in design view.

Figure 11.2
Notice that the name of the parameter is given in square brackets.

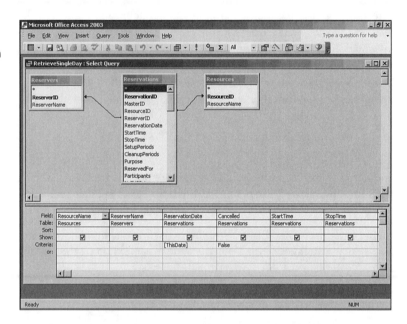

It's by way of the `RetrieveSingleDay` query and its parameter, `ThisDate`, that the code obtains data on reservations that have been made for a particular day. If you were to open the query directly, from within Access, you would be prompted for a value for the parameter. Then Access would respond by displaying all records that have the value you supplied on the field ReservationDate.

> **NOTE**
>
> In addition to the date parameter, the `RetrieveSingleDay` query uses another criterion. Notice in Figure 11.2 that the field named Cancelled has the criterion False. The query returns no record that has the value True on the Cancelled field. By using this field, reservations can be prevented from showing up on the worksheet without physically deleting them from the database. The Cancelled field is used later in this chapter, in "Deleting Records from the Database and from the Worksheet," where the `RemoveReservation()` subroutine is discussed.

Instead, the code gets the caption shown on the active worksheet's tab and passes that value as a parameter to the query. The query treats that value exactly as it does a value that you supply when you open the query directly.

> **TIP**
>
> Both ADO and DAO have an object named `Parameter`, and you can assign a value to it. But Excel also has an object named `Parameter`. If you declare an object variable to represent a parameter, be sure to qualify it with the object library you want. For example,
>
> ```
> Dim prmTheDate As Parameter
> Set prmTheDate = qdfRetrieveCurrent.Parameters("ThisDate")
> ```
>
> results in a type mismatch because VBA assumes that `prmTheDate` is an Excel parameter, not a DAO or ADO parameter. Instead, be sure to use
>
> ```
> Dim prmTheDate As DAO.Parameter
> ```
>
> or
>
> ```
> Dim prmTheDate As ADO.Parameter
> ```

Now the code executes the query and puts the results into a recordset that will be returned to the Excel worksheet. Again, the reason to put the results of the query into a recordset, instead of returning them directly to the worksheet, is that the latter approach brings the records back laid out as a list, instead of in the layout shown in Figure 11.1.

The recordset is opened as forward only. This is an efficient type of recordset, and it's appropriate because the code will not scroll back and forth through the records and will not edit them.

```
Set rsRecordsToRetrieve = _
qdfRetrieveCurrent.OpenRecordset(dbOpenForwardOnly)
```

Clearing the Worksheet

Now it's time to pick up information about the worksheet. The code begins by counting the resources listed in column A and using that to dimension `RoomArray`.

```
ResourceCount = ActiveSheet.Cells(600, 1).End(xlUp).Row - 1
ReDim RoomArray(ResourceCount)
```

The code assumes that there are no entries in column A farther down than row 600. It uses the `End(xlUp)` method to find the final entry in column A, and notes its row (in Figure 11.1 that's row 19). It subtracts 1 from that row number to account for the empty cell A1. So, using the layout shown in Figure 11.1, `ResourceCount` equals 18, and `ResourceArray` is redimensioned to contain 18 elements.

```
ActiveSheet.Range(Cells(2, 2), _
Cells(ResourceCount + 1, 72)).Clear
```

The code clears all cells in the worksheet that might contain data, removing information about reservations for the date that the worksheet currently represents. The range beginning with cell B2 and extending to the BT19 (19 because `ResourceCount` equals 18 in this example) is cleared of its contents, thus removing the cell values that identify the purpose of a reservation. The Clear method also removes cell comments and the cell colors that identify reservations, setup periods, and cleanup periods.

Populating the Memory Arrays

With the worksheet cleared of reservation data, the code picks up the names of the available resources, and times of day, and places them in memory arrays. These arrays will be useful in identifying the exact location on the worksheet where the information about each reservation should be placed.

First, though, it's best to check to see whether the date that the user has requested has any reservations established.

```
If Not rsRecordsToRetrieve.BOF Then
```

The code tests to see whether the query has returned an empty recordset. This can come about if the user specified a date that has no reservations in the database. In that event, subsequent code that makes reference to putative records will cause runtime errors; therefore, the subroutine executes that code only if there's at least one record in the recordset. One way to test for an empty recordset is to check whether the current position, immediately after the recordset has been populated, is BOF, or *Beginning Of File*. If that is not the current position, the recordset has at least one record and the code can proceed normally.

```
For i = 1 To 71
    TimeArray(i) = Application.Text _
    (ActiveSheet.Cells(1, i + 1), "h:mm AM/PM")
Next i
```

Populate the memory array TimeArray with the values found in cells B1:BT1 on the worksheet. Although they're displayed in h:mm AM/PM format, the cells' actual contents are date/time serial numbers. So, the code uses Excel's Text function to store the time values in TimeArray as strings, and using the same format the worksheet uses. The reason for this is that the code will subsequently search the array for time values in string format to determine which column it should use to enter reservation information.

```
For i = 1 To ResourceCount
    RoomArray(i) = ActiveSheet.Cells(i + 1, 1)
Next i
```

Similarly, the RoomArray array is populated with the names of the rooms found in column A. Note the use of ResourceCount as the final value used by the loop's counter. Also note that RoomArray's elements run from 1 through 18 because of the Option Explicit statement at the start of the module. In its absence, the array's elements would run from 0 through 17.

Finding the Reservation's Location

Next, a With block is established. Subsequent statements that refer to objects, properties, or methods qualified only with a dot (for example, .Fields) are deemed to belong to the With block's object—here, the recordset.

```
With rsRecordsToRetrieve
```

With the With block established, the code enters a loop that steps through the recordset, record by record. It terminates when the recordset's EOF (its *End Of File*) has been reached.

```
Do Until .EOF
```

Within the Do loop, each reservation record is checked to determine its start time, its stop time, and the room that it uses. This is done by getting the value in the record's StartTime field, its StopTime field, and its ResourceName field. These values are compared with the values in TimeArray and RoomArray to locate their positions within the arrays. The results of those comparisons inform the code which worksheet columns to use as the reservation's start and end times, and which worksheet row to use as the reservation's meeting room.

Begin by getting the value of StartTime and converting it to h:mm AM/PM format, once again using Excel's Text function.

```
TimeAsText = Application.WorksheetFunction.Text _
(.Fields("StartTime"), "h:mm AM/PM")
```

Then use Excel's Match function to locate the position of the reservation's start time within TimeArray. Recall from Chapter 2, "Excel's Data Management Features," that when used on a worksheet, the Match function returns the position of a value within a range of cells. Used in VBA code, it can—as here—return the position of a value within an array. So, if the time stored in the StartTime field were (in serial number format) 0.3125, the Text function would convert it to 7:30 AM. The Match function, searching TimeArray for 7:30 AM would return 5, which is the fifth value in the array. Because that's how the array was populated, 7:30 AM is also the fifth time shown in row 1 of the worksheet. But because the available times begin in column B, not column A, 1 is added to the result of the Match function.

```
StartCol = Application.Match _
(TimeAsText, TimeArray, 0) + 1
```

Similar logic is used to obtain the column of the reservation's stop time:

```
TimeAsText = Application.WorksheetFunction.Text _
(.Fields("StopTime"), "h:mm AM/PM")
StopCol = Application.Match(TimeAsText, TimeArray, 0)
```

But this time, the number 1 is not added to the result of the Match function. Suppose that a reservation's stop time is 12:00 p.m., as is the case with the YOGA reservation in row 17 of Figure 11.1. Then cell W17, corresponding to the 15-minute period beginning at 11:45 a.m., should be the reservation's final cell. By the time that 12:00 p.m. rolls around, the meeting is ending and is into its cleanup period. Therefore, 1 is not added, as it is to the result of the start time Match.

```
WhichRow = Application.Match(.Fields("ResourceName"), _
RoomArray, 0) + 1
```

The row that the reservation occupies on the worksheet is found in a similar way. The ResourceName field in the recordset contains the name of the reserved room. That value is matched to RoomArray to find its position in the array, corresponding (almost) to the worksheet row. That "almost" is handled by adding 1 to the result, accounting for the blank worksheet cell A1.

```
Set ReservationRange = ActiveSheet.Range _
(Cells(WhichRow, StartCol), Cells(WhichRow, StopCol))
```

The object variable `ReservationRange` is set to represent the columns beginning with `StartCol` and ending with `StopCol`, and occupying the row whose number is `WhichRow`. Now it's possible to refer repeatedly and conveniently to that range in subsequent statements.

Putting the Data on the Worksheet

Now that the code knows which cells the reservation should occupy, it puts the necessary data in those cells and provides the right formatting.

```
ReservationRange = UCase(.Fields("Purpose"))
```

Each cell in `ReservationRange` is filled with the value stored in the record's Purpose field. The VBA function `Ucase` is used to convert lowercase letters in the field to uppercase (for example, `Yoga` becomes `YOGA`).

```
If .Fields("ReserveHold") = "Reserve" Then
    ReservationRange.Interior.ColorIndex = 3
Else
    ReservationRange.Interior.ColorIndex = 6
End If
```

The application allows the user to fill a range of cells temporarily, not with a firm reservation but by holding a room until plans become more firm. If the record represents a firm reservation, the cells in the range are colored red (their `ColorIndex` is 3). Otherwise, the record represents a tentative hold and the cells are colored yellow (their `ColorIndex` is 6).

```
SetupPeriods = .Fields("SetupPeriods")
CleanupPeriods = .Fields("CleanupPeriods")
```

The recordset has two fields, SetupPeriods and CleanupPeriods, which store the number of 15-minute periods that should be reserved for setting a room up before the meeting and cleaning up afterward. These integer values (for example, two setup periods to allow 30 minutes for preparation) are assigned to two variables for later use.

```
If SetupPeriods > 0 Then
    ReservationRange.Offset(0, -SetupPeriods) _
    .Resize(1, SetupPeriods).Interior.ColorIndex = 48
End If
```

The cells that represent the meeting's setup period are colored gray. This is done by using Excel's `Offset` function. `Offset`'s usage on the worksheet is described in Chapter 2. Used here, it identifies a range that is offset from `ReservationRange` by zero rows and by as many columns as the value of `SetupPeriods`. Notice the minus sign before `SetupPeriods` as an argument to `Offset`. This means that if `SetupPeriods` contains 2, the range is offset from `ReservationRange` two columns to the left of the start of `ReservationRange`.

Additionally, the `Resize` method is used to make the offset range 1 row high and `SetupPeriods` columns wide. Then its `ColorIndex` is set to 48, or gray.

```
With ReservationRange.Offset(0, -SetupPeriods) _
    .Resize(1, 1).Borders(xlEdgeLeft)
```

```
    .LineStyle = xlContinuous
    .Weight = xlThick
    .ColorIndex = 1
End With
```

The first cell in the range that represents the setup periods is given a black border on its left edge. This cell is found in the same way that the setup range itself is found: by means of an offset by a negative number of setup periods. The sole difference is that the Resize method is used to specify a single cell, the first one in the range of setup periods.

```
If CleanupPeriods > 0 Then
    ReservationRange.Offset(0, ReservationRange.Columns _
    .Count).Resize(1, CleanupPeriods).Interior. _
    ColorIndex = 48
End If
With ReservationRange.Offset(0, ReservationRange.Columns. _
Count + CleanupPeriods - 1).Resize(1, 1) _
.Borders(xlEdgeRight)
    .LineStyle = xlContinuous
    .Weight = xlThick
    .ColorIndex = 1
End With
```

The same procedure is used to establish a range of cleanup periods and a black border. The differences from specifying the setup periods are as follows:

- The offset to ReservationRange takes the number of columns in the range into account so that the setup periods begin to the right of the final column in the range of reserved cells.

- The Resize method uses the positive number in CleanupPeriods to make the range extend to the right from ReservationRange instead of to the left, as is done with SetupPeriods.

- The right edge of the final setup period cell is given a black border, instead of its left edge.

A cell comment is added to the first cell in ReservationRange. That comment shows the name of the user who made the reservation, the name of the person for whom the reservation was made, and the date on which information about the reservation was most recently modified. These values are obtained from their respective fields in the recordset and concatenated into a comment, along with labels and carriage return characters.

The code does this by invoking the AddComment method on the first cell of ReservationRange.

```
ReservationRange.Resize(1, 1).AddComment _
("Reserved By: " & .Fields("ReserverName") & _
Chr(10) & "Reserved For: " & .Fields("ReservedFor") _
& Chr(10) & "Last Modified: " & Format _
(.Fields("MostRecentlyModified"), "m/d/yy"))
```

Chr(10) identifies a carriage return. Suppose that the person who made the reservation is named Joe, the person for whom the reservation was made is named Mary, and that the date that the reservation was last modified is 9/1/2004. In that case, the cell comment appears as follows:

```
Reserved By: Joe

Reserved For: Mary

Last Modified: 9/1/2004

If .Fields("Participants") = "External" Then _
    ReservationRange.Font.Bold = True
End If
```

The final chore for the current record in the recordset is to format `ReservationRange` in boldface font if the meeting participants are external to the organization, and to leave the font normal otherwise.

```
.MoveNext
Loop
```

Continuing Through the Recordset

The code moves to the next record in the recordset. (It can't move *back*, even if to do so fit the code's logic, because the recordset was opened as forward only.) The end of the loop is reached and control returns to the top of the loop, where the test for the recordset's EOF is made. If it's now at EOF, execution continues with the following `End With` statement, which terminates the `With rsRecordsToRetrieve` block.

```
End With
```

Then the `If` block is terminated. This `If` tested whether or not the recordset was at BOF at the outset, which would have indicated an empty recordset.

```
End If
```

Finally, the code releases the object variables by setting them equal to `Nothing` and the subroutine itself terminates.

```
Set qdfRetrieveCurrent = Nothing
Set rsRecordsToRetrieve = Nothing
Set ReservationRange = Nothing

End Sub
```

Returning Data from a Database to a User Form

It's not always desirable to return data to a worksheet from a database. Particularly when there are many fields that you want the user to see, to edit or to otherwise respond to, you should consider putting the data in a user form.

You establish a user form by switching to the Visual Basic Editor and choosing UserForm from the Insert menu. With an empty form active, you can use the Control Toolbox to place controls—text boxes, combo boxes, option buttons, multi-page controls, command buttons, and so on—on your form.

A multi-page control is useful when you have too many fields to conveniently fit on a normal user form. When you put a multi-page control on a form, you establish two or more tabs. Each tab has a different set of controls, very much like the dialog box that appears when you choose Options from Excel's Tools menu.

The main tab of the user form that is used in conjunction with the Reservations application appears in Figure 11.3. The user employs the form to supply data about a new reservation or to change data about an existing reservation.

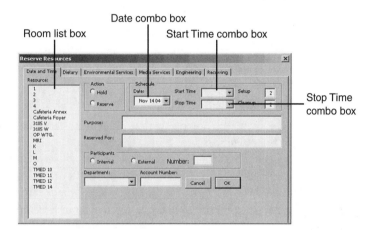

Figure 11.3
By enclosing the two option buttons *Hold* and *Reserve* in the same frame, labeled *Action*, you make them mutually exclusive.

When the user is making a new reservation, he chooses options and enters information on a blank user form. When he clicks the OK button, code gets the data from the user form and stores it in the database.

When the user is editing an existing reservation, information about the reservation is first obtained from the database and written to the user form. The user then can modify the value of any controls he wants. When he clicks OK, the code once again gets the data from the user form and puts it in the database.

Identifying the Reservation Record

The following code runs when the user has indicated that he wants to edit an existing reservation. It moves data from the database to the user form. The user begins by clicking any cell on the worksheet that represents a reservation, and then chooses a custom menu item that causes this procedure to run.

```
Sub FromDBtoForm(rsRecordsToEdit As Recordset)

Dim i As Integer
Dim ResourceCount As Integer
Dim WhichDate As Date, StartTime As Date
Dim WhichRoom As String
Dim WhichColumn As Integer
Dim qdfEditDetails As QueryDef
Dim rsRecordsToEdit As Recordset
```

```
DatabaseName = ThisWorkbook.Sheets("UserNames").Cells(1, 3)
Set dbReservation = OpenDatabase(DatabaseName, False, False, "MS Access")
```

After identifying the location and the name of the reservations database, it's opened and assigned to the object variable dbReservation. Now the code needs to retrieve from the database all the fields that describe the reservation the user has chosen to edit. Begin by collecting from the worksheet the information necessary to uniquely identify a reservation in the database: the date, the room, and the start time. Only one reservation can exist on a given date, in a given room, and commencing at a given start time.

```
WhichDate = ActiveSheet.Name
WhichRoom = ActiveSheet.Cells(ActiveCell.Row, 1).Value
```

The reservation's date is stored as the active sheet's name, which is also shown on the sheet tab. Because the user starts the process by clicking one of the cells that represents the reservation, the room that's reserved is shown in column A of the active cell's row. The sheet name is stored in WhichDate and the room name is stored in WhichRoom.

It remains to determine the reservation's start time. The user is allowed to begin this process by clicking any cell in the range that represents a reservation. Recall that the cells in the reservation range each contain a string that names the meeting—CASE MGMT TRAINING, for example. To find the leftmost cell for the reservation, all that's needed is to keep moving left from the active cell until a cell is found that does *not* contain the meeting's name. The leftmost cell that does contain the meeting's name is in the column that represents the reservation's start time.

So, identify the number of the column to the left of the active cell.

```
WhichColumn = ActiveCell.Column - 1
```

Use a Do loop to decrement the value of WhichColumn until the value of the cell in WhichColumn no longer equals the value in the active cell.

```
Do While Cells(ActiveCell.Row, WhichColumn) = _
Cells(ActiveCell.Row, ActiveCell.Column)
    WhichColumn = WhichColumn - 1
Loop
```

The start time for the reservation is found in row 1 of the prior value of WhichColumn. Store the start time in the StartTime variable.

```
StartTime = ActiveSheet.Cells(1, WhichColumn + 1).Value
```

Now set the query that will return all the information about the selected reservation from the database, and pass the values of the reservation date, the reserved room, and the start time as parameters to the query.

```
Set qdfEditDetails = dbReservation.QueryDefs("DetailRecords")
With qdfEditDetails
    .Parameters("WhichDate") = WhichDate
    .Parameters("WhichRoom") = WhichRoom
    .Parameters("WhichTime") = StartTime
```

Then set the object variable rsRecordsToEdit to the result of executing the query with its parameters.

```
Set rsRecordsToEdit = .OpenRecordset(dbOpenForwardOnly)
End With
```

Figure 11.4 shows the query in design view.

Figure 11.4
By including the Resources table, the code can use the room name instead of its ID as a parameter.

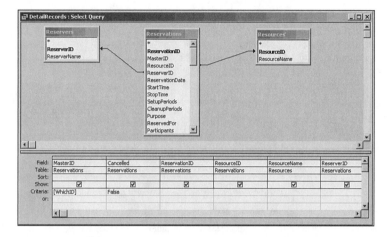

To review: The user has clicked a cell in an existing reservation on the Excel worksheet, and selected a custom menu item that calls the present procedure. The code notes the name of the worksheet (to get the reservation date), the name of the reserved room, and the column in which the reservation starts (to get its start time). These values are passed as parameters to a database query. Together they specify a single reservation.

That reservation's record is assigned to the object variable rsRecordsToEdit, and the next general step is to populate the user form with the reservation's information.

Populating the User Form

The values retrieved from the database are now assigned to the controls on the user form. Because the user form is involved in many of the assignment statements, a With block is initiated. Subsequently, objects that are used and that begin with a dot are deemed to belong to the With statement's object, the user form itself.

```
With ReservationForm
```

Now you need to populate the list box that shows the available rooms. It's handled a little differently from the date, the start time, and the stop time combo boxes. The reason is that the list of available rooms can change from time to time as one room becomes unavailable for meetings or a new room is added. In contrast, the number of available 15-minute periods, and their designations, are constants, as are the days in the year. Because dates and times are constants, their combo boxes can use static worksheet ranges as their data sources.

But because the list of available rooms can change unexpectedly, it's desirable to rebuild the contents of the list box each time the form is displayed.

Start by getting the number of rooms available from column A.

```
ResourceCount = ActiveSheet.Cells(600, 1).End(xlUp).Row - 1
```

Clear the current entries in the room list box. Then loop through the list of rooms on the active worksheet and populate the list box.

```
.lbResources.Clear
For i = 2 To ResourceCount
    .lbResources.AddItem (ActiveSheet.Cells(i, 1))
Next i
```

The database stores the reserved room as a numeric ID, not as the room's name. So, the code picks up the name of the reserved room from the worksheet and uses it to set the room list box's current selection.

```
.lbResources = ActiveSheet.Cells(ActiveCell.Row, 1)
```

TIP A list box can have its `MultiSelect` property set to a multiple selection. In this way, a user can select more than one of the items in the list. If you set that property to `fmMultiSelectMulti`, you must work with the list box's list index. For example, if it were possible to select more than one room in the list box, you would show that those rooms had been selected by setting the `Selected` property for that item to True. For example, to select both the 11th and the 13th items in a multi-select list box, use this:

```
.lbResources.Selected(10) = True
.lbResources.Selected(12) = True
```

NOTE In each case, 1 is subtracted from the calculated value of the `ListIndex` because the first element of the combo box's list is element number 0. This is unaffected by the use of `Option Base 1`. The same is true for the room list box, although it's the `Selected` property rather than the `ListIndex` property that's set.

Now set the combo boxes (informally known as *dropdowns*) to their proper values. The combo boxes display the reservation date and the start and stop times. The code sets the value of the combo boxes directly from the values of the fields in the recordset.

```
.cbDate = rsRecordsToEdit.Fields("ReservationDate")
.cbStartTime = rsRecordsToEdit.Fields("StartTime")
.cbStopTime = rsRecordsToEdit.Fields("StopTime")
```

Understanding the Combo Box

A combo box is perhaps more familiarly termed a *dropdown*. The combo box combines a text box with a list box. The text box is normally visible and shows the item that has been selected. The list box appears, or drops down, when you click its arrow. Using VBA code, you can set the value of a combo box in one of two ways. Either assign the value directly to the combo box (the approach used in the code described here) or set its `ListIndex` property. The `ListIndex` is the number of the item in the list box (starting with 0, not 1). If you assign a value directly, it need not be a member of the list, and the value of `ListIndex` is set to –1.

The first element of the combo box's list is element number 0. Thus, if you want to set the value of the combo box to its 15th element, you would use something like

```
ReservationForm.cbDate.ListIndex = 14
```

This is unaffected by the use of `Option Base 1`. The same is true for a pure list box.

Suppose that you want a combo box to display the value `7:00 AM`. You could use a statement such as this:

```
cbStartTime = "7:00 AM"
```

Alternatively, you could set the combo box's `ListIndex` property. Assuming that `7:00 AM` is the third value in the list, you would use this (remember, the first item in a list box is item number 0):

```
ReservationForm.cbStartTime.ListIndex = 2
```

The possible values for the three combo boxes are stored in a hidden worksheet, `UserNames`. (This is the same worksheet that stores the path to and name of the reservations database.) The worksheet is shown in Figure 11.5.

11

Figure 11.5
If you store values to be used by code in a sheet, it's a good idea to set the sheet's `Visible` property to `xlVeryHidden`.

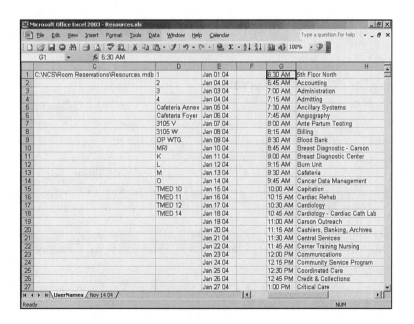

Compared to the choices involved in setting the values of list boxes and combo boxes, it's very straightforward to set the value of text boxes such as those that display the number of setup periods and cleanup periods. Just set the text box equal to the value you want it to display.

```
.tbSetupPeriods = rsRecordsToEdit.Fields("SetupPeriods")
.tbCleanupPeriods = rsRecordsToEdit.Fields("CleanupPeriods")
.tbPurposeBox.Value = rsRecordsToEdit.Fields("Purpose")
.tbReservedForBox.Value = rsRecordsToEdit.Fields("ReservedFor")
```

Of course, you can set values on the user form conditionally. Here, one option button or another gets set to True depending on the value of a field in the recordset.

```
If rsRecordsToEdit.Fields("Participants") = "Internal" Then
    .obInternal.Value = True
ElseIf rsRecordsToEdit.Fields("Participants") = "External" Then
    .obExternal.Value = True
End If
```

About 300 lines of code are omitted at this point. Their purpose is to set the values of other controls on the user form, controls that do not appear in Figure 11.5 because they're located on different tabs. The approach used is the same as this section has illustrated: Assign to a control the value found in the recordset, in the field that's associated with the control.

Just to finish the controls on the form's main tab, the responsible department and the account to be charged are set:

```
    .cbDept.Value = rsRecordsToEdit.Fields("Department")
    .tbAccount.Value = rsRecordsToEdit.Fields("Account")
End With
Set dbReservatioons = Nothing
Set rsRecordsToEdit = Nothing
End Sub
```

The With block is terminated, object variables are released, and the subroutine itself is ended.

Allowing for Recurring Reservations

One particularly useful aspect of the design of this reservations application is its capability to deal with recurring reservations. From the user's standpoint, a recurring reservation represents a meeting that occurs more than once, usually on a regular basis, in the same room, and with the same room setup requirements. For example, the user might make all the necessary arrangements for a meeting reservation and, in addition, request that those same arrangements apply to other dates. The other dates might be every other Wednesday, or the third weekday in every month, or on each day for five consecutive days.

From the application's standpoint, a recurring reservation consists of at least two records that share the same MasterID. In brief here's how individual reservations are grouped into a set of recurring reservations.

→ For more information on moving data from a workbook to a database, **see** "Using DAO Recordsets to Move Data from Excel to a Jet Database," **p. 337**.

The database contains a table, named Masters, whose sole purpose is to provide a new master ID for each reservation. The table has an AutoNumber field named MasterID. When the user establishes a new reservation, recurring or not, these statements are among the code that runs:

```
Sub GetMasterID(dbReservation As Database, _
MasterResID As Long)

Dim rsMasterTable As Recordset

Set rsMasterTable = dbReservation.TableDefs("Masters") _
.OpenRecordset(dbOpenDynaset)
With rsMasterTable
    .AddNew
    .Update
    .MoveLast
    MasterResID = .Fields("MasterID")
    .Close
End With
Set rsMasterTable = Nothing
End Sub
```

A new record is added to the table named Masters. When this is done, a new, unique value is automatically placed in the AutoNumber field MasterID. That value is assigned to the variable `MasterResID`.

> **NOTE**
> Notice that `MasterResID` is passed to the `GetMasterID` subroutine as a Long—that is, as a long integer. AutoNumber fields in Access are by default long integers, so it's best to give `MasterResID` the same variable type.

Milliseconds later, when the information about the reservation is stored in the database, the new reservation record stores the value of `MasterResID`:

```
rsReservation.Fields("MasterID") = MasterResID
```

Using that arrangement, when a user wants to edit a reservation—or even delete it—the code can obtain all the related, recurring reservations and at the user's option, apply the changes to all of them or only to the one that the user began by selecting.

Deleting Records from the Database and from the Worksheet

Here's how it works out in practice. Suppose that the user has clicked a cell in an existing reservation on the Excel worksheet, and chosen a custom menu item that initiates the cancellation of the reservation. It's necessary to take care of two broad tasks: indicating to the database that the reservation (or, if recurring, the reservations) has been cancelled, and removing the reservation from the worksheet, so that the room will be available for some other use on that day and at that time.

The following code manages those tasks.

Managing the Preliminaries

As usual, the procedure begins with a `Sub` statement and the declaration of the necessary variables.

```
Sub RemoveReservation()
```

It's good to check to make sure that the user has selected a cell in the reservation range before attempting to remove it. Such a cell has been colored either red to represent a firm reservation or yellow to represent a temporary hold. The `CellColor` variable is used to determine whether the user has started by selecting a cell in that range.

```
Dim CellColor As Integer
```

Three variables are declared to uniquely identify the reservation in question. As noted in the prior section, only one record can have a particular date, start time, and room. By determining their values for the reservation that the user wants to cancel, the code can find that specific reservation in the database and take the appropriate action. They are declared as `WhichDate`, `WhichRoom`, and `StartTime`.

```
Dim WhichDate As Date, WhichRoom As String, StartTime As Date
```

`WhichColumn` is used as in the prior section to help determine the reservation's start time.

```
Dim WhichColumn As Integer
```

It's best, after the reservation's record has been found but before actually canceling it, to ask the user whether he's sure he wants to go ahead. The `Confirm` variable is used to capture that information.

```
Dim Confirm As Integer
```

Two recordsets are declared: one to represent the Reservations table and one to associate the IDs that identify rooms with the names of the rooms.

```
Dim rsReservation As Recordset, rsRooms As Recordset
```

Two Long integers are declared, one to hold the reservation's master ID—the one that it shares with other records that are part of the same recurrence group—and a record ID that uniquely identifies one particular reservation.

```
Dim MasterResID As Long, RecordID As Long
```

Two object variables are used to represent database objects. The query that returns the reservation record (or records) is `qdfEditDetails`, and the recordset that holds the record (or records) is `rsRecordsToDelete`.

```
Dim qdfRecordDetails As QueryDef
Dim rsRecordsToDelete As Recordset
```

The next two variables required will contain the number of reservation records in the recordset: one if the reservation is nonrecurring, and an initially unknown number of records otherwise. Lastly, `ResourceID` is used to store the ID number that identifies a particular room.

```
Dim ReservationCount As Long
Dim ResourceID As Long
```

Four variables are declared to support communication with the user via a message box. The `Msg` variable stores the message itself, the `Style` variable contains an integer that determines the mix of buttons in the message box (for example, OK only, Yes/No/Cancel, and so on), `Title` to hold the string that's shown in the message box's title bar, and `Response` to capture the user's response to the message box.

```
Dim Msg As String, Style As Integer, Title As String, _
  Response As Integer
```

Verifying and Confirming the User's Request

The code then makes sure that the user has begun by selecting a cell within an existing reservation. A cell that represents a reservation has its color set to yellow (for a temporary hold) or to red (for a firm reservation). The code would not work properly if the user had not begun by identifying a reservation, so the code checks to see whether the cell's color is either yellow or red.

The code determines the numeric index that identifies the active cell's color—3 for red, 6 for yellow. If it is neither 3 nor 6, it displays a message box, complaining that the user has not selected a reservation cell. Then the subroutine is exited so that no more of its code runs.

```
CellColor = ActiveCell.Interior.ColorIndex
If CellColor <> 6 And CellColor <> 3 Then
    MsgBox "To remove a reservation, please begin by selecting a cell " _
        & "that's part of an existing reservation -- that is, a red " _
        & "cell or a yellow cell."
        Exit Sub
End If
```

The arguments for this message box do not call for a particular set of command buttons. Therefore VBA displays the default, which is a single OK button. Regardless of what the user does to dismiss the message box, the code then stops processing.

Assuming that the user began by selecting a reservation, the code next confirms that the user really does want to delete it. VBA displays a message box that asks the user if he's sure. The `vbOKCancel` argument causes the message box to have an OK button and a Cancel button.

```
Confirm = MsgBox("Are you sure you want to " _
& "delete this reservation?", vbOKCancel)
```

If the user clicks the Yes button, indicating that he wants to go ahead and delete the reservation, the message box returns a 1. So, if it returns anything else, the code stops processing by means of the `Exit Sub` statement.

```
If Confirm <> 1 Then
    Exit Sub
End If
```

11

Otherwise, the code continues by finding the path to and name of the reservations database, and opening it.

```
DatabaseName = ThisWorkbook.Sheets("UserNames").Cells(1, 3)
Set dbReservation = OpenDatabase(DatabaseName, False, False, "MS Access")
```

Establishing the Recordsets

Two recordsets are established. The database's Reservations table is needed because the reservation record needs to be deleted from that table. The Resources table is needed so that the code can determine the ID of the room that's been reserved. (The worksheet shows the names of the rooms, but the Reservations table stores their IDs rather than their names.)

```
Set rsReservation = dbReservation.TableDefs _
("Reservations").OpenRecordset(dbOpenDynaset)
Set rsRooms = dbReservation.TableDefs _
("Resources").OpenRecordset(dbOpenDynaset)
```

Finding the Reservation in the Database

It's time to get the information from the worksheet that will uniquely identify the reservation that the user selected. As noted in the "Identifying the Reservation Record" section, that information includes the reservation's date, its room, and its start time. The date and the time are obtained in precisely the same way they were in "Identifying the Reservation Record." It gets the active sheet name for the date. It gets the start time by backing up to the beginning of the reservation range to find its starting column—the start time is in row 1 of that column.

```
WhichDate = ActiveSheet.Name

WhichColumn = ActiveCell.Column - 1
Do While Cells(ActiveCell.Row, WhichColumn) = _
Cells(ActiveCell.Row, ActiveCell.Column)
    WhichColumn = WhichColumn - 1
Loop
StartTime = ActiveSheet.Cells(1, WhichColumn + 1).Value
```

In this case, though, it's more convenient to use the room's ID rather than its name. But that ID has to be obtained by using the room's name, and another subroutine, a brief one, is used to do that. The room's name is obtained as before from column A of the reservation's row.

```
WhichRoom = ActiveSheet.Cells(ActiveCell.Row, 1).Value
ConvertResource WhichRoom, ResourceID, rsRooms
```

Then the ConvertResource subroutine is called, with the room's name (WhichRoom), a variable to hold its ID (ResourceID), and the recordset that contains the names and IDs of rooms (rsRooms) as arguments. As yet, ResourceID has no value, but when it's returned from ConvertResource it will contain the ID of the selected room. Here's the code for that procedure:

```
Sub ConvertResource(RoomName As String, _
ResourceID As Long, rsRooms As Recordset)
Dim Criterion As String
```

```
Criterion = "ResourceName = '" & RoomName & "'"
With rsRooms
    .FindFirst Criterion
    ResourceID = .Fields("ResourceID")
End With
End Sub
```

The FindFirst method is used to locate the selected room name in the Resources table, represented by the rsRooms recordset. The code stores in Criterion a string comprised of the name of the field to be searched, ResourceName, and the name of the room to be found, stored in RoomName. Suppose that the name Cafeteria is in RoomName. The search string, Criterion, would be

```
ResourceName = 'Cafeteria'
```

The record with the value from RoomName in the ResourceName field is found, and its value on the ResourceID field is stored in the ResourceID variable. That variable is then returned to the calling procedure, RemoveReservation.

> **TIP**
>
> This code does not use the NoMatch property because the remainder of the application guarantees that a record will be found. If you use a search method such as FindFirst or Seek, consider using NoMatch. This property is True if the search method failed to find a record corresponding to the search criteria. For example,
>
> ```
> rsRooms.FindFirst Criterion
> If rsRooms.NoMatch Then
> [Code to recover from a failure to find a record]
> End If
> ```
>
> You could also use something such as If Not rsRooms.NoMatch to enable your code to continue processing. (The double negative does take a little getting used to.)

Checking for Recurring Reservations

Now that the room's ResourceID has been located, the code in the RemoveReservation subroutine continues. It first checks to see whether the record's MasterID is shared by any other records—that is, it checks whether the selected reservation is a recurring one. It does this by calling the function FindReservationMasterIDInDB, using the reservation database, the reservation date, the room ID, and the start time as arguments.

```
MasterResID = FindReservationMasterIDInDB _
(dbReservation, WhichDate, ResourceID, StartTime)
```

The function is not built-in, but is a user-defined function, or UDF. Here is its code.

```
Function FindReservationMasterIDInDB(dbReservation As Database, _
WhichDate As Date, WhichRoom As Long, StartTime As Date) As Long
```

Notice that the procedure's declaration begins with Function instead of Sub (*procedure* is a generic term for either a function or a subroutine). Also note that the function has a type; here, it's Long, so the value it returns is typed as a Long Integer.

Two object variables are declared in the function, a query that will return all records that share the same MasterID, and a recordset that will contain those records.

```
Dim qdfDetail As QueryDef
Dim rsDetail As Recordset

Set qdfDetail = dbReservation.QueryDefs("FindSingleReservation")
```

The query named `FindSingleReservation` appears in design view in Figure 11.6.

Figure 11.6
Notice the calculated field, which formats `StartTime` as Medium time (hh:mm AM/PM).

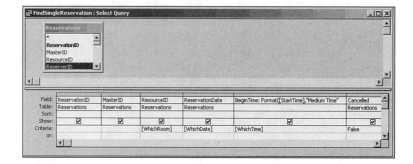

The code passes the room, the date, and the start time (formatted as Medium time) to the query, and its results are assigned to the recordset.

```
With qdfDetail
    .Parameters("WhichRoom") = WhichRoom
    .Parameters("WhichDate") = WhichDate
    .Parameters("WhichTime") = Format(StartTime, "Medium Time")
    Set rsDetail = .OpenRecordset(dbOpenDynaset)
End With
```

Then the function itself is set to the value of the MasterID field in the recordset. With that value available, it will be possible to find out whether there are other records in the database that share the same MasterID. If there are, the code will ask the user whether they should all be deleted, or just the one that was selected when the user initiated the process.

> **NOTE**
> The assignment of a value to the function is typical of UDFs and of functions in general. This aspect is what enables you to write your own functions in VBA and have them return values directly to the worksheet.

```
FindReservationMasterIDInDB = rsDetail.Fields("MasterID")
Set qdfDetail = Nothing
Set rsDetail = Nothing

End Function
```

Now the variable `MasterResID` has been set equal to the MasterID of the selected reservation. That value is passed as a parameter to the query named `DetailRecords`. The query will return only one record—the one chosen by the user—if it is not part of a group of recurring reservations. If the reservation *does* recur, the query will select all of them, and the code will ask the user whether he wants to delete all the reservations or only the one he selected.

The query is assigned to an object variable and its parameter is passed. Then the query's results are assigned to a recordset.

```
Set qdfRecordDetails = dbReservation.QueryDefs("DetailRecords")
qdfRecordDetails.Parameters("WhichID") = MasterResID
Set rsRecordsToDelete = qdfRecordDetails.OpenRecordset(dbOpenDynaset)
```

With the recordset established, go to its final record and then obtain the record count. It's necessary to first move to the final record: In a DAO recordset, the record count isn't available until the final record has been reached. Therefore, the code employs the `MoveLast` method on the recordset and then obtains the count of the number of records.

```
With rsRecordsToDelete
    .MoveLast
    ReservationCount = .RecordCount
End With
```

Now the code determines what to do if there is more than one reservation in the recordset.

```
If ReservationCount > 1 Then
```

If there are multiple records that share the same MasterID, a message box is prepared. The question to be posed to the user is assembled into the string variable `Msg`, which asks the user whether to delete all recurring reservations or only the selected reservation:

```
Msg = "This reservation is one of a recurring group " & _
"or a multi-room group. " & vbLf & _
"Do you want to delete all the records as a group? " & _
vbLf & "(If you click No, you will delete only " & _
"the reservation you selected.)"
```

The `vbLf` is a constant that represents a linefeed character. It's used here to break the message into three separate lines. The message box will offer a Yes, a No, and a Cancel button. This combination is specified by the `vbYesNoCancel` keyword and stored in the `Style` variable. A title is established, and the message box displayed.

```
Style = vbYesNoCancel
Title = "Delete multiple reservations"
```

The `Response` variable captures which button the user clicks.

```
Response = MsgBox(Msg, Style, Title)
```

If the user clicks the Cancel button, exit this subroutine.

```
If Response = vbCancel Then
    Exit Sub
```

If the user clicks the No button, that means he wants to delete only the selected reservation, and none of its related records. In that case, close the recordset that contains multiple records and re-establish it with only the selected record.

```
ElseIf Response = vbNo Then
    rsRecordsToDelete.Close
    RecordID = FindReservationDetailIDInDB _
    (dbReservation, WhichDate, ResourceID, StartTime)
```

The function `FindReservationDetailIDInDB` is identical to the function
`FindReservationMasterIDInDB`, discussed earlier in this section, except that it is set equal to
the ID of the selected reservation, not to its MasterID. That reservation ID is passed as a
parameter to a query that returns the single reservation record, and that query's results are
assigned to the `rsRecordsToDelete` recordset.

```
        Set qdfRecordDetails = dbReservation.QueryDefs _
        ("FindOneRecord")
        qdfRecordDetails.Parameters("WhichID") = RecordID
        Set rsRecordsToDelete = qdfRecordDetails _
        .OpenRecordset(dbOpenDynaset)
    End If

End If
```

To recap: If the user wants to delete all of a group of recurring reservations, he indicates
that by clicking the Yes button in the message box, and the `rsRecordsToDelete` recordset
remains as it was. If he wants to delete only the selected reservation, he clicks the No button
in the message box. In that case, the reservation's unique record ID is found using its date,
room, and start time, and that record is used to populate the `rsRecordsToDelete` recordset.

The code then loops through the recordset and sets the value of the Cancelled field to True
for each record. With that field set, a record will not subsequently be returned to the workbook. Note the use of the `Edit` and the `Update` methods:

```
With rsRecordsToDelete
    .MoveFirst
    Do While Not .EOF
        .Edit
        .Fields("Cancelled") = True
        .Update
        .MoveNext
    Loop
End With
```

Finishing Up

It remains to remove the reservation that was originally selected from the worksheet. That
can be done easily by calling the `GetSingleDayFromDB` subroutine, discussed earlier in this
chapter in the "Bringing Data Back from a Parameterized Query" section. Recall that the
subroutine clears the worksheet and then retrieves all reservations for the date shown on the
worksheet tab. But it does not retrieve any record for which the Cancelled field is True, so
the deleted reservation does not reappear on the worksheet.

```
GetSingleDayFromDB
```

Finally, clean up by releasing the object variables.

```
Set rsReservation = Nothing
Set rsRooms = Nothing
Set qdfRecordDetails = Nothing
Set rsRecordsToDelete = Nothing

End Sub
```

This subroutine employs a variety of techniques that you'll find useful in returning information from a database via a recordset. It calls other subroutines that modify the value of variables, as well as a UDF that finds record IDs. It uses queries to return specific records by means both of parameters passed to the queries as well as fixed criteria (such as the Cancelled field in the GetSingleDayFromDB subroutine).

It shows you how to use information in the workbook—in this instance, the date from the worksheet tab, room names from column A, and times of day from row 1—to determine the records that are returned from the database. It also demonstrates how to revise the contents of recordsets based on user responses to questions posed in message boxes.

This section concludes by providing you all the code it has discussed, unencumbered by commentary.

The Full Code

```
Sub GetSingleDayFromDB(Optional DateLastModified As Date)

Dim dbReservation As DAO.Database
Dim qdfRetrieveCurrent As DAO.QueryDef
Dim rsRecordsToRetrieve As DAO.Recordset

Dim StartCol As Integer, StopCol As Integer, WhichRow As Integer
Dim ReservationRange As Range
Dim SetupPeriods As Integer, CleanupPeriods As Integer
Dim TimeAsText As String
Dim TimeArray(71) As String, RoomArray() As String
Dim i As Integer
Dim ResourceCount As Integer

ResourceCount = ActiveSheet.Cells(600, 1).End(xlUp).Row - 1
ReDim RoomArray(ResourceCount)
DatabaseName = ThisWorkbook.Sheets("UserNames").Cells(1, 3)

Set dbReservation = OpenDatabase(DatabaseName, False, _
False, "MS Access;PWD=Nirmac")

Set qdfRetrieveCurrent = dbReservation.QueryDefs("RetrieveSingleDay")

Application.ScreenUpdating = False
qdfRetrieveCurrent.Parameters("ThisDate") = ActiveSheet.Name

Set rsRecordsToRetrieve = qdfRetrieveCurrent.OpenRecordset(dbOpenForwardOnly)

ActiveSheet.Range(Cells(2, 2), Cells(ResourceCount + 1, 73)).Clear
ActiveSheet.Range(Cells(2, 2), Cells(ResourceCount + 1, 73)) _
.Interior.ColorIndex = xlNone
```

11

```
If Not rsRecordsToRetrieve.BOF Then

    For i = 1 To 71
        TimeArray(i) = Application.Text(ActiveSheet.Cells(1, i + 1), "h:mm AM/PM")
    Next i
    For i = 1 To ResourceCount
        RoomArray(i) = ActiveSheet.Cells(i + 1, 1)
    Next i

    With rsRecordsToRetrieve

        Do While Not .EOF

            TimeAsText = Application.WorksheetFunction.Text _
            (.Fields("StartTime"), "h:mm AM/PM")
            StartCol = Application.Match(TimeAsText, TimeArray, 0) + 1

            TimeAsText = Application.WorksheetFunction.Text _
            (.Fields("StopTime"), "h:mm AM/PM")
            StopCol = Application.Match(TimeAsText, TimeArray, 0)

            WhichRow = Application.Match(.Fields("ResourceName"), _
            RoomArray, 0) + 1
            Set ReservationRange = ActiveSheet.Range(Cells(WhichRow, _
            StartCol), Cells(WhichRow, StopCol))
            ReservationRange.FormulaR1C1 = UCase(.Fields("Purpose"))
            If .Fields("ReserveHold") = "Reserve" Then
                ReservationRange.Interior.ColorIndex = 3
            Else
                ReservationRange.Interior.ColorIndex = 6
            End If

            SetupPeriods = .Fields("SetupPeriods")
            CleanupPeriods = .Fields("CleanupPeriods")
            If SetupPeriods > 0 Then
                ReservationRange.Offset(0, -SetupPeriods).Resize _
                (1, SetupPeriods).Interior.ColorIndex = 48
            End If
            With ReservationRange.Offset(0, -SetupPeriods) _
            .Resize(1, 1).Borders(xlEdgeLeft)
                .LineStyle = xlContinuous
                .Weight = xlThick
                .ColorIndex = 1
            End With
            If CleanupPeriods > 0 Then
                ReservationRange.Offset(0, ReservationRange.Columns.Count) _
                .Resize(1, CleanupPeriods).Interior.ColorIndex = 48
            End If
            With ReservationRange.Offset(0, ReservationRange.Columns.Count _
            + CleanupPeriods - 1).Resize(1, 1).Borders(xlEdgeRight)
                .LineStyle = xlContinuous
                .Weight = xlThick
                .ColorIndex = 1
            End With
            DateLastModified = .Fields("MostRecentlyModified")
            ReservationRange.Resize(1, 1).ClearComments
            ReservationRange.Resize(1, 1).AddComment ("Reserved By: " & _
```

```vba
                .Fields("ReserverName") & Chr(10) & "Reserved For: " & _
                .Fields("ReservedFor") & Chr(10) & "Last Modified: " & _
                Format(.Fields("MostRecentlyModified"), "m/d/yy"))
                If .Fields("Participants") = "External" Then
                    ReservationRange.Font.Bold = True
                End If
            .MoveNext
            Loop
        End With
    End If
Application.StatusBar = False
Set qdfRetrieveCurrent = Nothing
Set rsRecordsToRetrieve = Nothing
Set ReservationRange = Nothing

End Sub
Sub FromDBtoForm(rsRecordsToEdit As Recordset, WhichRoom As String)
Dim StopTime As Date, StartTime As Date
Dim RoomListIndex As Integer, StartTimeListIndex As Integer, i As Integer
Dim StopTimeListIndex As Integer, DateListIndex As Integer
Dim WhichDate As Date
Dim ResourceCount As Integer

ResourceCount = ActiveSheet.Cells(600, 1).End(xlUp).Row - 1
StartTime = rsRecordsToEdit.Fields("StartTime")
StopTime = rsRecordsToEdit.Fields("StopTime")
WhichDate = rsRecordsToEdit.Fields("ReservationDate")

GetDropdownIndices RoomListIndex, WhichRoom, StartTime, StartTimeListIndex, _
    StopTime, StopTimeListIndex, WhichDate, DateListIndex

With ReservationForm
    For i = 1 To ResourceCount
        .ResourceListBox.AddItem (Sheets("UserNames").Cells(i, 4).Value)
    Next i

    .DateDropDown.Value = Sheets("UserNames").Cells(DateListIndex, 5)
    .ResourceListBox.Selected(RoomListIndex - 1) = True
    .ddStartTime.ListIndex = StartTimeListIndex - 1
    .ddStopTime.ListIndex = StopTimeListIndex - 1
    .SetupPeriods = rsRecordsToEdit.Fields("SetupPeriods")
    .CleanupPeriods = rsRecordsToEdit.Fields("CleanupPeriods")

    If rsRecordsToEdit.Fields("RoundTables") = "Round Tables" Then
        .tbChairsPerTable.Visible = True
        .tbChairsPerTable.Text = rsRecordsToEdit.Fields("ChairsPerTable")
        .lblChairsPerTable.Visible = True
    Else
        .tbChairsPerTable.Visible = False
        .lblChairsPerTable.Visible = False
    End If

    .PurposeBox.Value = rsRecordsToEdit.Fields("Purpose")
    .ReservedForBox.Value = rsRecordsToEdit.Fields("ReservedFor")

    If rsRecordsToEdit.Fields("Participants") = "Internal" Then
        .obInternal.Value = True
```

11

```
            ElseIf rsRecordsToEdit.Fields("Participants") = "External" Then
                .obExternal.Value = True
            End If

    'Similar and repetitive code omitted here

        .cbDept.Value = rsRecordsToEdit.Fields("Department")
        .tbAccount.Value = rsRecordsToEdit.Fields("Account")
    End With
    Set dbReservatioons = Nothing
    Set rsRecordsToEdit = Nothing
    End Sub

    Sub GetMasterID(MasterResID As Long)

    Dim rsMasterTable As Recordset

    Set rsMasterTable = dbReservation.TableDefs("Masters") _
    .OpenRecordset(dbOpenDynaset)
    With rsMasterTable
        .AddNew
        .Update
        .MoveLast
        MasterResID = .Fields("MasterID")
        .Close
    End With

    End Sub


    Sub RemoveReservation()
    Dim MeetingRange As Range, SetUpRange As Range, CleanUpRange As Range
    Dim ICI As Integer, ReservationCount As Long, i As Long
    Dim WhichDate As Date, WhichRoom As String, StartTime As Date, StopTime As Date
    Dim WhichColumn As Integer
    Dim Confirm As Integer
    Dim rsReservation As Recordset, rsReserver As Recordset, _
        rsResource As Recordset
    Dim rsTableForSeek As Recordset
    Dim MasterResID As Long, ResourceID As Long
    Dim qdfEditDetails As QueryDef
    Dim rsRecordsToEdit As Recordset
    Dim RecordID As Long
    Dim Msg As String, Style As Integer, Title As String, Response As Integer
    Dim CanRemove As Boolean
    Dim CountSheets As Integer
    BookCheck = ActiveWorkbook Is ThisWorkbook
    If Not BookCheck Then
        MsgBox "Please use this command only with the Resources workbook active."
        End
    End If
    If Not SuppressWarning Then
        Confirm = MsgBox("Are you sure you want to delete this reservation?", _
        vbOKCancel)
        If Confirm <> 1 Then
            Exit Sub
        End If
    End If
```

```
DatabaseName = ThisWorkbook.Sheets("UserNames").Cells(1, 3)
Set dbReservation = OpenDatabase(DatabaseName, False, False, "MS Access")
Set rsReservation = dbReservation.TableDefs("Reservations") _
.OpenRecordset(dbOpenDynaset)
Set rsReserver = dbReservation.TableDefs("Reservers") _
.OpenRecordset(dbOpenDynaset)
Set rsResource = dbReservation.TableDefs("Resources") _
.OpenRecordset(dbOpenDynaset)

ICI = ActiveCell.Interior.ColorIndex
If ICI <> 6 And ICI <> 3 Then
    MsgBox "To remove a reservation, please begin by selecting a cell " _
        & "that's part of an existing reservation -- that is, a red " _
        & "cell or a yellow cell."
        Exit Sub
End If

WhichDate = ActiveSheet.Name
WhichRoom = ActiveSheet.Cells(ActiveCell.Row, 1).Value
ConvertResource WhichRoom, ResourceID, rsResource
WhichColumn = ActiveCell.Column - 1
Do While Cells(ActiveCell.Row, WhichColumn) = _
Cells(ActiveCell.Row, ActiveCell.Column)
    WhichColumn = WhichColumn - 1
Loop
StartTime = ActiveSheet.Cells(1, WhichColumn + 1).Value

MasterResID = FindReservationMasterIDInDB _
(dbReservation, WhichDate, ResourceID, StartTime)

Set qdfEditDetails = dbReservation.QueryDefs("DetailRecords")
qdfEditDetails.Parameters("WhichID") = MasterResID

Set rsRecordsToEdit = qdfEditDetails.OpenRecordset(dbOpenDynaset)
With rsRecordsToEdit
    .MoveLast
    ReservationCount = .RecordCount
    .MoveFirst
End With

If ReservationCount > 1 Then

    Msg = "This reservation is one of a recurring group or a multi-room " & _
    "group. " & Chr(10) & "Do you want to delete all the records " & _
    "as a group?" & Chr(10) & "(If you click No, you will delete " & _
    "only the reservation you selected.)"
    Style = vbYesNoCancel
    Title = "Delete multiple reservations"

    Response = MsgBox(Msg, Style, Title)

    If Response = vbCancel Then
        End
    ElseIf Response = vbNo Then
        rsRecordsToEdit.Close
        RecordID = FindReservationDetailIDInDB _
        (dbReservation, WhichDate, ResourceID, StartTime)
```

11

```
            Set qdfEditDetails = dbReservation.QueryDefs("EditOneRecord")
            qdfEditDetails.Parameters("WhichID") = RecordID
            Set rsRecordsToEdit = qdfEditDetails.OpenRecordset(dbOpenDynaset)
        End If

    End If

    Set MeetingRange = Selection
    GetFullReservationRange SetUpRange, MeetingRange, CleanUpRange

    rsRecordsToEdit.MoveFirst

    CanRemove = CheckEditPermits(MeetingRange)
    If Not CanRemove Then
        MsgBox "Only the person who made the reservation can delete it."
        End
    End If
    Sheets(MeetingRange.Parent.Name).Activate
    MeetingRange.Select
    SuppressWarning = True
    RemoveReservationFromWorksheet SetUpRange, MeetingRange, CleanUpRange
    SuppressWarning = False

    With rsRecordsToEdit
        Do While Not .EOF
            .Edit
            .Fields("Cancelled") = True
            .Update
            .MoveNext
        Loop
    End With
    GetSingleDayFromDB

    Set rsReservation = Nothing
    Set rsRooms = Nothing
    Set qdfRecordDetails = Nothing
    Set rsRecordsToDelete = Nothing

End Sub

Sub ConvertResource(ResourceName As String, ResourceID As Long, _
rsResource As Recordset)
Dim Criterion As String
Criterion = "ResourceName = '" & ResourceName & "'"
With rsResource
    .FindFirst Criterion
    ResourceID = .Fields("ResourceID")
End With
End Sub

Function FindReservationMasterIDInDB(dbReservation As Database, _
WhichDate As Date, WhichRoom As Long, StartTime As Date) As Long
Dim qdfDetail As QueryDef
Dim rsDetail As Recordset

Set qdfDetail = dbReservation.QueryDefs("FindSingleReservation")
qdfDetail.Parameters("WhichRoom") = WhichRoom
```

```
qdfDetail.Parameters("WhichDate") = WhichDate
qdfDetail.Parameters("WhichTime") = Format(StartTime, "Medium Time")
Set rsDetail = qdfDetail.OpenRecordset(dbOpenDynaset)

FindReservationMasterIDInDB = rsDetail.Fields("MasterID")
Set qdfDetail = Nothing
Set rsDetail = Nothing

End Function
```

Looking Ahead

This chapter has focused on bringing data into the workbook using recordsets. You've seen how to use the `CopyFromRecordset` method to acquire data *en masse*, and you have seen how to use queries and parameters to define recordsets that can be managed record-by-record.

The queries discussed in this chapter are *select* queries. Their sole purpose is to extract records and fields from tables, and to make the records and fields available to you for editing via recordsets. A select query makes no change to the underlying data, nor to the tables that contain the data.

There is another large class of queries, termed *action queries*. These queries do act on the data, by inserting or deleting records, or by modifying them. (Action queries are termed *stored procedures* in SQL Server.)

The final chapter in this book, "Controlling a Database from Excel Using ADO and DAO," focuses on moving data the direction opposite to that discussed in this chapter. It does so by making use of action queries, DAO, and the ADO Command object.

11

Controlling a Database from Excel Using ADO and DAO

12

Using DAO to Execute Action Queries

Action queries were discussed in some detail in Chapter 9, "Managing Database Objects," but from an interactive standpoint. There, in "Creating Queries," you saw how to use Update, Delete, and Append queries to change data, remove records, and add them to the underlying tables. The context was that of a user employing the queries directly from the database's user interface.

But just as you can combine VBA with DAO or ADO recordsets to return data via Select queries, you can cause VBA to run action queries from the Excel platform, and thereby update, delete, and append records in a database. You can do this with queries that have been saved in the database or you can submit the queries' SQL along with the commands to execute them.

The usual reason to execute an action query from Excel is that a user has done something in a workbook that requires something to occur in the database. For example, suppose that you want to replace a set of records in a table with new information. Particularly if others might be making use of that table, you need to be careful how you do this. You can't simply delete the table and rebuild it. No database worthy of the name would allow you to delete a table that another user has open, either directly or indirectly via a query or a form.

You have two options. One is to compare the old data with the new, record by record and field by field, updating any records for which the data has changed.

A much more straightforward approach is to simply delete all the old records from the table and then replace them with new records. The best way to do that is usually to put the new records into a temporary database table and execute a Delete query to remove the old records from the permanent table. Finally, you execute an Append query to move the new records into the permanent table from the temporary table.

> **CAUTION**
>
> A database *will* allow the deletion of records from an open table unless specific steps have been taken to prevent that action.

Using DAO to Execute an Existing Query

Here's an example of how you might use DAO to execute a Delete query. In this case, the query already exists in the database, and it accepts a parameter for its ReservationDate field. Figure 12.1 shows the query in design view.

Figure 12.1
If you run the query interactively, you're prompted for a date value. No prompt appears if you run it from code.

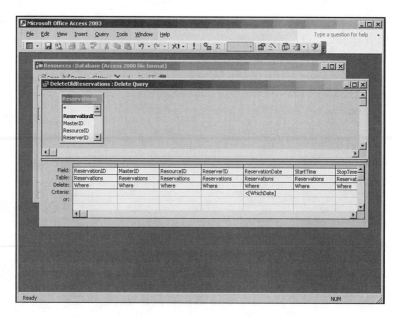

You would place code similar to the following in an Excel VBE module, and establish a reference to a DAO library by selecting References from the VBE's Tools menu. The code passes a value to the Delete query's parameter. When the code then executes the query, it deletes all records with values on ReservationDate earlier than January 1, 2004.

```
Sub DeleteOldRecords(FilePath As String)
Dim dbReservations As DAO.Database
Dim qdfDeleteRecords As DAO.QueryDef

Set dbReservations = OpenDatabase("I:\RM_RES\Resources.mdb")
Set qdfDeleteRecords = dbReservations.QueryDefs("DeleteOldReservations")
```

```
With qdfDeleteRecords
    .Parameters("WhichDate") = DateValue("1/1/2004")
    .Execute
End With

Set qdfDeleteRecords = Nothing
Set dbReservations = Nothing

End Sub
```

Notice the use of the VBA `DateValue` function to convert the parameter value from a text value that specifies a date to a true date value. This is *not* required. The statement could be this one:

```
.Parameters("WhichDate") = "1/1/2004"
```

because Access will constrain the value of the parameter to the type used by the criterion field, ReservationDate. You could also use this one:

```
.Parameters("WhichDate") = #1/1/2004#
```

because Access recognizes a value surrounded by pound signs as a date.

Using DAO to Define and Execute a Nonpersistent Query

At times you want to use a query that doesn't exist in the database. This can occur when the user takes an action that occurs only occasionally—for example, periodically clearing records out of a table because they're no longer needed.

In a case like that, you might prefer to create the query in your VBA code, rather than storing in your database a query that's needed only infrequently. One of the most maddening sources of clutter in a database is users' tendency to create queries that are used only once, or only once a year. You wind up with a lengthy list of queries with names like Al's Query, and Test Query, and Jane Query Feb 2004, and Query1, and Query2, and so on. You have no idea, looking at the names of the queries, what they're intended to accomplish, and they make it hard to locate useful queries.

So you sometimes create new queries in your code, rather than depending on the existence of a query in the database. (If things have gotten untidy enough, someone might have deleted *all* existing queries in exasperation.) To do that, you need to provide the SQL in your code, as in the following example:

```
Sub DeleteOldRecordsWithString1(FilePath As String, _
FirstDate As String)

Dim dbReservations As DAO.Database
Dim qdfTempQuery As DAO.QueryDef
Dim strQuery As String

strQuery = "DELETE Reservations.*, " & _
"Reservations.ReservationDate " & _
"FROM Reservations " & _
"WHERE ((Reservations.ReservationDate) < " & _
FirstDate & ");"
```

12

```
Set dbReservations = OpenDatabase(FilePath & "Resources.mdb")
Set qdfTempQuery = dbReservations.CreateQueryDef("", strQuery)
qdfTempQuery.Execute

End Sub
```

There are several points to note in this code:

- The SQL needed to carry out the query is supplied to the code. In this instance, it's stored in the string variable strQuery.

- It uses the CreateQueryDef method of the database object to create a new query. This method takes two arguments: the query's name and its SQL.

- The query is given a null name, indicated by the empty quote marks. This prevents the query from being saved in the database. It lasts only as long as the code is running. The object is *nonpersistent*.

- The procedure that calls the subroutine should pass the value of FirstDate enclosed in pound signs: for example, #1/1/2004#. That ensures that the value will be interpreted as a date.

Specifying Parameters in SQL

It's not necessary to declare a query's parameters in SQL, but it's not a bad idea, if only for purposes of documentation. An example follows:

```
Sub DeleteOldRecords(FilePath As String)
Dim dbReservations As DAO.Database
Dim qdfDeleteRecs As DAO.QueryDef
Dim strQuery As String

strQuery = "PARAMETERS [WhichDate] Date;" & _
"DELETE Reservations.*, Reservations.ReservationDate " & _
"FROM Reservations " & _
"WHERE (((Reservations.ReservationDate)<[WhichDate]));"

Set dbReservations = OpenDatabase(FilePath & "Resources.mdb")
Set qdfDeleteRecs = dbReservations.CreateQueryDef _
("DeleteOldRecs", strQuery)
With qdfDeleteRecs
    .Parameters("WhichDate") = #1/1/2004#
    .Execute
End With

End Sub
```

Notice that the first clause in the SQL names the parameter and specifies its type as Date. Also notice that this query *is* saved in the database, with the name DeleteOldRecs.

There would be little point in creating a nonpersistent query—one that is not saved in the database—that takes one or more parameters. The rationale for query parameters is that they enable users to execute the query repeatedly, with different values supplied to the parameter. For example, at the start of 2005, you might pass 1/1/2005 to the WhichDate parameter, calling for all records with a value prior to that date to be deleted. At the start of 2006, you could execute the same query, passing 1/1/2006 to the WhichDate parameter. The point is that after you've established the query, you can execute it repeatedly, with different parameter values to bring about different outcomes.

If the query is nonpersistent, though, it won't be saved, and therefore it won't be sitting in the database, patiently waiting for you to execute it again with a different parameter value. So, although it's certainly legal to create a temporary, nonpersistent query that has a parameter, there's little point to doing so. Instead, you would just dispense with the parameter and put the criterion value directly into the WHERE clause, as shown here:

```
"WHERE ((Reservations.ReservationDate) < #1/1/2004);"
```

and here:

```
"WHERE ((Reservations.ReservationDate) < FirstDate);"
```

Using DAO to Create and Execute an Append Query

Perhaps the fastest way to move data from an Excel worksheet to an Access table is by means of an Append query written in SQL. All other things being equal, SQL provides you the most efficient and speediest use of your system's resources for data manipulation.

When you work directly in Access and design a new Append query, Access wants to know the table that contains the source data. The assumption is that you have data in a table named, say, RecordsFrom2004, and that you want to append its contents to a table named, say, AllRecords.

That's not much help if you have data in an Excel worksheet and want to append it to an Access table. For that you need to find another way. DAO (and ADO) recordsets are one excellent method, but they're not as efficient as SQL. When you're not doing any fine-tuning, when all you want to do is stuff worksheet data into a database table as quickly and efficiently as possible, you want to use SQL.

The solution is to establish a temporary Append query and include the values that you want to append into the query's SQL. To do so, you need to use a version of an Append query's syntax that Access doesn't typically generate.

12

CASE STUDY

As director of an Employee Health Services department, one of your responsibilities is to make sure that the date on which an employee has a physical examination gets recorded in HR's Employees database.

You arrange for the receptionist to record the necessary information in an Excel worksheet after the physical has been completed. That information includes the employee's unique ID number, as well as the date and time that the physical was completed (see Figure 12.2).

Figure 12.2
Because the records enter the database with no special handling, an action query handles this situation efficiently.

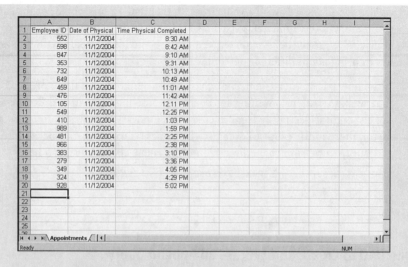

You use the workbook's `BeforeClose` event to execute the following code when the receptionist closes it at the end of each business day.

```
Private Sub Workbook_BeforeClose(Cancel As Boolean)

Dim dbEmpPhys As DAO.Database
Dim qdfTempQuery As DAO.QueryDef
Dim strQuery As String
Dim i As Integer
Dim EmpID As String, PhysDate As Date, PhysTime As Date
Dim LastEmployee As Long
Set dbEmpPhys = OpenDatabase _
(ThisWorkbook.Path & "\Employees.mdb")
Set qdfTempQuery = dbEmpPhys.CreateQueryDef("")
```

After declaring the necessary variables, your code sets the database and then sets a new, temporary query (note the empty string given as its name).

```
LastEmployee = ThisWorkbook.Sheets("Appointments") _
.Cells(65536,1).End(xlUp).Row
```

The number of employee records to be processed is obtained by going up from the last row of column A to the lowermost value in that column, and assigning its row number to `LastEmployee`.

A loop now begins, starting with 2 (because the actual data begins in row 2 of the worksheet) and ending with `LastEmployee`. The data in columns A, B, and C of the loop's current row are assigned to the variables `EmpID`, `PhysData`, and `PhysTime`.

```
For i = 2 To LastEmployee
    EmpID = ThisWorkbook.Sheets _
    ("Appointments").Cells(i, 1)
    PhysDate = ThisWorkbook.Sheets _
    ("Appointments").Cells(i, 2)
    PhysTime = ThisWorkbook.Sheets _
    ("Appointments").Cells(i, 3)
```

Now the query's SQL is built (the first time through the loop) and rebuilt (on subsequent cycles) using the current values of the employee ID and the date and time of the physical. The query inserts a new record into the table named Physicals, and specifies the fields named StaffID, DateOfPhysical, and TimeOfPhysical.

The SQL's VALUES clause provides the values that are to be inserted into those fields.

```
strQuery = "INSERT INTO Physicals" & _
"(StaffID, DateOfPhysical, TimeOfPhysical) " & _
"VALUES ('" & EmpID & "', '" & PhysDate & "', '" & _
 PhysTime & "');"
```

For a record in which the employee's ID is 314, the date is 2/5/2005, and the time is 10:00 AM, the value that's assigned to strQuery is

```
INSERT INTO Physicals (StaffID, DateOfPhysical, TimeOfPhysical) _
VALUES ('314', '2/5/2005', '10:00 AM');
```

So, each time the loop executes, different values are supplied to the SQL. The nonpersistent query itself has already been set, and only its SQL changes. The change to its SQL is accomplished in the following With block, which also causes the query to execute:

```
    With qdfTempQuery
        .Sql = strQuery
        .Execute
    End With

Next i

ThisWorkbook.Sheets("Appointments") _
.Range(Cells(2, 1), Cells(LastEmployee,3)).Clear

End Sub
```

After the final trip through the loop, the code clears the range that contained the data in preparation for the next day's appointments, and the subroutine terminates.

Using DAO to Define and Execute an Update Query

When you need to modify many records in a table, altering a field's values in the table, an Update query is often the best choice.

Suppose that, following the example introduced in the prior case study, you want to set the date of the next physical for *all* employees to June 30, 2005. You might use code like this:

```
Sub UpdatePhysicalDates(FilePath As String)
Dim dbEmployees As DAO.Database
Dim qdfUpdateDates As DAO.QueryDef
Dim strUpdateSQL As String
```

After declaring the necessary variables, your code sets the database.

```
Set dbEmployees = OpenDatabase(FilePath & "Employees.mdb")
```

Then you assign the appropriate SQL to a string variable. In this case, your SQL calls for all records in the Physicals table to have the value of the NextPhysical field set to 6/30/2005.

```
strUpdateSQL = "UPDATE Physicals SET " & _
"Physicals.NextPhysical = #6/30/2005#;"
```

You then set the query definition. You make it nonpersistent by naming it with an empty string, and you pass your SQL to the query in the form of the string variable strUpdateSQL.

```
Set qdfUpdateDates = dbEmployees.CreateQueryDef _
("", strUpdateSQL)
```

Finally, you execute the query and end the subroutine.

```
qdfUpdateDates.Execute
End Sub
```

This is, of course, unrealistic—you would not assign all employees to have their next physical on the same day—but it does serve to show how you can assign a constant to all records in a table.

A more realistic approach would be to assign all employees a date for their next physical that falls one year following their current physical. You could use exactly the same code as shown before, but you would modify the SQL as follows:

```
strUpdateSQL = "UPDATE Physicals SET " & _
"Physicals.NextPhysical = [DateOfPhysical]+365;"
```

Now the SQL instructs the database to add 365 to the value of the field named DateOfPhysical, and store the result in the field named NextPhysical. Because no criteria are applied, it carries out the update on all the records in the table.

Using ADO to Execute Action Queries and Stored Procedures

If you prefer to use ADO instead of DAO (or if you're not using a Jet database so that DAO isn't available), you'll need to adjust your VBA code to make use of ADO objects. The examples in this section use ADO's Command object which, along with the Connection and the Recordset objects, is one of the three fundamental objects in the ADO model. You generally use the Command object when your code will execute an action query—more broadly, a stored procedure.

> **NOTE**   ADO tends to follow SQL Server terminology in this area, and SQL Server uses the term *stored procedure* instead of *action query*. The two terms are not synonymous, however: SQL that Access would term action queries constitute part but not all of stored procedures.

Using ADO to Execute Delete Queries

The following VBA code, used in conjunction with ADO, looks a little different from that in use with DAO. Here's one way that you might use VBA and ADO to delete records with a date field's value that's earlier than 1/1/1997.

```
Sub DeleteOldOrders()
Dim cmd As New ADODB.Command
```

```
Dim cnn As New ADODB.Connection
Dim prm As ADODB.Parameter
```

Three ADO object variables are declared: `cmd` will represent the command to be carried out, `cnn` will represent the connection to the database, and `prm` will represent a parameter that accompanies the command.

Then the connection is defined by specifying the provider, the data source, and the catalog, and how security is handled. The SSPI specification, short for *Security Support Provider Interface*, calls for NT user authentication: NT authorizes the user on the basis of his logon.

```
cnn.Open _
    ConnectionString:="Provider=SQLOLEDB.1;" & _
    "Data Source=(local);" & _
    "Initial Catalog=NorthwindCS;Integrated Security=SSPI"
```

After the connection is opened, it's assigned to the Command object.

```
Set cmd.ActiveConnection = cnn
```

Then the code provides the specifics of the command. Its `CommandText` property, a string, either names the existing query or stored procedure that the command is to represent, or contains the SQL that the command will execute. The `CommandType` property specifies what `CommandText` contains. In the present example, it is a stored procedure named `DeleteOldOrders`. If instead the `CommandText` property included the actual SQL, the `CommandType` property would specify `adCmdText`—that is, it would indicate that `CommandText` included command text.

```
With cmd
    .CommandText = "DeleteOldOrders"
    .CommandType = adCmdStoredProc
```

Now a parameter is created. It's given the name `WhichDate` and a data type of `adDate`, meaning that a value assigned to it must be a date value. The `Direction` property might be new to you. In DAO and in Access SQL, parameters are unidirectional. They're input to the query and function as selection criteria. In ADO (and Transact-SQL and SQL Server), parameters can act as they do in DAO, as inputs, but they can also act as outputs, returning information about what happened when the query or other stored procedure executed. In this case, the parameter is of the familiar input type, as specified by the `adParamInput` value.

```
Set prm = .CreateParameter(Name:="WhichDate", _
    Type:=adDate, Direction:=adParamInput)
```

The parameter is appended to the command, and remains available to the command for as long as the command itself exists. The code gives the parameter a value—in this case, 1/1/97—and the command executes, deleting all records according to the requirements of the existing `DeleteOldOrders` query.

```
    .Parameters.Append prm
    prm.Value = "1/1/97"
    .Execute
End With

End Sub
```

12

It's not necessary to formally establish and append a parameter to the command object in order to use one (however, see the next section for an example of how doing so can make things more convenient). The prior example of deleting records using a date parameter could be written like this:

```
Sub DeleteOldOrdersWithSQL()
Dim cmd As New ADODB.Command
Dim cnn As New ADODB.Connection
Dim prm As ADODB.Parameter
Dim HowMany As Long

cnn.Open _
    ConnectionString:="Provider=SQLOLEDB.1;" & _
    "Data Source=(local);" & _
    "Initial Catalog=NorthwindCS;Integrated Security=SSPI"

Set cmd.ActiveConnection = cnn

With cmd
    .CommandText = "EXEC DeleteOldOrders '1/1/97'"
    .CommandType = adCmdText
    .Execute RecordsAffected:=HowMany
End With

MsgBox HowMany & " records were deleted."

End Sub
```

This example shows that you don't need to declare or set a parameter to make use of one that already exists in a stored procedure. There are three functional differences between the two procedures given in this section:

- The command object's CommandText property does not merely name the stored procedure, but provides SQL that names the query and also states that it should be executed.

- The CommandText property includes the value that VBA will pass to the stored procedure's parameter.

- The CommandType property states that the command's type is Text—that is, the command includes actual SQL syntax.

Another difference is that the second procedure shows the use of the Execute method's RecordsAffected property. It can be useful to know how many records were deleted (or, in the case of an Append or Update action query, how many records were inserted into a table or how many had their values modified). By declaring a variable as a Long integer and using it in the query's Execute method, you can view with a message box, or store in a worksheet cell, the number of records affected. If the number is zero, for example, you might know that something you expected to occur did not. And if you need an audit trail for changes that your code makes to the database, it can be valuable to know, as you move forward, the number of records that were affected by your code.

Using ADO to Execute Update Queries

Notice the use of the parameter object in the prior VBA code. The parameter used there, prm, is established with the Set statement. Then it is appended to the Parameters collection, which belongs to the Command object (cmd in the sample code). This is useful when you want to run a query several times, each time with a different value for the parameter.

"Querying Multiple Tables," in Chapter 5, "Using Microsoft Query," discussed the setup of a database containing information on the maintenance of doors in office buildings. The following case study shows how data might get into that database from Excel.

CASE STUDY

Your staff of maintenance technicians inspects fire doors in your company's office buildings on a regular schedule. At the end of each workday, you want the technicians to record the ID of each door that they inspected on that day. There is other information that the technicians are supposed to record, and it turns out that the most convenient location to record all the day's information is in an Excel worksheet, shown in Figure 12.3.

Figure 12.3
Excel lends itself well to this sort of informal data entry layout.

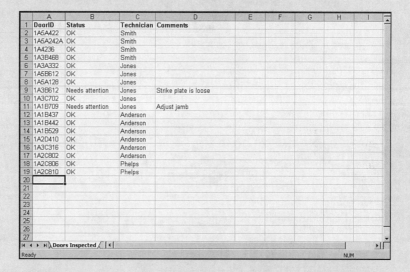

You want to move the doors' inspection date from the worksheet into an Access project. No special handling is needed of the sort that might require you to use a recordset. All you need to do is find each inspected door in the database and update its DateLastInspected field. You decide to use a stored procedure, one that Access would term an Update query. The query is shown in design view in Figure 12.4.

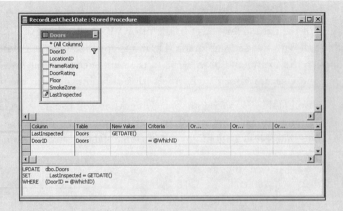

.4

in the table,
..or ID, indicates
. you've applied a cri-
.rion to that field.

The construction of stored procedures is in some ways different from the construction of action queries, even though they often accomplish the same ends. Notice in Figure 12.4, for example, that the parameter isn't identified as such by enclosing it in square brackets, but by preceding it with an ampersand. In an Access action query, the parameter's name could have an embedded blank, but you avoid this in a stored procedure. Also note the use of the GETDATE() function in place of the DATE() function. These differences are a direct result of the use of Transact-SQL instead of the SQL version used by Access MDB files.

After the technicians have finished recording the door IDs, they close the workbook. You've set the workbook's BeforeClose event to run the following code just before the workbook closes:

```
Option Explicit

Private Sub Workbook_BeforeClose(Cancel As Boolean)
Dim cmd As New ADODB.Command
Dim cnn As New ADODB.Connection
Dim prm As ADODB.Parameter
Dim i As Integer
Dim LastDoor As Long

LastDoor = ThisWorkbook.Sheets("Doors Inspected") _
.Cells(65536, 1).End(xlUp).Row
```

You set the variable LastDoor to the row in which the final entry is found on the worksheet. In Figure 12.3, that's 19. This will be the final counter value used as the code loops through the door IDs.

```
cnn.Open _
    ConnectionString:="Provider=SQLOLEDB.1;" & _
    "Data Source=Fran;" & _
    "Initial Catalog=FireDoors;Integrated Security=SSPI"

Set cmd.ActiveConnection = cnn
```

You define a connection by means of a string, specifying the provider, the server (the data source), the catalog, and the security. You open the connection and assign it to a Command object.

```
With cmd
    .CommandText = "RecordLastInspectDate"
    .CommandType = adCmdStoredProc
```

You use the Command object's `CommandText` property to identify the stored procedure to be run, `RecordLastInspectDate`. You also indicate that the Command object represents a stored procedure by means of `acCmdStoredProc`.

```
Set prm = .CreateParameter(Name:="WhichID", _
    Type:=adVarChar, Size:=10)
.Parameters.Append prm
```

You're going to use the door IDs found on the worksheet as parameter values: That is, you'll submit them to the query one by one in the following loop. Each time through the loop, the query executes after locating the record that's identified by the parameter's value.

In setting `prm` equal to a new parameter, you supply its name, which is the same as the one in the stored procedure. The `adVarChar` specification means that the parameter's value is a variable-length data type, roughly equivalent to a Text value. The `Size` parameter sets the maximum length of the value to 10 characters.

After you've set the parameter's properties, you append it to the collection of parameters that belong to this Command object. In this case, there's only one parameter in the collection, but it still must be appended. With that parameter in the collection you can use it repeatedly without having to respecify its properties. (Repeated usage is the principal reason for establishing the parameter in this way.)

```
    For i = 2 To LastDoor
        prm.Value = ThisWorkbook.Sheets("Doors Inspected") _
        .Cells(i, 1)
        .Execute
    Next i
End With

End Sub
```

Your code enters the loop that runs through each door ID found on the worksheet. Each time through the loop, the parameter's value is set equal to a different door's ID and the stored procedure is executed. The stored procedure locates the door in its table and sets its LastInspected field to the current date.

Using DAO Recordsets to Move Data from Excel to a Jet Database

As yet, this book has touched only very lightly on the topic of using recordsets to store data in a database. There are more efficient methods, discussed in the prior sections of this chapter as well as in earlier chapters. When you can use a Select query to return fields and records from a database, by all means do so. When you can use an existing action query, or create one temporarily, to modify records and fields, that's usually the method to use. SQL-based queries make more efficient use of your system's resources than do recordsets.

Append queries are fine when you want to add a group of records to a database table without a lot of intermediate processing. Delete queries work well when you want to remove records, or an easily identifiable group of records, from a table. Update queries are a good choice when you want to take the same action on some or all the records in a table. But when you need your code to examine each record individually and perhaps take action conditionally, you probably need to use a recordset.

Suppose that you want to put new records into a database table or to change the value of one or more fields in an existing record. These two very common actions call for the recordset's AddNew method and its Edit method; in DAO, both these methods require that you also use the recordset's Update method. The next two sections show examples of these methods.

Adding Data to a Recordset

There are many reasons that you would want to add data to a database from the Excel platform. One of the more important reasons is that although you or your users prefer to enter data directly into Excel, a database makes much more sense than a worksheet for long-term storage. The other reason of importance is that you want to use one or more of Excel's worksheet functions before storing the data elsewhere.

Suppose that you're tracking the performance of stocks in a retirement account. You find it useful to chart their daily per-share values against some broad-based index such as the S&P 500 or the NASDAQ, and to include trendlines on the charts. This is a fairly basic task in Excel, but clumsy at best in most database applications. So, you decide to perform your analysis in Excel and from time to time put the stock data into an Access database. You could automate that process with the following code:

```
Sub AddStocks()

Dim dbStocks As DAO.Database
Dim rs401k As DAO.Recordset
Dim wksStocks As WorkSheet
Dim i As Integer
Dim FinalRow As Long

Set dbStocks = OpenDatabas(ThisWorkbook.Path & _
"\Stocks.mdb")
Set rs401k = dbStocks.TableDefs("Retirement") _
.OpenRecordset(dbOpenDynaset)
Set wksStocks = ThisWorkbook.Worksheets("2004")
FinalRow = wksStocks.Cells(65536,1).End(xlUp).Row

With rs401k
    For i = 2 to FinalRow
    .AddNew
        .Fields("StockName") = wksStocks.Cells(i,1)
        .Fields("PriceDate") = wksStocks.Cells(i,2)
        .Fields("Price") = wksStocks.Cells(i,3)
```

```
        .Update
    Next i
End With

End Sub
```

The procedure named `AddStocks` begins by opening a DAO database named Stocks.mdb. It establishes a recordset based on a table named Retirement, located in Stocks.mdb. It uses a `For-Next` loop to add new records to the recordset, and thus to the table that the recordset represents. Each time a new record is added by means of the `AddNew` method, three fields in that new record are populated with values found in columns A, B, and C of the worksheet named 2004. The name of the stock is obtained from column A, the date on which the stock was priced from column B, and the price itself from column C.

After the three fields get their values, the `Update` method is called. When you use the `AddNew` method (or, as shown next, the `Edit` method), a record is placed in a buffer and changes are made to the record in the buffer. Only when you call the `Update` method are the record and the changes you've made to it moved from the buffer to the underlying data source.

After the current record has been updated, the loop continues, establishing a new record, populating its fields, and moving the record from the copy buffer into the Retirement table.

Editing Existing Data

When you already have all the necessary records available and the sole task is to edit the values in their fields, consider using an Update query. Suppose that you sell 100 shares of each holding in your retirement account. Because you're selling the same number of shares regardless of the holding, an Update query makes sense. You might provide SQL along these lines:

```
strSellShares = "UPDATE Retirement SET " & _
"Retirement.SharesHeld = Retirement.SharesHeld - 100;"
```

But if you wanted to record that you sold a different number of shares in each stock, an Update query might not make sense, and processing a recordset might be much more attractive. Suppose that your worksheet has the name of each stock in your retirement account in column A, and the number of shares you have sold in column B. Then the code might look like this:

```
Sub SellStocks()

Dim dbStocks As DAO.Database
Dim rs401k As DAO.Recordset
Dim wksStocks As Worksheet
Dim i As Integer
Dim FinalRow As Long

Set dbStocks = OpenDatabase(ThisWorkbook.Path & _
"\Stocks.mdb")
Set rs401k = dbStocks.TableDefs("Retirement") _
.OpenRecordset(dbOpenDynaset)
Set wksStocks = ThisWorkbook.Worksheets("2004")
FinalRow = wksStocks.Cells(65536,1).End(xlUp).Row
```

```
With rs401k
    For i = 2 To FinalRow
        .FindFirst "StockName = '" _
        & wksStocks.Cells(i, 1) & "'"
        If Not .NoMatch Then
            .Edit
                .Fields("SharesHeld") = _
                .Fields("SharesHeld") _
                - wksStocks.Cells(i, 2)
            .Update
        Else
            wksStocks.Cells(i,3) = _
            "Could not find this stock in database."
        End If
    Next i
End With

End Sub
```

The procedure named SellStocks differs in two fundamental ways from AddStocks. When stocks were being added to the database, it wasn't necessary to find a particular stock: The code just adds each stock's name, date, and price to the table.

But SellStocks edits the existing records, and (as is typical when you're editing existing data) it has to start by finding the record to be edited. So, the first major difference between the two procedures is that SellStocks uses the FindFirst method to locate each stock. It obtains the name of the stock from the worksheet and finds its record in the database. After the record has been found, it edits the record by subtracting a number, also taken from the worksheet, from the SharesHeld field. The FindFirst syntax is

```
Recordset.FindFirst Criterion
```

where Criterion is a string that consists of a field name, an operator, and a value to find. For example:

```
strCriterion = "SharesHeld = '" & _wksStocks.Cells(i, 1) & "'"
rs401k.FindFirst strCriterion
```

So, to use it, simply name the recordset that you want to search, followed by FindFirst. Supply a field name, an operator, and the value that you want to find. You don't need to use the equal sign as the operator: You can also use less than, greater than, does not equal, and so on.

The other major difference between the two procedures is that SellStocks has to make a provision for the possibility that a stock name found on the worksheet does not exist in the database. Therefore the NoMatch property is used.

NoMatch is a property that belongs to DAO recordsets. It's used after a Find (in SellStocks, it's used after FindFirst). If your code is successful in finding a record meeting the criterion, NoMatch is set to False. If your code cannot find such a record, NoMatch is set to True. You should provide for the case in which a record cannot be found. In the SellStocks procedure, the code writes a message that the stock couldn't be found. It puts that message on the same row as the stock's name, in the third column.

NOTE There are four `Find` methods in DAO. `FindFirst` starts at the beginning of a recordset and looks toward the end for a matching record. `FindLast` starts at the end and looks toward the beginning. `FindPrevious` looks from the current record toward the start of a recordset. `FindNext` looks from the current record toward the end.

Using ADO to Move Data from Excel to a Database

There are some minor differences between DAO and ADO when it comes to modifying data. This section examines how you might structure your code using ADO to perform the two tasks discussed in the prior section, adding records and editing existing records.

Using ADO to Add Records

As before, the intent is to scan the data on a worksheet, picking up the names and share prices of stocks and copying them to a database table.

The declarations in the subroutine are of course somewhat different in ADO. A new connection is established (the cnn object) and used to open the recordset.

```
Sub AddStocks()

Dim cnn As New ADODB.Connection
Dim rs401k As ADODB.Recordset
Dim wksStocks As Worksheet
Dim i As Integer
Dim FinalRow As Long

cnn.Open _
    ConnectionString:="Provider=SQLOLEDB.1;" & _
    "Data Source=(local);" & _
    "Initial Catalog=NorthwindCS;Integrated Security=SSPI"

Set rs401k = New ADODB.Recordset

rs401k.Open "Retirement", cnn, adOpenStatic, _
adLockOptimistic, adCmdTable
```

The prior statement contains a lot of functionality, as follows:

- It names the data source for the recordset: the Retirement table, as before.

- It supplies the connection object, cnn, so that the recordset can find the data source.

- It sets the recordset cursor to adOpenStatic. This setting means that the recordset can be modified, and you can move back and forth through it. You would not be able to see changes that other users might make.

- It sets record locking to optimistic: Your code will be able to modify the data, and any other users would be able to modify the same record that you're working on. When your modifications are saved, the record is locked until the database has finished saving the record.

- Via the adCmdTable option, it informs ADO that the source, already specified as Retirement, is a table or a Select query.

12

```
Set wksStocks = ThisWorkbook.Worksheets("2004")
FinalRow = wksStocks.Cells(65536, 4).End(xlUp).Row

With rs401k
    For i = 2 To FinalRow
        .AddNew
            .Fields("StockName") = wksStocks.Cells(i, 1)
            .Fields("PriceDate") = wksStocks.Cells(i, 2)
            .Fields("Price") = wksStocks.Cells(i, 3)
        .Update
    Next i
End With

End Sub
```

The code that actually adds the records looks identical to the DAO code, but there's a slight difference. Using ADO, the `Update` method isn't required. If you omit `Update` in DAO, following an `AddNew` or an `Edit`, the compiler will generate an error message.

This isn't the case in ADO, which treats `Update` as an optional statement. After a record has been added or edited, the update process occurs automatically *when you move to a different record*. (When you add a new record, it becomes the current record and you have therefore moved.) If you don't move to a different record, the changes you make aren't saved.

For example, suppose that your worksheet had data on stocks in rows 2 through 51, and that you omit the `Update` method in the code. For rows 2 through 50, the loop moves you to a new record each time it runs, so the automatic update occurs and the data is saved correctly. However, although the data in row 51 would be put into a new record, the record would not be saved because the loop is finished and doesn't move to a different record. Therefore the automatic update doesn't occur.

All of this is a lengthy way to say that although the compiler will let you get away without using `Update`, use it anyway.

Using ADO to Edit Records

In the following version of the `SellStocks` procedure, the declarations and preparations are identical to those in the prior `AddStocks` procedure using ADO instead of DAO:

```
Sub SellStocks()

Dim cnn As New ADODB.Connection
Dim rs401k As ADODB.Recordset
Dim wksStocks As Worksheet
Dim i As Integer
Dim FinalRow As Long

cnn.Open _
    ConnectionString:="Provider=SQLOLEDB.1;Data Source=(local);" & _
    "Initial Catalog=NorthwindCS;Integrated Security=SSPI"

Set rs401k = New ADODB.Recordset

rs401k.Open "Retirement", cnn, adOpenStatic, adLockOptimistic, adCmdTable
```

```
Set wksStocks = ThisWorkbook.Worksheets("2004")
FinalRow = wksStocks.Cells(65536, 1).End(xlUp).Row
```

There are more obvious differences in the loop using ADO when existing records are being edited. One is that instead of a `FindFirst` method, ADO has a `Find` method. Its full syntax is

```
Recordset.Find Criteria, SkipRows, SearchDirection, Start
```

All the arguments apart from `Criteria` are optional. Provide a numeric value for `SkipRows` if you want the search to skip over number of records as it checks for a match on the criterion. You can specify `adSearchForward` or `adSearchBackward` to control the direction of the search. And if you supply a bookmark, the search will start at that record instead of at the start of the recordset.

A real limitation to the use of `Find` in ADO is that you cannot supply multiple criteria. For example, the following `Find` would result in a runtime error:

```
Rst.Find "StockName = 'IBM' And StockPrice > 100"
```

Also notice that the failure to find a record matching the criterion is not tested by `NoMatch`. Instead, the recordset's `BOF` or its `EOF` property becomes True. Which one becomes true depends on the direction you were searching, either `adSearchForward`—a failure results in a True `EOF`—or `adSearchBackward`—a failure results in a True `BOF`. (`BOF` stands for *Beginning of File* and `EOF` stands for *End of File*.)

```
With rs401k
    For i = 2 To FinalRow
        .Find "StockName = '" _
        & wksStocks.Cells(i, 1) & "'"
        If Not .EOF Then
                .Fields("SharesHeld") = _
                .Fields("SharesHeld") _
                - wksStocks.Cells(i, 2)
        Else
            wksStocks.Cells(i, 3) = _
            "Could not find this stock in database."
        End If
    Next i
End With

End Sub
```

Although you can search only one field using ADO's `Find` method, a possible alternative is its `Filter` method. This would be legal:

```
Rst.Filter = "StockName = 'IBM' And StockPrice > 100"
```

and would limit the records in the recordset to those with a value of IBM in its StockName field, and with a value on StockPrice that's greater than 100.

Notice that the `Filter` method uses an equal sign, in contrast to the `Find` method.

If, after applying a filter, you need to have all the original records accessible, you can restore them with the `adFilterNone` constant:

```
Rst.Filter = adFilterNone
```

12

Bear in mind that if you use `Filter`, you might have several records accessible in the record-set. If you want to edit all of them, you'll want to loop through the remaining records. For example, suppose that you wanted to reduce your holdings in IBM by 100 shares in each account, without creating a negative number of shares in any account (selling short is too risky for a retirement portfolio):

```
With rs401k
    .Filter = "StockName = '" _
    & wksStocks.Cells(i, 1) & _
    "' And SharesHeld > 100"

    Do Until .EOF
        .Fields("SharesHeld") = _
        .Fields("SharesHeld") - 100
        .MoveNext
    Loop

    .Filter = adFilterNone
End With
```

Looking Ahead

You've reached EOF. This book can't offer you any more advice about using the Excel plat-form to manage your data. I can hope, though, that you've found the information useful. I've done a core dump here, including in this book everything I've found valuable about using Excel, VBA, DAO, ADO, Access databases, and Access projects to keep track of data.

Excel is a very powerful application, but 'twas not always thus. There was a time when Excel was best thought of as the JV version of 1-2-3. Believe it or not, there was a time that Microsoft was criticized in the personal computer media for not offering a spreadsheet application that supported more than one worksheet per file.

But Microsoft kept improving what had once been known as MultiPlan. Excel in 2004 is the gold standard. You can tell because new releases have fewer and fewer enhancements of any real value.

Access isn't yet there. Nor is SQL Server. As this book is written, Microsoft's attention is engaged in patching the holes in its operating systems, and devoting relatively little atten-tion to its end user applications. But every release of Access and SQL Server has enhanced their capabilities, and there's every reason to believe that they will follow the path estab-lished by Excel.

'Nuff said. If you keep on using Excel to analyze your data, and truly relational database management systems to store and retrieve it, it will pay off.

SQL (Structured Query Language), 114, 328-329

SQL Server Desktop Engine, 291

StartTime variable, 304

statements. *See also* functions

AddNew, 279-280
CreateDatabase, 257
Dim, 172-173, 196
End Sub, 170
End With, 302
loops
Do While, 178-181
For Each, 190-191
For-Next, 175-178
New, 196
On Error GoTo, 268
Option Explicit, 170
ReDim, 264
Set, 190, 196, 282
Sub, 170, 310
Update, 280
With, 182-184, 305

static range names, 68

Stop Recording command (Macro menu), 185

stored procedures, 332, 336. *See also* queries

string variables, 172

Structured Query Language (SQL), 114, 328-329

strUpdateSQL variable, 332

Sub statement, 170, 310

subroutines, 168-171

suppressing cache, 105

T

Table menu commands, Joins, 123

Table Options dialog box, 105

table-type recordsets, 283-285

tables, 227
creating with ADO, 272-277
NewShortStayTable function, 273, 276-277
object variables, 274
primary key, 274
creating with DAO, 260, 270-272
defined, 95
joins, 233-234
multiple tables, querying, 115-118
pivot tables, 12, 139
advantages of, 49
creating, 139-141
date/time fields, grouping, 147-148
importing data to, 104-110
null values, avoiding, 150-152
numeric fields, grouping, 149-150
populating, 105
reconfiguring, 141-144
retrieving data with GETPIVOTDATA function, 50-52
table options, 144-146
primary keys, 123, 238-239

referential integrity, 236-238
relationships
defining, 235-236
identifying, 235-236
one-to-many, 235
one-to-one, 235
viewing, 233-234

text, importing, 248, 250-252

Text function, 298-299

The Sisyphus Corporation case study, 10-14

time/date fields, grouping, 147-148

TimeArray array, 295, 298

Title parameter (GetOpenFilename method), 210

Tools menu commands
Macros, 168
Options, 170
References, 163
Security, 211

Total Row command (List menu), 60

TotalByVendor worksheet, 179-181

Transact-SQL, 114

TransferText method, 255

Transpose command (Paste Special menu), 47

TRANSPOSE function, 16, 29, 48-49

informIT

businesssolutions

If you like this book, you will love the rest of the books in the Business Solutions series! Remember, this series focuses ONLY on the specific function you are practicing and provides solutions to those needs through step-by-step descriptions of how to accomplish a task. Where possible, sample templates, examples, and macros are used, based on typical problems that you face on any given workday. Plus, case studies present the problem and offer solutions you can apply to actual situations!

Look for these titles at your favorite bookstore or online

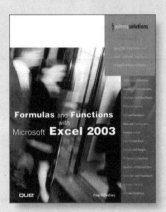

Formulas and Functions with Microsoft® Excel 2003

Paul McFedries
ISBN: 0-7897-3153-3
$34.99 U.S./ $42.99 CAN/ £25.50 UK
Available Summer 2004

This book not only takes you through Excel's intermediate and advanced options, it also tells why these options are useful and shows you how to use them in everyday situations and real-world models. This does all this with no-nonsense, step-by-step tutorials and lots of practical, useful examples.

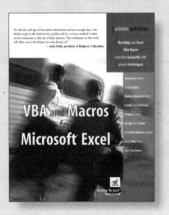

VBA and Macros for Microsoft® Excel

Bill Jelen
ISBN: 0-7897-3129-0
$39.99 U.S./ $57.99 CAN/ £28.99 UK
Available Spring 2004

This book teaches the skills necessary to use Microsoft VBA to customize the Excel spreadsheet. No prior programming knowledge is assumed. Soon you will be building macros and have a good understanding of the VBA language.

www.quepublishing.com